D0309989

AA

Explorer Canada

Tim Jepson

AA Publishing

Front Cover
Top: *Lakes, forests and the Rockie mountains* (C. Coe).
Centre (left to right): *(a) Wine bottles from the vineyards of the Okanagan* (C. Coe); *(b) A Mountie in full uniform* (C. Coe); *(c) Detail of the striking Goedesci Dome, Vancouver* (C. Coe); *(d) The Hockey Hall of Fame in Toronto* (J. Davison); *(e) Clapboard houses in St. John's* (N. Sumner)
Spine
Detail of an Inuit carving in Vancouver's Museum of Anthropology (C. Coe)
Back Cover
Left: *The modern skyline view of Toronto* (J. Davison)
Right: *Colorful Inuit mask* (J. Davison)

All pictures from AA World Travel Library

Page 2: *The Laurentides*
Page 3: *Hector Lake*
Page 4: *(a) O'Keefe's ranch, Okanagan; (b) Mounties*
Page 5: *(a) Fishing nets; (b) Racoon ; (c) Cape Spear lighthouse, Newfoundland*
Page 6/7: *Tombstone Mountains, Yukon*
Page 6: *Emerald Lake, Yoho National Park, B.C.*
Page 8: *Terra Nova National Park, Newfoundland*
Page 9: *(a) Vermillion Lake; (b) Science Centre, Vancouver*

Written by Tim Jepson
Updated by Tim Jepson

Published by AA Publishing, a trading name of Automobile Association Developments Limited, whose registered office is Fanum House, Basing View, Basingstoke, Hampshire, RG21 4EA. Registered number 1878835.

ISBN-10: 0 7495 4750 2
ISBN-13: 978-0-7495-4750-9

A CIP catalogue record for this book is available from the British Library.

Color separation by KDP, Kingsclere, UK
Printed and bound in Italy by Printer Trento Srl

Find out more about AA Publishing and the wide range of travel publications and services the AA provides by visiting our website at www.theAA.com/bookshop.

Revised fourth edition Jan 2006
First published 1997

Titles in the Explorer series:
Australia • Boston & New England • Britain • Brittany
California • Canada • Caribbean • China • Costa Rica • Crete
Cuba • Cyprus • Egypt • Florence & Tuscany • Florida
France • Germany • Greek Islands • Hawaii • India • Ireland
Italy • Japan • London • Mallorca • Mexico • New York
New Zealand • Paris • Portugal • Provence • Rome
San Francisco • Scotland • South Africa • Spain • Thailand
Tunisia • Turkey • Venice • Vietnam

A02413

How to use this book

ORGANIZATION

Canada Is, Canada Was
Discusses aspects of life and culture in contemporary Canada, and explores significant periods in its history.

A–Z
For ease of use, the book is divided into geographical regions, arranged province by province from west to east. Places of interest are listed alphabetically within each section. Suggested drives and tours, as well as the Focus On articles, which consider a variety of topics in greater detail, are also included.

Travel Facts
Contains the practical information that is vital for a successful trip.

Accommodations & Restaurants
Lists recommended establishments in Canada, region by region. Entries are graded budget, moderate or expensive.

Admission charges
Inexpensive is under $4
Moderate is between $4 and $7
Expensive is $7 and over

ABOUT THE RATINGS
Most places described in this book have been given a separate rating. These are as follows:

►►► **Do not miss**

►► **Highly recommended**

► **Worth seeing**

MAP REFERENCES
To make the location of a particular place easier to find, every main entry in this book is given a map reference, such as 66B3. The first number (66) indicates the page on which the map can be found; the letter (B) and the second number (3) pinpoint the square in which the main entry is located. The map on the inside front cover and inside back cover is referred to as IFC–IBC.

Contents

Tim Jepson's passion for highlands and wild places has taken him not only to the Canadian Rockies and the windswept tundra of the Yukon, but also to Umbria, where he learned to speak Italian from the children of a tiny mountain hamlet. Tim's future plans include walking the length and breadth of the Pyrenees, in addition to exploring South America and the Arctic. He has written several Exploring guides, including *Italy*, *Florence & Tuscany* and *Venice*.

My Canada

How does one go about researching a guide to the world's second-largest country? On the face of it, it looks an impossible task, requiring one—among other things—to trail across almost half a continent, tramp the farthest reaches of the frozen north, or explore over 30 national parks, one of which alone (Wood Buffalo) is larger than Switzerland. In fact, the brief is less daunting than it appears; for while Canada is undoubtedly huge, much of the country is pristine wilderness, many of its settlements little more than a collection of homes gathered in a forest clearing. Time and again I budgeted a couple of days to explore a town or village, only to find that its half-dozen houses, small museum and motel could be "seen" in half an hour.

This is not to say that Canada's urban side is disappointing: cities like Montréal, Québec and Vancouver are a revelation—dynamic, sophisticated and cosmopolitan; the sort of places in which, in the words of travel writer Jan Morris, anyone would be happy to live. Yet it was Canada's landscapes, and the immensity of its wilderness, that left the greatest impression. The country's scale struck me before I had even set foot in the place, as I glanced down from a Calgary-bound 747 on to the vast spread of the Prairies, a checkerboard of wheat fields that rolled on unbroken for almost three hours: in the same time, I mused, I could have traveled from London to Rome.

What struck me still more strongly was how new everything is, how recently many towns and cities have been carved from the wilderness, and how close this wilderness is to civilization: lying in bed in Whitehorse, for example, and listening to the howl of wolves; flying into Montréal airport, looking for a city and finding an expanse of lakes and woods; or stepping into a bus in downtown Vancouver and finding pine needles on the floor, shaken off by passengers who had boarded in the forest heights of the city's outskirts. Canada is vast, but also spectacularly wild and gloriously empty: this made it easy to research; it should make it easy, and pleasant, to explore.

Tim Jepson

Canada Is

9

Canada is a young country and, like many young countries, it is forever grappling with its sense of national identity. Its complex and multiethnic population—now increasingly restless—only adds to the uncertainties, making it difficult to identify precisely the qualities that define a "Canadian."

SOUL-SEARCHING Bookstores across Canada often have a puzzling little section called "Canadiana," its shelves full of learned and worthy tomes on "The Canadian Question," or some similarly worded title aimed at untangling the difficult question of Canada's future. Such books are merely the tip of the iceberg, the intellectual expression of a debate that sooner or later involves virtually every Canadian. For outsiders this constant soul-searching can seem something of an irrelevance, but for Canadians—with their particular history and multiethnic population—the question goes right to the heart of their heritage and cultural identity.

THE UNITED STATES One of the main problems affecting Canada's view of itself is the proximity of the United States, a neighbor whose national self-confidence is in marked contrast to Canada's more reticent demeanor. Former Prime Minister Pierre Trudeau touched on the problem in 1969 in a speech in Washington: "Living next to you," he observed, "is in some ways like sleeping next to an elephant; no matter how friendly and even-tempered the beast, one is affected by every twitch and grunt." The "beast" affects Canada in every arena, from its cultural dominance to its undoubted economic prowess, something that has become more of an issue in the light of the North American free trade agreements.

Top: The Toronto Blue Jays
Right: Many Canadians are of Scottish descent

❑ "A Canadian is somebody who knows how to make love in a canoe."—Pierre Berton, Canadian writer (1973) ❑

MULTICULTURAL In many ways the whole "Canadian" debate is a flawed one (as Pierre Berton's mischievous definition, see above, subtly suggests), not least because Canadians are not a single people but rather a vast medley of ethnic and native groups. In the US, the melting-pot idea of nationality has encouraged such groups to see themselves primarily as Americans. In Canada, by contrast, the approach has been more determinedly multicultural, encouraging ethnic groups to acknowledge rather than disown their origins. As a result, Canada has emerged not as a melting pot but—in its own definition—as an ethnic "mosaic."

TENSIONS This is not to say that the model is without flaws. Many argue that the mosaic merely reinforces the country's traditional structures, forcing ethnic groups into "occupational ghettos" and concealing the fact that Canada remains a hierarchical and class-bound society. These flaws—for they do exist—have profoundly affected the country's aboriginal peoples, who, despite growing political autonomy, remain a marginalized and often impoverished minority. The same was once also true of French Canadians, whose drive for independence from Canada has brought a new immediacy to the old "Canadian question" (see pages 22–23).

CANADIANS For French *Canadiens*, being part of the mosaic is not enough; as founding partners of modern Canada they seek recognition that goes beyond simple integration with the whole. In terms of numbers they have a point, for French-speakers make up 23 percent of the 29,639,030 population (2001 census). Canadians of so-called English descent (English, Irish, Scots, American) make up 58.9 percent. Native, or aboriginal, Canadians number 976,305, or about 3 percent of the total. Behind them come the Chinese (2.5), Italians (1.7), Germans (1.6), Polish (0.75), Spanish (0.74), Portuguese (0.74), Punjabi (0.7), Ukrainians (0.6), Chinese (1.4) and many others. But to pay attention simply to the numbers would be to miss the point of Canada, to overlook the charms of the country and its people, whose friendliness, well-mannered reserve and pride in the beauty of their landscape often transcend ethnic divisions to become, for want of a better word, Canadian.

❏ "You have to know a man awfully well in Canada to know his surname."—John Buchan, the *Observer* (1950) ❏

Many Canadians are united in their love of the great outdoors

In some countries, geography is merely a matter of incidental interest. In a country like Canada, whose size and scale are greater even than those of the United States, it is a factor that has shaped the country's history and settlement, and that today colors the political and cultural outlook of its widely flung population.

❑ "If some countries have too much history, we have too much geography."—William Lyon Mackenzie King, Canadian Prime Minister (1936) ❑

SIZE Since the demise of the Soviet Union, Canada has become the world's second-largest country, spreading across 9,997,000sq km (3.84 million square miles), or roughly the area occupied by Europe as far east as the Urals. Its most northerly point lies just 800km (500 miles) from the North Pole, while its most southerly point (on Lake Erie) occupies the same latitude as Rome and northern California. The total distance from north to south is around 4,600km (2,800 miles), and from east to west the distance is 5,500km (3,400 miles). Three oceans border its shores: the Pacific, the Arctic and the Atlantic. Six time zones separate its east and west coasts.

EMPTINESS Canada's dominant geographical feature is the Canadian Shield, a region that occupies much of the north and east of the country (or around 43 percent of its surface area). Its rocks—mostly granite and gneiss—are over 500 million years old, some of the oldest on the continent. Its landscapes are a rugged combination of forest, lake and tundra, interspersed with vast swathes of impenetrable "muskeg" bog. Few people live here, and farming is scarce, but the region contains huge amounts of mineral and hydroelectric wealth, and some 15 percent of the world's fresh water is locked in its lakes and rivers. To the north, the region merges with the still more inhospitable wastes of the Arctic Lowlands, a region covering almost 10 percent of Canada's land mass.

Top: Colors of fall in Yukon
Above: The Laurentides near Montréal

GEOGRAPHY The area of Ontario around the Great Lakes—a region known as the St. Lawrence Lowlands—by contrast covers just 3 percent of Canada, but contains over 60 percent of its population. It was created 200–500 million years ago by flooding, seaborne deposits forming the rich soils that attracted the country's earliest settlers. Similar deposits, washed from the Canadian Shield over the millennia, also settled over the Prairies (Manitoba, Saskatchewan, Alberta). These rippling heartlands, which cover just 15 percent of the country's land mass, produce colossal amounts of wheat, not to mention significant quantities of oil and natural gas. To the west

lie the Cordillera, Canada's main mountain ranges, whose great northern sweep covers over 13 percent of the country. The best known of their ranges are the Canadian Rockies, mountains that dwarf the country's only other significant peaks, the Appalachians, which stretch through much of Newfoundland and the Maritime Provinces.

ISOLATION Canada's geography makes it easy to understand how many Canadians might feel isolated from the mainstream of national life. People in Newfoundland, for example, are physically closer to Ireland than to vast areas of Canada. Inhabitants of Vancouver are five hours' flying time from Ottawa, their country's capital. In some areas, notably the far north, distance has bred a hardy and self-contained outlook. In others, notably British Columbia—cut off by the Rockies and Prairies—it has created a sense of psychological detachment. At its most benign, this has produced a laid-back attitude such as California and the West Coast (and an economic bias toward the new markets of the Pacific Rim). At its worst, it has produced the first stirrings of factionalism in the west, and of a desire for independence from a country from which many people already feel a sense of physical detachment.

❑ "It is impossible to describe the country, for it is built on a scale outside that of humanity."—John Buchan, Governor-General of Canada 1935–1940 ❑

Hector Lake: The Canadian Rockies contain some of North America's most majestic scenery

Canada's vast empty spaces make up one of the world's last areas of virgin wilderness. Huge tracts of country in the north and west remain untouched by human hand. Wolves, bears and other animals inhabit the windswept tundra, rippling grasslands and the unending mantle of the northern forests.

POPULATION The scale of the Canadian wilderness is almost impossible to comprehend. In the Northwest Territories and Nunavut, which cover an area the size of India (around a third of Canada's land mass), the population is just 68,600—roughly the same as an average-sized town. Across the country as a whole, the population is around 29,639,000, with a population density of about one person per square mile. In the United Kingdom—the "mother country" for some Canadians—the figure is 85. Furthermore, the vast majority of Canadians live in a tiny area, most of them (about two-thirds) in just two provinces—Ontario and Québec. Of these the bulk are concentrated in a corridor along the US border.

FOREST Around 50 percent of Canada is covered in forest, from the so-called boreal coniferous forest of the north (80 percent of the total) to the magnificent old-growth rain forests of the west coast, and from the deciduous forests of the east to the montane and sub-alpine forests of the Rockies. Roaming these arboreal expanses are some of the creatures most commonly associated with the Canadian wilderness. Wolves, bears, moose and elk are the most prominent, along with smaller mammals such as marmots, beavers and coyotes. Rarer and, for some, more beautiful animals, such as the cougar and lynx, also inhabit these wooded sanctuaries.

❏ Around 90 percent of Canadians live within 150km (100 miles) of the US border. Yet the country stretches over 4,600km (2,800 miles) from north to south. ❏

A trip along the Dempster Highway is one way to experience something of the Yukon wilderness: below left, looking toward the Ogilvie Mountains; above, the Tombstone Mountains

GRASSLAND Canada's true grasslands have been shrinking for decades, plowed up and lost under the Prairies' sprawling wheat fields. Today only around 10 percent of the country remains covered in traditional grassland. Farming has also destroyed some of the region's former fauna, notably pronghorns, elk and mule-deer. No recent loss, however, has been as dramatic as the disappearance of the buffalo (or bison). Before European settlement some 60 million of these animals roamed the Prairies. By 1830 the number was down to 40 million, and by 1900 it had fallen to just 1,000. Something similar appears to be happening to the caribou, denizens of Canada's sweeping tundra, a region whose waste of ice and emptiness conforms most closely to the image of the Canadian wild. Numbers have fallen from 2.5 million in 1938 to around 800,000 today.

PROBLEMS The disappearance of the bison and the depletion of the caribou are the most obvious manifestations of the problems facing the Canadian wilderness. Less obvious—but no less potent—problems include forestry, in particular the wholesale felling of trees (or "clear-cutting"), a practice that is especially common in the rain forests of British Columbia (see pages 78–79). Against the need for conservation must be set the need for jobs, which are scarce in remote country areas. Much the same goes for regions touched by tourism, notably the Rockies, where planning restraints are being eroded in the face of local lobbying. Controversy also surrounds hunting—some 60,000 black bears are shot each year in North America—and in particular the activities of seal-hunters on the northern pack ice. Mining is another problem area, as much of Canada's vast mineral wealth lies locked away at the heart of its deepest wilderness. Roads and pipelines built to exploit resources have invariably compromised the environment. Canada's wilderness may be vast, but its size should not blind outsiders to its precariousness.

❑ Only 11 percent of Canada's land mass is either populated or cultivated. ❑

Canada's immense natural wilderness—its lakes, rivers, mountains and forests—makes it a magnet for those who enjoy the great outdoors. You can hike, ski, fish, climb, canoe or pursue any of a host of other sports virtually anywhere, especially in the country's unspoiled national and provincial parks.

ALL OUTDOORS So much of Canada is wilderness that at times the whole country can seem like the great outdoors. On the Alaska Highway, for example, you can drive for long stretches knowing that no other human sullies the landscape for hundreds of miles. Few things leave such an impression on visitors as this immensity, yet this huge empty space is as much a playground as a wilderness.

PLAYGROUND Even if Canada is also many other things, no visitor can truly appreciate Canada without spending some time at play outdoors. This does not necessarily mean tramping across the tundra, ice-climbing, or any of Canada's other more strenuous activities (canoeing, mountaineering, white-water rafting, bungee-jumping…). It can also mean biking, whale-watching or enjoying the country's idyllically located golf courses. It could mean skiing, hiking or camping. It might involve scuba-diving or boating. Tourist offices across the country have information on the many possibilities. For the adventurous, tour operators are available to organize the bigger projects—anything from a week's fishing trip to tracking polar bears in the far north.

❑ Banff, founded in 1885, was Canada's first, and the world's third, national park. ❑

❑ The outdoors is so close to cities such as Vancouver that the floors of public buses are often scattered with pine needles brought in on the shoes of passengers who have boarded at outlying stops. ❑

Top: Time for reflection on Pyramid Lake, Jasper National Park
Below: Horseback-riding near Montréal

WALKING Hiking is a revelation almost everywhere in Canada, with hikes to suit every age group and ability. Easy hikes are available throughout the country, even in areas where the terrain might suggest otherwise. Trail networks, with good signage and maps, are often extensively developed, especially in national parks, so it's easy to turn up and start walking with a minimum of preparation. Visitors' centers can advise on suitable hikes, most of which are so well-worn and signposted that detailed maps are unnecessary. More demanding options are there for those who want them in mountainous regions' national parks. Try some of the walks in Yoho National Park or the tougher hikes around Moraine Lake.

SKIING Where there is hiking in Canada there is usually also skiing. Resorts in the Rockies and in British Columbia are recognized as some of the world's best. Many cities are close to downhill and cross-country runs: Vancouver, for example, is a 90-minute drive from Whistler; Calgary is the same distance from Rockies resorts such as Lake Louise and Banff; and Montréal is just an hour from over 400 runs in L'Estrie and the Laurentians. Few things illustrate more clearly the ever-present proximity of Canada's outdoors.

Wildlife watchers will revel in the wilderness of Nova Scotia's Cape Breton Island National Park

FISHING Much the same applies to fishing, where scarcely a town or village is without a lake or local river teeming with fish. Again, tourist offices can advise on permits and regulations, while outfitters and tackle shops can provide equipment or help with chartering boats and guides.

NATIONAL PARKS Landscapes that anywhere else might be a country's scenic highlight are often just another patch of wilderness in Canada. Only the finest countryside achieves national park status, an accolade that suggests the exalted nature of Canada's finest scenery. The first park, Banff, was created in 1885, inspired partly by the US example, Yellowstone National Park, which was founded in 1872. Today there are more than 40 superlative national parks, together with over 1,200 provincial parks and around 100 national historic sites.

❑ Wood Buffalo National Park, straddling the Alberta/NWT border, is Canada's largest park and covers an area bigger than Switzerland. ❑

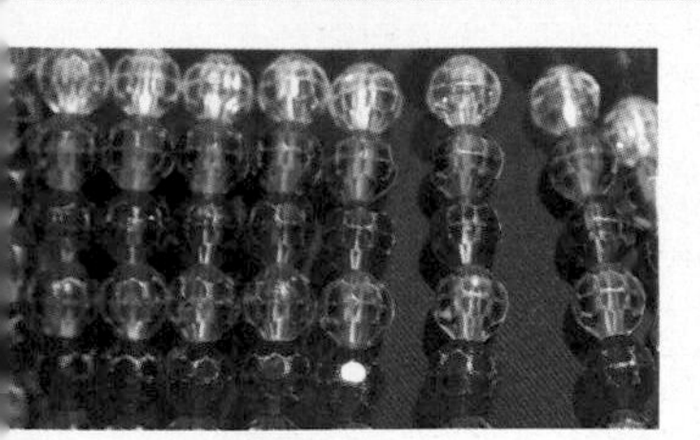

Although Canada's contribution to the arts may be overshadowed by the United States, the country has produced many stars in several artistic fields. Its cultural good health is reflected in a wealth of countrywide festivals and colorful outdoor events, including festivals of jazz, film and comedy.

GRASS ROOTS One of the great surprises that many small Canadian towns offer is the sheer variety and vitality of their cultural life. Most villages have a lovingly presented museum, or a modest gallery of arts and crafts. Few are without an arts center or community theater, and many are dotted with posters proclaiming a recital or exhibition.

WILDERNESS A young country needs to work harder—and quicker—to establish its cultural credentials (which in turn contribute to its sense of national identity). The isolation of rural communities is also a significant factor in the development of culture, for wilderness means not only that you have to make your own entertainment, but that survival itself is often dependent on the type of cooperation and community that is engendered by shared culture.

LITERATURE Canada's highbrow cultural contribution has perhaps been most marked in the fields of poetry and literature. Writers of international renown include the novelists Margaret Atwood, Mordecai Richler and Robertson Davies, while Alice Munro ranks among the world's finest living short-story writers. Poets include Leonard Cohen—better known as a crooner of angst-filled ballads—and Robert Service, whose gold-rush poems have remained in print for over 50 years. Other authors of note include Elizabeth Smart (*By Grand Central Station I Sat Down and Wept*) and L. M. Montgomery (*Anne of Green Gables*), while in the field of social and narrative history few can match the outstanding works of Pierre Berton (for example, *Flames Across the Frontier*, *The Arctic Grail* and *Klondike: the Last Great Goldrush; The Last Spike*).

See page 270 for a list of suggested further reading.

❑ Canadian culture is not merely the culture of mainstream Canada, for its native populations have also been producing sublime works of art for centuries. ❑

Right: The Native Canadian artistic heritage dates back millennia.
Top: Detail from a traditional costume

Donald Sutherland, one of many Canadians who have made their name in the United States

PERFORMING ARTS Most Canadian cities have fine orchestras, in particular Montréal, whose Orchestre Symphonique has achieved worldwide renown. Past musicians include the virtuoso pianist Glenn Gould, while in popular music Neil Young, Joni Mitchell, Celine Dion and k.d. lang all have Canadian roots. Film actors Michael J. Fox and Donald Sutherland hail from Canada, having started their careers in the flourishing world of Canadian theater (Toronto is surpassed only by London and New York as a theater city). Canada's film industry is in its infancy, though US films are increasingly shot in Canada to capitalize on its lower costs and outstanding locations. Ballet companies thrive in most cities, especially Winnipeg and Vancouver, while opera—notably in Toronto—attracts large audiences and world-class performers.

❑ Famous "Americans" who are actually Canadians include Raymond Burr (Perry Mason) and William Shatner (Star Trek's Captain Kirk). Even Rambo, an all-American hero, was created by a Canadian (David Morrell). ❑

FESTIVALS Canada probably hosts more festivals than anywhere else in the world. Some of these are small-time affairs, events that form part of the same cultural impetus as a village's museum or arts center. Others have achieved worldwide fame. Among the latter are Montréal's *Juste Pour Rire* ("Just For Laughs"), the world's largest festival of comedy, and the Montréal International Jazz Festival (the world's largest jazz festival of its type). Toronto, Montréal and Vancouver all have major film festivals, and in Québec the Festival d'Été is the largest celebration of francophone culture in North America. Other festivals include Calgary's famous Stampede; Ontario's Glengarry Games, North America's largest Highland gathering; and Whitehorse's Festival of Storytelling.

The Vancouver Symphony Orchestra. Many Canadian orchestras have achieved international success

Canada has a wonderfully eclectic cuisine based on fine ingredients and the varied influences of its multiethnic population. There are distinct regional variations in cuisine, depending on the ingredients available locally and the area's traditions and cultural influences.

IMPROVEMENT For years "Canadian" and "cuisine" rarely appeared in the same sentence unless it was to lament the paucity of decent restaurants and the stodgy anonymity of the country's cooking. While backwoods areas are often still culinary deserts—served only by diners, pizza joints and fast-food chains—Canada's towns and cities these days are a cornucopia of ethnically varied restaurants that can hold their own with any in the world. An influx of immigrants in recent years has done much to promote this culinary renaissance, as has the rediscovery of dishes and ingredients bequeathed by the country's native population and European settlers.

NEW WORLD Perhaps the area where this rebirth is most apparent is on the West Coast, where the influence of California chefs has been making itself felt on former staples such as salmon and seafood to produce an innovative and healthy cuisine. The west is also the area where native cooking is in the ascendant—venison, elk and buffalo are again appearing on menus, together with wild rice, exotic grains and strange local fruits such as chokecherries and Saskatoons. Japanese and Chinese restaurants are also enjoying considerable popularity, together with a vast range of Southeast Asian outlets (especially Korean, Thai, Malaysian and Vietnamese).

❑ Montréal has over 5,000 restaurants serving some 75 types of ethnic cuisine. ❑

PRAIRIES In the Prairies, beef has always been superb thanks to the quality of Prairie grazing, while some of the innovations of the west—notably game and other more unusual meats—are finding their way into local restaurants. You can still find traditional Native American food, including turkey, venison, cornbread and popcorn, and barbecues are popular in summer.

Top: Crab, a Maritimes delicacy
Right: Part of the rich bounty of Canada's seas

It takes 40 liters (40 gallons) of sugar-maple sap to produce a litre (gallon) of maple syrup

❑ The Ordre de Bon Temps, North America's first dining club, was founded as early as 1605 in Nova Scotia by Samuel de Champlain. ❑

The region can also draw on the Ukrainian, German and Scandinavian traditions of much of its population, and on exotica such as caribou and Arctic char.

QUÉBEC AND MONTRÉAL Cooking in the east has developed over centuries from its early French roots. Not only are there more regional dishes here, together with a greater preponderance of outstanding produce, but there is as much ethnic variety as is found in the west. Québec's food is predictably French at heart, but boasts specialties of its own, such as maple syrup, *cipâte* (beef pie), *cretons* (spicy pâté), *tourtière* (meat and potato pie), *trempette* (bread, cream and maple syrup) and *poutine* (home-made *frites*, cheese and gravy). Montréal is well known for its smoked meats, beef sandwiches and crispy roast chicken. Pea, onion and cabbage soups and apple pie are popular everywhere.

MARITIMES Fish and seafood are the Maritimes' great staples, in particular the region's renowned lobsters, Digby scallops and Malpeque oysters. More unusual dishes include Solomon Gundy (marinated herring), finnan haddie (smoked haddock), rappie pie (potatoes and salt pork), fiddlehead (an edible fern), marakin (a Cape Breton sausage), Lunenburg pudding (a German sausage), scrapple (fried pork) and dulse (an edible seaweed). Desserts include such delicacies as fat archies (biscuits and dates), grunt (stewed fruits and dumplings) and forach (oatmeal, cream and sugar).

NEWFOUNDLAND Whole books have been devoted to Newfoundland's often bizarre cuisine. Cod tongues are a favorite, along with capelin (tiny fish) and brewis (soaked hard-tack biscuit boiled up with cod). Capelin are smoked, pickled or pinned to fences to dry, while brewis is eaten with fried salt-pork squares known as scrunchions. Seal-flipper pie is another specialty. Also common is summer savory, a spicy herb that is added to stews and stuffings. Moose, rabbit pie and seal soup are occasionally available. Desserts include partridgeberries (a relative of the cranberry) and bakeapples (yellowy-red berries). Both are eaten with ice cream or as jam on fresh-baked bread.

The divisions between French-speaking Québec and the rest of the country—a rift that has its roots in an antipathy dating back centuries—have often brought Canada to the brink of disintegration. The present difficulties have sparked wider debate elsewhere in Canada on the issues of national sovereignty.

❑ "The world's dumbest and most unnecessary constitutional crisis."—Mordecai Richler, contemporary Canadian writer ❑

SEEDS OF DIVISION Canada was in trouble from the moment its shores were contested by Britain and France almost 500 years ago. Long-standing historical animosities between the two countries were exported to the New World, where they remained largely under wraps until the defeat of the French at Québec in 1759. Up to that point French settlers had lived safely within the confines of New France (see pages 32–33), their language, culture and Catholic faith guaranteed by firm ties with the mother country. After 1759, however, they became British subjects, albeit ones who retained certain rights and remained in a French-speaking majority. With the slow evolution of the Canadian State, however, the Québécois increasingly found themselves marginalized in an English-dominated Confederation.

Top: President de Gaulle's "free Québec" speech in Montréal (1967)
Below: Québec separatist supporters

QUIET REVOLUTION For years their reaction was to retreat, keeping themselves to themselves in Québec's francophone redoubts. In

Confederation Square in Ottawa, Canada's federal capital

❑ *"Vive le Québec libre."*—French President Charles de Gaulle, Montréal (1967) ❑

the process many became part of an underclass, destined to be either farmers or blue-collar providers of cheap labor for industries owned and financed by English-speaking Canadians. Things began to change in the 1960s, when artists, writers and politicians (including Pierre Trudeau) began to breed a new sense of Québécois purpose and identity, a period now referred to as the *révolution tranquille*, or "quiet revolution." Social change followed hard on its heels, as the new Liberal-led provincial government wrested control of welfare, health and education from the Church (previously a force of reaction), and began the process of seeking greater political and economic autonomy.

❑ "Romance is the political currency of the independence camp. Seldom do they deviate into reason."—John Carlin, writing in the *Independent* newspaper (1995) ❑

TERRORISM Other, darker forces sought to lend a hand in this process, namely the Front de Libération du Québec (FLQ), a terrorist group whose actions culminated in 1970 with the kidnap and murder of Pierre Laporte, a Québécois minister. Within days the War Measures Act was invoked, troops were sent on to the streets, and 500 separatists had been rounded up and thrown into jail. Such events jolted the rest of the country from complacency, undermined what was, in many respects, a good Québécois case, and further worsened relations between French- and English-speakers.

BETTER OR WORSE A sign of how things were changing in Québec's favor, however, came with the Official Language Act of 1969, which gave French equal status to English, and made all of Canada officially bilingual. In 1977, things went further in Québec with the infamous *Charte de la langue française*, or Law 101, which made French the *only* official language in the province. Henceforth a "hot-dog," for example, had to be described as *un chien chaud*, and all street signs had to be in

French, producing such anomalies as Montréal's rue McTavish. Needless to say, English-speakers began to leave in droves, taking money and management skills with them, precipitating a provincial economic crisis that continues to this day.

MONEY Ultimately money will probably decide whether Québec remains part of Canada. Outside investment has faltered in the face of continuing uncertainty; and Canada has suggested that if Québec goes, it must pay a quarter of the country's multi-billion dollar national debt (as it has a quarter of the country's population). The province's farmers fear the loss of national subsidies, while its federal employees would have to surrender their Ottawa-linked jobs. As a result, separatist politicians are trying to sell a vision of a Québec that will acquire independence yet remain part of Canada.

The Canadian flag, symbol of a troubled country

Many hope that after secession they will keep the Canadian dollar (complete with portrait of the British Queen), retain their passports, and continue to trade with the rest of Canada as if nothing had happened.

DISINTEGRATION Federalists are openly scathing about these ideas. If Québec secedes, they say, it will spell disaster for Canada, not least in the economic sphere: the Canadian dollar might plunge, interest rates would soar, and the economy would be reduced to tatters. Other anomalies would come to the fore—for example, the Maritime provinces would be separated from the rest of Canada by over 563 km (350 miles) of "foreign territory." The Québécois, for their part, would be on their own.

WESTERN ALIENATION Most other provinces feel powerless to intervene, and at the mercy of any referendum decision. This has caused growing disenchantment with federalism. The phenomenon known as "Western alienation" is particularly strong in Alberta and British Columbia, where it is felt that federal effort and funds should be spent on all Canadians and not on trying to keep Québec in Canada. In many ways, Western alienation poses more of a threat to Canadian unity than does separatism in Québec. Since the defeat of the last Québec referendum in 1995, support for separatism has declined there. Despite the strength of the Parti Québécois, which is pledged to secede from Canada, recent polls show that the vast majority of Québécois prefer to remain part of Canada but they want their government to fight for increased powers, a factor that may well further alienate Westerners. Thus, it seems, the threat to Canada's integrity may never go away.

❑ In response to the question "What does Québec want?", Québec bard and humorist, Gilles Vigneault, said: "Why that's easy. They want to be totally independent in a strong and united Canada." ❑

Canada Was

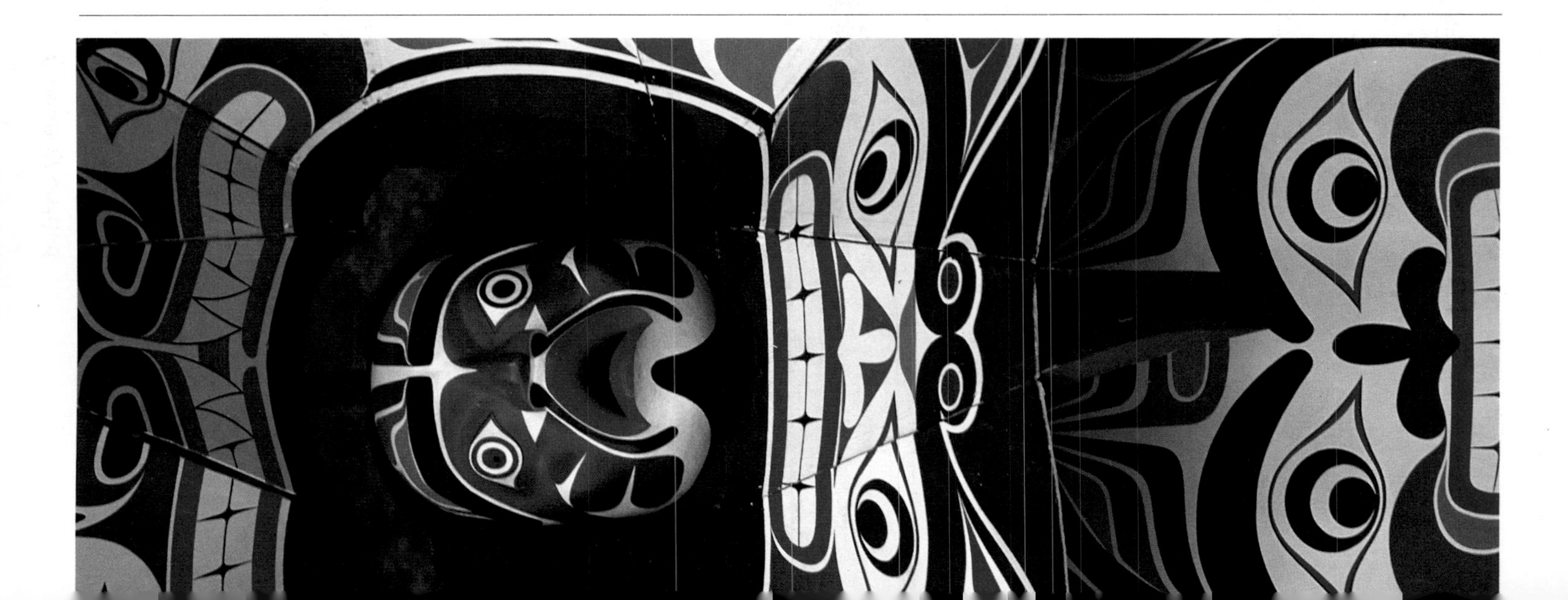

Canada's history begins not with its gradual colonization and exploitation by European settlers, but with the spread, over thousands of years, of its native peoples, for whom the arrival of foreigners was to spell tragedy and the near extinction of an ancient way of life.

LAND BRIDGE There was a time when not a soul roamed North America. Only around 25,000 years ago, close to the end of the last Ice Age, did the continent's first inhabitants arrive, by way of a vast land bridge which then existed between Asia and North America. Most were probably nomads from the Siberian steppes or from the mountains of Mongolia, who crossed today's Bering Strait (sea levels were then lower) to wander the ice-covered wastes of Alaska and the Yukon. Most came in search of food, hunting the buffalo, mammoth and hairy rhino that formed the basis of their diet. Few memorials now survive of their passing, save a handful of graves and the distinctive carved spear-heads that have seen them christened the "Fluted Point People."

> ❑ *"Quelques arpents de neige"* ("a few acres of snow").—Voltaire on Canada, *Candide* (1759) ❑

Top: Modern Inuit painting
Below: Native Canadian chieftain painted by Paul Kane (1848)

A CONTINENT COLONIZED Fresh waves of immigration from such peoples washed over North America for thousands of years, spreading south across the isthmus of Panama until a genetically related group of tribes spanned the continent. Individual tribes then developed their own languages and cultures, each group evolving according to the natural resources close at hand. In Canada only the Inuit still preserve traces of their ancient way of life (see pages 132–133), the traditions of other aboriginal peoples, or First Nations, having been almost obliterated. Improvization and creative adaptability were all in Inuit culture. Sled runners, for example, might be made from sealskin or frozen fish, while the Inuits' distinctive facial tattoos were made by drawing a soot-soaked sinew through the flesh.

WEST COAST Some of the most sophisticated of the First Nations were the tribes of the Pacific coast, whose access to abundant natural resources, such as wood, fish, furs and forest animals, allowed a way of life far in

The way of life for Canada's aboriginal peoples remained unchanged for thousands of years

advance of the near-subsistence level of other native groups. The ease with which food and raw materials could be gathered, together with a benign climate, resulted in a relatively sedentary lifestyle. This in turn left tribes-people with time for art and ceremony. The result was some of the most sophisticated ceremonials of almost any aboriginal peoples in North America, and some of the greatest woodcarving—of which totem poles were the ultimate expression.

PLAINS TRIBES In the interior plains of central Canada, by contrast, native tribes relied on the buffalo for most of their creature comforts. Where the buffalo roamed, therefore, so roamed the Cree, Assiniboine and Blackfoot. The animal was hunted for its meat, its bones (for tools), its skins (for clothes and tepees)—even for its hooves (boiled down to make glue). Tribes were often mutually hostile, their languages so different—despite their shared nomadic habits—that sign language was often needed to trade.

❏ "They be like to Tartars, with longe blacke haire, broad faces and flatte noses, and tawnie in colour, wearing seale skinnes..."—Officer on the Frobisher expedition describing the Inuit (1576) ❏

WOODLAND TRIBES Eastern Canada's aboriginal tribes were mostly sedentary, agricultural peoples (see pages 184–185). They lived in "longhouse" villages and supplemented a diet of corn, beans and squash with forays into river country and the eastern woodlands for fish, meat and berries. Although often linked by language, the main tribes had distinct characteristics, none more so than the enterprising Algonquin and the warlike Iroquois. The latter were to become the scourge of early French settlers, and were implacable enemies of the Huron, another Iroquoian tribe. None of these centuries-old cultures, however, was ultimately to prove a match for the Europeans, whose first envoys began to tread Canadian shores about 1,000 years ago.

Some claim 6th-century Irish sailors were the first Europeans to find the "New World," others that Basque fishermen and Bristol mariners trawled its North Atlantic coast in the 15th century. All the signs are, however, that it was the Vikings who, 500 years before Columbus, first set foot on Canadian shores.

THE VIKINGS Although there are no contemporary written records of the event, it was probably around AD 870 that Viking longboats nosed through the icy waters of the North Atlantic and made landfall on the island now known as Iceland. From here, according to the Icelandic Sagas, they pushed west to Greenland, introducing some 3,000 settlers to its shores by the beginning of the 11th century. One of these, Bjarne Herjolfsen, so the story goes, found himself lost between Iceland and Greenland some time around AD 986. Caught in the teeth of a gale, and blown off course, he glimpsed a distant coastline through the raging weather. Escaping the storm, he returned home with tales of the strange land.

VINLAND About AD 995 Leif Eriksson, "The Lucky," set off to explore this new land. In time he landed at Helluland (Baffin Island), Markland (Labrador) and Vinland (Newfoundland). His accounts of the region's salmon and teeming forests soon prompted others to follow. Attempts at settlement, however, were thwarted by encounters with local tribes, wild people whom the Vikings christened the *skraelings*, or "wretches" (probably Algonquin natives). As a result, the Vikings appear to have established only temporary settlements, using them as bases to gather wood and other resources for export to Greenland

John and Sebastian Cabot leaving Bristol for the New World in 1497

Jacques Cartier, who visited two Native Canadian villages on the sites of the future Montréal and Québec

and Scandinavia. This pattern continued until about 1410, when something—possibly Inuit attacks, or a change in climate—seems to have made the sea voyage too dangerous. Isolated, and wracked by disease, the last Vikings died out almost at the moment Columbus was to set sail across the Atlantic for his "New World."

JOHN CABOT The success of Columbus's voyage, which had been prompted by the search for a new route to the Orient, encouraged other European monarchs to chance their arm in state-sponsored voyages across the "western sea." In 1497 John Cabot, an Italian navigator, received the blessing of Henry VII of England for such a trip. Cabot set sail with just 18 men, and landed on Cape Breton Island 52 days later—the first European "officially" to have set foot in Canada. Having claimed the land for England (and mistaken it for northeast Asia), he returned home to regale a disappointed Henry with tales not of silks and spices, but of fish and forestry. Henry paid him £10 for his troubles. Others paid more heed to the tales, and within a few years the waters off Newfoundland were filled with the boats of English, Basque, French, Spanish and Portuguese fishermen.

❑ "I believe that this was the land that God allotted to Cain."—Jacques Cartier (quoted) *The First Relation* (1534) ❑

JACQUES CARTIER Little attempt was made to settle the new lands until the voyage of Jacques Cartier in 1534, an expedition—also made in the hope of finding a route to the East—that was sponsored by the French crown. Cartier landed further south than Cabot, claiming the Gaspé Peninsula for France before pushing up the St. Lawrence River. Here he stopped at two Iroquois villages, Hochelaga (modern Montréal) and Stadacona (present-day Québec). After wintering near the latter, he returned to France with two Iroquois natives as "booty" and tales of the vast mineral wealth in the new land. Some of these minerals (probably fool's gold) were collected by Cartier on a subsequent voyage (in 1542), only for them to be declared worthless on his return. The disappointment killed interest in the region until about 1600, when a growing interest in furs sparked the events that were to shape Canadian history for centuries.

❑ "Canada is said to have got its name from the two Spanish words *Aca* and *Nada*, as signifying 'there is nothing here.'"—R. B. Graham, *Mogreb-el-Acksa* (1898) ❑

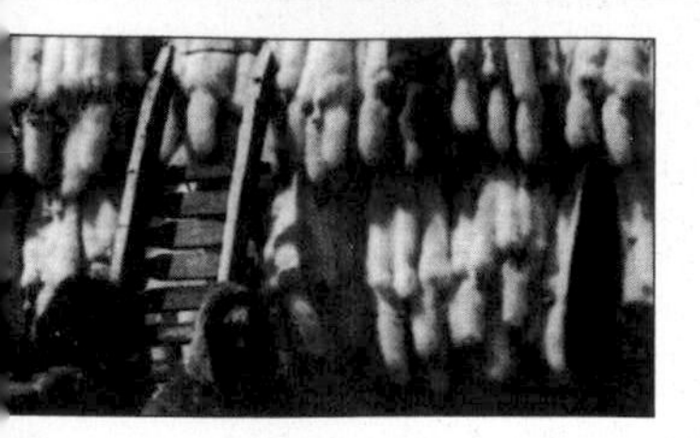

Modern Canada was virtually born on the back of its lucrative fur trade. Hunters drove trails through virgin territory in search of pelts; explorers blazed continent-wide routes to secure lines of supply; and towns across the country grew out of the network of trading posts built to barter furs with native trappers.

BEGINNINGS Realizing that Canada would yield little in the way of gold, silks and spices, most Europeans turned to the more mundane rewards of fish and timber. Trading in furs began as a sideline for the fishermen who made seasonal visits to Canadian waters. From the camps that many established on shore to cure their catch, they would hunt, trade a few pelts with natives, then use the furs as barter among themselves.

FOUNDER The first post designed specifically for the purpose of trading furs—near present-day Tadoussac—was established in 1600 by the Frenchman Pierre Chauvin. Another Frenchman, however, Samuel de Champlain, is usually awarded the title "Father of New France." An explorer and surveyor, de Champlain had been commissioned to chart the St. Lawrence River, forming part of an expedition which, encouraged by the French king (who was anxious to emulate Spanish success elsewhere in the New World) sought to establish permanent settlement in the lands claimed by Cartier for France.

Below: The new season's furs are brought into storage
Top: A collection of white fox furs

SETTLEMENT The expedition settled first in New Brunswick (see pages 224–225, moving to Port Royal in Nova Scotia in 1605 (present-day Annapolis). Although a settlement survived here, the region's rugged countryside made it impossible to enforce the fur-trading concessions awarded by the French king. Such concessions were offered as incentives to encourage settlement in

White trappers were unusual: Fur companies usually employed aboriginal peoples

otherwise hostile environments. Settlement, in turn, was vital to making good the claims of France to her new lands. Foiled in Nova Scotia, therefore, de Champlain moved to the St. Lawrence, where he established a *habitation* at a site that natives called *kebec* (present-day Québec).

BEAVER BOOM From this point on the importance of the fur trade became immense, inextricably linked with the growth of Canada, and with the rivalry between Britain and France for control of the new country. Demand for the beaver, in particular, became almost insatiable, thanks to its use in the fashions promulgated by European hat-makers. However, the battle to monopolize the market—which remained voracious for over 200 years—not only engaged the merchants of Europe, but changed forever the life of the continent's aboriginal populations.

TAKING SIDES While Europeans could trap furs themselves, they could hardly compete with the natives' local knowledge and sheer expertise. De Champlain understood this from the outset, quickly identifying tribes who would prove the most reliable suppliers. To this end he allied himself (and France) with the Huron, traditional enemies of the Iroquois, exacerbating the existing antipathies between the tribes. In one famous episode in 1609, de Champlain and three armed companions accompanied the Huron in a raid against the Mohawks, a tribe in the Iroquois confederation. French guns killed many (some accounts say 300), a massacre that left a lasting impression on the Iroquois, who eventually joined forces with the Dutch and the British.

WAY OF LIFE While later fur companies (the North West and Hudson's Bay) were larger than earlier French concerns, the manner in which native ways of life were undermined remained unchanged from day one. Polarization of tribes along European lines was one consequence; the arrival of guns was another. Furs bought first one, and then the other side muskets, tools and metal-bladed weapons, each a huge leap from the stone and wood technology that had served the native tribes for centuries. In the long run this was to engender a subtle dependence from which they would never recover. In the short term it seemed to the benefit of all, especially the French, who for decades appeared to have the vast resources of the new country at their mercy.

After beginning life as a trading venture, the lands claimed by de Champlain for the French king were eventually recognized as the crown colony of "New France." For much of its 100-year existence, this domain found itself at the heart of a broader struggle for supremacy in North America between Britain and France.

CONSOLIDATION France's new lands were plagued from the outset by skirmishes with Britain and by disputes with their native populations. In 1627, for example, a pair of English adventurers, the Kirke brothers, blockaded the St. Lawrence River, seriously disrupting the French trade in furs. In 1649 French missionaries were massacred by the Iroquois, while in 1660 Montréal was only narrowly saved from destruction by hostile tribes.

In response to these problems, Louis XIV moved to put the new lands—until then little more than a fur traders' fiefdom—on to a more formal footing. The result was the establishment of the crown colony of "Nouvelle France," or "New France."

AUTHORITY Louis's action introduced firm government to the region for the first time. Until then, native raids and a lack of central authority had frightened off potential settlers. In 1640, for example, more than a century after Cartier's pioneering voyage, the new lands' population totaled a mere 240 (compared with 40,000 elsewhere in the New World). More rigorous control soon paid dividends, and by 1685 the population had risen to some 10,000. Prosperity soon followed, bolstered not only by absolutist government, but also by the authority of the Catholic Church and a rigidly structured system of settlement.

❑ Lands on the St. Lawrence were claimed for France in 1535 but were only declared a crown colony in 1663. ❑

General James Wolfe, British hero of the French and Indian War

SETTLEMENT Most French settlers conformed to a seigneurial way of life, a feudal system that was introduced to the colony from the mother country and that survived until the 1850s (though in France it ended with the revolution in 1789). Under its terms, the king granted land, or a *seigneurie*, to nobles, merchants and religious orders in return for loyalty (in New France land was also available to those of more humble birth). These *seigneurs* then rented their land to a series of tenant farmers, or *habitants*, whose security of tenure rested on payment of a yearly tithe, payment in kind (usually grain), work on roads and ditches, and a willingness, when called upon, to join the militia.

DECLINE Trade rather than settlement, however, remained New France's main *raison d'être*. While explorers

extended French influence across the continent, settlers were discouraged from following them, remaining confined to settlements on the St. Lawrence River such as Québec, Montréal and Trois-Rivières. This left New France vulnerable to more populous British territories to the south, notably New England, while political neglect of the west allowed the British greater freedom of action. Consequences of this included the founding of the Hudson's Bay Company in 1670, whose importance was to be constantly underestimated by the French (see pages 168–169).

DEFEAT By the time France realized the danger posed by Britain, it was too late. Countless raids and battles to protect their possessions proved unsuccessful, leading only to the 1713 Treaty of Utrecht, whose terms—designed to bring the skirmishing to an end—saw Britain gain Acadia, a French territory in the Maritimes (renamed Nova Scotia), and all of Hudson Bay and the lands south of the Great Lakes.

By 1744 fighting broke out again, culminating in the French and Indian War (1754–1763). France's execution of the war proved singularly half-hearted. New France's surviving borders were lightly defended, while the fleet remained in France to protect the mother country. Québec City—the key to New France—was taken by General James Wolfe in 1759. Montréal fell a year later. In 1763 France surrendered, ceding her North American territories to the British. The newly named colony of "Québec" became a British territory.

Wolfe died shortly after learning that his attack on Québec had been successful

For decades after the capitulation of New France, Britain struggled to come to terms with her new and largely French-speaking subjects. This struggle acquired new twists with the American Revolution and the increasingly vocal opposition to political corruption within the nascent colonies.

FOREIGN SUBJECTS Britain's victory over France left it master of "Canada" but not of its people, most of whom were French-speaking *Canadiens* who deeply resented their new rulers. English-speaking enclaves existed only in Halifax, Nova Scotia and a few parts of Newfoundland. Elsewhere across the country, notably in the great lands of the west, exploration, let alone settlement, was still in its infancy. James Cook made the first Pacific landing in 1778, just 15 years after France's surrender, while the first crossing of the Rockies by a European took place in 1793.

Top: The signing of the US Declaration of Independence had profound effects on Canada's history
Below: British "Loyalists" arriving in Canada after the American Revolution

THE QUÉBEC ACT Britain's first thought was to flood her new colony with British settlers. This, it was hoped, would dilute French influence at a stroke. Willing pioneers, however, proved to be in short supply. Matters were made more pressing by rumblings from the south, where Britain's American colonies were becoming increasingly restless. If the American colonies

❏ The first act of the new American Congress in 1775 was not to declare independence from Britain, but to declare war on Canada. ❏

were to rebel, the loyalty of Britain's 80,000 *Canadiens*—around 99 percent of the population—might prove crucial. This led more astute politicians, among them Sir Guy Carleton, Québec's governor, to replace immigration with a more diplomatic approach. The result was the 1774 Québec Act, a document granting French-speakers economic, political and cultural guarantees.

INDEPENDENCE The concessions proved timely, for just a year later the American colonies rose up against British rule. Most *Canadiens*, mollified by the Québec Act, refused to join the American Revolutionary War (1775–1783), though they also refused to fight for the Crown. Businesses also sided with the British, deciding—despite the Americans' success—that continued contact with Britain promised greater economic benefits.

CANADA After the war many thousands of "Loyalists"—American colonists who had supported the British—swarmed across the border to settle in what remained of British North America. *Canadien* dominance was thus removed by the influx of English-speaking Protestants, dramatically altering Québec's balance of ethnic and political power. The resulting stand-off between French- and English-speakers was resolved by the Constitutional Act (1791), which provided for the division of Québec into two. One part, Upper Canada (present-day Ontario), was to be predominantly English (or Loyalist). The other, Lower Canada (modern Québec), was to be mainly French.

REVOLT Each province had an elected assembly, together with a council appointed from Britain. However, final executive power resided with the latter, an arrangement that meant Assembly decisions were invariably overruled. Worse still, powerful cliques developed around the appointed councils, leading to corruption and numerous abuses of power and privilege. Upper Canada's ruling faction was known as the "Family Compact," Lower Canada's as the "Château Clique." Both caused growing resentment, giving rise to reform movements headed by William Lyon Mackenzie and Louis-Joseph Papineau, respectively.

"Radical Jack" (Lord Durham)

TOWARD UNION Both movements spawned armed revolts, and, though neither proved successful, the disturbances forced Britain to re-examine the provinces' political grievances. Lord Durham—"radical Jack" to his friends—was appointed Governor of Upper and Lower Canada and the "Canadian" colonies (Nova Scotia, New Brunswick and Prince Edward Island). His report on the situation underlined the colonies' problems, concluding that some form of unity was vital to meet the growing economic (and thus political) challenge of the US

The result was the union of Upper and Lower Canada into the "Province of Canada," a halfway house to confederation and the birth of modern Canada.

Centuries of Canadian history elapsed before Canada itself was born. Until Confederation in 1867, and the "Dominion" it brought into being, the country was a collection of separate British-owned colonies, its peoples an ethnic mosaic of indigenous Canadians and French, British and other disparate settlers.

SEPARATE COLONIES Despite the union of Upper and Lower Canada, British North America in the middle of the 19th century remained a collection of separate colonies. Most of these became ever more prosperous, forging increasingly distinct identities as the century progressed. Fishing flourished in Newfoundland, shipbuilding thrived in Nova Scotia and New Brunswick, farming flowered in Prince Edward Island, and immigration fueled economic growth in the former Upper and Lower Canada. Elsewhere, industry and commerce blossomed in the colonies' larger towns, nurtured by the vast resources of the interior and the ever-flowing flood of furs from the north.

Top: Prince Edward Island, where confederation was agreed
Below: George Étienne Cartier

DIVIDED Across the continent the first stirrings of trade and settlement had also started in what was to become British Columbia (Vancouver Island was declared a Crown colony in 1858). Alberta, the Yukon and the Prairie provinces, however, together with the lands to the north, remained virtually unknown. Much of this domain was the former Rupert's Land, still under the nominal control of the Hudson's Bay Company (see pages 168–169), the vast vacuum of power at the center of the continent a symbol of the gulf that separated the disparate colonies.

❏ *A mari usque ad mare*—"From sea to sea" (Canada's motto). ❏

AMERICAN THREAT This state of affairs provoked bitter political debate during the 1850s and early 1860s. Many politicians argued for some form of confederation, only to see the issue sidelined by political infighting. Hard-headed reality finally intruded during the Civil War (1861–1865) in the United States, an event that brought with it the possibility of renewed Anglo-American conflict. This eventuality, together with alarm at US progress (a fact that had long worried Canadian politicians), quickly focused minds on the need for change. Previously antipathetic factions soon reached a consensus, allowing George Étienne Cartier, George Brown and John A. Macdonald—previously implacable political foes—to unite on a platform of confederation.

CONFEDERATION COCKTAILS In the meantime, the maritime colonies had quietly been discussing an affiliation of their own (to include Nova Scotia, New Brunswick, Newfoundland and Prince Edward Island). When Brown and Macdonald caught wind of the discussions they immediately decided to join them (uninvited). They quickly chartered a boat, the *Queen Victoria*, and loaded it with $13,000 worth of champagne by way of a peace offering.

The boat and its booty landed at Charlottetown (Prince Edward Island) in 1864, where the visiting worthies were somewhat disappointed to be met by a delegation of one: a single official sent out in an oyster boat. Ignoring this inauspicious start, the delegation set to work, and within days the so-called "Fathers of Confederation" had laid the groundwork for a union of all British North American colonies.

John A. Macdonald, one of the "Fathers of Confederation"

CANADA BORN The proposed merger was debated by the British parliament for three years. Final ratification was granted by the British North America Act in 1867. This brought together Nova Scotia and New Brunswick, and divided the Province of Canada into Québec and Ontario. Cartier and Macdonald's hopes for the "Dominion," however, had been of a country across the continent, and the door to new members was left firmly ajar.

In 1868 Rupert's Land was bought from the Hudson's Bay Company, clearing the way for the creation of a fifth province, Manitoba (see page 38). British Columbia, independently minded, but fearful of its US neighbor, joined in 1871. Prince Edward Island signed up in 1873. Alberta and Saskatchewan were created in 1905. Plucky little Newfoundland was to remain an outsider until 1949.

Provincial shields: Ontario (top) and Québec

While creating Canada was easy, creating Canadians to fill it was to prove more difficult. Settlers were first lured with the offer of free land, using territory bought from the Hudson's Bay Company. Much of this land was already settled by Native Canadians and Métis, however, a fact that was to lead to rebellion and long-standing recriminations.

LAND Confederation left several large pieces missing from the Canadian jigsaw puzzle. Chief of these were lands still administered by the Hudson's Bay Company (see pages 168–169), territories eventually bought by the Canadian government for $1.5 million dollars. Unfortunately the deal—concluded in 1870—failed to acknowledge the area's 170,000 existing inhabitants, the majority of them tribes who had roamed the region for millennia, and some 5,000 Métis, the mainly Catholic and French-speaking offspring of mixed aboriginal and European parentage.

❑ Canada's purchase of the Hudson's Bay Company territories was the largest land deal in history. ❑

TROUBLE Hints of trouble began to surface immediately, as government surveyors, backed by troops, started to square up Métis land for distribution to immigrants. More coherent in their opposition than tribal members, who were already being bought off with high-sounding treaties, the Métis proceeded to seize Fort Garry (a British outpost) and formed a provisional government under the inspirational leadership of Louis Riel (1844–1885).

LEADER Even today Riel remains one of the most charismatic and controversial characters in Canadian history. Born near Red River, in the heart of Métis country, he trained first as a priest and then as a lawyer, nurturing an almost obsessive desire

Louis Riel, inspirational leader of the Métis rebellions

to establish Catholicism in Canada. In championing the Métis cause—a largely worthy one—he led a model and initially successful campaign, refusing to shed blood and showing a willingness to negotiate.

SUCCESS Riel enjoyed little support from the English-speaking Métis, however, or from the mainly Irish-born Ontarians who had drifted into Métis regions in anticipation of their annexation. One of the latter, the Orangeman Thomas Scott, tried to assassinate Riel, who—making his one fatal blunder—had him court-martialed and executed. A white Protestant "murdered" by French Catholic "half-breeds" caused outrage in Ontario and resulted in long-lasting bad feeling. Riel's position remained strong, however, and in the light of negotiations the

province of Manitoba was created in 1870. Equal rights were granted to English- and French-speakers, and 57ha (140 acres) of land were set aside for each Métis.

RETREAT Despite his success, Riel fled before the arrival of British troops, and was sentenced *in absentia* to two years' imprisonment. He was then elected to parliament in 1874, but remained unable to take his seat in the wake of continuing anger at Scott's death. In 1875 he was granted a pardon, but on condition he remained in exile for four years, a period of banishment he spent in the US.

REBELLION Elsewhere the early high hopes of the Métis were being dashed. Only 20 percent ever received their allotted land, much being bought by speculators at a fraction of its worth. Many of the dispossessed drifted into Saskatchewan, keen to pursue a life away from the settlers and survey troops. When this proved impossible, Riel was summoned once more. He

Métis and Native Canadian forces outgunned at Frenchman's Butte (1885)

formed another provisional government and linked up with the Cree. This alliance—in another unfortunate incident—was to lead to the deaths of several policemen. Responding to public outrage in the east, and fearing full-scale insurrection, Prime Minister John Macdonald dispatched a force that duly crushed the revolt and captured its leader. At Riel's trial the defense pleaded insanity (Riel was almost certainly mentally ill), while pleas for clemency flooded in from both sides. After weeks of debate, however, Riel was hanged on November 16, 1885, a controversial death (martyrdom to some) that still arouses the strongest passions.

❑ "He shall hang though every dog in Québec should bark in his favor."—Prime Minister Macdonald (1815–1891), responding to appeals for Louis Riel's life ❑

Having created a country and tamed its rebellious heart through force of arms, Canada's next task was to create a transcontinental railroad, a great thread of steel that would open up the Prairies, bind together its far-flung provinces and symbolically unite the country in one grand, sweeping gesture.

STRATEGY Plans for a transcontinental railroad had been hatched well before Confederation, its strategic as well as psychological importance to the Canadian colonies having long been apparent. Before its arrival, the natural movement of trade and people was southward, attracted by the obvious proximity of the USA. No country could survive where it was easier to reach a foreign country (and a largely hostile one at that), than it was to reach neighboring provinces in one's own country. This was particularly true in the west, where British Columbia had made the construction of a railroad a condition of its joining the Confederation. The Maritimes, equally worried by their peripheral position, had voiced similar concerns.

The Canadian Pacific Railway was the thread which helped unite a nation

TRADE As well as having a strategic role, the line was also seen as a basic prerequisite for trade, particularly around the St. Lawrence, whose transportation links were becoming inferior to those south of the border. Railroad building in the United States was already well under way, the first transcontinental line having been completed in 1869. A Canadian line would also carry pioneers to their promised land, and tap into the colossal agricultural (and later mineral) wealth of the Prairies and Canadian Shield. French-speaking politicians, for their part, saw the line as a means of spreading French cultural influence across the new lands to the west.

SLOW START British Columbia's promise to join the Confederation, with its insistence on a rail link to the east, was made in 1871. Work on the link eventually began in 1881.

❑ Between 1896 and 1913 over a million settlers used the Canadian Pacific Railway to travel to a new life in the Prairies. ❑

Progress was hamstrung by political infighting, the opposition parties in 1871 having labeled the project "an act of insane recklessness." Finance presented still greater problems. Private enterprise was won over by cash subsidies of $25 million, and by the promise of 10 million hectare (25 million acres) of free land. The latter was to be chosen from lots within a 40km (24-mile) corridor along the railroad. Once the line was built, this land—now covered by cities such as Calgary—was to become some of the most valuable in the country.

SLEAZE The line's problems eventually brought down Prime Minister John A. Macdonald, one of the line's staunchest advocates. He stood accused of accepting election funds from Sir Hugh Allan, a prominent Montréal shipping magnate organizing the line's construction. Worse still, Allan's consortium included heavy US backing, suggesting the railroad might eventually finish up under US control, but Macdonald fell because of the suspicion that Allan might have received the railroad contract for services rendered. Macdonald's successor, Alexander Mackenzie, then proceeded so slowly with the line that British Columbia threatened secession if matters continued to drag on. The railroad finally reached Vancouver in 1887.

❑ The ceremonial "last spike" of Canada's transcontinental railway was made of iron. That of the US was made of gold. ❑

JOINING THE WHOLE Over the intervening decades, Canada's transcontinental railroad came to be seen as a thread that helped unite the sprawling country. There is romance in the idea of a cross-country rail journey. Yet today the once-proud line, built in the face of such hardships, is in a sorry state. By 1992 so much business had been lost to air and road that Canadian Pacific closed the line to passengers. The mighty railroad is now a freightline: only wheat, oil and minerals ride its hallowed rails. Its passenger services have merged with those of the Canadian National Railways under the auspices of VIA Rail.

Modern Canada has a population of around 30 million, of whom only 810,000 belong to the country's aboriginal peoples. All the rest are immigrants or descendants of immigrants, a vast multiethnic patchwork whose pattern and development over four centuries have done much to shape the country.

SETTLEMENT Canada's first pioneers were a sorry bunch—a few fishermen, a handful of hunters and a scattering of half-starved Vikings. More organized settlers arrived around 1600, introduced by the Norman entrepreneur Pierre Chauvin, who obtained a ten-year trading monopoly from Henri IV in return for settling 50 French men and women a year. Behind the deal lay the thinking that was to drive immigration policy in Canada for centuries: the idea that only permanent settlement could make good a country's territorial claims against those of rival powers.

FRANCE In the first instance this meant the claim of France to the lands of the St. Lawrence. Her main challengers in the region were the British—there were already British settlers in Newfoundland and the Maritimes—but for the most part her rival's efforts were concentrated in the "American" colonies to the south. France's next move was the settlement of "Acadia" (Nova Scotia) in 1604 (see pages 224–225), and the creation of the first fur post on the site of modern-day Québec (in 1608). This was followed in the 1620s by the creation of the "Hundred Associates," a company whose fur monopoly was granted on condition that 400 pioneers were settled each year.

❑ New France's population: 1642 (240); 1663 (2,500); 1666 (3,200); 1676 (8,500); 1713 (19,000); 1739 (48,000); 1759 (70,000). ❑

BRITAIN At the fall of New France in 1759 (see pages 32–33) some 99 percent of Canada's settlers were French, a proportion that saw the British strive to introduce English-speaking settlers from the old "American" colonies. Few felt inclined to move until the American Revolution, when the influx of English-speaking "Loyalists" altered Québec's ethnic complexion at a stroke (and dramatically increased the population of the Maritimes).

❑ Population in 1806: Prince Edward Island (9,700); Newfoundland (26,000); New Brunswick (35,000); Nova Scotia (65,000); Upper Canada/Ontario (71,000); Lower Canada/Québec (250,000). ❑

BIG WAVE The first waves of mass immigration from Britain and Ireland began around 1830, prompted by the high price of grain there, Britain's post-Napoleonic unrest and poverty, and then the potato famines. These were the migrations of popular imagination: thousands crammed into the holds of usually filthy, ill-equipped lumber boats, short of food, warmth and sanitation, and wracked by the diseases that killed hundreds in the quarantine and immigration reception huts of Montréal and Québec. Some 800,000 rode this human wave to a new life across the Atlantic between 1815 and 1850 (more than doubling the population). In 1832 alone, around 66,000 arrived in Upper Canada (Ontario) whose entire population had been 71,000 in 1806.

❑ Population in 1840: Prince Edward Island (32,000); Newfoundland (73,000); New Brunswick (157,000); Nova Scotia (203,000); Upper Canada/Ontario (716,000); Lower Canada/Québec (432,000). ❑

LAND RUSH Canada's second great period of immigration came after 1885, in the rush of British and European emigrants to the Prairies, drawn by offers of free land, transported by the new transcontinental railroad, and aided by Canadian officials who trawled Europe actively recruiting immigrants. Some 16,800 arrived in 1896: by 1913 the annual figure was 500,000. In 1914 Canada's population was about 8 million, almost 3 million of whom had arrived in the preceding 20 years. Today, immigration—though tempered—continues to be the motor driving Canada: since 1945, for example, the country's population has doubled, while these days around 15 percent of all "Canadians" were born in another country.

Top: Newcomers' tents at Dawson in 1898
Below: An immigrant family stands in front of its new home near Lake St. John

Canada's immigrant population has continued to soar during the 20th century, and the country has struggled to forge a sense of national identity—distinct from those of Britain and the US—despite growing separatist ambitions among its French-speaking population.

PRAIRIE PROMISE Canada's immigrant flood continued during the early years of the 20th century. On the Prairies, settlers brought two new provinces into existence, Alberta and Saskatchewan, ruthlessly supplanting their native populations in the process. Newcomers paid a registration fee of $10, and promised to remain on a farm for at least six months of the year for three years in a row. In return they received 160 acres of free land and—in most cases—Canadian citizenship. Places that had previously been little more than railside clearings—notably Calgary and Vancouver—suddenly sprang to life, while in the far north the discovery of gold on the Klondike attracted pioneers to previously uncharted lands.

❑ "Canada is a political expression."—Goldwin Smith, *Canada and the Canadian Question* (1891) ❑

❑ "Canada is really two countries held together by three nation-saving bywords—conservatism, caution and compromise—bequeathed to us by Britain."—William Toye, *A Book of Canada* (1962) ❑

ALLIES Canada's deep links with Britain were underlined during World War I, when Canadians fought hard for the Allied cause (though many of Québec's French Canadians proved reluctant to enlist). The participation of Canadian soldiers in several great battles, notably Vimy Ridge, has been seen as an almost symbolic coming of age for the country (though one that cost it 60,611 lives). However, postwar euphoria, symbolized by new directions in art and culture, quickly gave way to the privations of the Depression.

Top: Calgary in 1889
Below: Canadian troops in the trenches of the Somme during World War I

Former Prime Minister Pierre Trudeau and his then wife, Margaret

SMALL-TOWN BLUES The Depression hit particularly hard in the Prairies, which had enjoyed a boom during World War I after the disruption of Russian wheat supplies. The country's heartland was struck first by a world glut of wheat (which meant Australian, Argentinian and Russian wheat was cheaper), and then by the same string of droughts and poor harvests that created the Dust Bowl in the United States. Prairie settlements in the 1930s were a microcosm of Canada, a country that—with a few exceptions—was then still a patchwork of quiet and deeply conservative towns. Thus, while the 1931 Statute of Westminster finally made Canada an autonomous state within the British Empire, the country remained a worthy but basically ineffectual player on the world stage.

❑ "I don't even know what street Canada is on."—
Al Capone (1931) ❑

BOOM All this began to change after World War II, when Canada had again stood alongside Britain (with the usual Québécois exceptions). Cities such as Toronto, Montréal and Vancouver began to boom; and immigration soared again. Canada took a leading role in NATO, the United Nations and the Korean War. The consumer booms of the 1950s brought prosperity, and the country's huge natural resources were greedily sought by the world's industrialized nations (Canada is now a member of the G7 group of the world's seven leading economic powers).

NEW CONFEDERATION During the 1960s, the cultural revolution that touched much of the developed world also touched Canada. Changes in Québec were particularly profound, where the so-called "quiet revolution" paved the way for more radical French separatist ambitions (see pages 22–23). On the broader stage, Pierre Trudeau, one of Canada's most charismatic politicians, attempted to bridge the country's growing ethnic divisions by championing bilingual and multicultural policies. In this he was only partially successful, and today Canada is still increasingly divided between those seeking a stronger federation, and those whose desire for greater provincial autonomy once again threatens Canada's fragile sense of nationhood.

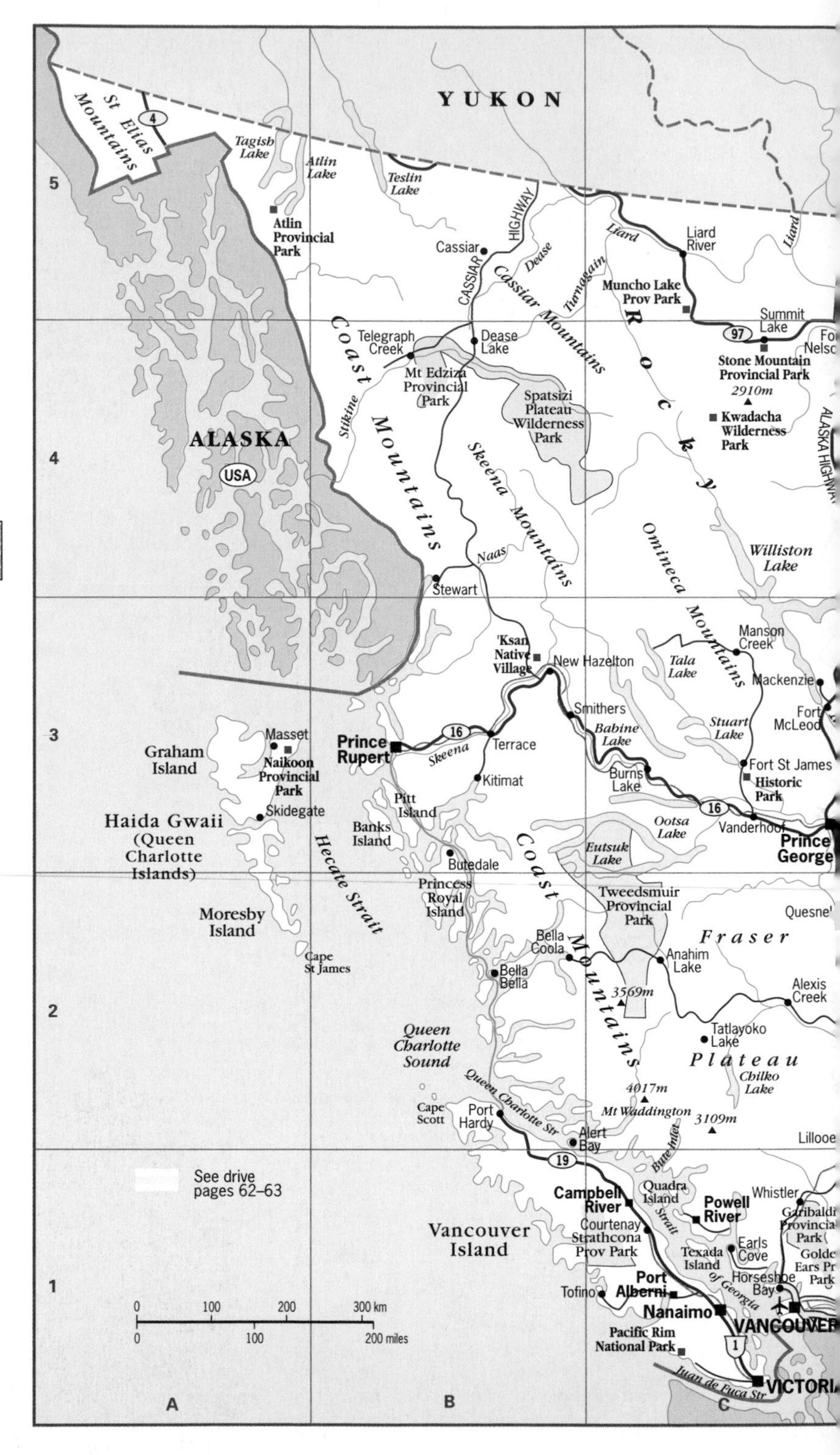

YUKON
St Elias Mountains
Tagish Lake
Atlin Lake
Teslin Lake
Atlin Provincial Park
Cassiar
CASSIAR HIGHWAY
Dease
Cassiar Mountains
Turnagain
Liard
Liard River
Muncho Lake Prov Park
Summit Lake
Stone Mountain Provincial Park
2910m
Kwadacha Wilderness Park
ALASKA HIGHWAY
Coast Mountains
Telegraph Creek
Dease Lake
Mt Edziza Provincial Park
Spatsizi Plateau Wilderness Park
Stikine
Skeena Mountains
Rocky
ALASKA
USA
Omineca Mountains
Williston Lake
Naas
Stewart
'Ksan Native Village
New Hazelton
Tala Lake
Manson Creek
Mackenzie
Fort McLeod
Smithers
Babine Lake
Stuart Lake
Masset
Graham Island
Naikoon Provincial Park
Prince Rupert
Skeena
Terrace
Kitimat
Burns Lake
Fort St James
Historic Park
Haida Gwaii (Queen Charlotte Islands)
Skidegate
Pitt Island
Banks Island
Hecate Strait
Ootsa Lake
Vanderhoof
Prince George
Butedale
Eutsuk Lake
Princess Royal Island
Moresby Island
Tweedsmuir Provincial Park
Quesnel
Fraser
Cape St James
Bella Coola
Anahim Lake
Bella Bella
3569m
Alexis Creek
Queen Charlotte Sound
Tatlayoko Lake
Plateau
Chilko Lake
Queen Charlotte Str
4017m
Mt Waddington
3109m
Cape Scott
Port Hardy
Alert Bay
Bute Inlet
Lillooet
See drive pages 62–63
Campbell River
Quadra Island
Powell River
Whistler
Garibaldi Provincial Park
Vancouver Island
Courtenay
Strathcona Prov Park
Strait
Texada Island
Earls Cove
Golden Ears Prov Park
of Georgia
Horseshoe Bay
Tofino
Port Alberni
Nanaimo
VANCOUVER
Pacific Rim National Park
Juan de Fuca Str
VICTORIA
0 100 200 300 km
0 100 200 miles
16
97
19
1
4
A B C
1 2 3 4 5
46

British Columbia

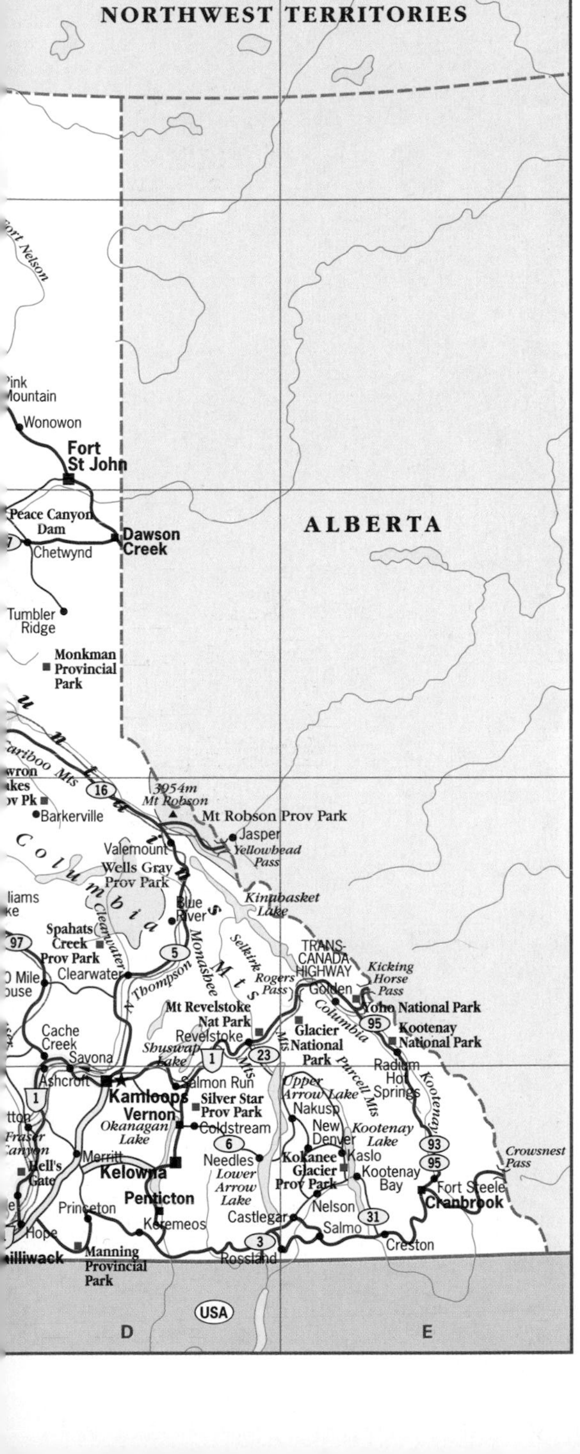

Great Slave Lake
NORTHWEST TERRITORIES
ALBERTA
Fort Nelson
Pink Mountain
Wonowon
Fort St John
Peace Canyon Dam
Dawson Creek
Chetwynd
Tumbler Ridge
Monkman Provincial Park
Cariboo Mts
16
3954m Mt Robson
Mt Robson Prov Park
Barkerville
Jasper
Yellowhead Pass
Valemount
Wells Gray Prov Park
Columbia
Kinbasket Lake
Blue River
Clearwater
Spahats Creek Prov Park
97
5
Thompson
Monashee Mts
Selkirk Mts
TRANS-CANADA HIGHWAY
Kicking Horse Pass
Rogers Pass
Golden
Yoho National Park
Mt Revelstoke Nat Park
Glacier National Park
Kootenay National Park
Revelstoke
95
Cache Creek
Savona
Shuswap Lake
1
23
Radium Hot Springs
Ashcroft
Kamloops
Salmon Run
Upper Arrow Lake
Purcell Mts
Nakusp
Vernon
Silver Star Prov Park
Okanagan Lake
Coldstream
New Denver
Kootenay Lake
Kootenay
93
Fraser Canyon
Hell's Gate
Merritt
6
Needles
Lower Arrow Lake
Kokanee Glacier Prov Park
Kaslo
Kootenay Bay
Crowsnest Pass
Kelowna
Penticton
Princeton
Keremeos
Castlegar
Nelson
31
Fort Steele
Cranbrook
Hope
Salmo
Chilliwack
Manning Provincial Park
3
Rossland
Creston
USA
D
E

2860
BRITISH COLUMBIA
CANADA

DRAMATIC CONTRASTS Of all Canada's provinces perhaps only Alberta comes close to matching the beauty and grandeur of British Columbia (BC). Not all the region's landscapes are the patchwork of snow-tinged mountains, tranquil lakes and deep-green forests of popular imagination, for scattered between the far-reaching majesty of the Rockies and the splendor of a great fjord-cut coastline lie swathes of pastoral farmland, patches of near desert, huge tracts of ranching country—even a Mediterranean enclave of vineyards and fruit orchards.

FIRST CONTACT For more than 12,000 years before the coming of Europeans, British Columbia's vast natural bounty supported the most sophisticated of all Canada's native tribes. Small pockets of living native culture survive to this day, while the superb museums of Victoria and Vancouver contain magnificent displays devoted to native art and history. The earliest white contact with the area was probably made by Francis Drake in 1579, though the first recorded landing was achieved by Captain Cook in 1778. Spanish claims to the region were relinquished, in 1790, following intense diplomatic wrangling, clearing the way for Captain George Vancouver to take possession of Vancouver Island in 1792.

EXPANSION Exploration of the interior was then prompted by the dictates of the fur trade, the need to find trade routes from the east driving men such as Mackenzie, Fraser and Thompson, to breathtaking feats of discovery (see pages 66–67). Power in the region then passed to the Hudson's Bay Company, and more direct control was established when the British formalized the region's boundaries to forestall US expansion. Settlement of the area, however, was slow in coming. As late as 1855, for example, Vancouver Island had a white population of only 774, half of whom were under the age of 20. The figure did not begin to increase significantly until 1858, when prospectors flooded in following the discovery of gold on the mainland. Britain declared the region a Crown colony in the same year, though it was not until 1871 that a reluctant British Columbia joined the Dominion.

ECONOMY British Columbia's economy rests on lumber, minerals and energy, all primary resources whose exploitation carries a heavy environmental price. As a result, conservation issues increasingly dominate the province's political agenda, particularly in the area of forestry, where friction between the industry and conservationists has occasionally ended in violent standoff. Traditionally, much of the lumber has gone to the US and Europe; however, with the province increasingly concentrating on the markets of the West Coast and Far East, trade is now more focused on the countries of the Pacific Rim. This, in turn, has reinforced the province's natural tendency to ignore the rest of Canada—a stance long helped by the formidable natural barrier of the Rockies, and by the vast empty expanse of the Prairies.

MULTICULTURAL British Columbia's predominantly British ethnic mix—some 60 percent of the population have British forebears—is mingled with its large and

▶▶▶ REGION HIGHLIGHTS

FACTS AND FIGURES
British Columbia covers 9.4 percent of Canada and is the country's third-largest province after Québec and Ontario. It is larger than every US state except Alaska. Half of its 3.7 million population were born outside the province. It has Canada's wettest and driest climates, and more species of flora and fauna than the rest of the country put together. It produces about a quarter of North America's lumber, and most of the world's chopsticks.

OUTDOOR PARADISE
British Columbia's natural splendor allows for a wealth of outdoor activities, from hiking, climbing and skiing (the province has the country's largest ski areas) to sailing, canoeing and some of the greatest fishing in the world. Local tourist offices, known in BC as "info centers," offer full details of all activities.

Opposite page: The snow-capped peaks of the Canadian Rockies dominate the horizon in Yoho National Park

LAND FOR LOAFING
"Such a land is good for an energetic man. It is also not so bad for the loafer."—Rudyard Kipling, *Letters to the Family* (1908)

CLIMATIC PERFECTION
"An ideal home for the human race: not too cold, not too hot, not too wet and not too dry..."—Stephen Leacock on British Columbia, *My Discovery of the West* (1937)

INSIDE PASSAGE
To take a ferry through the "Inside Passage" or along the Discovery Coast is to make one of North America's great journeys. BC Ferries (tel: 250/386–3431 or 888/223–3779 in British Columbia; www.bcferries.com) operates the route from Port Hardy on Vancouver Island to Prince Rupert, together with boats of the Alaska Marine Highway network, tel: 250/627–1744 or 800/642–0066, www.dot.state.ak/amhs (which continue to Skagway and the ports of the Alaskan "Panhandle"). BC Ferries' boats run every two days, and the journey takes 20 hours. Reservations are always essential in summer if you want a cabin or are taking a car.

long-established Italian, Chinese, Greek and Japanese communities. Recent waves of immigration from Hong Kong, however, which pushed up property prices, have caused a rare ripple of trouble in the region's generally excellent multicultural relations. Relations with Native Canadians—which have never been comfortable—have also deteriorated, largely because claims on aboriginal lands (including some urban areas of Vancouver) are being pressed ever more vigorously.

TOWNS AND CITIES British Columbia's scenic splendor and vast leisure potential make the province notoriously more laid back and hedonistic than many Canadian regions. It shares the easy-going outlook of California and other West Coast areas, an outlook exemplified by Vancouver, a magnificent city whose beautiful natural setting is matched by its sophisticated atmosphere and cosmopolitan population. Victoria, the provincial capital across the water, sits on the southern tip of Vancouver Island, a tiny outpost of easy-going charm and quiet beauty. Other BC towns are rather more functional, though Nelson, in the Kootenays, has considerable appeal (see pages 52–53), while the towns of the Okanagan—Vernon, Kelowna and Penticton—attract visitors by virtue of their summer resort facilities.

EXPLORING Most people tackling BC do so either from Vancouver, which is the main point of entry by air, or from the Rockies, whose roads offer the most logical itineraries from the east. Both main transprovincial routes between Alberta and Vancouver, however—the Trans-Canada Highway and Highway 3—are relatively dull, so making the most of any tour requires a more meandering course through the province. The best of the lakes and mountains are found in the Kootenays, a pristine little enclave with lovely villages and a fascinating mining and pioneer heritage. To its west lies the lush lakeland scenery of the Okanagan, a mild-weathered redoubt of orchards, vineyards and busy summer beach resorts. Wells Gray Provincial Park, by contrast, perhaps the finest of BC's many mountain parks, offers some of the country's best wilderness landscapes. The so-called Cariboo, a vast ranching and forestry region sprawled across the province's interior plateau, is duller, though in the Skeena Valley and Prince Rupert on its northern extremes there is another pocket of outstanding landscapes.

VANCOUVER ISLAND The largest of the vast archipelago of islands scattered off BC's fractured coastline, Vancouver Island enjoys a slightly over-pitched reputation, for its landscapes are rarely the equal of any on the mainland. Its ease of access attracts a disproportionate number of US visitors and weekenders, particularly to Victoria, its self-consciously quaint capital, and to the nearby Gulf and San Juan islands. This said, the Strathcona Provincial Park, which protects the island's mountainous heart, is wonderful, while the Pacific Rim National Park embraces some of the country's greatest coastal landscapes. Vancouver Island is also the jumping-off point for the Inside Passage and Discovery Coast, two extremely scenic ferry trips through the fjords and islands of the west coast (see panel).

▶▶▶ The Kootenays *47E1*

Of all British Columbia's scenic enclaves, perhaps none is as pretty and unspoiled as the rivers, lakes and mountains of the Kootenays (not to be confused with the Kootenay National Park to the north—see pages 108–111). A vaguely defined region, the area centers on two parallel valleys, the Kootenay and Columbia—dominated respectively by Kootenay Lake and Upper and Lower Arrow lakes—and on three great dividing mountain ranges: the Purcells, Selkirks and Monashees. White settlers first came to the area to mine its veins of lead, copper and silver, a side to the Kootenays that can still be glimpsed in its ghost towns, sternwheeler boats and pioneer museums.

Exploring the Kootenays The Kootenays have no real center, and no single route that takes in the best of the region. A car is therefore essential, as is a willingness to explore some of the area's back roads. Nelson is the biggest and prettiest town, while Kaslo, Nakusp and New Denver are the nicest of the villages. The best approach is from the east, entering the region at Creston. You can see Kaslo and Kootenay Lake, and then drive west to take in Nelson, New Denver and Nakusp. This leaves you well placed for the Okanagan (see pages 56–59), which is reached via Highway 6, a more scenic route than Highway 1, or Highway 3 to the north and south.

Creston to Kaslo Scenic Highway 31 starts its meandering course up the eastern shore of Kootenay Lake from **Creston**, a bland town at the edge of fertile fruit-growing country. In its early stages the road passes little of interest—except bucolic views of lake and mountains—until Boswell's wonderfully bizarre **Glass House** (see panel, page 52). Gray Creek boasts the **Gray Creek Store**, an intriguing backwoods shop that purveys everything from diapers to chainsaws.

Crawford Bay and Kootenay Bay, hamlets with pleasant places to stay, are the eastern departure points for the

RUSSIAN CANOES

The canoes once used by the natives of the Kootenay region had an almost unique peculiarity: their bows and sterns came to a point at or under the waterline. The only other place in the world where similar boats are found is the Amur River region of southeast Russia. This fact is used to lend weight to the theory that Asiatic peoples migrated to North America via Siberia and Alaska.

Looking across the Kootenay River to Nelson

SEASONAL TOURIST OFFICES
Creston 1711 Canyon Street tel: 250/428–4342); *Kaslo* 324 Front Street, (tel: 250/353–2525, www.klhs.bc.ca); *New Denver* 202–6th Avenue (tel: 250/358–2719, www.newdenver.ca); *Nelson* 225 Hall Street (tel: 250/352–3433, www.nelsonchamber.bc.ca); *Nakusp* 92 West and 6th Avenue (tel:250/265–4234, www.nakusphotsprings.com).

THE GLASS HOUSE
British Columbia's most bizarre building was constructed by a certain Mr. Brown, who after 35 years as a mortician spent his retirement indulging "a whim of peculiar nature": visiting friends in the funeral business to collect 500,000 embalming bottles (some 250 tons-worth). These were then used to build his retirement home (*Open* May–end Oct daily 9–5; Jul–end Aug daily 8–8. *Admission: moderate).*

The town hall, one of Kaslo's many heritage buildings

Kootenay ferry▶▶; the 45-minute crossing provides a super oportunity to relax and admire the fine lake scenery. **Balfour**, on the western shore, has plenty of motels and campsites, though more attractive options await you at nearby **Ainsworth Hot Springs▶▶**. Here you can take a dip in the hot springs (*Open* daily 8.30am–9.30pm. *Admission: moderate*), visit the nearby **Cody Caves** (for details of guided tours, dial 250/353–7425.

Kaslo▶▶▶ You would have to travel far to find a friendlier or prettier spot than lakeside Kaslo. The mountain-ringed village began as just a sawmill in 1889, springing to life following the discovery of silver in 1893. Explore the grid of well-kept streets—and especially the lovely old church and wooden town hall—and visit the **SS *Moyie*** (*Open* mid-May to mid-Sep daily 9–5, tel: 250/353–2525. *Admission: moderate*), the oldest surviving paddle steamer in North America. Built in 1867, the boat was one of a fleet of Kootenay steamers ferrying people and supplies before the improvement of local roads; it retired from service in 1957 and is now a museum. To get a feel for local community arts, it is well worth dropping into the Langham Cultural Centre (A Aveneue, tel: 250/353–2661), a thriving arts center in a prettily restored 1890's hotel. Among other things, it organizes an annual summer jazz festival.

Kokanee Glacier Provincial Park▶▶ If you have time, drive to Howser at the northern end of Kootenay Lake, worthwhile for the scenery alone, but also watch for ospreys: the 100 or more local pairs are the largest concentration of the birds in North America. Better still, drive the rough 29km (18-mile) road from Kaslo into the heart of the Kokanee Glacier Provincial Park, a magnificent swathe of the Selkirk mountains full of scenic trails (most start from the Joker Miller parking lot at the end of the road).

Kaslo to New Denver One route from Kaslo takes you north on rough roads through wild country before swinging south to Nakusp; a second takes you past Ainsworth Hot Springs before heading west to Nelson; a third takes you west to New Denver on Highway 31a. The last is the best, climbing through tremendous scenery, skirting the crashing waters of the Kaslo River, and passing a beautiful little trio of lakes: Fish, Bear and Beaver.

As the road begins to drop toward New Denver, look out for signs to **Sandon▶**, a battered ghost town at the end of a 13km (8-mile) gravel road. At the height of the 1890s' mining boom, the town had 2,000 inhabitants, 24 hotels, 23 saloons and an opera house. Most of the town was destroyed by a flood in 1955.

New Denver▶▶ was born during the same mining boom that created Kaslo and other Kootenay villages. It started life with the hopeful name "Eldorado." In 1892 it was renamed New Denver, this time in the hope—a forlorn one—that it would develop into a greater mining town than its American namesake. By the end of World War I the mines were all but played out. Today the lakeside village is quieter than Kaslo, if not as pretty, its somnolent little streets dotted with old pioneer buildings and the modest **Silvery Slocan Museum** (*Open* Jul–Aug daily 10–4; mid-May to mid-Oct Sat–Sun. *Admission: inexpensive*).

Idyllic Kootenay Lake and one of its many beaches

Nelson▶▶▶ Few towns in BC are worth a trip for their own sake. Most provincial centers are functional spots to sleep, eat and stock up, before exploring the next stretch of scenery. Not so lakeside Nelson, self-proclaimed "Queen of the Kootenays," which has several galleries and interesting little shops, and 350 beautiful "heritage" buildings. Most of these lovingly restored properties date from the 1880s and 1890s, and have been used as the setting for several films, most famously Steve Martin's Cyrano de Bergerac spoof, *Roxanne.* To explore the "Heritage Capital of Western Canada," pick up the Heritage Walking Tour pamphlet from the tourist office (see panel opposite); there is also a self-guided *Roxanne* walk. To learn something of the area's mining heritage, visit the **Chamber of Mines of Eastern BC** at 215 Hall Street (tel: 250/352–5242. *Open* daily 10–4/5. *Admission free*). Nelson's outlying Civic Museum (tel: 250/352–9813. *Open* Jul–end Aug daily 1–6; Sep–end Jun Mon–Sat 1–4. *Admission: inexpensive*) is small and slightly haphazard, but contains a few interesting exhibits on mining and the local Doukhobor population (see page 157).

Nakusp▶▶ Nakusp nestles on the shores of Upper Arrow Lake. The village offers swimming, boating, fishing and a museum of pioneer memorabilia (6th Avenue and First Street. *Open* May–end Sep 9–5; Sep–end May Mon–Fri 12–5. *Admission free*). The **Nakusp Hot Springs▶▶**—some of the best of western Canada's many thermal pools (tel: 250/265–4528. *Open* Jun–end Sep 9.30am–10pm; Oct–end May 11–9.30. *Admission: moderate)*—are located 13km (8 miles) northeast of the town and clearly signed. They become busy in summer, but are regularly cleaned (unlike many), and the surroundings and changing facilities are excellent. Highway 23 strikes north to link with the Trans-Canada Highway, while the beautiful **Highway 6▶▶** runs along the shores of Lower Arrow Lake to the free ferry at Needles, then climbs through the superlative scenery of the Monashee Mountains before descending to the Coldstream Valley and the Okanagan.

BOOM AND BUST

The discovery of silver, which launched the Kootenays mining boom of the 1890s, was made by two grizzled prospectors, Eli Carpenter and Jack Seaton. Having discovered the vein—on the ridges between Ainsworth and Slocan—they later fell out while celebrating the find in a Slocan bar. Both rushed from the saloon to stake a proper claim. Seaton arrived first, and went on to become a hugely wealthy silver baron. Carpenter, by contrast, was forced to return to his earlier profession as a tightrope walker. He died in poverty.

SILVERY SLOCAN

In the 1890s, villages in the Kootenays, and around Slocan in particular, produced virtually all of Canada's silver, earning the region the title of "Silvery Slocan." "Silver, lead and hell are raised in the Slocan," claimed a local newspaper in 1891, "and unless you can take a hand in producing these articles, your services are not required."

REVELSTOKE DAM
Many people also come to Revelstoke for its vast dam. Much of the dam complex is open to the public: highlights include a viewing platform and high-tech visitors' interpretative center. It is located 5km (3 miles) north of the town on Highway 23.

GLACIER TRAILS
The best short walk in Glacier National Park is the 1.6km (1-mile) Loop Brook Trail, a path with good views and interpretative panels describing the old rail route over the pass. It is clearly marked off Highway 1 near the Loop Brook campsite 6km (4 miles) west of Rogers Pass. Another easy stroll is the 1km (0.6-mile) Meeting of the Water Trail from the Illecillewaet campsite, which is also the start of longer climbs (notably the Avalanche Crest and Abbott's Ridge trails) that offer jaw-dropping views of the Illecillewaet Glacier.

AVALANCHES
Some of the world's highest snowfall figures make Glacier dangerously prone to avalanches. Tunnels, dams and rubble barriers usually protect the region's roads and railway, but during dangerous build-ups of snow the roads are closed and artillery is brought in to fire howitzer shells into the mountains to dislodge the snow under "controlled conditions."

►► Mount Revelstoke and Glacier national parks *47D2/E2*

Although Glacier and Mount Revelstoke national parks protect country within the Columbia Mountains (a separate range that parallels the Rockies), they are often visited and bracketed together with the Rockies national parks to the east. Both are therefore best seen in conjunction with Banff (see pages 96–99) or Yoho (pages 112–115), though approaches from the south (the Okanagan), or the west (the Trans-Canada Highway), are equally possible. Both parks are relatively small, and easily seen in a day. Golden is the nearest town to Glacier, but is less attractive than Revelstoke, which makes the best overall base.

Mount Revelstoke National Park Mount Revelstoke's tiny park was created in 1914, at the behest of local people, to protect the Clachnacudainn Range of the Columbia Mountains. It is named after Lord Revelstoke, head of the British bank Barings, who saved the Canadian Pacific Railway from bankruptcy during the construction of the transcontinental railway in the 1880s. The park's only vehicle access is the 26km (16-mile) **Summit Road►►►**, or Summit Parkway, which is reached on Trans-Canada Highway 1 from nearby **Revelstoke►**. A wonderfully scenic drive, the road switchbacks through forest and alpine meadows almost to the summit of Mount Revelstoke (1,938m/6,357ft). Views from the top are magnificent, and in late spring and early summer the area is renowned for its wild flowers. Damage to the area through overuse, however, means that a shuttle bus is sometimes used to ferry people to the summit parking area at Balsam Lake.

If you want to walk, the best of the upland meadows can be seen on the **Meadows in the Sky Trail**, an easy loop that kicks off from the parking area. Other trails from the same spot include the more demanding Miller Lake Trail (6km/4 miles one way), and a path that cuts back down toward Revelstoke shadowing the route of Summit Road. The **Inspiration Woods Trail** provides an easy loop marked off Summit Road near its junction with Highway 23. Perhaps the best short walk, however, is the **Giant Cedars Trail**, a 1km (0.62 miles) loop through an ancient forest of 600-year-old Western Red Cedars. The path is signed off the Trans-Canada close to the park's eastern border, some 25km (15 miles) east of Revelstoke.

Glacier National Park The scenery in the Columbia Mountains is spectacular, but they bear the brunt of some appalling weather. Local wits say that it rains or snows four days out of three (the real figure is three days out of five). Weather stations regularly record over 20m (60ft) of snow a year, while annual rainfall figures invariably top 152cm (60in). Compare this to the 50cm (20in) a year recorded at Golden, just a few miles to the east, which lies sheltered in the Columbias' rain shadow. The region's rain and snow conspire to produce glaciers, 422 of them in the appropriately named Glacier National Park alone (14 percent of the park is permanently covered in snow and ice). They also produce avalanches.

Such were the hardships of life in the region that it remained virtually uninhabited until 1881, when Major A. B. Rogers surveyed the area in readiness for the

transcontinental railroad (blasted over the pass that bears his name in 1885). Rail remained the sole means of seeing the park, which was created in 1886, until the completion of the Trans-Canada Highway in 1962. Today the road's window on the wilderness provides the only way to see an otherwise inaccessible region (the section over the Rogers Pass is one of the world's most spectacular highways). There's nothing much en route, but be sure to stop at the **Rogers Pass Visitors' Centre** (tel: 250/837–7500. *Open* Apr–end Oct daily 9–5 (mid-Jun to mid-Sep 8/9am–8/9pm; Nov Thu–Mon 9–5; Dec–end Mar Thu–Mon 7–5), which has details of walks (see panel opposite), and videos and displays on geology, wildlife, bears and avalanche control.

Meadows in the Sky, Mount Revelstoke National Park

A traditional barn in the hills above Okanagan Lake

OGOPOGO
Ogopogo is a monster that is said to inhabit the depths of Okanagan Lake. The myth has its roots in a Salish native story, which tells of a lake monster called N'ha-a-tik which lived in a cave near present-day Squally Point. The Salish kept well away from the spot, and when forced to canoe near it cast an animal overboard as a placatory sacrifice. The present name was coined in 1924, reputedly because the creature—like the word—looked the same at both ends. The beastie is said to be between 9m (30ft) and 21m (60ft) long, and to have the head of a sheep, goat or horse.

Horseshoe-throwing: old-style Okanagan entertainment

►► The Okanagan *47D1*

After touring the mountain regions of British Columbia, few things are more surprising than to stumble across the Okanagan, a region of low hills, mild-watered lakes, vineyards, orchards and pastoral countryside. Hours of summer sunshine, countless fairs and festivals, warm sandy beaches and a wealth of hiking and watersports possibilities have turned the area into one of Canada's most popular resort destinations; the region is busy and crowded, and its brash beach life and busy resorts are at odds with the rural calm and tranquility to be found elsewhere in British Columbia. This said, the crowds thin out off-season, and if you can come in spring the area offers blossom-filled orchards and winsome lakeside villages.

Where to go Exploring the region is straightforward, for it centers on Vernon, Kelowna and Penticton, three large towns ranged north to south along Okanagan Lake. The best approach is from the Kootenays, following Highway 6 along the beautiful Coldstream Valley. Almost equally pretty is Highway 97 from the north, a road that cuts down from the Trans-Canada Highway through pristine farming country. Kelowna makes the best large base for exploration, though to get the most from the region you should drive some of the quieter back roads, and aim to explore the smaller villages, lakes and provincial parks away from Highway 97.

O'Keefe Historic Ranch►►► Canada has many historic sites, but few that suggest the rigors and reality of 19th-century pioneer life quite as vividly or as poignantly as the O'Keefe Historic Ranch, 11km (7 miles) north of Vernon. (tel: 250/542–7868. *Open* May–mid-Oct 9–5; Jul and Aug 9–7. *Admission: moderate*). The lovely 20ha (50-acre) site sits at the heart of farming country, as attractive today as it must have been when Cornelius O'Keefe first settled here in 1867. Pride of place goes to the 19th-century ranch building, which still preserves much of its original furniture, books, silverware and chandeliers. Other monuments to the past include a reconstructed forge, post office and general store (complete with staff in period dress), and a display devoted to the old Shuswap and Okanagan Railroad. The fine little museum runs through the background to 19th-century life, with a particularly interesting section on the little-known role of aboriginal peoples during the two world wars (when over a quarter of eligible men signed up for duty). Perhaps the most poignant corner of the site, however, is **St. Ann's Church** (1899), a lovely wooden building whose handful of graves contains three generations of O'Keefes (the family lived here until 1977); the grandchildren all died in the 1980s.

Vernon▶▶ Vernon relies less heavily than its neighbors on tourism, trusting instead to forestry and agriculture for its civic well-being. As a result its streets and lakeside beaches are quieter than elsewhere though there is still no shortage of motels, fast-food joints and neon signs cluttering the town's approaches.

The settlement is named after the Vernon brothers, who in 1864 decided to try their hand at farming after failing as prospectors in the Monashee Mountains. Their farm, on the site of the present-day Coldstream Ranch, was soon joined by the BX Ranch, which specialized in providing horses for mail coaches in the Cariboo country to the north.

The **Greater Vernon Museum and Archives** (3009 32nd Avenue. *Open* Mon–Sat 10–5. *Closed:* Mon in winter. *Admission: donation*) offers a neat roster of pioneer ephemera, native Salish artifacts, natural history displays, a livery-stable coach and a double-cutter sleigh. Escape from the crowds at the town's southern entrance, where **Polson Park▶▶** features a replica Japanese tea house, formal Japanese gardens and a 9m (30-ft) floral clock comprising 3,500 plants. The best of the beaches, together with some fine viewpoints and hiking trails, are found at **Kalamalka Lake Provincial Park**, located on Kalamalka Lake a few miles south of the town.

CHEESE COUNTRY
The dairy farms around Vernon are renowned for their cheese. Some 3 million tons of Canada's famous mature cheddar is produced here annually.

SILVER STAR PROVINCIAL PARK
This little mountain park lies 21km (13 miles) northeast of Vernon, and can be reached by following 48th Avenue off Highway 97. In summer you can use the ski lifts to take you to the top of Silver Star Mountain (1,915m/6,281ft) for magnificent views and a variety of easy hiking trails.

The old post office at the O'Keefe Historic Ranch

FRUITFUL
Kelowna grows a third of all Canada's apples, while the Okanagan produces all the country's apricots, half its plums, and 40 percent of its cherries, pears and peaches.

VINEYARD TOURS
Many Kelowna vineyards, orchards and fruit and juice plants offer guided tours. Contact the info center or vineyards for full details. British Columbia's largest and oldest winery is Calona Wines Ltd, 1125 Richter Street (tel: 250/762-9144). The region's wineries join together in May and September to present spring and fall wine festivals, with many tastings, tours and other events.
Visit www.owfs.com for more details.

SUNNY SPOT
Penticton enjoys an average of ten hours of sunshine a day during July and August.

Kelowna The Okanagan's largest town comes as a bit of a shock, particularly if you approach it from Vernon on Highway 97, which is choked for many miles by a huge sprawl of suburbs, motels and neon-fronted clutter. For a gentler introduction to Kelowna—a pleasant resort center at heart despite its summer rush—drive out of Vernon and take the more scenic country road along the western shore of Lake Okanagan.

Kelowna takes its name from a Salish native word meaning "grizzly bear." The Salish inhabited the region long before the arrival of Europeans Kelowna was one of the most important of their inland settlements. Fur traders aside, the first white presence in the region came in 1859, when Father Charles Pandosy, a French Catholic missionary, opened a mission with two theological students at Mission Creek. Two years later he planted a small apple orchard, an enterprise whose success attracted further European immigrants and provided the kernel of the Okanagan's modern fruit industry (see panel). You can still visit the mission, the **Father Pandosy Mission Historical Site▶** (3685 Benvoulin Road. *Open* Easter–mid-Oct daily sunrise to sunset. *Admission: donation*), a modest collection of school, church and cabin buildings, located just south of the town.

Downtown Kelowna, with its lakefront beach and gardens, is pleasant enough to wander around, though the only "sight" is the 1,400m (4,500-ft) lake bridge. Built in 1958, it is Canada's longest "floating bridge." Be sure to visit the info center (see panel opposite), which has details of the numerous vineyards and fruit-processing plants in the region that offer guided tours and free tastings (see panel). Another worthwhile place to stop is the Laurel

Packinghouse, a heritage building at 1304 Ellis Street, which houses the BC Orchard Museum (*Open* Jul–end Aug Mon–Sat 10–5; Sep–end Jun Tue–Sat 10–5) and the Wine Museum and VQA shop (tel: 250/868–0441. *Open* Mon–Sat 10–5, Sun 12–5). Both have displays on these two important local industries. (*Admission free.*)

Penticton Also known as "Peach City," Penticton is the most tourist-battered of the Okanagan's towns, its 2,000 hours of sunshine a year providing a magnet for armies of US and Canadian visitors anxious for beaches, watersports and guaranteed good weather. As a result, the town's winter population of 25,000 mushrooms to a frightening 130,000 in the summer.

In its day the area must have been idyllic, the town's name being a corruption of the Salish *pen tak tin*, meaning a "place to stay for ever." Its first white settler, Irishman Thomas Ellis, laid out an orchard in 1866; some of his farm equipment, along with other pioneer ephemera, can be seen in the **Penticton Museum and Archives▶** (785 Main Street. *Open* Tue–Sat 10–5. *Admission donation*). Beached on the lake shore lies another historic relic, the *SS Sicamous*, an old Canadian Pacific boat that plied up and down Okanagan Lake between 1914 and 1951. (*Open* May–end Sep daily 9–7/9; Oct–end Apr 9–5. *Admission: moderate.*)

Elsewhere, waterslides abound, an increasingly common feature of western Canadian resorts and highways. If you simply want to stretch out or swim, however, the best beaches are Okanagan Beach (the closest to downtown) and Skaha Beach (4km/2.5 miles south of downtown). You can also take boat trips on the lake (details from the info center), visit various festivals, sample wine or just wander.

KELOWNA'S BEACHES

The best beaches are the public beach off City Park; Bear Creek (over the bridge and 2km/1mile north up Okanagan Lake's west bank); and Rotary Beach and Boyce Gyro Park, off Lakeshore Road south of the bridge.

TOURIST OFFICES

Thompson Okanagan Tourist Association (Regional Office) 1332 Water Street, Kelowna, VIY 9P4 (tel: 250/860–5999); *Vernon* 701 Highway 97S (tel: 250/542–1415, www.vernontourism.com); *Kelowna* 544 Harvey (tel: 250/861–1515, www.kelownachamber.org); *Penticton* 888 Westminster Avenue West (tel: 250/493–4055, www.penticton.org).

Vineyards on the Okanagan's balmy slopes

Visit British Columbia at the right time of year and you may be lucky enough to see one of several species of salmon running upriver. The still-prolific fish is vital to the region's economy, and remains inescapable both in the province's restaurants and in the trophy cabinets of its countless fishing communities.

FIVE SPECIES
Five species of salmon are indigenous to the Pacific and the waters of British Columbia. The largest is the chinook, which can weigh in at 55kg (120 lb); the smallest is the pink, which rarely exceeds a far more modest 2.5kg (5 lb). In between are the coho (up to 10kg/22 lb), the chum (5kg/11 lb) and the sockeye (3.5kg/8 lb). Across the country, a sixth species, the Atlantic salmon, can be found in the Maritimes and eastern seaboard.

Salmon have entered the mythology of British Columbia. Once so plentiful they were shoveled onto land as fertilizer, they were also said to swarm so thickly in the straits between Vancouver Island and the mainland that it was possible to walk across them. These days canning and their sheer ubiquity has reduced their romantic allure—salmon soup and sandwiches top the menu in many a BC diner—though the fish's extraordinary lifestyle, and its prodigious reproductive exploits, continue to draw visitors to the province's many hatcheries and salmon runs.

Swimming for sex Evolution has dealt the salmon a tough hand. During spawning both the male and female fish swim from the open sea to the rivers of their birth, battling head-on against waterfalls, landslips, rapids and a malevolent current before expiring on completion of their reproductive cycle. These epic migrations can involve swimming up to 50km (30 miles) a day and, in the case of fish unlucky enough to be born in the headwaters of the Fraser River, a total journey of some 1,400km (850 miles). Before this they have spent anything between two and five years in the open sea, a period of relative calm sandwiched between the traumas of their birth and extended demise.

Traditional fishing methods on the Fraser River

Fishing in British Columbia's teeming offshore waters

The early years Once returned to their breeding grounds, each female salmon lays anything up to 4,000 eggs, of which only a fraction are likely to yield mature fish. In one of the region's most famous spawning grounds, for example, the Adams River near Salmon Arm, an estimated 2 million sockeye return to spawn annually, turning the river a deep crimson during the early weeks of October. Of the 4 billion eggs laid and buried in the river's stony bed, only a quarter will survive to emerge as "fry" (hatched fish about an inch long). Of these only another quarter will survive the predators of Lake Shuswap, where the young fish spend about a year before becoming "smolts" (year-old fish). A mere twentieth of these will then survive their journey as "fingerlings" along the Fraser to the open sea.

Commercial fishing Of the $1 billion British Columbia generates from fishing (the largest of any Canadian province), two-thirds derives from the canning and export of salmon. This makes it the region's third most valuable money-earner behind forestry and energy. It is also, however, one of the most susceptible industries to natural and human interference.

One of the earliest blows to the industry came in 1913, when huge rock slides on the Fraser River blocked the path to the salmon's traditional spawning grounds. More recently mining, logging and the dumping of waste, together with intensive agricultural methods, have further reduced the numbers of BC salmon. Fish on the high sea are equally threatened, particularly by overfishing and the indiscriminate use of drift nets by foreign fleets.

Helping hand Awareness of the razor's edge on which the salmon industry operates, underlined by the grim statistical evidence as to a salmon's chances of survival (see panel), have led to increased efforts to lend Nature a helping hand. Landslips and waterfalls on rivers have been bypassed by salmon runs, while hatcheries (many of which are open to the public) have been built on rivers to try to increase the percentage of eggs, fry and smolt that survive to reach the open sea.

SURVIVAL STAKES
A salmon's chances of survival are slim: each pair of spawning salmon produces ten mature fish; of these, eight are caught over the next four years by commercial fishing, while only two survive to return to their spawning grounds to reproduce.

DO AND DIE
Salmon reach sexual maturity after about four years, at which point they return to their spawning grounds, guided, it is thought, by an extraordinary sense of smell. Many undergo dramatic changes *en route:* sockeye, for example, change color from a silvery blue to a deep red. Many die on the journey, a brutal form of natural selection. At their destination, surviving females scoop a depression in the river bed and lay their eggs, which are then fertilized by the male. Duty done, both fish wither away and die within a few days.

Drive

Kamloops to Hope

See map on pages 46–47.

A drive along two of Canada's greatest rivers, exploring the desert-like terrain of the Thompson River, the gold-rush country around Lytton, and the tremendous Hell's Gate gorge of Fraser Canyon (325km/200 miles).

Almost any itinerary through BC will eventually bring you to **Kamloops▶**, a former fur-trading post whose name comes from the native word *cume-loups*, meaning "meeting of the waters" (the North and South Thompson rivers merge here). It is still a meeting place for road and rail links from all corners of the province, and the starting point of the Coquihalla Highway (Highway 5), a fast toll road to Hope (see below). While this is a scenic enough route, the older Trans-Canada Highway (Highway 1) route is more interesting and varied.

Kamloops itself, a sprawling, functional place, distinguished by the strange bare hills and dry, dusty terrain that surrounds it on all sides, is not somewhere to linger, but it does have a couple of interesting little museums: the **Kamloops Museum** (207 Seymour Street. tel: 250/828–3576. *Open* Tue–Sat, 9.30–4.30. *Admission donation*), full of archive displays and pioneer exhibits; and the **Secwepemec Museum and Heritage Park** (355 Yellowhead Highway (Highway 5), tel: 250/372–1127. *Open* summer daily 9–5; winter Mon–Fri 8.30–4.30. *Admission: moderate*), which explores the history and culture of the local Shuswap natives. Another attraction is the chance to explore the river on the ***Wanda Sue***, a renovated sternwheeler (tel: 250/374–7447. *Open* daily from mid-Jun to mid-Sep). It departs from the wharf on River Street.

The desert-like scenery around Kamloops

West of Kamloops the highway enters some arid country, parched by the rain shadow effect of the Coast Mountains to the west. Sagebrush, scrub and cacti dot the dry hills, home to herds of cattle, eerily abandoned farmsteads and the occasional irrigated oasis. Some 50km (30 miles) from Kamloops, beyond Kamloops Lake and the pretty little Savona Provincial Park, a side-road leads into **Deadman Valley**, scattered with small lakes, caves, the fissured crags of Split Rock, and several dramatic rock pinnacles, or "hoodoos." **Cache Creek▶▶** (80km/50 miles from Kamloops), the "Arizona of Canada," takes its name from a cache of gold reputedly abandoned here by prospectors in the 1860s. In fact it was probably named after the prospectors' habit of leaving a "cache" of supplies on the trail to be used later. Nearby **Ashcroft▶▶**, "Copper Capital of Canada," offers tours round the mines.

After Spence's Bridge the road becomes increasingly spectacular, snaking above the river before meeting the Fraser River at **Lytton▶▶**, a staging post on the old Cariboo Road to the 1858 gold fields. Today it is a center for river rafting, with numerous companies offering trips of varying lengths on any of four local rivers. About 50km (30 miles) farther south, just beyond Boston Bar, lies **Hell's Gate▶▶▶**, where the Fraser Canyon—here 180m (600ft) deep but just 30m (100ft) wide—squeezes the river into a seething channel of water over 60m (195ft) deep and 8m (26ft wide). A cable-car, the "Air Tram" (tel: 604/867–9277. *Open* mid-Apr to mid-Oct daily), descends into the gorge to give you a better view. Close by are the fish ladders built to help spawning salmon bypass the gorge (see pages 60–61).

Yale▶▶, which closes the canyon's southern maw, is another pleasant gold-rush remnant, its 20,000 population in 1858 having made it one of the largest towns in North America west of Chicago. Visit the **Yale Museum** (*Open* Jun–end Sep 9–6, tel: 604/863–2324 for hours. *Admission: moderate*) on Douglas Street for displays on the gold rush and the building of the Canadian Pacific Railway. **Hope▶▶**, a lovely mountain-ringed town, marks the beginning of the flat run on to Vancouver. It has plenty of accommodation options, the usual little pioneer museum (919 Water Avenue. *Open* mid-May–early Sep), alongside the info center (tel: 604/869–2021), fine views across the Fraser River, and pleasant hikes in the provincial parks dotted around its hinterland.

The Fraser River near Hell's Gate

A beautiful day on the Skeena River, belying its title of "the river of mists"

SPEECHLESS CHIEF
Among the exhibits in Prince Rupert's museum is the famous "talking stick," used by the native Chief Shakes during a visit to England to meet Queen Victoria. He was reputedly so overcome by the occasion that he was unable to speak, leaving the stick to do his talking for him.

►► Skeena Valley *46B3*

Like much of Canada, the Skeena Valley can be seen only as part of a much longer itinerary. Here the choice is either an Inside Passage boat from Vancouver Island to Prince Rupert, the area's main town, or a trip from Prince George by car, VIA Rail or Greyhound bus. If you are driving, and have not reserved a place on the Inside Passage ferries (see panel, page 50), the only options at Prince Rupert are to double back to Prince George, or to head north on the Cassiar Highway to the Yukon. This said, the valley's scenery is majestic, Prince Rupert is vibrant and lively, and the journey from Prince George, though dull in its early stages, improves immeasurably between New Hazelton and Prince Rupert.

Prince Rupert►► Prince Rupert began life as a Hudson's Bay Company post, blossoming when it was chosen as the terminus of the Grand Trunk Railway, begun in 1906. Despite the death of the railroad's chairman Charles Hays on the *Titanic* in 1912, the line was completed in 1914—too late, in the event, to realize Hays's dream of turning Prince Rupert into a city to rival Vancouver. Nonetheless, Prince Rupert is today British Columbia's second port after Vancouver, and—despite its modest appearance—one of the largest deep-water terminals in the world.

It is a good-looking town, full of rough, salty charm and surrounded by vast mountains, deep-cut fjords and a sprinkling of tiny islands. An air of prosperity pervades the port, derived from the fishing fleet, the flow of passengers off the

BC and Alaskan ferries, and the torrent of natural resources that pours through its spectacular natural harbor.

Leave time to visit the fascinating **Museum of Northern British Columbia▶▶** (100 First Avenue and McBride Street, tel: 250/624-5637. *Open* Jun–end Aug Mon–Sat 9–8, Sun 9–5; Sep–end May Mon–Sat 9–5. *Admission: donation*). In the Tsimshian language, this museum is called a "Treasure House of the Ancient Ones," which is a very appropriate name. The museum has a small gallery, bookstore, several fascinating archive films, and the exhibits feature a longhouse and an excellent collection of Tsimshian native art. In summer, the museum also runs two-hour archeology tours of the harbor (telephone for details and reservations).

The Skeena Estuary▶▶▶ The largely monotonous road from Prince George takes a scenic turn for the better with the sudden rearing of the Coast Mountains and the valley carved through them by the Skeena River. Beyond New Hazleton the road follows the river for a couple of hours, its asphalt framed by snow-capped peaks, dark, mysterious valleys, and vast waterfalls that thread their way through distant forested slopes. Tiny islands and log-jams scatter the often mist-shrouded river, perches for dozens of bald eagles and home to countless beavers that can be seen from the shore-hugging highway.

While you could ride the road simply for the scenery, it is worth making a slight detour at New Hazelton to see four restored Gitxsan native villages. The best (although it is also the most commercialized) is the 'Ksan Native Village▶▶▶ (tel: 250/842–5544 *Open* mid-Apr–end Sep daily 9–5; limited winter opening. *Admission: inexpensive*), an open-air museum created by the native population in the 1960s to help preserve their rapidly vanishing culture. Seven tribal longhouses form its core, several of which are open to the public as part of a guided tour. You can also learn about potlatches, carving, clothes and masks, and hear snippets of Gitxsan local history. Another nearby village, Gitanyow (formerly Kitwancool) has what is reputedly the world's largest standing totem pole, the so-called "Hole-through-the-Ice." Elsewhere, stranger things can be just as appealing. At Kitimat, for example, about 190km (120 miles) east of Prince Rupert, you can take a guided tour around the town's Alcan aluminum smelter, whose 330,000-ton annual production makes it one of the largest such plants in the world. (*Tours:* Jun–end Aug, Mon–Fri 10.30 and 1.30; tel: 250/639–8259.)

THE GITXSAN

'Ksan was the native word for the Skeena, the "River of Mists". The Gitxsan were the most easterly of the great Northwest Coast native tribes, a group that relied more on fishing and hunting than on the cultivation of land. The natural abundance of the Skeena allowed the Gitxsan a relatively tranquil life, leaving them time to develop elaborate arts and crafts, and sophisticated music and dance.

Totem-pole carving (left) and barn wall decoration (below) at Ksan Native Village, near New Hazelton

Canada's first great wave of exploration came in the 16th century with John Cabot, Jacques Cartier and Samuel de Champlain. With its second, two centuries later, the exploits of Alexander Mackenzie, Simon Fraser and David Thompson opened up previously impenetrable wastes of the country's western wilderness.

HENRY HUDSON
Little is known of the early life of the man who gave his name to Hudson Bay. In 1607 he twice searched for a route to Asia via Norway and Russia. In 1609, commissioned by the Dutch East India Company, he sailed to Iceland and then to the bay that was to take his name. That winter his ship, the *Discovery*, froze solid in the ice, prompting a mutiny. The following spring, Hudson, his son, and seven crew members were set adrift in a boat and never seen again.

SIR JOHN FRANKLIN
Franklin was one of many explorers who perished in Canadian waters. He made two expeditions (in 1819 and 1825) to explore the Northwest Passage, the largely ice-bound route across the roof of the North American continent. In 1845, having set out to explore its eastern margins, he disappeared into the ice with 129 men and his two vessels, HMS *Erebus* and HMS *Terror*. Over the years 38 separate expeditions set out to find the missing ships, with no success.

SIR MARTIN FROBISHER
In 1576, on the orders of Elizabeth I of England, this dashing British explorer and privateer made one of the earliest attempts to find a route through the Northwest Passage. The first recorded exploration of the Arctic produced neither riches nor the hoped-for ice-free route.

Alexander Mackenzie Where land and conquest had spurred Canada's early explorers, its later discoverers were driven by the demands of the fur trade. The industry's greatest need was for a route to the Pacific, a link that would remove the need to carry furs by canoe and pack-animal across a continent to the ports of eastern Canada. The search for such a route came to obsess Alexander Mackenzie (1755–1820), a Scot who had arrived in New York with his father at the age of ten. In later life he joined the Montréal Company, later the North West Company, rivals of the mighty Hudson's Bay Company (see pages 168–169). Mackenzie set off on his first trans-Canadian quest in 1789, battling for almost four months through 3,000km (1,860 miles) of forest and desolate wilderness. His reward was to end up on the Arctic Ocean, having mistakenly followed the Mackenzie, North America's second longest river (named after him). Chastened by his "failure," Mackenzie christened the waterway the "river of disappointment." Undeterred, he launched a second expedition, and this time arrived at the Pacific just north of Vancouver Island on July 22, 1793. This was the first documented journey across the North American continent.

Simon Fraser In 1801 Simon Fraser (1776–1862) joined the North West Company's Athabaska Department and assumed responsibility for territories in the Rockies (a region all but unknown to foreign settlers). He established the area's first white settlement, and went on to forge trading posts at Fort McCleod (1805), Fort St. James (1806), Fort Fraser (1806) and Fort George—present-day Prince George (1807). Having retraced Mackenzie's route, he followed a river he believed to be the Columbia, seeking to establish a route to the Pacific and secure it for Britain against rival claims of the United States.

Instead, he found himself following the river that now bears his name, a 1,300km (800-mile) odyssey that took him, as he put it, "where no human should venture." Some 35 days were needed to negotiate the Fraser Canyon (see page 63), where he slithered along narrow ledges and used ladders and ropeways to bypass rapids

too treacherous to cross by boat. Reaching the river's mouth (where he would have glimpsed the site of modern Vancouver), he realized his error, and deemed the venture a commercial failure. However, he had successfully navigated one of the continent's greatest rivers.

David Thompson Thompson was born in London in 1770. After moving to Canada, he joined the Hudson's Bay Company in 1784. He then worked as a clerk until 1796, when he made an expedition on the company's behalf to Lake Athabasca. A year later, he left to become a partner in the rival North West Company. During subsequent expeditions, he negotiated part of the Missouri River and discovered Turtle Lake, one of the headwaters of the Mississippi. In 1807 his attention turned to the Rockies, and to the Columbia, the river for which Fraser had searched in vain. He crossed the Rockies, built the first-ever trading post on the Columbia, and traveled the river in its entirety in 1811. Perhaps his greatest achievement, however, was to map and survey huge areas of the west, work that provided a basis for maps of the region for decades to come. He also led a commission that established the United States–Canada border, which he fixed and surveyed between 1818 and 1826.

SIR FRANCIS DRAKE
During his round-the-world voyage of 1579, this famous Elizabethan courtier may have been the first European to glimpse the coast of British Columbia, but not land on it.

CAPTAIN COOK
Cook made the first recorded European landing on Canada's Pacific Coast on Vancouver Island in 1778. Here he traded several fur pelts with the natives, which he later sold at vast profit in China. News of his success soon attracted other English and Spanish traders to the area in search of furs.

HMS Terror *trapped in ice in 1837 during a trading journey*

ARRIVING BY AIR
Vancouver International Airport (tel: 604/207–7077, www.yvr.ca) is located 13km (8 miles) south of the city. To reach downtown take a taxi or use the Airporter bus (tel: 604/946–8866 or 800/668–3141, www.yvrairporter.com) from outside international arrivals and the domestic terminal between 6.45 and 1.10 every 30 minutes. It stops at the main downtown hotels, and there are transfers to the bus and rail stations. Purchase tickets at the bus stop kiosk.

GETTING AROUND
Translink (tel: 604/953–3333), www.translink.bc.ca) runs Vancouver's integrated public transportation system. Tickets for buses, SkyTrain (the metro) and the SeaBus (the ferry to North Vancouver) can be bought in advance from shops with a "Faredealer" sticker, or from machines on station platforms, or at the SeaBus terminal. To buy a ticket on buses you *must* have the right change to put into a box by the driver: *no* change is given. Tickets are valid for 90 minutes from time of issue for use throughout the system. More expensive two- and three-zone tickets are required for longer rides and for use on the SeaBus during peak periods. Day passes are available for use after 9.30am weekdays and all day Saturday or Sunday.

YOUNG CITY
"Vancouver is an aged city, for only a few days previous to my arrival the Vancouver Baby—*i.e.* the first child born in Vancouver—had been married."—Rudyard Kipling, *Letters to the Family*, 1907

►►► Vancouver *46C1*

Few cities can match Vancouver's dazzling setting, its gleaming downtown skyline ringed by the waters of the Pacific, and the vast snow-capped peaks of the Coast Mountains. Fewer still can match its combination of laid-back hedonism and cultural sophistication, or the vast range of recreational opportunities available to its enterprising population (the third largest of any Canadian city). Play and pleasure are not the only allures, however, for the city's dynamic port and booming economy make it a key player in the markets of the Pacific Rim (the panoply of West Coast and Southeast Asian economies earmarked for 21st-century success). In addition, a busy multicultural population lends the city a cosmopolitan air (as well as providing some wonderful restaurants), while a mild, if sometimes damp, climate allows for plenty of outdoor festivals of music and dance.

Exploring Vancouver's glittering downtown is bounded by Stanley Park to the west and Gastown and Chinatown to the east. After visiting its highlight, Canada Place, it's a five-minute stroll to Gastown, the city's renovated but rather bland historic core. A longer walk (or short bus ride) takes you to Chinatown, an essential port of call if you enjoy streetlife, while at the other extreme lies Stanley Park, an astonishing oasis of calm and semi-wilderness. Vibrant Granville Island—Vancouver's best people-watching spot—is crammed with interesting stores, restaurants, a superb indoor market, and even a small brewery. Close by lie two of Vancouver's best museums, the Vancouver Museum and Maritime Museum, though a visit to the city's cultural highlight, the excellent Museum of Anthropology, requires a longer excursion into the western suburbs.

Downtown No better introduction to Vancouver exists than **Canada Place►►►**, whose magnificent canopied profile is one of the most distinctive features of the city's famous skyline. Built as the Canadian Pavilion for Expo '86, and since converted into a hotel and convention center, its broad promenades offer superlative views of the city's port, Stanley Park, and the encircling mountains. The tourist office is just around the corner (see panel, page 70), so it's a good place to come after stocking up on information. And plaques along the walkways describe the history of the cityscape before you. An equally good viewpoint, "The Lookout," exists at the top of the nearby **Harbour Centre Building►** (555 West Hastings Street, tel: 604/689–0421 *Open* May–end Sep daily 8.30am–10.30pm; Oct–end Apr daily 9–9. *Admission: expensive*), reached by vertigo-inducing, glass-fronted elevators that climb the side of the building to a 40th-story observation platform.

From the waterfront it's a short walk to **Robson Street**, Vancouver's main shopping street and the focus of much of its streetlife on balmy summer evenings. The cultural highlight here is the **Vancouver Art Gallery►►** (750 Hornby Street, tel: 604/662–4700. *Open* May–end Sep daily 10–5.30, Thu 10–9; Oct–end Apr Tue–Sun 10–5.30, Thu 10–9. *Admission: expensive*), whose only modestly interesting collection is redeemed by a superb café and several powerful works by Emily Carr. Other downtown sights worth catching include the **Marine Building**, often described as Canada's finest piece of art deco architecture (close to the tourist office at the foot of Burrard Street), and other sights on and just off Burrard Street such as Christ Church Cathedral, begun in 1888, and the distinctive Hotel Vancouver, whose-French-style architecture dominates central downtown's skyline. Finally, don't miss the superb Vancouver Public Library complex (on Robson between Homer and Hamilton streets).

Gastown▶ After seeing Canada Place most visitors make for Gastown, a self-conscious and rather overwrought piece of urban rejuvenation. The district takes its name from "Gassy" Jack Leighton, a publican who opened a bar close to the area's lumber yards in 1867 (see panel, page 78). In time a ramshackle hamlet sprang up around the bars, an area which by 1886, and the arrival of the transcontinental railroad, had become the heart of a rapidly expanding port. By the middle of this century, however, when the city's downtown focus moved west, the area had become semi-derelict. Dubious spots still exist on the area's fringes, but restoration has tidied up most vestiges of the district's Victorian heritage. It is pleasant enough to stroll around here, though the only thing to see is an eccentric steam-powered clock at the western end of Water Street.

Chinatown▶▶ Nowhere is Canada's much-touted multiculturalism more in evidence than in Vancouver's Chinatown, where the 100,000-strong Chinese population forms the second-largest Chinese community outside the

BUS AND RAIL
Greyhound (tel: 604/482–8747 or 800/661–8747) and other bus companies use the new bus depot alongside the Pacific Central Station, 1150 Station Street, which is also the rail terminus for VIA Rail (tel: 800/561–8630) services from Jasper and eastern Canada. To reach downtown take a taxi from the forecourt or take a "Waterfront" train from the Science World–Main Street "SkyTrain" station (150m/160 yards from the station).

URBAN IDYLL
"The sort of city nearly everyone would want to live in."—Jan Morris on Vancouver

Vancouver: Spectacular by nature

New Year festivities in Vancouver's Chinatown

TOURIST INFORMATION
The Vancouver Touristinfo Centre is located in the Waterfront Centre (200 Burrard Street, tel: 604/683–2000 or 800/663–6000, www.tourismvancouver.com. *Open* Jun–end Aug daily 8–6; Sep–end May Mon–Sat 8.30–5), at the street's northern end on the corner with Canada Place Way. The center offers maps, an accommodations service, foreign exchange and tickets for BC Transit, cultural and sporting events.

NARROW FRONTAGE
At just 2m (6.5ft) across, the 1913 Sam Kee Building at 8 West Pender Street in Vancouver's Chinatown is reputed to be the narrowest building in the world.

PERFECT CITY
"Vancouver...had the combined excellence of Nature's gift and man's handiwork. God did a lot for Montréal, but man didn't add to it. Québec is historical and has a majesty of situation, but a lot of it is squalid. Toronto is a village, and always will be, if it spreads out a hundred miles wide: the prairie cities are impressive in their isolation and extension—fill in houses and they will be wonderful—but Vancouver is wonderful right now."—Stephen Leacock, *My Discovery of the West* (1937)

Far East (just behind that of San Francisco). Many of the present inhabitants' ancestors arrived during the 1858 gold rush, or were among the 15,000 Chinese laborers who worked on the transcontinental railroad in the 1880s. Shabby treatment awaited their descendants, who obtained legal and voting rights only in 1947.

Today Chinatown is wonderful to explore, its sights and sounds centered on Pender Street (between Carrall and Gore streets) and Keefer Street (between Main and Gore streets). Wander the area, dipping into some of the many exotic shops and markets; to add some focus, visit the **Dr. Sun Yat-Sen Gardens▶▶** (578 Carrall Street near Pender, tel: 604/662–3207. *Open* mid–Jun–end Aug daily 9.30–7; mid–May to mid-Jun and Sep daily 10–6; Oct daily 10–4.30; Nov–end Apr Tue–Sun 10–4.30. *Admission: moderate*). Begun in the 1960s, and completed for the '86 Expo, the gardens are named after the founder of the Chinese Republic, a frequent visitor to Vancouver. Some 57 artisans from Suzhou, China's Garden City, spent 13 months putting the finishing touches to these classical gardens, the first ever built outside China. No nails, screws or power tools were used in the project, which reproduces the subtle balance of *yin* and *yang*—hard and soft, light and dark, large and small—of a typical 14th-century Ming garden.

Stanley Park▶▶▶ As if it were not enough that Vancouver is surrounded by water and majestic mountains, forest and wilderness sweeps through the countryside just a few blocks from its downtown core. The largest urban park in North America (at over 400ha/1,000 acres), with stands of first-growth cedar, hemlock and Douglas fir, Stanley was set aside as a city park in 1888, having previously been a military reserve created to counter the threat of a US invasion. Most people come simply to walk and enjoy the views. Others come to tour Vancouver's most popular sight, the outstanding **aquarium▶** (*Open* late Jun–early Sep daily 9.30–7; early Sep–late Jun daily 10–5.30. *Admission: expensive*), whose collection of over 6,000 marine species is Canada's largest. Seals, otters, and the feeding of beluga and killer whales, are the star attractions.

Take bus 23 (Mon–Sat, daytime), or buses 25, 35 or 240 (Mon–Sat evenings, Sun and holidays) from the corner of Burrard and Pender to the park's main pedestrian entrance near Lost Lagoon, where on weekends in summer the free Stanley Park Shuttle bus connects the major attractions. Beach Avenue to the south is also a good point of entry for the area's wonderful sandy beaches. You can also rent bikes from various stores on Denman Street (take identification or a credit card to hand over as a deposit). A 9km (6-mile) walkway and cycle path run around the edge of the park, and a maze of trails meander through the woods.

Granville Island▶▶▶ Granville Island, like Chinatown and Stanley Park, offers an unexpected contrast to Vancouver's high-rise heart. A tiny island hideaway beneath the Granville Street Bridge, it started life as a sandbar at the turn of the century, when sludge dredged from False Creek was heaped up to form the foundations for an ironworks and shipyard. Dereliction in the 1960s saw the site turned into a rubbish dump, but in the 1970s, the federal government implemented an imaginative and highly successful program of regeneration. Part of the area's industrial infrastructure has been left in place, lending the island a gritty edge that saves it from the self-consciousness of Gastown. There's no better place to be on a sunny morning, when the indoor market is laden with food, and people spill out onto the wooden promenades to eat, chat and watch the world go by. Bars, cafés, a brewery, a children's playground, bookstores and a host of interesting stores and small businesses complete the picture.

MUSEUMS The Vancouver Museum▶▶, Canada's largest civic museum, offers a comprehensive, if occasionally old-fashioned, account of the history of Vancouver and its

GRANVILLE ISLAND PRACTICALITIES

The walk to Granville Island across the Granville Street Bridge is not terribly pleasant. The best way to approach on foot is to walk to the small dock behind the Vancouver Aquatic Centre at the southern end of Thurlow Street. Tiny ferries ply from here to Granville Island across False Creek every few minutes. To reach it by public transport, take bus 50 south on Granville Mall, and stroll onto the island. The Granville Island Information Centre (1592 Johnston Street, tel: 604/666–5784. *Open* daily, 9–6) provides maps and background material on the island. The best way to get to the Vancouver and Maritime museums and the Space Centre is by ferry from Granville Island to the small quay by the Maritime Museum.

A cyclist in Stanley Park appears oblivious to the city's famous downtown skyline

SCENIC SEABUS
The mountainous setting of North and West Vancouver makes a beautiful backdrop for downtown Vancouver. As mainly residential areas, they have few sights, but you can find fantastic views of the port and downtown by taking the SeaBus across the Burrard Inlet to "North Van" from the SeaBus terminal near Canada Place. Lonsdale Quay, the terminal in North Vancouver, has an indoor market which is well worth an hour's browsing before returning downtown by SeaBus.

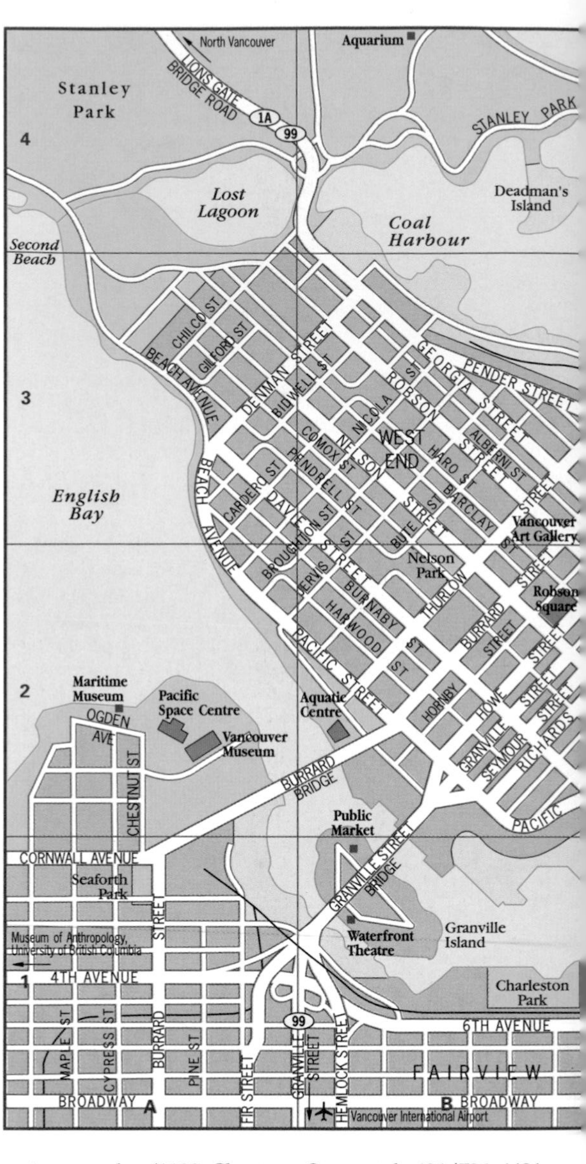

Entertaining the crowds on Granville Island

native peoples (1100 Chestnut Street, tel: 604/736–4431. *Open* Tue–Sun 10–5 (also Thu 5–9). *Admission: expensive*). The highlights are a huge dugout canoe, the only one of its type in existence, and displays on early pioneer life and the extreme hardships endured by the region's earliest white explorers. Next door, at the exciting Pacific Space Centre, you can take a "virtual" ride to Mars or other parts of the universe, watch multimedia and laser shows and view displays. (1100 Chestnut Street, tel: 604/738–7827 for show times. *Open* Jul–end Aug daily 10–5; Sep–end Jun Tue–Sun 10–5. *Admission: expensive.*) Nearby is the equally dated, but lovingly presented **Maritime Museum▶▶** (1905 Ogden Avenue, tel: 604/257–8300. *Open* mid-May–end Aug daily 10–5; Sep–mid-May Tue–Sun 10–5. *Admission: moderate*).

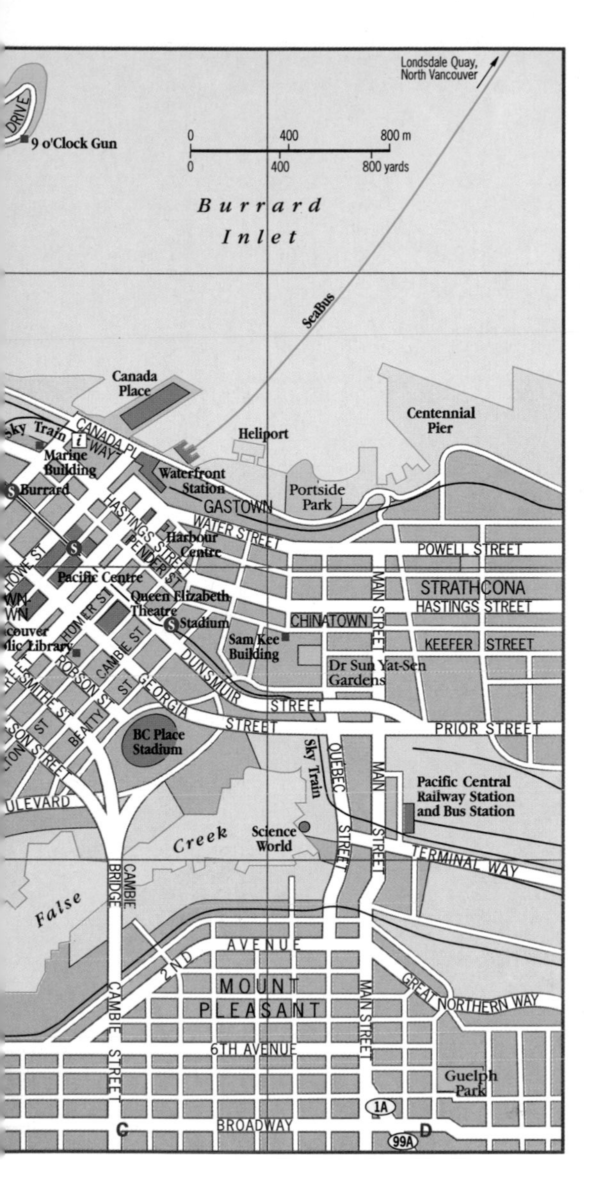

Dominating the maritime ephemera on display is the *St. Roch*, a schooner that in 1944 became the first vessel to sail the feared Northwest Passage in a single season.

If you can visit only one Vancouver museum, make it the **Museum of Anthropology▶▶▶** (6393 Northwest Marine Drive, tel: 604/822–5087. *Open* mid-May to early Sep Wed–Mon 10–5 and Tue 10–9; early Sep–mid-May Wed–Sun 11–5, Tue 11–9. *Admission: moderate*). Sited on the University of British Columbia campus, in a building designed by Arthur Erickson, the museum contains an unrivaled collection of totem poles, Haida houses, monolithic sculptures and smaller objects. Take bus 4 or 10 south on Granville Street to the campus (a 30-minute ride), then a 15-minute walk to the museum; follow signs, or ask for directions.

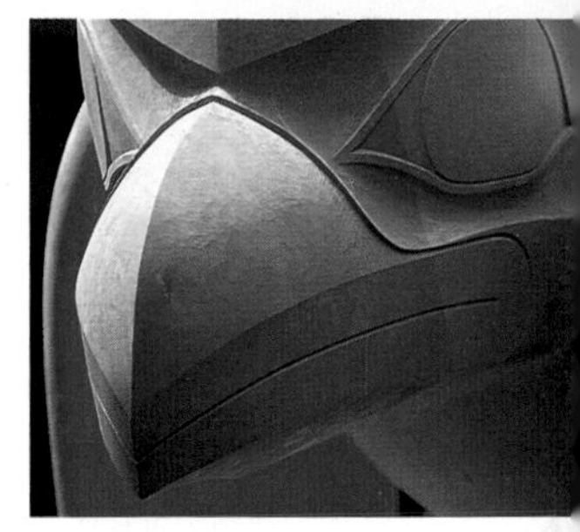

GASSY JACK

Vancouver's boozy founding father, Jack Leighton (1830–1875), was a sailor turned publican who arrived in Burrard Inlet in 1867 with a native wife and a single barrel of whiskey. His bar, Deighton's House (on the corner of Water and Carrall streets), took just 24 hours to build, with the help of lumberjacks who were paid in raw spirit. Business was brisk: drinking was banned in the lumber yards and the only other place to get drunk was over 12km (7 miles) away in New Westminster. Jack soon opened a second bar, and it was here that his rambling and bragging monologues earned him the nickname "Gassy."

SCIENCE WORLD

Science World's distinctive geodesic dome, built for Expo '86, is one of the city's modern landmarks. The modest but high-tech science museum inside is aimed at children (1455 Québec Street, tel: 604/443–7440. *Open* Mon–Fri 10–5, Sat–Sun 10–6. *Admission: expensive*).

PARK INFORMATION
Be certain to visit Clearwater's information center (tel: 250/674–2646, www.ntvalley.com), located at the junction of Highway 5 and the park access road. As well as the free *BC Parks* map-pamphlet on Wells Gray, there is a wealth of detailed information on hiking, accommodations and white-water rafting (one of the park's big draws).

►►► Wells Gray Provincial Park *47D2*

With scenery equal to that in many national parks, Wells Gray is by far the most tempting of British Columbia's many provincial parks. You can approach the area on Highway 5 from Jasper and Mount Robson to the north, a magnificently scenic mountain route or from Kamloops and the Okanagan to the south (a quicker and gentler road that follows the course of the North Thompson River). The accommodations amount only to campsites and a couple of small lodges, but a few hotels and motels are available at Clearwater, a village south of the park, and at the hamlets of Valemount and Blue River on Highway 5.

Clearwater Access to the park begins at **Clearwater►**, the start of a 60km (37-mile) road (gravel only for its last 30km/19 miles) that strikes north from the village past waterfalls, crashing rivers, deep forest and mountain viewpoints. Everything of note in the park, together with a handful of strolls and day hikes, can be accessed from this road. Accommodations, food and fuel are all available at Clearwater, where you'll also find the small **Yellowhead Museum** (*Open* summer months, tel: 250/674–3660 for hours), housed in one of the area's first white homesteads. Its displays include a proficient account of early pioneer life, with special reference to the exploits of the famous Overlanders (see panel opposite). The local tourist office is a vital port of call before leaving for the park (see panel).

Clearwater to Green Mountain Some 8km (5 miles) north of Clearwater, a sign from the access road directs you to **Spahats Creek Provincial Park**. A short walk from the parking lot brings you to a pair of observation platforms that look on to the 61m (200ft) **Spahats Falls►►**, a

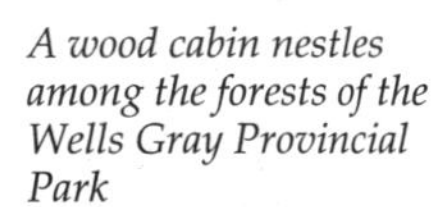

A wood cabin nestles among the forests of the Wells Gray Provincial Park

The Helmcken Falls are taller than the Vancouver skyline, and two and a half times the height of Niagara Falls

waterfall that cascades out of a deep gorge cut by Spahat Creek. As an added bonus, brightly colored layers of pinky-gray volcanic rock—much of Wells Gray is scattered with such volcanic remnants—frame a superb and unexpected view of the Clearwater River below.

Returning to the main access road, various minor gravel lanes branch off into the wilderness, most giving access to some of the park's longer day hikes and backpacking routes. Unless you are hiking, ignore these until you come to the signed turn (just after the park entrance) for the **Green Mountain Lookout▶▶▶**, where a winding gravel road leads to an absolutely phenomenal viewpoint. Mountains, forests and lakes, many still unnamed or unclimbed, stretch in all directions as far as the eye can see.

Dawson Falls to Clearwater Lake One of the more famous of the park's dozen or so waterfalls, **Dawson Falls** is the next sight to look for: there are "Viewpoint" signs shortly before the road crosses the Clearwater River on a large iron bridge. Broad and tumultuous, rather than spectacularly high (91m/300ft wide and 18m/60ft high), they provide a stocky contrast to the park's premier waterfall, the 137m (450-ft) **Helmcken Falls▶▶▶**. Reached via a cul-de-sac off the access road, this cascade—two and a half times the height of Niagara Falls—arches into a deep-cut, tree-fringed bowl in a single graceful plume, throwing up vast veils of spray into its green-shrouded amphitheater.

Back on the park road the scenery becomes better and better, with some lovely stretches of the fast-flowing Clearwater River accessible from the road for picnics and easy strolls. Watch for the sign to **Ray Farm▶**, a picturesque cluster of remote, half-ruined pioneer buildings a couple of minutes' walk from the road. Once owned by John Bunyon Ray—the first man to homestead the area in 1912—they provide a graphic illustration of the hardships that typified pioneer life. Clearwater Lake, at the end of the park road, offers a campsite, boat launch and well-marked short trails. There is no further vehicle access beyond this.

THE OVERLANDERS
Most prospectors lured to British Columbia by the 1860s gold rush came by boat to Vancouver Island. Around 200 innocents, however, were lured overland from Québec and Ontario by one company's promise of the "speediest, safest and most economical route to the gold diggings." After a bone-crunching cart journey across the Prairies, the group struggled over the Rockies on foot. At the Fraser River the party split into two groups: one attempted to run the river in rafts and canoes, many drowning in the attempt; the other—36 people in all—followed the North Thompson River past Clearwater, arriving half-starved in Fort Kamloops after a five-month journey. Only one of the original 200 "Overlanders" ever found gold.

WHAT'S IN A NAME?
Western Canada long went under the name New Caledonia, a title coined by an explorer of Scottish origins, Simon Fraser. Sadly it was also the name of a French colony in the Pacific. Britain's Queen Victoria came up with "Columbia," a title eventually rejected because it was the name of a South American country (and the river to which it referred spent most of its time in the US). After more thought Victoria came up with something that qualified matters suitably: British Columbia.

GETTING THERE

Foot passengers to Vancouver Island from Vancouver should take the hourly Pacific Coach Lines (tel: 604/662–8074 or 800/661–1725) service (inclusive of ferry) from the city's bus terminal. The total journey time is 3½ hours. By car, reserve crossings with BC Ferries (tel: 250/386–3431 or, BC only, 888/223–3779). The chief routes are Tsawwassen (30 minutes south of Vancouver) to Sidney (30 minutes north of Victoria); Tsawwassen to Nanaimo (2½ hours north of Victoria); and Horseshoe Bay (30 minutes north of Vancouver) to Nanaimo. In the US, ferries, hydrofoils and buses operate to Victoria from Seattle, Anacortes and Port Angeles.

Vancouver Island

Vancouver Island stretches almost 500km (300 miles) from north to south, making it the largest of North America's many west coast islands. Yet it musters a population of only half a million, most of whom live in Victoria, British Columbia's intimate and beautifully situated capital (see pages 84–87). The city shamelessly plays up to its image of an old British outpost, luring several million visitors a year with its pastiche of pubs, tea shops and bagpipers. Although a touch less enticing than its reputation suggests, the city is the obvious place to start a tour of the island, and in the Royal British Columbia Museum (see pages 86–87) it can claim to have one of the country's greatest museums, with superb displays on the natural history of the province's magnificent landscapes and marine environment, and on the history of its aboriginal peoples.

Elsewhere, the south of the island is disappointing, especially after the sublime landscapes of the British Columbian interior. The mountains of the Strathcona Provincial Park, however, midway up the island, and the seascapes of the Pacific Rim National Park (on its west coast, see pages 82–83) are unmissable. Further north the land becomes starker and less populated, culminating in the wild country around Port Hardy, the southern terminus of the BC Ferries' route through the Inside Passage (see panel, page 50).

Drive

Victoria to Nanaimo

See map on page 76.

A drive through villages and gentle countryside to Vancouver Island's second-largest town 220km (136 miles).

The drive from Victoria forms the main route north if you are headed for the Pacific Rim National Park and the ferries of the Inside Passage. After a whirl through Victoria's suburbs, the first sign of open country comes with **Goldstream Provincial Park▶▶**, created partly to protect evocative old mine workings dating from the 1855 gold rush. Stands of arbutus, Canada's only broad-leaved evergreen and glades of Douglas fir—some over 600 years old—can be seen on the park's Arbutus Ridge Trail (3km/2 miles). The path to Mount Finlayson offers fine panoramas of the ocean.

Duncan▶, 60km (37 miles) north of Victoria, merits a stop for the **Quw'utsun Cultural Centre** (*Open* daily. *Admission: expensive*), an attractive riverside complex with a shop, restaurant and displays and demonstrations of native carving, crafts, dance and cooking.

Less than 1.6km (1 mile) north lies the **British Columbia Forest Discovery Centre▶▶** (tel: 250/715–1113. *Open* early May–early Sep daily 10–6. *Admission: moderate*), a 40ha (100-acre) open-air museum that traces forestry's history from the first logging camps to today's high-tech sawmills.

A pleasant 30km (20-mile) detour west at Duncan takes you to **Lake Cowichan▶**, named after a native word meaning "warmed by the sun." A 75km (45-mile) scenic road circles the lake, passing several pretty forest parks. For more background on the area contact the info center at Lake Cowichan village (tel: 250/ 749–3244,www. cowichanlakecc.ca. *Open* summer months only).

Another short diversion from Highway 1 brings you to **Chemainus▶▶▶**, the "Little Town That Did," as signs along the highway tell you. Its achievement was to turn around a village in terminal decline, a downhill slide precipitated by the closure of the local sawmill, once one of the world's largest. The about-face began in 1983, when the local council commissioned a mural to record episodes from the area's past. More panels followed, attracting tourists. All manner of international awards have been foisted on Chemainus in recognition of its handiwork.

One of the many award-winning murals in Chemainus

Nanaimo▶▶, a large town gathered around a harbor, marks the watershed between Vancouver Island's inhabited south and its wilder northern reaches. Coal first brought settlers to the area, while its earlier native inhabitants produced petroglyphs (rock drawings) in the surrounding countryside. The **District Museum** (100 Cameron Street, tel: 250/753–1821. *Open* May–end Sep daily 10–5; Oct–end Apr Tue–Sat 10–5. *Admission: inexpensive*) has details of these, together with pioneer and natural history exhibits. Other sights include the **Bastion** (1853) a fort and store built by the Hudson's Bay Company and now a small museum (*Open* Jul–early Sep Wed–Sun 10–4). For more on Nanaimo, contact the info center at Beban House, 2290 Bowen Road (tel: 250/756–0106, www.tourism.nanaimo.com).

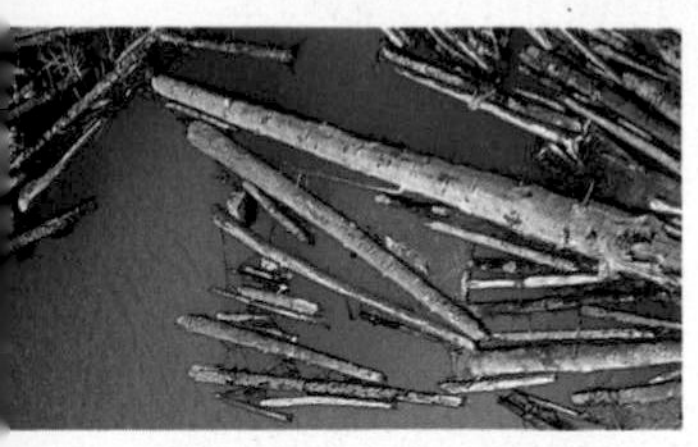

Nowhere are the bristling battle lines between conservationists and Canada's lumber industry more sharply drawn than in British Columbia and Vancouver Island. While some Canadians see forestry as a form of "harvesting" and a vital source of jobs, others condemn it as wanton desecration of a unique and vanishing environment.

NEWSPAPERS
Over 50 percent of all the world's newspapers are produced using paper made from Canadian trees.

CLEAR-CUTTING
Nothing raises the blood pressure of Canada's environmentalists more than the Canadian habit of "clear-cutting." This involves stripping forests completely to leave a bare, blasted hillside. In Europe, by contrast, forests tend to be partially and selectively felled, a solution that is easier on the eye and kinder to the environment.

Facts and figures There is no doubting forestry's importance to Canada's economy. There are good years and bad years, but the industry is worth around $40 billion annually, and accounts for almost 20 percent of the country's exports. In British Columbia, one of the country's richest provinces, its importance is even more marked: here some 48 percent of its export income derives from wood and wood products (a total of $16.8 billion). The region supplies around 45 percent of all Canada's usable lumber, thanks to forests that cover two-thirds of the province (only 1 percent of BC consists of cultivated land). Almost 10 percent of the world's newspapers are made using BC cellulose and wood pulp, while around 292,000 (or 17 percent) of the province's workforce are employed in the industry either directly or indirectly.

Priceless forests British Columbia's appeal to the lumber industry in the early days—apart from the obvious wealth of trees—was its preponderance of temperate rain forest, a vast belt of huge "old-growth" (or "first-growth") trees that once stretched from Alaska to the forests of northern California. This "Pacific rain forest" is considered one of the world's most productive ecosystems, producing up to ten times more biomass per acre than its tropical counterpart. The huge trees from these forests—sitka, cedar, spruce and Douglas fir—command enormous prices: a single trunk of sitka, for example, can fetch anything up to $60,000.

Trees awaiting processing in a Prince Rupert lumberyard

One of the many Vancouver Island lumber plants

Dilemma British Columbia's forests are being felled at a greater rate, but with less publicity, than their South American counterparts. At precisely what rate, however, is open to question. Conservationists claim two-thirds of BC's Pacific rain forest are now gone, and that the surviving old-growth trees are "the last cookies in the jar." Forestry apologists claim two-thirds of the old forest still survive. The Canadian government, by contrast, which remains a staunch defender of, and stakeholder in, the industry, concedes that only about a seventh of BC coastal rain forest enjoys environmental protection.

Jobs or trees At stake are not only profits, but numerous jobs—a vital concern in a province where rural employment is scarce. Environmentally friendly observations are unwelcome in logging communities. Recent advances in forestry automation, however, have confused arguments for and against logging, as lumbermen now see their jobs being lost to machines rather than to conservationists. Increased efficiency means half as many people are needed per volume of wood cut in BC as in the rest of Canada (in other words, twice as many trees have to be cut down to provide the same number of jobs). Some of the more enlightened unions now realize that more sustainable approaches to forestry—less clear-cutting and more replanting—might result in more jobs.

Dissent Passions run high in environmental circles, where demonstrators have been joined in clashes with loggers by native groups angry at the desecration of sacred sites. Opposition has occasionally taken a dangerous turn, with nails being left in trees to wreck lumber equipment when the trees are felled or processed (workers can also be killed or maimed when machinery hits the nails). Others direct their energies at stressing forestry's peripheral dangers, notably the damage done by landslides on clear-cut slopes, or the destruction of salmon habitats. Still others monitor the dioxin pollution from pulp mills (which ruins fishing for coastal shellfish) or point out the lumber companies' perennial failure to meet statutory cutting or replanting targets.

END OF THE LINE

Environmentalists claim that of Vancouver Island's 91 forest-covered watersheds of 5,000ha (12,000 acres) or more, only eight have escaped the attentions of the lumber industry.

A LOW PROFILE

The Canadian government commissioned a report on the image of the country's forestry industry in the United Kingdom, which imports a third of Canada's paper pulp, half of BC's plywood exports, and three-quarters of its lumber shipments. "UK public opinion," the report stated, "appears to be highly uncritical of Canadian forestry, largely because awareness of the subject is low... [There is] a reassuringly romantic and simplistic image of Canadian forestry based on a lumberjack in a checked shirt, felling a single tree." The report concluded that the public should remain of this opinion, stating that "media attention and coverage of Canadian forestry management issues should not be sought."

Coves and sandy beaches dot the shores of Vancouver Island

FORBIDDEN PLATEAU
This eerie wilderness is located in the eastern area of Strathcona Provincial Park above Buttle Lake. It takes its name from a Comox native legend, which tells how Comox women and children disappeared without trace after being sent to the plateau for safekeeping during an attack on their village by Cowichan natives. It was believed they had been devoured by evil spirits, and thereafter the plateau became taboo, or forbidden territory.

BIG BANG
Ripple Rock and the treacherous waters off Quadra Island were a ships' graveyard until 1958, when the vast navigational nightmare was blasted from existence in Canada's biggest-ever controlled explosion.

►► North Vancouver Island *76B2–A3*

For many people, the north of Vancouver Island is merely somewhere they pass through en route to pick up the Inside Passage ferries at Port Hardy. In fact, the area contains the best of the island's scenery, an assortment of winsome villages, and a medley of easily accessible islands. It also boasts some of the finest salmon fishing in British Columbia, which is to say some of the finest in the world.

Campbell River► No one can be in any doubt why people come to Campbell River. Self-proclaimed "Salmon-Fishing Capital of the World," the town is a shrine to all things fishy, its every corner festooned with pictures of proud anglers and their mammoth catches. A hotel sprang up here as early as 1904 to accommodate the first handful of fishermen, angling pioneers tempted west by tales of the gargantuan chinook salmon local Cape Mudge natives pulled from the sea almost at will (the fish are particularly plentiful here because shoals of salmon are squeezed into the narrow strait between the town and the mainland). Dozens of tackle shops and guides are on hand. You can also fish from the 200m (660ft) **Discovery Pier**, an exceptionally deep saltwater fishing pier. The town's outskirts are scrappy and unappealing, however, so if you do not want to fish, don't bother to come here unless to visit Quadra Island (see panel opposite).

Strathcona Provincial Park►► British Columbia's oldest protected area, Strathcona Provincial Park was created in 1911 to safeguard the best of Vancouver Island's mountain scenery. The island's highest point, Golden Hinde (2,200m/7,216 ft) is here, together with waterfalls, small glaciers, rugged mountain peaks and over 100km (60 miles) of hiking trails. If you approach from Campbell River, detour briefly to **Elk Falls Provincial Park**, 10km (6 miles) northwest of the town, where stands of vast Douglas firs and several impressive waterfalls make the diversion worthwhile. Some 5km (3 miles) further west on

Highway 28 (the main approach to Strathcona), stop at the **Quinsam River Salmon Hatchery**, which was built in 1976 to help counteract the effects of the nearby John Hart Dam.

An access road strikes south from Highway 28 at the head of **Buttle Lake**, site of the Strathcona Park Visitor Centre. This provides a source of information on hiking, flora, fauna and the area's outdoor activities. Most of the hikes start from the access road, which runs along the entire eastern shore of Buttle Lake. Be certain to pick up one of the excellent blue *BC Parks* guides, available free from visitors' centers.

Telegraph Cove▶▶ North of Campbell River, Highway 19 meanders through increasingly rugged scenery, avoiding settlements of any size until **Port McNeill** (200km/120 miles from Campbell River). From here it is just 8km (5 miles) to Telegraph Cove, an attractive "boardwalk village" raised above the ocean on wooden stilts. Visitors come here both to admire the village, and in the hope of seeing whales, for the area is renowned for its pods of killer whales. Some 20 whale "families" calve at nearby Robson Bight, which was established as an ecological reserve in 1982. Whale-watching trips here quickly fill up, so reserve in advance, especially if you visit in mid-summer; one of the best operators is Stubbs Island Charters (tel: 250/928–3185 or 3117 or 800/665–3066).

Alert Bay▶▶ Numerous ferries ply back and forth between Port McNeill and Cormorant Island. The crossing, which takes 50 minutes, brings you to Alert Bay, a fetching little fishing village known for the **U'Mista Cultural Centre** (tel: 250/974–5403. *Open* mid-May–early Sep 9–5; early Sep–mid-May Mon–Fri 9–5. *Admission: moderate*). The center contains numerous Kwakiutl native artifacts, and claims to have the world's tallest fully carved totem pole (239ft/73m). Further poles can be seen in the village's native cemetery.

TOURIST INFORMATION

Campbell River
1235 Shoppers' Row (tel: 250/287–4636, www.campbellriverchamber.ca);
Alert Bay 116 Fir Street (tel: 250/974–5213, www.alertbay.bc.ca);
Port Hardy 7250 Market Street (tel: 250/949–7622).

QUADRA ISLAND

Just 15 minutes by ferry from Port McNeill, this island is best known for the Kwagiulth Museum (tel: 250/285–3733. *Open* Jun–early Sep Mon–Sat 10–4.30, Sun 12–4.30; mid-Sep–end May Tue–Sat 10–4.30. *Admission: inexpensive*), where you'll find an outstanding collection of native masks, costumes and totem poles. Cape Mudge, on the island's southern tip, has the most important petroglyphs or native rock carvings, on the Pacific coast. You can also swim, boat or hike at Rebecca Spit Provincial Park.

Spring flowers in Strathcona Provincial Park

BAMFIELD
Tucked into the lee of Bamfield Inlet, this snug little village has no main street, just a 1km (1,100-yard) boardwalk raised on stilts above the ocean. It is best known as a trail-head for the West Coast Trail, but is also worth visiting for its own sake. Several easy hikes are possible, the best targets being Keeha Bay and the lighthouse at Cape Beale. Access to the village is via a 100km (60-mile) gravel road, float-plane or the MV *Lady Rose*. Bamfield has several accommodation options, but all need to be reserved in advance in high season.

Long Beach offers one of the loveliest seascapes on Vancouver Island

►►► Pacific Rim National Park *76B1*

This outstanding park, one of the chief reasons to visit Vancouver Island, was Canada's first national marine park. A cornucopia of magnificent islands, beaches and dramatic seascapes, it divides into three basic components: Long Beach (see below), the Broken Group Islands and the West Coast Trail (see panels opposite). Two towns, Tofino and Ucluelet, sit at the northern and southern ends of Long Beach, the park's most accessible area for casual visitors, while a small village, Bamfield (see panel), marks the northern end of the West Coast Trail. Long Beach could easily be seen in a day but, if you want to stay, Tofino makes the best and prettiest base.

Long Beach►►► Long Beach stretches south from Tofino for 10 miles, a glorious strand of wild, windblown beaches and crashing Pacific breakers backed by lush, vegetation-choked rain forest and the snow-covered peaks of the Mackenzie Mountains. Sculpted driftwood and splintered trees scatter the white-sanded foreshore, a happy hunting ground for beachcombers (the water is too cold and rough for swimming). The numerous islets and rock pools burst with shells, marine life and exotic flora; the BC coastline is reputedly home to more marine species than any other temperate shoreline in the world. Whales (see pages 212–213), sea lions and thousands of migrating birds can often be seen, especially in October and November; the best vantage points are nine marked trails accessed off Highway 4, which parallels the beach at a distance. South Beach Trail (Number 4; 1.6km/1 mile) is best for admiring the surf, while Half Moon Bay (Number 2; 10km/6 miles) explores a quieter sandy bay. Contact the park centers for more details (see panel opposite).

Fishing wharf close to picturesque Tofino

Tofino▶▶ Easily the prettiest, and also one of the oldest villages on Vancouver Island, Tofino began life in 1875 as a small trading post serving local settlers. Perched on a narrow promontory surrounded by water and tree-covered islands, its easy-going charm attracts ever-increasing numbers of summer visitors. Most are here to admire the fishing boats, harbor views and pleasant streets or to take boat rides, join whale-watching trips or ride out to **Meare's Island**▶▶▶ and several other scenic points accessible by boat. Just 15 minutes away, it is an idyllic spot, its shores swathed with 1,000-year-old forest, some of whose trees are over 6m (20ft) in diameter. Plans to log the island unleashed a cacophony of protest, and though they have been forestalled, the pressure to log may not be contained indefinitely, so the chance to wander through the woods (take the marked Tribal Park Trail) continues to be under threat. Another popular trip is the one-hour boat ride to **Hotsprings Cove**, where a half-hour walk from the landing stage brings you to Vancouver Island's only hot springs.

MV *Lady Rose*▶▶▶ The best way to see the scenery is aboard the MV *Frances Barkley* or its sister ship, the MV *Lady Rose* (*Open* Sep–end Jun Tue, Thu, Sat 8am; Jul–end Aug Tue, Thu–Sun), an old Scottish-built freighter that ferries supplies and up to 100 passengers between Kildonan, Bamfield, Ucluelet and the Broken Group Islands. Based in **Port Alberni** (east of the park), it leaves the town's Argyle Street Dock at the Alberni Harbour Quay, arriving at Bamfield (via Kildonan) at lunchtime before its return trip to Port Alberni (arriving 5.30pm). In June and September there are additional sailings on both boats (Mon, Wed, Fri 8am) which take in the Broken Group Islands en route to Ucluelet (arriving 12.30pm), and which return to Port Alberni (7pm). Given the lovely scenery visible from the boat, the trips fill up quickly, so try to reserve a ticket through Alberni Marine Transportation (tel: 205/723–8313 or 800/663–7192 Apr–end Sep only). You can buy one-way or round-trip tickets to all destinations.

INFORMATION

Park information is available at the visitor center close to the Ucluelet junction of Highway 4 (tel: 250/726–4212, www.parkscanada.gc.ca); and the *Wickaninnish* Interpretative Centre (tel: 250/726–4212). *Ucluelet* info center is on Highway 4 (tel: 250/726–4641, www.ucluelетinfo.com. *Open* May–end Sep); *Tofino* info center is at 380 Campbell Street (tel: 250/725–3414, www.tofinobc.org).

BROKEN GROUP ISLANDS

These wild and beautiful islands are a densely wooded archipelago scattered across Barkley Sound between Bamfield and Ucluelet. The only way for casual visitors to see them is aboard the MV *Lady Rose*. You can often see whales and harbor seals here, and there are colonies of ospreys, pelagic cormorants, and around 170 pairs of bald eagles.

WEST COAST TRAIL

This increasingly popular 77km (48-mile) coastal path between Bamfield and Port Renfew is one of North America's great marked trails. It was first blazed in 1906 as an escape route for shipwrecked sailors, who would otherwise have stood no chance of traversing the interior's forest and mountains. The full six- to ten-day walk is difficult and requires careful planning, but many people walk the first stage from Bamfield, which can be accomplished in a day (tel: 250/387–1642 or 800/435–5622). Reservations are essential.

WHALE-WATCHING
Whale-watching is one of Victoria's most popular activities. Local waters are not as whale-rich as those of the Pacific Rim National Park (see pages 82–83), but there's still an excellent chance of spotting orcas (killer whales), grays and humpbacks, as well as Harbour and Dall's porpoises, harbor or elephant seals and California and Steller sealions. Most companies offer similar trips at similar prices. Most offer full protective gear, and towels and gloves when required, and all offer life jackets and other safety essentials. Most have a naturalist or knowledgeable crew member to act as a guide. The only real variables are the **boats**: either rigid hull cruisers (covered or uncovered), which are more comfortable, or high-speed inflatables known as zodiacs, which are more exhilarating but offer a sometimes bumpy ride that makes them unsuitable for pregnant women, young children or people with back problems. Also enquire whether your chosen company has hydrophone equipment to listen to the whales' underwater vocalizing. *Other tips* Morning trips can be less choppy than afternoon excursions. Be sure to take sunglasses, sun-block, a tight-fitting hat, good soft-soled footwear, a sound plastic bag for camera and films and a warm sweater. Smoking is not usually allowed on boats. If you're using zodiacs you might want to bring a change of clothing. Trips often run over the scheduled time, so don't make any hard and fast travel plans. Drop by the Victoria info center (see panel opposite) for details of the tours and options. It has all the companies' P.R. material, and staff can book you on any tour.

▶▶▶ Victoria *76C1*

Victoria sprang to life in 1843, when the Hudson's Bay Company established a trading post on the southeastern tip of Vancouver Island. Settlers soon followed, and in time the harbor became a major staging post for the British Navy's Pacific fleet. The gold rush of the 1860s saw the town blossom, its population bolstered by prospectors en route to the mainland gold fields. Although the rush petered out, the town continued to prosper, and in 1866 was declared capital of the newly formed Crown colony of British Columbia (Vancouver was then still non-existent). Today it remains a prosperous, elegant and mild-weathered little corner, as well as a favored retirement and second-home retreat. Its prosperity derives from tourism, fishing and civil service jobs.

The Inner Harbour▶▶▶ Most of what you want to see in Victoria is on or around the Inner Harbour, a pleasant garden-fronted arc that fringes the city's downtown grid

to its rear. Following the pedestrian pathway around the horse-shoe shape of the Inner Harbour is a great way to see the major sights and appreciate Victoria's location. The stolid Gothic lines of the **Empress Hotel▶▶**, which rises imperiously over the waterfront, provide a perfect symbol of the city and its echoes of colonial grandeur. Built by the Canadian Pacific Railway in 1908, it survives today on the backs of mainly US and Japanese tourists, though anyone who is suitably dressed (no jeans, shorts or T-shirts), is welcome to take tea in one of the palatial lounges.

A short distance to the south lie the Crystal Gardens, designed by the hotel's architect, Francis Rattenbury. Created to emulate London's Crystal Palace, the complex opened in 1925, when it had the dubious distinction of containing the British Empire's "largest saltwater swimming pool." The pool has since been converted into a conservatory stuffed with plants, flowers, squawking birds and even live monkeys (713 Douglas Street, 250/381–1213. *Open* daily 10–4.30; later Jul–end Aug. *Admission: expensive*).

Countless tiny bulbs illuminate the Parliament Buildings on Victoria's Inner Harbour

TOURIST INFORMATION
Victoria's excellent info center is situated in front of the Empress Hotel on the Inner Harbour at 812 Wharf Street (tel: 250/953–2033, www.tourismvictoria.bc.ca; reservations, tel: 800/663-3883 in North America). It advises on tours, whale-watching and accommodations, and offers a wealth of information on the rest of Vancouver Island.

EXILED ENGLISH
"The heat, the slowness, the thick foliage, the bungalows with the nice drives, blossoms on the trees, blossoms on the sidewalk and roads, the large gardens, the blue mountains with snow on top across the water... [Victoria] was provincial middle-class English in exile."—Norman Levine, *Canada Made Me* (1958)

BRITS GALORE
Victoria has more British-born residents than any other town or city in Canada.

EXOTIC CITY
"Brighton Pavilion with the Himalayas for a back-drop."—Rudyard Kipling on Victoria, *Letters to the Family* (1907)

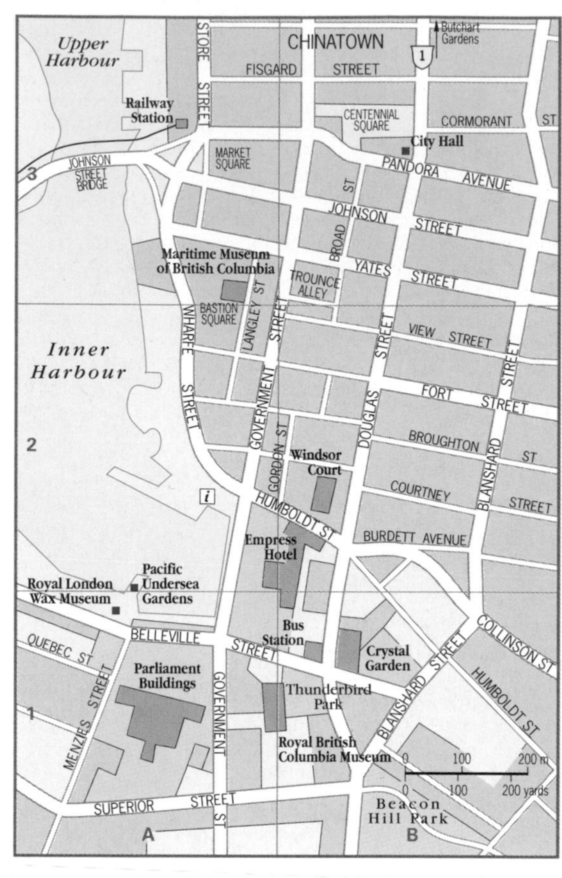

Other sights dotted around the harbor are rather more commercial, often dubiously so. Think carefully, therefore, before being lured into any tourist traps.

Parliament Buildings►► Francis Rattenbury's Parliament Buildings, built in 1897, dominate the southern curve of the Inner Harbour. They are best seen at night, when countless tiny bulbs trace the provincial government buildings' outline in pinpricks of light. A statue of Queen Victoria, shaded by a giant sequoia, overlooks the formal gardens to the front, while George Vancouver gazes down from a lofty perch atop the central dome. Various luminaries from the province's past adorn the facade, their stories regaled by official guides during tours of the opulently decorated interior (501 Belleville Street, tel: 250/387-3046). *Open* Jul–end Aug daily 9–5; Sep–end Jun Mon–Fri 9–5. *Admission free*. Regular free tours.

Mammoth opening exhibit at the Royal British Columbia Museum

Royal British Columbia Museum►►► This superlative museum, which is regularly ranked among the top ten museums in North America, would alone make a visit to Victoria worthwhile. Two days are needed to do the exhibits justice (the admission ticket is valid for 48 hours). Complete floors are dedicated to natural history displays, to the province's history, and to a definitive account of the

Pacific Northwest's native peoples. Remarkable dioramas show BC's coastal, rain forest and delta landscapes—replicating virtually every natural detail, even down to bird song and dripping leaves; other displays cover every historical aspect imaginable, from mining and fishing (with reconstructions of mines and an old salmon cannery) to early homesteads and a turn-of-the-century street. Between floors is the high-tech and highly popular **Open Ocean**►►►, a state-of-the-art array of dark tunnels, films and gripping audiovisuals on the mysteries of the ocean (675 Belleville Street, tel: 250/356–7226 or 888/447–7977. *Open* daily 9–5 all year round. *Admission: moderate*).

Downtown►► While many of downtown Victoria's streets—notably Government and Douglas—contain a predictable roster of shops, restaurants and mock-English pubs, much of the area is well worth casual exploration. Make a point of seeing **Chinatown**►, centered on Fisgard Street (once renowned for its brothels and gambling and opium dens), especially the tiny Fan Tan Alley; and wander around **Market Square**►►, a picturesque warehouse district restored to Victorian splendor (and full of interesting shops, galleries and restaurants), as well as Trounce Alley (between Government and Broad streets). Also leave time for **Bastion Square**, another lovely little corner of old Victoria, and the spot chosen by James Douglas in 1843 for the original Hudson's Bay post, Fort Victoria. The attractive building on its eastern flank, once the city's court house, contains the **Maritime Museum of British Columbia**►► (28 Bastion Square. *Open* daily 9.30–4.30. *Admission: moderate*), home to an excellent collection of model ships, uniforms, old photographs and maritime ephemera.

BUTCHART GARDENS

These breathtaking internationally renowned gardens, among the finest in Canada, were begun in 1904 by the wife of a Victorian mine-owner in an attempt to reclaim one of her husband's former quarries. Today, their 20ha (50-acre) site supports several hundred species and over 1 million individual plants. The gardens lie 22km (14 miles) north of downtown (800 Benvenuto Avenue, Brentwood Bay, tel: 250/652–5256. *Open* daily 9–sunset. *Admission: expensive*). Regular shuttle buses to the gardens leave in summer from outside the town's main bus terminal behind the Empress Hotel on Douglas Street.

Roses in full bloom at the glorious Butchart Gardens

The Rockies

UNPARALLELED GRANDEUR Few landscapes have a reputation to match that of the Canadian Rockies. Their very name suggests mountains of stunning beauty, so it comes as a wonderful surprise to find that they deserve every word of the praise lavished upon them. Gigantic glaciers, peaks rimed with snow and ice, huge forests and emerald-green lakes conspire to produce some of the world's most majestic scenery. Bears, wolves and a host of other magnificent animals and birds range through the wilderness, which extends for some 1,500km (900 miles) from the the southern border with the US to the distant reaches of Alaska and Yukon.

PLANNING Around 2,0235,000ha (5 million acres) of this domain have been set aside for posterity—one of the world's largest protected areas. At its heart lie four contiguous parks—Banff, Jasper, Yoho and Kootenay—the region most people mean when they talk about the Canadian Rockies. None of the parks will disappoint, though as all are wild—despite occasional impressions to the contrary—planning a trip and organizing accommodations are both vital. Distances are also considerable, so a car and several days are necessary to do the region any sort of justice. In an ideal world you would approach the area from Calgary, just 90 minutes from Banff, or from Edmonton, around four hours from Jasper. Access from the south or west, whether from British Columbia or the US, means visiting the more minor parks of Yoho or Kootenay before Banff or Jasper. Calgary is the best option if you're flying into the region, though Edmonton and Vancouver (about 12 hours' drive from Banff) are also reasonably convenient.

WHAT TO SEE The layout of the parks, and the road links between them, mean that it is impossible to see the major parks without retracing your steps. The most important consideration is to visit Banff and Lake Louise, and to plan an itinerary that takes you along the Icefields Parkway, a breathtaking highway through the Rockies' grandest scenery. Bear in mind, however, that Banff and Lake Louise are the popular face of the Rockies: places you have to see, but places with too many visitors for their own good (around 4 million a year). Therefore, plan to explore some of the less-frequented corners of Jasper, Yoho and Kootenay. Also note the region's shortage of accommodations, which means you should always reserve rooms well in advance, particularly if you intend to stay in Banff and Lake Louise.

WHAT TO DO Large and majestic swathes of all the parks can be admired from the road, but you should also be certain to explore some of the Rockies on foot, whatever your fitness level. All four parks are crisscrossed with well-marked trails, most of them so well worn and well documented that you can tackle them with little advance planning. Many are quite short, and you do not need to move far from your vehicle, or climb terribly high, to be rewarded with views or sights you would miss from the road. All the parks have at least one visitors' center, staffed by rangers who are happy to advise on walks and other outdoor activities. Most also have bundles of maps

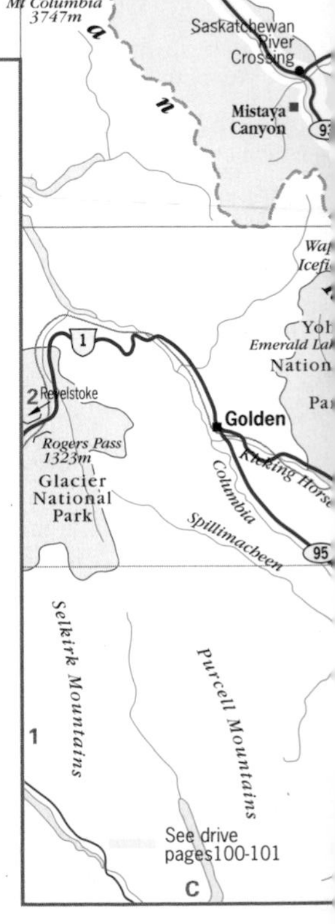

▶▶▶ REGION HIGHLIGHTS

Page 88: Moraine Lake, near Banff
Page 89: Hoo Doo formations, Banff
Page 90: View of the Rockies from Banff National Park

and miscellaneous pamphlets, together with a range of audio-visual displays. Numerous trail guides and handbooks are also available if you want to tackle something more ambitious (entries on the next few pages suggest the best shorter walks in each area). Most larger centers, notably Banff, Lake Louise and Jasper, also have facilities for renting bikes and other equipment.

ITINERARIES The most common Rockies itinerary, and the one that offers a good taste of the scenery and the differences between parks, takes you to Banff Townsite (see pages 94–95) and Lake Louise, and then follows the Icefields Parkway to Jasper and the Jasper National Park (see pages 102–105). From here you head westward into Mount Robson Provincial Park, home to the highest peak in the Rockies (see page 105). Thereafter you have to either leave the Rockies and head for Wells Gray (see pages 74–75), or retrace your steps to Lake Louise via the Icefields Parkway. From here you can pick up the Trans-Canada Highway through Yoho National Park (see pages 112–115) and then head south to Radium Hot Springs to loop back through Kootenay National Park (see pages 108–111) to Banff. At Lake Louise, if your itinerary is westward, you could also head for Glacier and Mount Revelstoke national parks (see pages 54–55).

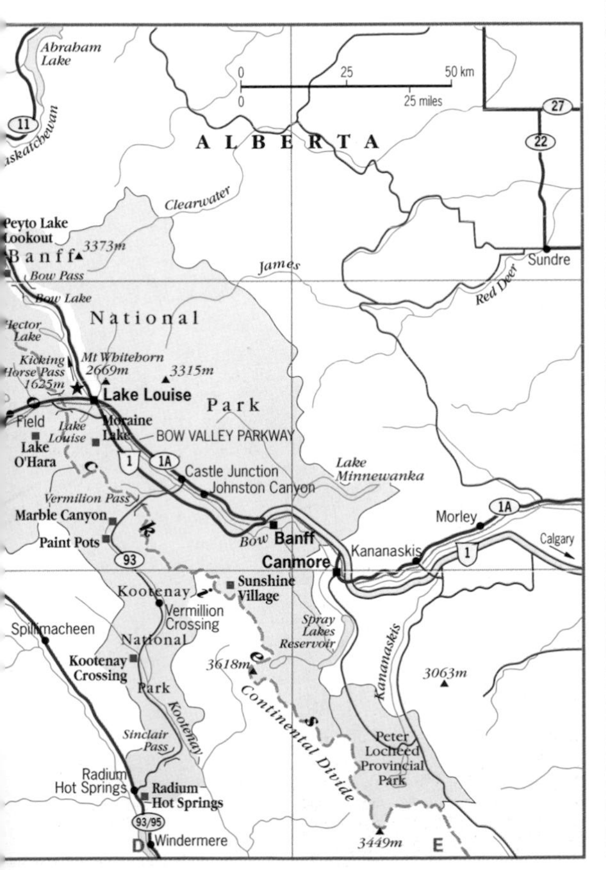

LONG-LASTING LITTER
This is how long litter lasts when dropped in the Rockies:
Orange peel up to 2 years
Cigarette butts 1–5 years
Wool socks 1–5 years
Coated paper 5 years
Plastic bags 10–20 years
Film canisters 20–30 years
Nylon fabric 30–40 years
Leather up to 50 years
Tin cans 50 years
Aluminum cans 500 years
Glass bottles 1,000 years
Plastic bottles indefinitely
Styrofoam cups indefinitely

PARK PERMITS
Anyone "using" any of the Rockies and other national parks, regardless of mode of entry, must buy a permit. The cost of a National Parks of Canada Pass (valid for 28 parks) is $45. Individual day passes (valid until 4pm following day of purchase) cost $7 for Banff, Yoho, Jasper and Kootenay; and $5 for Waterton Lakes, Glacier and Mount Revelstoke parks. Passes and permits can be bought at the entrances to all parks (compulsory for people in cars or on bikes), information centers, some campgrounds and (in summer) at automated pass machines within parks. If you buy several day passes you can redeem their cost against a year's pass at park centers on presentation of receipts. There's no fee to enter provincial parks. A separate backcountry wilderness pass ($8 per person per night), available from any park visitor center or info center, is required for all overnight backcountry use.

The Canadian Rockies are the result of huge global cataclysms dating back almost 600 million years. Woven within the apparent chaos of their creation lies the thread of a story, a geological tale that helps make sense of their convoluted evolution and distinctive modern appearance.

ICY REFINEMENTS
There have been three major ice ages in the last 250,000 years. Although they have occupied only a fraction of the Rockies' 600-million-year history, their effect on the mountains has been dramatic. They would have covered the high and then-rounded mountains to produce a region resembling modern-day Antarctica. Below the ice and snow, glaciers would then have carved and etched the cirques and castellated profiles that characterize the mountains today.

CASTELLATED MOUNTAINS
Castellated mountain profiles are a Rockies' trademark, and are formed where resistant strata of limestone, dolomite and quartzite are interspersed with weaker layers of shale. The stronger formations become cliffs, while the shales are eroded to form ledges. The result is the Rockies' distinctive "layer cake" mountain scenery.

DOGTOOTH MOUNTAINS
The "dog tooth" appearance of many Rockies peaks was formed when horizontal layers of sedimentary rocks were thrust into an almost vertical position. Weaker rock was then eroded, leaving the more resistant strata as vast vertical spires and pillars.

Conundrum High in the mountains of Yoho National Park, many hundreds of kilometers from the sea, lie the fractured and contorted strata of the Burgess Shales, a series of rocks that hold the fossilized bodies of marine creatures many millions of years old. In order to understand how these rocks came to rest where they did, so high and so far from any ocean, and why the Rockies rise with such sudden majesty from the rippling Prairies, it is necessary to describe the dramatic chain of events that led to the creation of one of the world's greatest mountain ranges.

Erosion Around 600 million years ago, North America was covered from Greenland to Guatemala by an immense range of granite mountains known as the Canadian Shield (today its ancient and smoothly eroded rump is largely confined to the wilds of northern Canada). Over the course of some 400 million years this mighty dome was gradually eroded, its vast debris of mud, sand and gravel washed westward by rivers and streams (the rivers flowed west because of the Shield's westerly tilt). Once this stream of mountain debris reached the land's edge it was deposited offshore on the so-called continental shelf.

Compression Over the millennia these deposits accumulated to a depth of some 19km (12 miles). As they did so, their enormous weight, and the pressure they generated, converted sand to sandstone, mud to shale and the natural deposits of the sea (such as reefs rich in limeproducing algae) into neatly arranged layers of limestone. In time these layers were to become the buckled and folded strata now visible in the Rockies. Two more dramatic episodes were required, however, to lift the newly formed rocks to their present position many thousands of feet above the sea.

Collision The first event was the collision of the Pacific and North American tectonic plates, a pair of vast floating platforms poised on the earth's crust. Around 200 million years ago, two separate chains of islands on the Pacific plate began to move eastward toward the North American mainland. As the first chain approached the coast, so their supporting plate slid under the more resilient North American plate into the earth's interior. The islands themselves, however, became detached from the disappearing plate, and continued their eastward progress, crashing into the coast and its ordered offshore deposits with catastrophic effect.

Mountains in the Rockies have been formed and shaped over a period of 600 million years

Mountains The collision bulldozed and crumpled the deposits, their layers fracturing and climbing over one another to produce the present-day Columbia Mountains. More mountains were produced as the aftershock of the collision continued inland, throwing up the old sedimentary layers over the next 70 million years to produce the Rockies' Western Main Ranges (the mountains on a line with Yoho and Kootenay national parks). Farther inland, the continuing aftershock then pushed up the Eastern Main Ranges (those mountains on a line with Lake Louise). The tale's final twist came when the islands shuddered to a halt, breaking up in a tangle of "exotic" rocks whose remains can be found inland as far east as Salmon Arm, British Columbia.

Finishing touches By this time the second chain of islands had also collided with the continent. This created further uplifting and geological chaos, strata once again being raised, rumpled and ruptured. The aftershock from this second collision moved inland to form the Eastern Front Ranges, the line of mountains that rears up so dramatically from the Prairies close to Calgary and Waterton Lakes. As for the rest of the Rockies, all that now remained was for erosion and the glaciers of the ice ages to apply their finishing touches (see panel opposite).

HORN MOUNTAINS

A "horn" peak has the perfect pyramid shape of a child's picture-book mountain, and is formed when large glaciers on several sides of a mountain erode it simultaneously. The scooped bowls around the summit are called cwms or cirques, while the sharp ridges between them are known as arêtes.

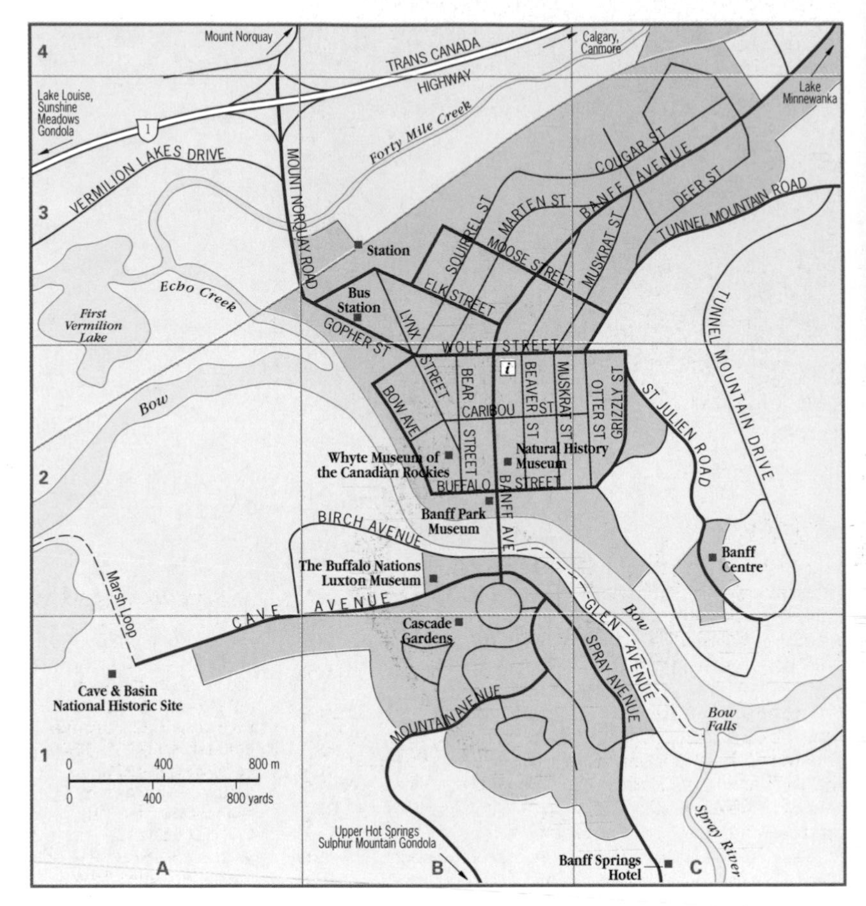

STROLLS

Banff's nicest piece of downtown greenery is the park behind the Banff Park Museum. A stroll that's a little more demanding takes you along the south bank of the Bow River to Bow Falls (1km/0.6 miles), a powerful set of cascades and rapids below the Banff Springs Hotel (start from the road bridge at the junction with Glen Avenue). Slightly out of town, the Fenland Trail (1km/0.6 miles) near First Vermilion Lake offers the chance to see ospreys, bald eagles and other wildlife on the lake's montane wetlands.

►► Banff Townsite (Banff) *91D2*

As the region's principal center, Banff, or Banff Townsite—the "Capital of the Canadian Rockies"—is a service, accommodations, and souvenir center that attracts many thousands of visitors in summer. Though the town is brash in itself, its surroundings and setting are lovely.

MUSEUMS Banff's premier museum is the **Banff Park Museum►►** (93 Banff Avenue, tel: 403/762–1558. *Open* mid-May–end Sep daily 10–6; Oct–mid-May 1–5. *Admission: inexpensive*). Most of its two floors are devoted to stuffed animals whose living counterparts inhabit the surrounding wilderness. Although game hunting was banned in the park in 1890, wolves, lynx, eagles and cougars continued to be hounded until the 1930s as part of the park's predator-control program. Most of the museum's exhibits date from those bad old days. The **Whyte Museum of the Canadian Rockies►►** (111 Bear Street, tel: 403/762–2291. *Open* daily 10–5. *Admission: inexpensive*) takes a more highbrow approach to the region's history. Its 4,000-volume archive of the Canadian Rockies includes paintings and period photographs offering an interesting trawl through the Rockies' past. The **Buffalo Nations Luxton Museum** (1 Birch Avenue, tel: 403/762–2388. *Open*

Banff's hot springs led directly to the creation of the national park

mid-May–end Oct daily 1–5; Nov–mid-May Wed–Sun 1–5. *Admission: moderate*) has exhibits on native history and culture, while the **Natural History Museum** (112 Banff Avenue, tel: 403/762–2388 for opening hours. *Admission free*) explores the formation and topography of the Rockies.

Hot springs The discovery of the Cave and Basin Springs (one of eight hot springs in Banff's vicinity) spurred the creation of the Banff National Park (see pages 96–99). Today the **Cave and Basin National Historic Site▶▶** (Cave Avenue, tel: 403/762–1566. *Open* daily. *Admission: moderate*) offers interpretative displays on the park's history and wildlife. It is also the trailhead for two short hikes—Marsh Loop (2km/1 mile) and Sundance Canyon (4km/2 miles)—that offer fascinating glimpses of the area's flora and fauna. For a dip in real hot springs, head for the **Upper Hot Springs▶**, 2km (1 mile) south of the town center, whose sulfurous waters emerge at a steamy 108°F (42°C) (Mountain Avenue, tel: 403/762–1515. *Open* daily. *Admission: moderate*).

Sulphur Mountain Gondola▶▶ The Upper Hot Springs can occasionally be busy, mainly because they attract a large amount of passing trade from the nearby Sulphur Mountain Gondola (tel: 403/762–5438. *Open* daily, seasonally varying opening times–sunset. *Admission: expensive*). This is a popular 8-minute cable-car ride up Sulphur Mountain (2,348m/7,701ft) to fine views and a restaurant.

Around Banff Mountain-ringed **Lake Minnewanka▶▶**, the park's largest lake, is best seen as a summer boat trip with Minnewanka Boat Tours (tel: 403/762–3473). On dry land, you can take one of the scenic drives that allow you to explore the area around Banff. Vermilion Lakes Drive, a 9km (5.5-mile) loop, offers good chances of seeing wildlife (sunrise and sunset are the best times), and takes in the three Vermilion Lakes that spread across the Bow Valley immediately west of Banff. Norquay Road offers a broad panorama over the town, while Tunnel Mountain Drive is a 5km (3-mile) scenic drive through the country to the east of Banff.

TOURIST INFORMATION
Banff's Chamber of Commerce and the excellent Park Visitor Center share the same building at 224 Banff Avenue. For park information, tel: 403/762–1550 or 800/651–7959; for details of the town or accommodations, tel: 403/762–8421; www.banfflakelouise.com. The former offers help finding accommodations; the latter provides information on walks, campsites and all manner of park-related activities.

BANFF SPRINGS HOTEL
This huge Gothic building, though 2km (1 mile) out of Banff, dominates much of the town's skyline. Built by the Canadian Pacific Railway in 1888, it was begun the wrong way round: when the architect arrived to supervise building, he found the rooms facing into the forest while the kitchens afforded magnificent views of the mountains. The maze-like interior has 770 rooms, plus one "lost" room reputedly sealed up by a plasterer during renovations.

ACCOMMODATIONS
Between June and early September it is absolutely vital to reserve the limited accommodations available in Banff, Lake Louise, Moraine Lake and the lodges along the Bow Valley and Icefields parkways. Hotels are also available at Canmore, 40km (25 miles) east of Banff, a far less scenic option, but one with more choice and more reasonably priced accommodations. The same goes for Golden, 80km (50 miles) west of Lake Louise on Highway 1, which is also convenient for Yoho and Glacier national parks. Radium Hot Springs, 128km (80 miles) southwest of Banff, is another option (and is also convenient for Kootenay National Park). These towns, though, are little more than glorified truck stops: places to stay, but not to explore.

INFORMATION
The Lake Louise Visitor Centre in the village's Samson Mall area (tel: 403/522–3833. *Open* daily).

PLANT LIFE
The species of vegetation in Banff and Jasper national parks include 996 vascular plants (trees, grasses and flowers), 407 lichens, 243 mosses and 53 liverworts.

▶▶▶ Banff National Park *91D2*

The first, the most famous, and arguably the most beautiful, of Canada's national parks, Banff National Park contains all the emerald lakes, mighty forests, white-water rivers and majestic, snow-covered mountains you would expect of the Canadian Rockies. Given the amount of literature on the park, however, and the number of visitors you encounter in Banff Townsite (see pages 94–95), it's easy to forget that virtually all of the park's 6,641sq km (2,553sq miles) are near-pristine wilderness. Roads penetrate only a limited area, but within that area are enough walks and sublime landscapes to last a lifetime.

Exploring the park Banff, the best place to begin a tour of the park, is a good spot to pick up supplies and background information (see pages 94–95). From here you can head north to Lake Louise, 60km (37 miles) from Banff, which can be reached via Highway 1 or the Bow Valley Parkway, two parallel and almost equally picturesque roads. Lake Louise divides into a small "village" with stores and hotels and Lake Louise itself, an incomparably beautiful ensemble of lake and mountain views. A few miles west of the lake and village lies Moraine Lake, a slightly more intimate but scarcely less stunning enclave.

The areas around both lakes offer some of the finest hiking in North America, and it would be a crime to leave the park without having ventured from your car, especially since you do not need to be fantastically fit to walk most paths. All but the toughest trails are well worn and well marked, though you should always wear sturdy shoes or boots, and take spare food and adequate protective clothing. Hundreds of walks are available (the following pages mention some of the best), most of which can be accomplished without maps. For more information be sure to contact the visitors' centers at Banff and Lake Louise Village (see panel).

The Icefields Parkway Beyond Lake Louise, Highway 1 branches west into Yoho National Park (see pages 112–115), an obvious destination if time is short and you are heading onwards to Vancouver and British Columbia. Taking this route, however, would mean missing the Icefields Parkway (Highway 93), one of the world's great drives, and one of the highlights of any Canadian trip (see pages 100–101). The road cuts through some of the country's most spectacular scenery on its 230km (142-mile) journey from Lake Louise to Jasper, cresting vertiginous mountain passes, skirting endless lakes and forests and penetrating one of the largest glacial icefields in North America. On arriving in Jasper Townsite (see pages 103-104), choose between exploring the Jasper National Park, visiting Mount Robson Provincial Park (see page 105), or retracing your route back down the Icefields Parkway.

History Excavations in the Vermilion Lakes area around Banff have uncovered traces of human habitation in the Bow Valley dating back at least 11,000 years. Stoney, Kootenay and Blackfoot natives roamed the region long before the coming of the first white "tourist," a visitor widely held to have been one George Simpson, governor of the Hudson's Bay Company (led across the Bow River by a native guide in 1841). Trappers and fur traders remained the only other visitors until the arrival of the Canadian Pacific Railway (CPR), which reached Banff—then known simply as "Siding 29"—in 1883. In the same year a group of railway workers, ostensibly looking for minerals, stumbled across the Cave and Basin Springs (see page 95), whose warm waters were soon soothing the aches and pains of fellow workers. However, disputes as to who exactly owned the springs (they had long been sacred to the Stoney natives) led to the creation of the Hot Springs Reserve in 1885. Two years later this became the Rocky Mountains Park, Canada's first national park, and the world's third. Its present name was coined in 1930.

Scenic routes Highway 1 from Banff to Lake Louise provides scenery enough for most visitors, whisking them between the two resorts past towering peaks and jade-green rivers that hint at the splendor to come on the Icefields Parkway. The 48km (30-mile) **Bow Valley Parkway▶▶▶** (Highway 1a), however, provides a quieter and even more majestic alternative. Specifically designed as an attractive drive, it is dotted with campsites, picnic spots and stopping places, together with marked trails and a series of interpretative boards intended to make sense of the area's topography and natural history. One of the many highlights is the **Johnston Canyon▶▶**, some 30km (20 miles) west of Banff, which can best be seen on the highly recommended **Johnston Canyon Trail** (3km/2 miles each way). Another good walk is the 15-minute stroll to Silverton Falls, which starts from close to the park ranger station at Castle Junction.

Lake Louise Village▶ Just off Highway 1, Lake Louise Village amounts to little more than a mall, garage, visitors' center (tel: 403/522–3833) and a dozen or so expensive

GUIDED TOURS
Traveling without a car, or leaving your vehicle in Banff, need not stop you seeing the national park. Regular Greyhound buses run to Banff and Lake Louise from Calgary and Vancouver, while Brewster Transportation runs daily buses in summer between Banff and Jasper along the Icefields Parkway. Brewster also organizes half-, full- and multi-day bus tours from Banff, Jasper and Calgary, with trips to Lake Louise, the Columbia Icefield and elsewhere. To contact Brewster tel: 877/791–5500, www.brewster.ca

"Snocoach" tours offer a first-hand glimpse of the Rockies' largest icefield

One way to escape the crowds attracted to the sublime Lake Louise

LAKE LOUISE WALKS
The simplest walk at Lake Louise takes you along the lake's northern shore, a stroll that can be extended to the "tea house," a rustic café at the Plain of the Six Glaciers (6.5km /4 miles one way from the hotel; 365m/ 1,200ft of ascent). This provides a first-hand look at the stark glaciated scenery beyond the lake. Better is the shorter climb to Lake Agnes, a popular but highly recommended, steep switchback trail through the woods, with magnificent views, to a tea house on the edge of little Lake Agnes (3km/ 2 miles; 400m/1,300ft). Two short walks from Lake Agnes continue to still-grander aeries at Little Beehive and Big Beehive. The latter walk can be continued to meet the Plain of the Six Glaciers trail, completing a satisfying return loop to Château Lake Louise. All paths are well marked.

MATCHLESS SCENE
Tom Wilson, the first Canadian of European origin to see Lake Louise, describes his reaction on seeing the lake in 1882: "I never, in all my explorations of these five chains of mountains throughout western Canada, saw such a matchless scene...I felt puny in body, but glorified in spirit and soul."

motels. The only thing to do locally, other than eating and sleeping, is to take the **Lake Louise Gondola**►► (tel: 403/522–3555. *Open* May–end Sep daily. *Admission: expensive*) up Mount Whitehorn (2,669m/8,754ft). Views from the summit embrace over a dozen glaciers, best enjoyed from the friendly Whitehorn Tea House. After refreshments you have the option of hiking back. The gondola—nicknamed the "Friendly Giant"—is marked north off Highway 1 just outside the village.

Lake Louise►►► More photographs are probably taken in front of Lake Louise than in the rest of the Rockies put together. Located around 6.5km (4 miles) from its eponymous village, the picture-perfect lake sits beneath a bowl of mountains and glaciers, its eastern shore—site of a giant glacial moraine—dominated by the Château Lake Louise hotel. Built in 1924, after fire had destroyed an earlier structure, the building is a major eyesore. Such is the lake's splendor, however, that it remains miraculously unsullied by its crude sentinel.

Information boards on the shore recount lake-related anecdotes, among them the story of its discovery. Christened the "Lake of the Little Fishes" by the Stoney, the lake was "discovered" for white Canada by Tom Wilson (see panel), a survey packer for the CPR (then driving the transcontinental railroad through the area). A native guide led him to the lake in 1882, which he named,

rather unimaginatively, Emerald Lake. Its present title derives from Princess Louise Alberta, Queen Victoria's fourth daughter, and the wife of Canada's then Governor-General, Lord Lorne.

Renting a canoe on the lake shore is one way of fleeing the 2 million or more visitors lured here every year. A better means of escape is to follow one of the trails from the lake shore (see panel opposite). But be warned, these are some of the most-tramped paths in the Rockies.

Moraine Lake▶▶▶ That fewer people visit Moraine Lake than Lake Louise is no reflection on its scenery, which is more intimate and more sublime than that of its neighbor. A beautifully designed lodge, with cabins, restaurant and café, a few information boards and a small parking lot are the only concessions to visitors. The lake shimmers an almost surreal turquoise, backed by screes, forested slopes and the jagged peaks of the Wenkchemna Mountains (a scene that graces older versions of the Canadian $20 bill). As at Lake Louise you should aim to tackle a few hikes to make the most of the scenery. Wander along the lake shore if you want a gentle stroll; walk to Consolation Lake if you can manage a modest 3km (2-mile) hike; or go up to Larch Valley (3km/2 miles; 300m 1,000ft ascent) and Sentinel Pass (8km/5 miles; 700m/2,300ft ascent) or Eiffel Lake (5km/3 miles; 365m/1,200ft ascent) if you are prepared for a full morning's hike.

COLOR

The peacock-blue of the Rockies' lakes is caused by the particles of glacial silt, or "till," which are washed into them by spring melt water. These fine flour-like particles absorb all the visible colors in the incoming spectrum of light except those in the blue-green range. In winter or early spring, before the snows have melted, the lakes are a more normal sky-blue color.

The Icefields Parkway

See map on pages 90–91.

A magnificent drive between Lake Louise and Jasper through the most majestic scenery in the Canadian Rockies (230km/143 miles).

On no account miss this drive, which traces an old native and fur-trappers' route up the Bow River (the present road was begun as a public works program during the Depression). At its midway point the Parkway crosses into the Jasper National Park, but it is generally treated as a single journey, as described here. Walks long and short start from numerous points along the road, together with a host of short strolls to well-marked viewpoints and places of interest. Full details of these are given in *The Icefields Parkway*, an excellent Canadian Parks pamphlet available free from visitors' centers.

The road's first major landmark is **Hector Lake** (17km/11 miles), named after the geologist James Hector, in 1858 the first European to pass through this part of the region. Notice the great scars carved by avalanches on Pulpit Peak (2,724m/8,935ft), the summit at the lake's southern tip. At Bow Lake (37km/23 miles) you might tackle one of the highway's best lake walks, the **Bow Lake and Bow Glacier Falls Trail** (5km/3 miles; 155m/500ft ascent). If you decide against this, on no account pass up the chance to walk to the **Peyto Lake Lookout▶▶▶**, an easy 20-minute stroll to one of the Rockies' most astounding viewpoints. Look for signs to the trail about 3km (2 miles) beyond the 2,609m (6,786-ft) Bow Pass, the highest point reached by any Canadian highway.

Beyond the pass the road falls some 700m (2,300ft), the drop in altitude bringing noticeable changes in vegetation, particularly around Saskatchewan Crossing (a scrappy hotel and service station). Something of the altered habitats can be seen from the short trail that leads to **Mistaya Canyon▶**. Moving north, the next landmark is the so-called "Big Hill," where the road climbs in a vast sweeping curve, offering dramatic views over mountains stretching back to Banff and Lake Louise. Just beyond (117km/72 miles) is the trailhead for

Trees and lakes: Two components in the Rockies' magnificent natural ensemble

the **Parker Ridge Trail▶▶**, which is probably the one path on the whole trip (after Peyto Lake) that you should make an effort to walk (2.5km/1.5 miles; 275m/900ft ascent). In summer the ridge is swathed in flowers, while the breathtaking views from its summit include a huge portion of the Saskatchewan Glacier.

This glacier forms part of the famous **Columbia Icefield▶▶▶**, the largest sheet of ice and snow in the Rockies, covering 389sq m (150sq miles), and the largest glacial area anywhere in the Northern Hemisphere below the Arctic Circle. Ice in the six main glaciers, three of which are visible from the road, is anything up to 900m (3,000ft) thick, while melt water from Mount Snowdome (3,520m/11,546ft) flows into three oceans (the Arctic, Pacific and Atlantic). For more background information, drop into the **Icefield Center** (*Open* May–end Oct daily) an interpretative and information complex, or join one of the popular "Snocoach" tours onto the ice

Sunwapta Falls, easily seen on a short trail off the Icefields Parkway

sheet itself (May–end Oct daily 9–5, every 15 minutes. *Admission: expensive*). For more information on the latter, contact Brewster Transportation (tel: 877/ICE RIDE).

Although the scenery continues in majestic vein all the way to Jasper, landscape fatigue may well set in beyond the Icefield. Two waterfalls, however, deserve attention: the **Sunwapta Falls**, visible from a short trail; and the more spectacular **Athabasca Falls▶▶**, where the Athabasca River has carved through seams of tough quartzite rock.

The only food and fuel on the highway is available at Saskatchewan Crossing (77km/48 miles from Lake Louise) and the Columbia Icefield (127km/79 miles). The only accommodation options are a few youth hostels and campsites, and the individual lodges located at Bow Lake, Saskatchewan Crossing, the Columbia Icefield and Sunwapta Falls.

Take the Jasper Tramway for superb views of the national park

►►► Jasper National Park 90B4

Jasper National Park covers a greater area than Banff, Yoho and Kootenay national parks combined (10,878sq km/4,181sq miles), yet plays second fiddle to Banff in the minds of most visitors. Its mountains, lakes and forests, however, are the equal of anything in the Rockies, and have the added advantage that they lack some of the cars, crowds and commercialization of their southern counterparts. While hiking opportunities are relatively scarce (at least for casual visitors), good roads still provide easy access to some magnificent country.

EXPLORING Jasper is the main base and only town of any size in the park. The best scenery includes Maligne Lake (see page 105), some 50km (30 miles) southeast of the town; the Maligne Canyon, reached via Maligne Road en route for Maligne Lake; Mount Edith Cavell, a scenic road and viewpoint 30km (20 miles) south of Jasper; the Icefields Parkway (see pages 100–101); and the Miette Hot Springs area, 65km (40 miles) north of Jasper. Beyond the park you can head for Edmonton, Prince George (for the Skeena Valley—see pages 64–65—and the Alaska Highway) or follow the Yellowhead Highway into British Columbia to see Mount Robson Provincial Park (see page 105).

EARLY SETTLEMENT Jasper was the first area in the Rockies to be reached by Europeans. Some of its earliest visitors arrived in 1811, members of David Thompson's expedition to find a northern route over the mountains. One of Thompson's companions, William Henry, remained in the region to establish a supply depot for the North West Company (NWC), Thompson's employer. The depot took the name Henry House, though its precise

INFORMATION
The excellent Canadian Parks Service Visitors' Centre is situated almost opposite the railroad station. It is set back from the road at 500 Connaught Drive (tel: 780/852-6176; www.pc.gc.ca).
The town's Chamber of Commerce office is at 409 Patricia Street (tel: 780/852-3858, www.jaspercanadianrockies.com

location—probably close to present-day Old Fort Point—has since been lost. Two years later the depot was replaced by Jasper House, named after Jasper Hawes, a long-term employee of the NWC In 1829, following the amalgamation of the NWC and Hudson's Bay Company, the post was superseded by yet another building, this time situated closer to the position of the present townsite.

THE RAILROAD A fall-off in trade during the 19th century saw life at the post dwindle to almost nothing. By the end of the century it was being visited by a few prospectors and the occasional painter (most notably Paul Kane). Other visitors included the explorer Mary Schäffer, the first European to see Maligne Lake, which remained unknown to Europeans until as late as 1908. All this changed with the coming of the Grand Trunk Pacific Railway, a competitor to the Canadian Pacific, whose route through the southern Rockies had opened up places such as Banff and Yoho to a lucrative tourist trade. Seeking a similar success further north, the Grand Trunk pushed its own route west, reaching the area around Jasper in 1908. The Jasper Forest Park was duly instigated, and within three years a sprawling tent city had developed on Jasper's present site. It initially took the title Fitzhugh, after Grand Trunk's vice-president, but changed its name to Jasper following the site's first formal survey.

Jasper Townsite▶▶ Jasper has less to recommend it scenically than Banff, mainly because the mountains are set farther back from its streets. Yet its quieter, small-town feel somehow seems more in keeping with the Rockies than does its more cosmopolitan neighbor. For background on the town, first visit the information centers (see

ARRIVING
By car you can approach Jasper from the south via the Icefields Parkway (from Lake Louise), and on the Yellowhead Highway from Edmonton (to the east), Prince George (to the north) and Kamloops (to the west). Greyhound buses (www.greyhound.ca) run to Jasper from Edmonton and Kamloops (four daily) and from Prince George (two daily). In the summer Brewster Transportation runs one bus daily to Jasper from Banff (see panel, page 97). Both bus companies operate from the VIA Rail station at 314 Connaught Drive (tel: 780/852–4102 or 888/VIA RAIL, www.viarail.ca), which has train services to Vancouver, Edmonton and Prince Rupert (several times a week).

MIDDLE-AGED MOUNTAINS
The average age of the Rockies is 120 million years, which makes them younger than the Appalachians, but older than the Alps, Himalayas and American Rockies.

The peaceful environs of Pyramid Lake are just a few minutes from Jasper

White-water rafting trips on the Maligne River can be arranged in Jasper

panel, page 102) and then head for the **Yellowhead Museum** (400 Pyramid Road, tel: 780/852–3013. *Open* mid-May–early Sep, 10–9; early Sep–end Oct 10–5; Nov–mid-May Thu–Sun 10–5. *Admission: inexpensive*), which provides a competent summary of the region's fur trading and railway history. For a more literal overview, try the **Jasper Tramway▶▶** (Whistlers Mountain Road, tel: 780/852–3093. *Open* mid–Apr to mid-Oct, varying hours. *Admission: expensive*), a cable-car about 7km (4 miles) south of town. The 2.5km (1.5 mile), seven-minute ride whisks you up to a 2,2285m (7,495ft) viewpoint, a belvedere with all-embracing views of the Jasper area. For more extensive views still, follow the steep one-hour trail to Whistlers summit (2,470m/8,102ft).

Another popular outing is the 5km (3-mile) drive to **Patricia and Pyramid lakes▶**, two recreational areas filled with beaches and trails, where you can rent bikes and canoes. East of town (and easily seen en route to Maligne Lake) are **Edith and Annete lakes▶**, both busy day-use areas with numerous sandy beaches and shady nooks. Otherwise, Jasper has relatively little to see or do, as its main function is as a place to eat and sleep. Most of the action takes place on Connaught Drive, the main street, which boasts a sprinkling of cafés, stores and restaurants. The grid of streets to its west contains a host of bed and breakfast options, most in old-style wooden homes, while the bulk of the town's motels lie at its northern edge.

FINDING ACCOMMODATIONS

Contact the Chamber of Commerce (see "Information") if you need help finding a motel or one of Jasper's many bed and breakfasts. Alternatively, use one of the town's specialist accommodations agencies, such as Jasper Travel (tel: 780/852–4400). For those on a lower budget there are four park-run campsites and four youth hostels within 7 miiles of the town (tel: 780/852–3215, www.hihostels.ca for hostel reservations).

Maligne Lake Road▶▶▶ Short of a mountain walk, there is no better day out in Jasper National Park than a drive along the 48km (30-mile) Maligne Lake Road. It is a popular excursion and can be busy. Maligne Tours (626 Connaught Drive, tel: 780/852–3370) runs trips along the road during the summer months.

The first stop is **Maligne Canyon▶▶**, 11km (8 miles) from Jasper, a gorge that's not quite as dramatic as it's often painted (though it is 50m/165ft deep in places). Its 20-minute trail is still worth walking, however, as it takes you past several waterfalls and a series of interpretive panels explaining the forces that have shaped the canyon. The walk can be extended with another 45-minute loop.

Not quite as many people stop at **Medicine Lake▶▶**, which is 32km (20 miles) from Jasper, and both scenically and geologically interesting in that it has no outlet but loses water instead via a system of sink-holes on the lake bed. The result is a constantly fluctuating water level, a mystery that suggested to aboriginal medicine men that the lake had magical properties—hence its name. The water feeds into a vast system of limestone caves, emerging again somewhere in the vicinity of Jasper.

Maligne Lake▶▶▶, 48km (30 miles) from Jasper, is well worth the journey. At an altitude of some 1,673m (5,487ft), and ringed by snow-dusted mountains, it is both the largest lake in the Rockies and the largest glacially formed lake in North America (22km/13.5 miles long, 2km/1 mile wide and 92m/300ft deep). The road ends at the lake shore, where there is a picnic area, restaurant and easy walk, the 3km (2-mile) Lake Trail. Be certain to take a **boat trip▶▶▶** (reserve your place with Maligne Tours, tel: 780/852–3370. *Open* Jun–mid-Oct daily every hour. *Admission: expensive*) from the landing stage, for spine-tingling views of the lake and its mountains.

Mount Robson Provincial Park▶▶ West of Jasper the Yellowhead Highway climbs gently through ever-more-beautiful countryside, breasts the Yellowhead Pass after 20km (12 miles), and eventually comes to Mount Robson (3,954m/12,969ft), the highest and most awe-inspiring peak in the Rockies. There is a Travel Infocentre (tel: 250/566–4325. *Open* May–end Oct) at the western edge of the park, offering the best view of the mountain. About 1.6km (1 mile) away lies the trailhead for the Berg Lake Trail, the only way to get closer to the peak (22km/13.5 miles each way; 795m/2,600ft ascent). Too long for a day walk, it is reputedly the most popular backpacking hike in the Rockies. If you don't have that much time, tackle the 6.5km (4 miles) to Kinney Lake, the first leg of the journey.

The Mount Robson Provincial Park protects the highest peak in the Canadian Rockies

ANGRY CLERIC

Maligne Lake takes its name from Maligne River, christened in 1846 by a French missionary, Father de Smet, who encountered problems in his attempt to cross it downstream (*maligne* is French for "wicked").

WALK—OLD FORT POINT

Jasper's rather flat surroundings mean that most short walks from the town are relatively unremarkable. The best, however—Old Fort Point Loop—proves the exception to the rule, offering 360-degree views and plenty of peaceful corners (6.5km/4-mile round trip). To reach the trailhead (1.6km /1 mile east of town) leave the town via Old Fort Exit and follow Highway 93a/Highway 16 across the railway to the turn-off for Old Fort Point-Lac Beauvert.

No animal so symbolizes primeval wilderness as the bear. As a result, no animal seems to hold quite as much fascination for visitors. Encounters with bears are relatively rare—hunting is reducing their numbers—but a meeting with a grizzly is not to be taken lightly.

HIBERNATION
About November the grizzly digs its den, usually on a steep north- or east-facing slope, where deep snow will provide winter insulation. No food is stored in the den, for the bear will live off the reserves of fat built up over the summer. During hibernation the animal's temperature drops by several degrees, and respiration falls to just two to four breaths a minute. The bear's intestines are blocked by a thick plug of food, and for several months the animal will neither urinate nor defecate. On warm winter days the bear may occasionally come round to eat or stretch its legs, but hibernation generally continues until April.

Below: Take care—there's a bear about
Top: Another grizzly

Bear essentials Canada has three types of bear—grizzly (or brown), black and polar. All are big, and all are dangerous. The biggest and best known is the grizzly, distinguished by its brownish fur and the pronounced hump on its back. Black bears are smaller (but no less dangerous), darker, lack a hump and are slightly more common. Polar bears, of course, stick to the country's frozen margins, though they often parade for casual visitors around Churchill on Hudson Bay (see pages 144–145). All three types exist mainly on fruits, plants and berries, but they will also kill live prey.

Myths The bear's almost mythical place in our view of the wild—not to mention the danger they are perceived to present—has led to a plethora of tall tales and potentially dangerous misconceptions. One is that they are slow and lumbering. They are not. Turning tail and running for your life when confronted by a curious bear will avail you nothing; if anything it will make matters worse, for while bears may be slow off the mark they can run surprisingly fast once started, and they almost always give chase. Another popular notion is that they cannot climb trees. Grizzlies may be lazy and give up the pursuit after a few yards of trunk-climbing, but black bears can shinny up trees with remarkable ease, as films in park centers rather worryingly confirm.

Dangers Bear attacks are not confined only to the deepest depths of the Canadian backwoods. Not so many years ago a man was killed in Banff as he walked from the railway station. Almost yearly, incidents occur on major highways, usually as a result of people leaping from cars,

Black bears rummaging in a town dump: the park authorities now take more care with waste disposal

camcorder in hand, to pursue a bear along the hard shoulder. For all their cuddly appearance, bears are wild animals. They attack when frightened, surprised or provoked, or when they are attempting to protect their young. If attacked you are likely to be mauled, raked by claws and, as a *coup de grace*, have your scalp peeled from your head. Bears that become used to humans—such as those that used to cluster around Banff's garbage dumps—are not tame; if anything they are more dangerous than ever, and every effort is now made to discourage bears and humans from getting too close to one another. Left alone, and warned of your coming, bears will generally live and let live.

Avoidance Bears would be quite happy never to meet humans, and to keep them happy you should always make a noise when hiking (singing or blowing a whistle are the best: the famous tinkling bear bells people wear round necks are not loud enough). Be especially careful when walking into the wind (bears will not pick up your scent), and stay away from berry patches and dead animals, both important sources of food. Watch out for tracks, diggings and droppings, and camp away from running water and animal tracks.

Disgrace Despite the extent of the Canadian wilderness, grizzly bears are in decline. They are extinct in many original habitats, and are now largely confined to the remoter slopes of the Rockies and British Columbia. Hunting of both grizzly and black bears is often still allowed in many areas—apart from wolves, humans are the bears' only predators—and hunters bag an estimated 30,000 black bears in North America every year. Worse still, thousands of bears are shot to obtain glands and "tokens" which find their way—illegally—to the Far East to be used as charms and remedies.

ATTACK

If confronted by a bear never approach it, never feed it, and on no account run, scream or make sudden movements: all will probably provoke an attack. Stay still even if charged (a tall order, admittedly) as bears bluff, and may stop or veer off before reaching you. Remain calm. Forget about trees. Wait for the bear to leave, and try to allow it an escape route. Otherwise, abandon your pack on the ground as a possible distraction and talk quietly to the bear—and then back off very slowly. If actually attacked, playing dead may help with a grizzly. Fighting back will only increase the ferocity of the attack. Intimidation using anything at hand is really only the very last resort.

INFORMATION
Kootenay National Park's visitor center is in Radium Hot Springs town at the corner of Main Street East and Redstreak Road at 755b Main Street (tel: 250/347–9505. *Open* daily mid-May to mid-Oct). An information office occasionally opens at Marble Canyon in summer, when there are also park staff on hand at the park-run campsites at Marble Canyon and McLeod Meadows.

NAMES
Kootenay National Park probably takes its name from the area's Kootenai Native Canadian tribes. *Kootenay* means "people from beyond the hills," though some scholars believe the name may derive from *kootemik*, which means "places of hot water."

►► Kootenay National Park 91D1

Kootenay is often called the least spectacular of the Rockies' national parks, dismissed as a rather perfunctory strip of scenic splendor on the British Columbian side of the Continental Divide. But while its opportunities for walking and other outdoor activities are limited, its seductive blend of jagged peaks and river-cut forests is the equal of anything in Banff or Jasper. It is also the easiest of the national parks to explore, thanks to the Banff–Windermere Parkway (Highway 93), which runs through the park for 105km (65 miles) from Castle Junction (28km/17 miles northwest of Banff) to Radium Hot Springs (one of the park's potential bases). The road is an easy three-hour drive (depending on stops and hikes en route), and means you can see Kootenay as a day excursion from Banff, or as part of a loop that takes in Yoho National Park (via Golden and the Trans-Canada Highway).

HISTORY Kootenay's mountains appear grander than their equivalents on the Icefields Parkway, partly because you see them while crossing the Continental Divide, which brings the high peaks closer, and partly because the park's origins guaranteed a close relationship between the landscape and its principal highway. Archaeological evidence, notably ancient rock carvings at Radium Hot Springs, suggests that the park's passes served as vital routes for Plains and Coastal natives for thousands of years. White influence in the area arrived in the 19th century with the Hudson's Bay Company, and the peregrinations of David Thompson, one of several explorers who sought a route through the region to the Pacific.

In 1910 similar concerns drove Randolph Bruce, a local businessman, to lobby the Canadian government for a road route from Banff to the west (no major road then existed through the mountains). The idea was to link the Prairies with the Pacific, and in the process bolster Bruce's

A superb vista of the Vermilion mountains from Kootenay National Park

Marble Canyon's dramatic gorge can be seen on an easy trail close to the highway

MATTERHORN MOUNTAINEER
Mount Whymper 2,844m (9,330ft), to the west of Vermilion Pass, is named after the British mountaineer Edward Whymper, the first person to conquer the Matterhorn, and who also scaled many Canadian mountain summits. He once described the Rockies as "fifty Switzerlands in one."

plans for a fruit-growing business in the Columbia valley, west of the present park. The road was launched a year later, but progressed just 22km (14 miles) before the money ran out. In return for more federal funds, British Columbia agreed to surrender around 6.5km/4 miles of land either side of the new highway to the Canadian government, land that became a new national park in 1920.

Vermilion Pass▶▶▶ Highway 93 enters Kootenay from the east at Vermilion Pass (1,651m/5,417ft). The pass marks the site of the Alberta–British Columbia border, and of the Continental Divide, the watershed from which rivers flow into the Pacific one way, and into the Atlantic the other. An expanse of blackened trees and new undergrowth surrounds the pass, the legacy of a forest fire that ravaged the area for four days in 1968 (an inferno unleashed by a single bolt of lightning). Amidst the destruction, signs of Nature's phoenix-like regeneration are now well established, with lodge-pole pines, shrubs and young plants taking tentative root among the scorched trunks. New undergrowth such as this—known as "doghair" forest—provides important new food sources for deer, elk, moose and even bears, attracting animals back to what had previously been a forest in decline (see panel). The short **Firewood Trail** (1km/0.6 miles) from the parking area provides a first-hand look at this transformation.

Stanley Glacier▶▶ A parking area on the highway's eastern side, 3km (2 miles) south of the Vermilion Pass is the start of the Stanley Glacier Trail (4km/2.5miles; 365m/1,198ft of ascent); allow an hour and a half for the climb.

BURNING ISSUE
Forest fires such as the 1968 blaze at Vermilion Pass are not always the natural disaster they appear. Trees such as lodge-pole pines require the heat of a fire to release the seeds from their resin-sealed cones. Some forests also need to burn regularly to remain healthy. Natural "fire return cycles" for montane forests are a mere 42–46 years, 75–130 years in lower sub-alpine woods, and 180 years for the highest sub-alpine areas. Older growth contains few plant species and provides poor habitats for wildlife. Ironically, the national parks' fire services have been so successful in preventing fires that modern thinking has turned to controlled burning to ensure healthy woodland.

HEALTHY INVESTMENT
Radium Hot Springs' thermal pools had been enjoyed for centuries by Native Canadians when they were bought in 1890 by Roland Stuart for a mere $160. When traces of radium—then thought to be therapeutic—were discovered in the springs, Stuart found himself sitting on a gold mine as people flocked in to take the cure. When the government slapped a compulsory purchase order on the pools (during the creation of the national park) Stuart was paid $40,000. The pools' market value was estimated at $500,000.

HOT SPRINGS
The hot springs found all over western Canada begin life as surface water—rain, snow and ice—which then trickles through cracks and porous rocks deep into the earth's crust. At depths of anything up to 5km (3 miles) it meets hot or molten rock, where it is heated to temperatures as high as 1,830°F (1,000°C). The superheated steam then rises through cracks and faults, condensing into water before re-emerging at the surface. Thirty-thousand gallons of water a day rush from the springs at Radium Hot Springs.

Although fairly strenuous the path leads to a wonderful view of the famous Stanley Glacier and the hanging valley below Stanley Peak (3,155m/10,350ft). The 2km/1 mile) of the trail, incidentally, negotiate part of the Vermilion Pass Burn (see page 109).

Marble Canyon▶▶▶ Marble Canyon, 3km (5 miles) south of Vermilion Pass, is the main point of interest for one-stop visitors to the park. A narrow and precipitous gorge (66m/216ft long and 37m/120ft deep), the canyon takes its name from its dolomite and marble walls, polished smooth over 8,000 years by the rushing waters of Tokumm Creek. An easy 1km (0.6-mile) trail follows the gorge, crossing back and forth over a series of log bridges before emerging at the thunderous waterfall that closes its narrowest point. In summer a small information center complements the trail's interpretative boards.

The Paint Pots▶▶ Just 2km (1 mile) south of the Marble Canyon parking area is a pull-in for a trail to the Paint Pots, an atmospheric collection of ocher pools immersed in a gladed forest. The easy approach path 1km (0.6 miles) crosses the Vermilion River, whose open expanse of rushing white water frames fine views of the mountains. Across the bridge, the path crosses the Ochre Beds, a series of strangely colored muds and shales, before arriving at the pools themselves. The area is underpinned by numerous mineral springs, whose waters seep upward through iron-rich clays (laid down on the bed of an ancient glacial lake). This results in the pools' mysterious orangey-yellow hue.

There is little to see apart from the colors, though few places are as strange or as atmospheric, especially on overcast days, or when you have the pools to yourself. On such occasions it is easy to understand the glade's importance to Native Canadians, who believed that the pools were inhabited by animal and thunder spirits. Tribes came from far and wide to collect the colored earth, which they then baked into clay cakes and ground into different colored powders. The powder, or "ocher," was then mixed with animal fat or fish oil, producing a medium that could be used for rock, body or tepee painting. In the 1920s, white businessmen—showing a complete disdain for native sensibilities—mined the clays to produce dyes and paints in Calgary.

Sinclair Pass▶▶ About 20km (12 miles) beyond the Paint Pots rest-stop lies **Vermilion Crossing**, the only place on the highway that provides food, gas and (limited) lodgings. A further 15km (9 miles) brings you to **Kootenay Crossing▶**, the point where the ribbon was cut in 1923 to open the Banff–Windermere Parkway. The inevitable information boards at the rest-stop explain the background to the opening of the road and the creation of the national park. Nearby **Wardle Creek** makes a good spot for a picnic, while **Kootenay Viewpoint**, one of the park's broader panoramas, always attracts a gaggle of onlookers. Some 80km (50 miles) of the mighty Kootenay Valley is visible from this point. The highway's swan song comes with **Sinclair Pass**, a red-rock gorge that funnels into the steep-walled scenery of Sinclair Creek. Trails branch off the road here, including the park's best day hike (the Kindersley Pass Trail) and the easier Juniper Trail (3km/2 miles).

Radium Hot Springs▶ Radium Hot Springs' name may conjure all sorts of exotic visions, but in fact the town is a tacky and scrappy mix of motels and garages, somewhere to stock up and stay only if you have to. To take a dip in the springs, however, there's no need to touch the town at all, for the park-administered complex, or **Aquacourt▶** (tel: 250/347–9485. *Open* daily. *Admission: moderate*) lies 2km (1 mile) north, just outside the park boundary on the Banff–Windermere Parkway (you can rent towels and swimsuits outside the changing facilities). Be prepared for crowds: in high summer thousands of people a day use the pools (which to look at are no more than normal swimming pools). The radium content, incidentally, produces no more radioactivity than the dial of an illuminated watch. Unlike many hot springs, however, these are almost odorless.

BIG RIFT

Immediately west of Kootenay you leave the Rockies and enter the Rocky Mountain Trench, a major rift in the earth's crust that separates the Rockies from the Columbia Mountains.

Radium's hot springs are less radioactive than a luminous watch

Winter comes early to the magnificent Yoho National Park

INFORMATION
National Park Visitor Centre (tel: 250/343–6783, www.pc.gc.ca) for Yoho National Park is located on the Trans-Canada Highway about 1km (0.62 miles) east of Field. It offers lectures, displays and background on the park, issues back-country permits, and takes reservations for places on the Lake O'Hara bus (see panel below).

ACCESS TO LAKE O'HARA
Visiting Lake O'Hara requires pre-planning. Access to the lake, which is reached on an 13km (8-mile) road from the Trans-Canada, is restricted to those with reserved accommodations at the Lake O'Hara Lodge; those with reservations at the Lake O'Hara Campground; or those who reserve a place on the twice-daily park bus (tel: 250/343–6433 for reservations. *Open* late Jun–early Sep). Bikes and private cars are not allowed. You may hike in, but this is dull and time-consuming, especially as the whole point of reaching the lake is to walk the magnificent trails in the mountains above.

▶▶▶ Yoho National Park *90C2*

Yoho is a park for connoisseurs: small and intimate, but containing some of the most varied and sublime scenery in North America. Nestled on the Rockies' western flanks, it adjoins Banff and Kootenay parks, and is bisected by the Trans-Canada Highway, a magnificently scenic road that links other areas of the park accessible by car. Among these are Emerald Lake and the Yoho Valley, both starting points for a network of day hikes, and the Lake O'Hara region, which has more stringent access restrictions (see panel). Accommodations in all three areas are very limited and expensive. The park's only settlement to speak of is Field, home to the park information center (see panel). More accommodations are available in Lake Louise Village (see pages 97–98), or Golden, a nondescript town 54km (35 miles) west of Field.

Sir James Hector Long before the arrival of Europeans, Native Canadians had reveled in the majesty of Yoho, which takes its name from a Cree word meaning "awe" or "wonder." As with Banff and Jasper, it was the building of the railroad that first brought outsiders to the region. Sir James Hector was a member of an expedition detailed to reconnoiter road and rail routes through the Rockies. Crossing the Vermilion Pass into present-day Kootenay

National Park (see pages 108–111), Hector and his party struggled over the mountains into Yoho at Wapta Falls (see page 115). Here Hector was kicked by a horse, and sustained injuries so severe that he was initially taken for dead. Undeterred, the party battled on toward Lake Louise, following the Kicking Horse River and the route of the modern Trans-Canada Highway. The Continental Divide was breasted at Kicking Horse Pass, named—along with the river—after Hector's brush with death.

The railroad While Hector's efforts laid the railroad's foundations, the final groundwork was completed by Sandford Fleming, the Canadian Pacific's chief surveyor. Following Hector's route over the Kicking Horse Pass, Fleming was moved to say that he would "never forget that walk; it was the greatest trial I ever experienced." Believing the pass was barely passable on foot, let alone by rail, Fleming shared the opinion of many in the company that the railroad should take a more northerly route. His preferred option was the Yellowhead Pass, a route eventually taken by the C.P.R.'s rivals (see page 103). Such a route, however, lay well to the north of valuable land on the US border. This option ignored one of the railroad's main political imperatives: to prevent border territory slipping into the hands of the US Against all engineering advice, therefore, the line was

DARING DAME
Lady Agnes Macdonald, the remarkable wife of Canada's first prime minister and railroad promoter, rode down Yoho's Big Hill by train in 1886. She was not in the slow-moving train, however, but on the *front* of it: in a chair clamped to the engine's cowcatcher. The ride, she declared, presented "a delightful opportunity for a new sensation."

HIDING PLACE
Until the arrival of the railroad in 1884, the Yoho Valley was used by Cree people to hide the women and children while the men crossed the mountains into Alberta to trade and hunt buffalo.

FIELD
This village began life as a railroad construction camp in 1884. In 1886 a hotel, Mount Stephen House, was built. Its purpose was to provide meals for train travelers so that a heavy buffet car would not have to be hauled up and down the Big Hill. The village grew up soon after, taking its name from Cyrus Field, sponsor of the first transatlantic communication cable, who paid a visit to the village in 1884.

BURGESS SHALES
These fossil beds east of Field are some of the most important in the world. Fossils up to 530 million years old have been found in their unique and undisturbed strata. Access is restricted. Contact the visitor center at Field for details of guided visits.

blasted through Yoho in 1884, creating the notorious "Big Hill" (see below) and a series of gradients steeper than those of any other railroad of the period.

Kicking Horse Pass to Field Following the Trans-Canada westward from Lake Louise you cross into Yoho at the 1,625m (5,330ft) **Kicking Horse Pass** (see above). Soon afterward comes a picnic area at the Great Divide, the watershed between rivers that flow west to the Pacific and those that flow east to Hudson Bay. About 1.6km (1 mile) beyond lies the first of several short trails that can be accessed off the highway. These are ideal if you do not want to tackle any of the longer hikes from Emerald Lake and the Yoho Valley. Here they include **Ross Lake Trail** (1.6km/1 mile), which leads to a small upland lake, a remarkable little stroll given the grandeur of the scenery it reveals. The **Sherbrooke Lake Trail** (3km/2 miles), which winds to a quiet sub-alpine lake, departs from the Wapta Lake picnic area (5km (3 miles) west of the Great Divide).

A short way beyond comes the Old Bridge, part of the former railroad route over the **Big Hill**, a stretch of line between Wapta Lake and Field where the track dropped over 300m (1,000ft) in just 6km (4 miles). A taste of the problems it would pose came when a construction train attempted the first descent: the engine simply careered into the canyon and killed the three railroad workers aboard. Problems continued with exploding boilers that burst under the strain of the hill, while four locomotives were required to pull cars up the slope (the 6km/4-mile ride took more than an hour). Runaways were so common that four blasts on the whistle quickly became the standard warning for trains careering out of control.

The Kicking Horse River forms the heart of Yoho National Park

Some of these problems were solved by the building of the famous Spiral Tunnels, a pair of figure-of-eight tunnels that curl round on themselves inside Yoho's mountains. Look for the **Lower Spiral Tunnel Viewpoint**, where freight trains often emerge from the tunnels before their rear wagons have entered. A belvedere of a different sort, the **Mount Stephen Viewpoint**, lies farther down the road, offering views of the hanging glacier on Mount Stephen (3,199m/10,492ft). Below the glacier to the right is the entrance to the old Monarch Mine, a lead, zinc and silver working that operated until 1952.

Yoho Valley▶▶▶ The tortuous 13km (8-mile) access road up the Yoho Valley strikes north from the Trans-Canada shortly after the highway crosses the Kicking Horse River (about 2km/1 mile) west of the information center; see panel, page 112). At its head are found the **Takakkaw Falls▶▶▶**, named after the Cree for "it is wonderful." At 254m/1,250ft the cascade is one of the highest road-accessible falls in North America. Adding to their splendor are the peaks and icefields of mounts Yoho (2,790m/9,151ft), President (3,139m/10,296ft) and Balfour (3,246m/10,647ft).

A trail network totaling some 360km (235 miles) allows you to get a closer look at this scenery. The most popular path is the **Twin Falls Trail**, which is an easy day hike to a pair of cataracts at the head of the valley (8km/5 miles one way; 290m/950ft ascent). Countless other walks are possible, including some that take you into the Emerald Lake region to the west.

Emerald Lake▶▶ The Emerald Lake Road turns off the Trans-Canada Highway 2km (1 mile) west of Field to Emerald Lake. This is a more commercialized region than the Yoho Valley, thanks mainly to the Emerald Lake Lodge, an upscale "railroad hotel" designed to emulate the Banff Springs and Château Lake Louise. You can sample the hotel's bars and restaurants even if you're not staying there. If you want to expend a touch more energy, either amble around the lake shore or tackle the more demanding **Emerald Basin Trail**, which climbs from the lake shore to an imposing rocky amphitheater (5km/3 miles one way; 290m/1,000ft ascent). Or try the fascinating **Hamilton Lake Trail**, a quiet walk to an idyllic upland lake (5.5km/3.5 miles one way; 850m/2,800ft ascent). Both walks start from the parking area at the end of Emerald Lake Road.

Field to the Wapta Falls▶▶▶ Whether or not you branch off to Emerald Lake or the Yoho Valley, the Trans-Canada beyond Field continues to offer a string of big viewpoints and off-highway trails. Information boards at **Ottertail Viewpoint** explain the rock formations exposed by the Ottertail and Kicking Horse rivers, while similar boards at the **Misko Viewpoint** outline the glacial effects to be seen on Mount Hunter and Mount King. The best of the short walks off the road is the **Hoodoo Creek Trail** (3km/2 miles) close to the park's western border (22km/14 miles west of Field). This leads from the Hoodoo Creek Campground to strangely eroded rock pinnacles known as "hoodoos." The park's westernmost trail is the **Wapta Falls Trail** (2.5km/1.5 miles), a level 40-minute stroll that takes you to Yoho's largest waterfalls (in terms of volume of water).

The Takakkaw Falls are some of the highest road-accessible falls in North America

HELL'S BELLS

Major A. B. Rogers was in charge of finding a route over the Rockies for the transcontinental railroad. Although commemorated in Glacier National Park, where the Rogers Pass was named after him, he also did sterling work in Yoho. He was a remarkable man, renowned for his profanity (his nickname was "Hell's Bells"), the extraordinary length of his moustache, his tobacco chewing and his diet of raw beans. He was paid $5,000 for discovering Rogers Pass, but framed the check and never cashed it.

Yukon

VISION OF WILDERNESS The Yukon is a revelation, its people, scenery and almost unimaginable wilderness likely to provide some of the most exhilarating moments of a Canadian visit. Wedged between Alaska and the vast expanse of the Northwest Territories (NWT), the region contains the country's highest mountains, grandiose swaths of forest and tundra and a fascinating historical nugget in the shape of Dawson City, a town that formed the focus of the famous Klondike gold rush (see pages 126–127).

ARRIVING Getting to the area is a pleasure in itself, whether you follow the great Alaska Highway from British Columbia, fly directly to Whitehorse, the region's bustling capital or follow the route of the old prospectors by taking a boat up the west coast to the Alaskan port of Skagway. Itineraries within the region are easily planned, and, given the proximity of Alaska, can easily be extended to incorporate loops into US territory.

Road routes are long, though scenically rewarding; the Cassiar Highway offers one of North America's last great wilderness drives. Major domestic airlines fly to Whitehorse from Edmonton, while numerous smaller companies fly services between regional airstrips. Car and foot passengers riding the Inside Passage and Alaskan Panhandle ferries experience the continent's greatest sea voyage, linking up at Skagway with bus and train services to Whitehorse and beyond. Buses also run along the Alaska Highway, and from Whitehorse to Dawson City. Cars can be rented in Whitehorse.

FURS AND GOLD Prior to exploration by Europeans, the Yukon, like the rest of Canada, was the preserve of its native populations. Foreign encroachment began around 1670, when the Hudson's Bay Company began to exploit the region for its furs. Such was the area's remoteness, however, that the trade did not reach sizeable proportions until the 1850s.

It was at about the same time that the first gold prospectors appeared: grizzled old-timers who had moved on from the Californian and British Columbian gold fields. Discovery of gold in 1896, on a creek close to present-day Dawson, triggered the Klondike gold rush, a tumultuous stampede of people that saw Dawson's population soar to 25,000 (some estimates put the figure as high as 50,000). Flushed by its gold finds, Yukon declared itself a "Territory" in 1898, riding the crest of a wave until the boom began to fade in 1904.

ROADS AND MINES After the rush, Yukon, and Dawson in particular (then the Territory's capital), remained a forgotten backwater until 1942. In that year the building of the Alaska Highway brought a fresh influx of newcomers (see pages 120–121). Most settled in Whitehorse, one of the road's principal construction camps, which in 1953 was declared the region's new capital. The area then continued to prosper, bolstered by its mineral wealth and the discovery of oil in the Arctic during the 1970s. The drive to exploit these resources led to the building of the Dempster Highway (opened in 1978), one of only two public roads in North America to cross the Arctic Circle.

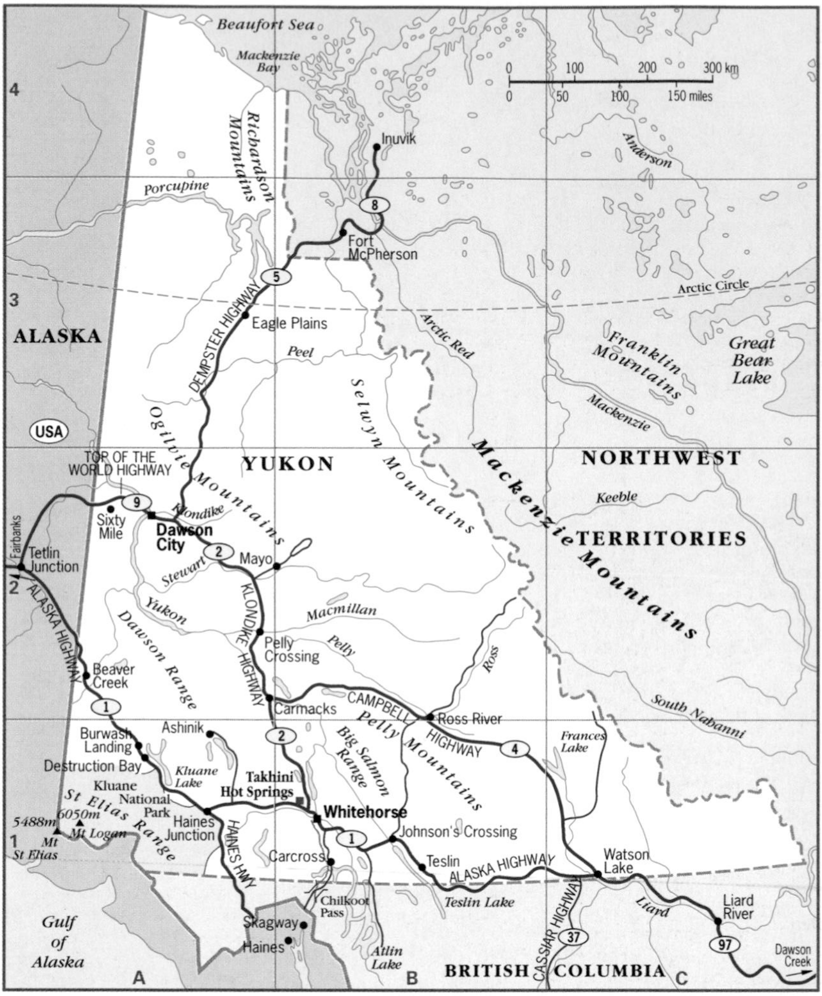

REGION HIGHLIGHTS

Alaska Highway *pages 120–123*

Dawson City *pages 124–127*

Dempster Highway *page 118*

Kluane National Park *page 129*

Whitehorse *pages 130–131*

Page 116: Yukon's St. Elias Mountains, Kluane National Park

A BREED APART Yukoners are an appealing breed, and the robust character of Canada's "northerners" is one of the more interesting aspects of traveling in the region. Despite the extremes of climate, and the apparent hardships of northern life, most are here out of choice, and most share a keen enthusiasm for their region, whether they are incomers or locals born and bred "North of 60," the 60th Parallel, the line of latitude that forms Yukon's border with British Columbia.

EXPLORING Distances might be long, but getting around Yukon is surprisingly easy. Most people kick off a tour from Whitehorse, attracted by its position on the Alaska Highway and by convenient road links to Skagway. From here you should follow the Klondike Highway to Dawson City, a distance of some 500km (300 miles) (see page 128). This is not only a fine ride in its own right, but also allows you to see Dawson and then choose between two further breathtaking drives. One, the Dempster Highway, crosses the Arctic Circle and the tundra north of Dawson to Inuvik on the Beaufort Sea, a total distance of 740km (460 miles). This is a gravel highway with potentially treacherous weather, and few accommodations, so ensure you are well prepared before setting off. Contact the NWT Department of Tourism before you go (see page 269) or the NWT tourist office in Dawson (see panel, page 124).

At Inuvik you will need to retrace your steps to Dawson, unless you are in a rental car that you can drop at the end of the Dempster (a tall order). Flying out of Inuvik is another option. But if you simply want a taste of tundra scenery, you could drive 100km (60 miles) or so from Dawson before turning back. This would enable you to take the second option on from Dawson, which is to drive the Top of the World Highway (see panel, page 128) across the US border to Tetlin Junction in Alaska. From there you could loop back to Whitehorse on the Alaska Highway, taking in the Kluane National Park en route (see page 129).

GOVERNMENT
Canada is made up of ten semi-autonomous provinces, and three territories dependent on the federal government in Ottawa. Although Yukon strictly falls into the second category, the people of Yukon directly elect their government, which has many of the powers of the provincial governments. Certain responsibilities—natural resources, for example—remain in the hands of the federal government.

NATIVE NAME
The Yukon takes its name from the Dene word *you-kon*, meaning "great water," a reference to the 3,185km/2,200-mile Yukon River. This mighty waterway rises in the south of the region, flows northward through Whitehorse and Dawson City, and then sweeps west across Alaska to empty into the Bering Sea through a delta covering some 30,000sq km (11,500sq miles).

PEOPLE
The Yukon has a population of around 30,000. Of these about 20 percent are of British extraction. Some 10 percent are Native Canadians (a mere 0.4 percent of the country's indigenous population). A few Inuit aside, the majority belong to the Athapaskan tribes, members of the large Na-Dené language family, a group that also embraces the Navajo and Apache in the south.

HIGHEST POINT
The Yukon has Canada's highest mountain, the 6,050m (19,844ft) Mount Logan.

Some 250 steamers once plied the Yukon River; now only two originals remain

Once dubbed the "junkyard of the American automobile," the great 2,446km (1,520-mile) Alaska Highway is now one of the world's ultimate drives, a long, mainly blacktop odyssey between Dawson Creek (BC) and Fairbanks (Alaska) through the wilderness of one of North America's most forbidding frontier regions.

NORTHWEST STAGING ROUTE
This line of air bases through Alaska and northern Canada played a vital but little-known role during World War II. Some 8,000 planes were moved along the route from Montana to Edmonton, and then from Edmonton to Fairbanks. Here they were collected by Soviet pilots and pressed into action on the Siberian front.

COLDEST SPOT
The north to south alignment of the mountains in Yukon acts as a funnel for polar air, which in winter rushes south unhindered to produce the coldest temperatures on the North American continent:around –60°C, or –76°F. Whitehorse's average January temperature is –25°C (–13°F), its maximum just –16°C (3°F).

Undefended outpost Roads came late to much of Canada. Few were longer coming than the link to the Yukon. Less than a century ago the only way north, bar elusive wilderness trails, was the sea journey from the West Coast to isolated harbors on the Alaskan coast. No road route existed. All this changed in World War II, when the Japanese invaded the Aleutians, a string of islands lying just off the Alaskan coast. The invasion not only threatened northern sea lanes, cutting off supplies to the region, but also left Alaska at the mercy of Japanese troops.

The route A joint US–Canadian venture was immediately launched to defend Alaska. The first requirement was for a road, essential to ferry in troops and provisions. Choosing a suitable route, however—in an area of almost complete wilderness—proved no easy task. The quickest route—one that hugged the British Columbian coast—was considered too prone to enemy attack (it has since been built as the Cassiar Highway). An inland route, along the line of the Rockies, would have taken more than five years to build. This left the so-called "Prairie Route," a compromise that had the advantage of following a line of air bases through Alaska and northern Canada known as the Northwest Staging Route (see panel).

Construction Work on the road began on March 9, 1942, and was completed just eight months later. Some 27,000 men were involved on the project, one of the marvels of modern engineering. Work progressed in the face of horrifying weather and some of the worst terrain imaginable. Forests, mountains and rivers had to be confronted, along with the swarms of black flies that infested the worst barrier of all: the unending mud and marsh of the north's "muskeg" bog. Two crews did the groundwork, one working east, the other west, the two gangs meeting at Contact Creek in September 1942. A final leg, the spur to Fairbanks, was polished off in a month. Despite the hardships, over 8 miles of road were built per day.

Unexplained bends Much of the Alaska Highway stretches across the wilderness in a straight, uncompromising ribbon. Every now and again, however, it lurches around an inexplicable bend, or curves as if to avoid some unseen obstacle. Several myths have sprung up to explain the serpentine curves. The best known is that the bends were introduced to prevent Japanese pilots using the road to land their aircraft. Another claims

that workers simply pointed their bulldozers at the line of least resistance. One section, it was rumored, was plotted to follow the course of a rutting moose. In fact, the meanderings were probably the result of hurried surveying, for often the route was only sketched from a plane the day before. Tools on the ground, moreover, often amounted to no more than a cord stretched across a marsh or a finger aimed at a distant horizon.

Tidying up Many of the highway's kinks were ironed out during subsequent rebuilding, a process that began in 1943, only months after the road's completion. Much of the work was done in the seven years to 1950, a couple of years after the road opened to civilian traffic. Bridges replaced pontoons, gradients were reduced and some of the curves were straightened (see panel). The road's 50th anniversary also brought a reappraisal of more controversial aspects, notably the effect on the region's hitherto isolated native population, which was ravaged by diseases introduced by workers, and the mass slaughter of wildlife wrought by trigger-happy GIs.

MISSING MILES
The straightening of the Alaska Highway's notorious curves means that it is now only 2,395km (1,488 miles) from Dawson City (Mile Zero) to the old Mile 2,445km (1,520 miles), marker post at Fairbanks.

Top: The Alaska Highway at Teslin
Below: US soldiers building the Alaska Highway over glacial swamp in 1942

Drive

The Alaska Highway

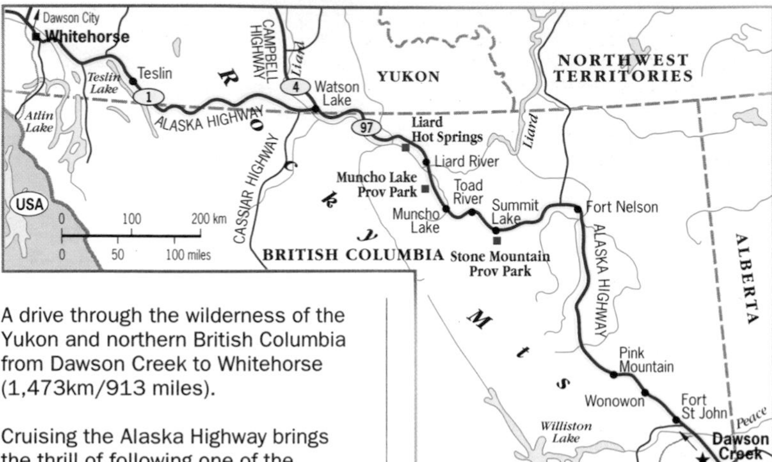

A drive through the wilderness of the Yukon and northern British Columbia from Dawson Creek to Whitehorse (1,473km/913 miles).

Cruising the Alaska Highway brings the thrill of following one of the world's great drives, the romance of the far north and the particular satisfaction of completing a journey of epic status. Today, however, the highway is tamer than it was, and no longer tests human and mechanical endurance to the limits. These days it's an all-weather road, with fuel stations, motels and service areas at anything between 40km (25-mile) and 80km (50-mile) intervals. This said, certain stretches still have only gravel or semi-consolidated surfaces, and there are only three villages worthy of the name before Whitehorse: Fort St. John, Fort Nelson and Watson Lake. None is terribly attractive, so if possible aim to stay at some of the smaller motels dotted along the highway (though be sure to reserve a room in advance). Ensure your car is in good condition, and check weather conditions if you are setting out between October and May. Drive with your headlights on, keep to a maximum of 80kph/50mph, and pay special attention when passing (or being passed by) large trucks.

Dawson Creek▶ is famous only for its Mile Zero cairn (be sure to take the obligatory photograph) but makes an obvious (if uninspiring) motel stop before the drive. If you have time to kill, visit the local info center (900 Alaska Avenue, tel: 250/782–9595. *Open* daily 9–6, longer hours in summer. *Admission: inexpensive*) and the adjoining info center (tel: 250/782–9595) for more background on the Highway. The town sits at the heart of gentle farming country, a pastoral accompaniment to the road that continues as far as the Peace River (72km/45 miles), where the highway suddenly drops into a dramatically eroded canyon.

Soon after comes **Fort St. John** (80km/50 miles), a functional settlement, typical of those you will encounter all the way to Whitehorse. During the building of the road, it served as the headquarters of the eastern construction gangs; before that it was the preserve of the local Sikanni and Beaver people. More recent stimulus has come from the exploitation of nearby oil fields (British Columbia's largest). Filling up with gas aside, however, there is no reason to stop. Much the same goes for the smaller settlements of Wonowon (161km/100 miles) and Pink Mountain (226km/140 miles).

Beyond these points the landscape—the main point of the drive—begins to pick up considerably. Huge forests stretch away to distant, mountain-lined horizons, the trees becoming noticeably more stunted as you approach their northern growing limits. The transformation becomes more marked around **Fort Nelson** (480km/300 miles), an obvious if uninteresting place to break your journey (contact the info center for lodging details at 5500 50th Avenue, tel: 250/774–2956, summer months). Here you enter the **northern Rockies▶▶▶**, and with them some of the grandest landscapes in British Columbia. Summit Lake (630km/396 miles) and Toad River (690km/425 miles), both one-horse towns, have atmospheric motels, as does the larger **Muncho Lake▶▶**, which sits at the heart of an impressive provincial park. Perhaps the best stop is **Liard Hot Springs▶▶**, two popular thermal pools surrounded by a lush floral carpet containing over 250 plant species, including 14 species of orchid.

Watson Lake, 137km (85 miles) beyond the springs, heralds the Yukon border and houses the **Alaska Highway Interpretative Centre▶▶**, which recounts the highway's history through audiovisual displays and archive material (tel: 867/536–7469. *Open* May–Sep daily 8–8). Although it was established in the 1890s, the settlement found its feet during the building of the road, when 25,000 workers were based here. Its main sight, the slightly gimmicky "Sign Post Forest," dates from this time, when a homesick worker put up a sign pointing to his home town (Danville, Illinois). His example has since been followed by some 10,000 people.

Beyond Watson Lake the road again picks up magnificent lake and mountain landscapes, a scenic feast that continues almost unbroken to Yukon's capital, **Whitehorse▶▶**.

A lonely road—over 2,000km/1,200 miles of wilderness and little traffic

INFORMATION
Dawson's superb Visitor Reception Centre is on Front Street. It provides a wealth of background material and offers free screenings of modern and archive films about the town (tel: 867/993–5566, www.dawsoncity.com). It also organizes free tours of heritage buildings. For information on the Dempster Highway, contact the Western Artic–NWT Information Centre opposite (tel: 867/993–6167 or 800/661–0750).

MIDNIGHT DOME
Midnight Dome—the mountain above Dawson—is so called because at midnight on June 21 (the longest day) Dawson's northerly position allows you to watch the sun dip to the horizon and rise again without setting. Views are magnificent at any time. Access is via the 8km (5-mile) Midnight Dome Road, leaving the Klondike Highway just out of town.

►►► Dawson (Dawson City) *118A2*

For three years at the end of the 19th century, Dawson City was one of the most famous places on earth. From humble origins (it was once a patch of moose pasture) the town sprang to life almost overnight in 1896, hard on the heels of massive gold strikes on the Klondike River. Gold-hungry hopefuls swarmed here in their thousands, disembarking from a raggle-taggle of boats at Dawson before succumbing to the lure of the gold-rich creeks close by. Just three years later it was all over, the "stampeders" long gone, the prospectors lured west by new finds in Alaska. By the 1950s the town was all but dead, its people gone, its role as Yukon's capital surrendered to Whitehorse.

Past preserved That might have been the end of the story, but for a public campaign begun in the 1950s to preserve a poignant part of Canada's recent past. As a result some 30-plus buildings have been saved, and Dawson looks like something out of a Hollywood Western. The only difference here is that everything is real, from the false-fronted houses to the dirt streets and wooden boardwalks. Leaning buildings, many close to collapse, strike a still more genuine note, tottering monuments to the permafrost that lurks beneath the town's streets (the frozen subsoil buckles their foundations). Future gentrification or prettification is unlikely, for winter temperatures plummet to –59° C (–75° F), and the proximity of the Arctic Circle results in months of almost perpetual seasonal gloom.

Heritage buildings Most pleasure in the town comes from wandering its evocative streets. The best place to start is by the Yukon River on Front Street. This plays host to the tourist office (see panel) and heritage buildings such as the Federal Building, the Old Post Office (1901) and the Canadian Bank of Commerce, where prospectors' gold was weighed and melted down. Also here is the SS *Keno*, one of only two surviving paddle-steamers on the Yukon (the other is Whitehorse's SS *Klondike*).

The cabin in Dawson once owned by poet Robert Service

Wonderfully restored old wooden buildings still give Dawson the look of a genuine frontier town

Other old buildings include Harrington's Store on 3rd Avenue and Princess; Diamond Tooth Gertie's Gambling House, Queen Street, once Canada's only legal casino (profits go toward Dawson's restoration); the Anglican Church (1902), built with donations from miners; and the **Palace Grand Theatre** (1899) on King Street. To place the buildings in their historical context, visit the **Dawson City Museum▸▸**, a competent if slightly dated account of the town's gold-rush heyday (595 5th Avenue and Church Street. *Open* mid-May–early Sep daily 10–6. *Admission: moderate*). Here you should also catch the award-winning *City of Gold*, a wistful film that brought Dawson's decline to public attention in the 1950s.

Literary heritage Dawson's gold-rush fever drew two literary figures to the Klondike. The better known of the two was Jack London, who spent time as a ferryman on Whitehorse's Miles Canyon before moving to a cabin on one of Dawson's gold-seamed creeks. Although he returned to California penniless, his fund of memories would eventually be woven into classics such as *The Call of the Wild*, *White Fang* and *A Daughter of the Snows*. A partial reconstruction of his **cabin▸**, together with a small museum of memorabilia, can be seen on 8th Avenue (*Open* mid-May to mid-Sep, daily 10–6. *Admission: donation*).

The other figure was poet Robert Service, a character held in high esteem in Canada as well as in the US Service experienced little of the Klondike's rowdy heyday, as he arrived in Whitehorse in 1904 (long after the rush was over). Recitals of his gold-rush classics—notably *The Shooting of Dan McGrew*—are given in the theater on Front Street and you can visit his quaint little **cabin▸▸** (8th Avenue. *Open* Jun–end Sep daily 9–12, 1–5. *Admission:* free).

GOLDFIELDS
The epicenters of the Klondike gold rush, Bonanza and Eldorado creeks, lie 20km (12 miles) by road from Dawson. Although neither has any big working mines, both make fascinating excursions. Visit Discovery Claim, the spot where the first gold was found, and follow the road to King Solomon's Dome for a compelling panorama of the whole area. Also see some of the vast abandoned dredges used to extract gold commercially once the small-time prospectors had left. Gold City Tours on Front Street organizes guided tours of the area (tel: 867/993–5175).

Gold rushes in the 19th century were nothing new, but none generated the delirium of the Klondike, when an estimated 1 million people left home for the goldfields. Of these, 100,000 reached the Yukon, 20,000 panned the creeks, 4,000 struck lucky and a few dozen made—and usually lost—vast fortunes.

HINTS OF RICHES
Anecdotes as much as figures hint at the scale of the Klondike riches. In 1897, for example, $200 of gold was panned nightly from the beer mats of a Dawson saloon; destitutes in the Great Depression, 35 years after the rush, panned $40 of gold a day from beneath Dawson's boardwalks; and $1,000-worth of gold was panned in a morning during rebuilding of the Orpheum Theatre in the 1940s, taken from where it had fallen from miners' pockets 50 years earlier.

Up to $1 million-worth of gold a day was extracted by some miners at the height of the gold rush

First hints The discovery of gold on the Klondike, an obscure tributary of the Yukon River, followed some 20 years of prospecting in the far north. Fur traders and missionaries had first noticed gold traces in the 1840s, but it was not until the 1880s that mining took place on any scale. Camps sprang up on the Yukon at places such as Forty Mile, Sixty Mile and Circle City, home to a few hundred hardened men raised on the earlier Californian and British Columbian strikes.

The big one The first man to prospect the Klondike region was Robert Henderson, a dour Nova Scotian and the very embodiment of the lone pioneer. In early 1896 he panned out 8¢-worth of gold on a local creek—an excellent return for the time. After accumulating $750-worth of gold, he returned downriver to pick up supplies. On his return, looking for a route up the Klondike to his earlier creek, he met George Washington Carmack, a more sociable figure, and two of Carmack's native friends, Skookum Jim and Tagish Charley. Explaining his high hopes for the area, but with a glance at Jim and Charley, he reputedly uttered the phrase that cost him a fortune: "There's a chance for you, George," he said, "but I don't want any damn Siwashes [natives] staking on that creek."

There is still gold to be found in the Klondike, if you know where to look

Discovery Henderson wandered off to the hills; Carmack, nettled by the remark, prospected a different set of creeks—the right ones, as it turned out. On the eve of August 16, Skookum Jim found a nugget the size of his thumb, and then proceeded to sift $4 worth of gold, from a single pan. Carmack registered a claim the next day, leaving Henderson to prospect almost barren ground on the other side of the hills. By the end of the month all of Bonanza and Eldorado—as the two key creeks were christened—had been staked, and all the real fortunes secured. When winter came, freezing the Yukon solid, the area was left cut off from the outside world.

The rush Rumors of the awaiting riches nonetheless began to trickle out, and when the ice melted around 1,000 miners from up and down the Yukon congregated on the Klondike. The populist rush was unleashed only a few months later, however, in July 1897, when the *Portland* and *Excelsior* docked in Seattle and San Francisco. Weary Klondike miners staggered from the *Excelsior*, dragging bags, boxes and sacks literally bursting with gold. The press, now alerted, met the *Portland*, which contained a staggering two tons of gold. The rush was on.

Disillusion Thousands of miles away the creeks were all staked, the fortunes already won (and in many cases already lost). Countless hopefuls set off undeterred, whipped up by the media frenzy and the hard-sell of West Coast outfitters. Indeed, the departure of 1 million or more people for Yukon was the largest single mass movement of people in the 19th century. Some trudged overland from Edmonton (a pitiless route). Others traveled by boat to Skagway, where they had to climb the dreaded Chilkoot Pass before finding a boat for the 800km (500-mile) journey to Dawson and the Klondike. The largest influx came in May 1898 after the melting of the winter ice, a full 21 months after the rush began, carried on a ramshackle armada that nestled six boats deep along 3km (2 miles) of the Dawson waterfront. For most it was a fruitless journey and by 1899 the rush was over, the most easily reached gold long gone. Rich pickings still awaited industrial mining, however, and gold continues to be mined in the Klondike to this day.

UNTOLD RICHES
The Klondike was probably the richest goldfield of all time, but how much gold left the area is almost impossible to fathom (it was in miners' interests to undervalue their finds when dealing with officials). Estimates say $600 million-worth was extracted between 1897 and 1904 (in the prices of the day). Each 152m (500ft) claim on Bonanza and Eldorado creeks yielded 3,000kg/ 6,500 lb (worth $25 million at 1900 prices). One miner took 100kg (220 lb) of gold in a day from one "fraction" of a claim—about $1 million-worth. Mechanical dredges introduced after 1913 took 25kg (55 lb) a day; modern mines are lucky to extract a quarter as much in a week.

RITE OF PASSAGE
For many "stampeders" the Klondike was as much a rite of passage as a quest for gold. Canadian writer Pierre Berton observed: "There were large numbers who spent only a few days in Dawson and did not bother to visit the hypnotic creeks that had tugged at them all winter long. They turned their faces home again, their adventure over... It was as if they had, without quite knowing it, completed the job they had set out to do and come to understand that it was not the gold they were seeking after all." *Klondike: The Last Great Goldrush 1896–1899.*

Stretches of the Klondike Highway are wilder even than the Alaska Highway

NORTHERN LIGHTS
The shimmering red-green lights of the *aurora borealis* can be seen across large parts of Yukon and northern Canada. The effect, which takes its name from the Roman goddess of dawn, was long thought to have been produced by light refracted like a rainbow, or by sunlight reflected from the polar snow and ice. Now it is believed to be caused by radiation emitted as light in the upper atmosphere. This is caused in turn by electrons and protons thrown out with the "solar wind" striking atoms in the atmosphere. The effect is strongest two days after intense solar activity, the time it takes the wind's radiation to reach the earth from the sun.

TOP OF THE WORLD HIGHWAY
This highway (Highway 9) abuts the Klondike Highway at Dawson, linking it to the US border (107km/66 miles) and Tetlin Junction in Alaska (181km/112 miles beyond the border). It takes its name from the many ridges and plateaux en route, a high-level journey that offers quite phenomenal views over rows of bare-backed mountains. The road is gravel-surfaced and open only in the summer, while border crossing is possible only when the customs post is open (daily 9–9, Yukon time). If you are not driving the whole route, there are stunning viewpoints just 5km (3 miles) and 14km (9 miles) from Dawson.

►► Klondike Highway *118A2*

Gold-rush stampeders made the journey from Whitehorse to Dawson along the Yukon River, a route that remained the towns' main lifeline until the building of the Klondike Highway in 1979. In its entirety, the 717km (430-mile) highway runs from Skagway to Dawson, though for most people the 500km (300-mile) section between Whitehorse and Dawson is the one that counts. Part of a potentially much longer itinerary (see pages 118–119), the drive offers not only a first-hand taste of the Yukon wilderness, but also links Whitehorse with the gold-rush area of the Klondike (see pages 124–125).

The first point of interest west of Whitehorse is **Takhini Hot Springs**, a place to take a dip before the long drive ahead. Braeburn Lodge (83km/51 miles beyond) is one of only a handful of service stops on a road that is still far wilder than the Alaska Highway. Primeval scenery opens up on a vast scale from here on, with seemingly endless ranks of conifers carpeting the slopes of the Pelly and Big Salmon mountains. **Carmacks**, 86km (53 miles) beyond, is a native village named for the co-discoverer of Yukon gold. The village straddles the Yukon River, just 24km (14 miles) from Five Finger Rapids, a point where Klondike stampeders once hauled their boats downriver with ropes.

About 100km (60 miles) from Dawson in gentler hilly country, the road quietly picks up the **Klondike**—the river that started it all. At first it is no more than an inconsequential stream, rather disappointing given the romance that surrounds its name. In time, however, small tailings begin to appear on the surrounding hills, the first hints of the tumult that hit the region a century ago. Before long the river is lost amid a confusion of spoil heaps and old workings, a scene of devastation that continues until Dawson looms wonderfully into view.

▶▶▶ Kluane National Park *118A1*

The pocket of territory in southwest Yukon known as Kluane Country takes its name from the Tutchone native word meaning a "place of many fish." It is not so much fish, however, that brings people to the region, as the Kluane National Park, Canada's largest protected mountain sanctuary. A United Nations World Heritage Site, it embraces the country's highest mountains and the world's largest icefields outside the polar regions, site of a total of over 4,000 glaciers. While most of the park is inaccessible wilderness, the Alaska Highway between Whitehorse and Beaver Creek (a 491km/295-mile drive) offers stunning views of the distant mountains, together with a handful of trailheads and opportunities to spot wildlife.

The park's main center is **Haines Junction**, a functional town well to the west of Whitehorse at the junction of the Alaska Highway and the Haines Road, a highway that links with the Alaskan port of Haines 174km (108 miles) to the southeast. Other small settlements further west on the Alaska Highway, all of which have campsites and accommodations, include Kluane Lake, Destruction Bay, Burwash Landing and Beaver Creek.

The road between these points provides a viewpoint for the park's distant mountains (almost 160km/100 miles away), which include the mighty **St. Elias Range▶▶▶**, home not only to the highest peak in Canada, Mount Logan (6,050m/19,844ft), but also to Alaska's Mount McKinley (6,193m/20,313ft), the highest point in North America. In front of the St. Elias rises the Lower Kluane Range, at only around 2,500m (8,000ft). About 60km (46 miles) west of Haines Junction the vast **Kluane Lake▶▶** is a beautiful stretch of glacier-fed water some 60km (37 miles) long and 400sq km (145sq miles) in area. Boating and fishing (Artic char and trout) are available on its shores, notably at Destruction Bay and Burwash Landing.

INFORMATION

The national park visitor center is in Haines Junction on Logan Street (tel: 867/634–2345 or 7207. www.kluane.com). It has information on numerous activities, and details of the easier hikes available from the Alaska Highway. There is another, summer-only, office, the Sheep Mountain Information Kiosk (mid-May–Sep), at the southern tip of Kluane Lake, 74km (46 miles) northwest of Haines Junction. Beaver Creek also has a Yukon Visitor Information Centre (tel: 867/862–7321. *Open* mid-May to mid-Sep).

ICEFIELD TOURS

For details of surprisingly well-priced plane tours over the region, contact the Haines Junction visitor center.

The St. Elias Mountains boast the highest peaks in North America

INFORMATION
Whitehorse's Yukon Visitor Reception Centre is on 2nd Avenue and Hanson Street (tel: 867/667–3084, www.visitwhitehorse.com. *Open* mid-May to mid-Sep daily 8–8; rest of the year Mon–Fri 9–12, 1–4.30). Up on the Alaska Highway by the airport, away from the town center, lies the Yukon Beringia Interpretive Centre (*Open* May–end Sep daily 8.30–7, www.beringia.com. *Admission: expensive*), which looks at the history, flora, fauna and other aspects of the region. Next door is the new and excellent Yukon Transportation Museum (*Open* May–end Sep daily 10–6. *Admission: moderate*), devoted to aspects of transport and its history in the region. Stores selling books and maps can be found on Main Street, near Second Avenue.

▶▶ Whitehorse *118B1*

The Yukon's capital is a surprisingly lively and appealing little town, its downtown grid containing a mixture of homey wooden buildings—a legacy of its frontier origins—and a collection of sleek shops and booming businesses. Two-thirds of the province's population live here, some in the suburbs that straggle along the Alaska Highway, others in the town proper, which sits below a curious bluff on the banks of the Yukon River. It is a key point in northern itineraries, its location making it convenient for trips on to Alaska and the Klondike, with a range of accommodations.

Rapids and railroads During the Klondike gold rush, prospectors picked up the headwaters of the Yukon River after climbing the Chilkoot Pass. From here they rode by boat to the gold fields at Dawson. En route, however, they had to navigate their way through the Miles Canyon and White Horse rapids, obstacles located just south of present-day Whitehorse. This they did by creating a tramway around the rapids, and this diversion soon spawned a settlement at the canyon's northern head. In time this new village, Whitehorse, was consolidated by the arrival of the White Pass and Yukon Railroad from Skagway. No sooner had the railroad arrived, however, than the gold rush petered out, with the result that the town's population plummeted, almost overnight, from 10,000 to 400. Numbers remained at this level until the building of the Alaska Highway, when the arrival of some 20,000 newcomers prompted a recovery that still continues today.

SS *Klondike* Over 250 paddle-steamers once plied the Yukon River, and until comparatively recently they remained the region's most important form of transportation. Now only two remain, Dawson City's SS *Keno* (see page 124), and Whitehorse's SS *Klondike* (2nd Avenue,

The SS Klondike, *one of only two of the Yukon's former 250 paddle-steamers to have survived*

Abandoned workings at White Pass Silver Mine

tel: 867/667–3910. *Open* May–Sep daily tours. *Admission: moderate*). The SS *Klondike*, which now lies beached just south of downtown, is a National Historic Site administered by the Canadian Parks Service. The largest of all the old steamers, she was built in 1929, sunk in 1936, and rebuilt in 1937. Thereafter, she battled against the river until 1955, when an inexperienced pilot ran her aground. Most of the time she carried ore from mines near Mayo, or moved passengers and cargo up to Dawson. The journey, fully laden, took her 36 hours; the return, against the current, took five days. Today, guided tours take you around the lovingly restored boat.

McBride Museum▶▶ For all its hotels, cafés and restaurants, Whitehorse makes relatively little play for tourists. After the SS *Klondike* the biggest draw is the McBride Museum (1st Avenue and Wood Street, tel: 867/667–2709. *Open* daily. *Admission: moderate*), an appealing assortment of natural history displays, old machinery, archive material and gold-rush memorabilia. Its evocative period photographs are particularly compelling. For more detailed background on Whitehorse, contact the Yukon Historical Society (tel: 867/667–4704), which provides guided tours (Jun–Aug Mon–Sat).

Miles Canyon▶▶ Whitehorse's liveliest outings are the river tours that shoot the Miles Canyon, scourge of the old gold-rush pioneers (note that you can also admire the canyon from viewpoints along Canyon Road). Hydroelectric works have calmed the rapids' former ferocity, but the two-hour trips aboard the MV *Schwatka* still offer a good idea of the perils faced by pioneers (tel: 867/668–4716. *Open* Jun–mid-Sep daily 2pm, mid-Jun to mid-Aug, also at 7pm daily. *Admission: expensive*). The boat leaves from a dock nearly 3km (2 miles) south of town on Canyon Road. You can buy tickets at the dock.

GETTING THERE

There are direct flights to Whitehorse from Calgary, Edmonton and Vancouver. Road access is via the Cassiar or Alaska highways. Car ferries operate on the Alaska Marine Highway network from Prince Rupert and US West Coast ports to Skagway on the Alaskan Panhandle. Alaska Direct Bus Lines (tel: 867/668–4833 or 800/770–6652) runs from Skagway to Whitehorse (May–Sep daily), and on to Anchorage (May–Sep, three per week). Greyhound buses (www.greyhound.ca; six per week in summer, three in winter) run from Dawson Creek (journey time 20 hours) with connections from Edmonton and Vancouver. The White Pass and Yukon Railroad (tel: 907/983-2217 or 800/343–7373. *Open* summer only) is a highly scenic private line from Skagway to the top of the White Pass (Canadian border). The remainder of the trip is done by bus.

The Inuit are one of the most resilient and distinctive of all Native Canadian groups, far removed from the mainstream of national life by their art, culture and language, and by the sheer hostility of their domain, a largely frozen territory that stretches across the far north of the continent from Alaska to Greenland.

Background The Inuit pay little heed to national borders. For centuries they were a nomadic people, crossing the world's Arctic regions into Russia, Canada, Alaska and Greenland. Today they number around 100,000, a scattered population linked by a roughly similar language (Inuktitut). Unlike Native Canadians to the south they have few tribal ties, but divide instead into seven groups, each distinguished by subtly different circumstances of culture and subsistence (the Copper, Caribou, Iglulik, Mackenzie, Baffin, Labrador and Netselik). Sadly, even these vague differences are beginning to blur as the old ways of life—including the igloo, ice-hole fishing and the dog-pulled sledge—are pushed aside by the less romantic intrusions of the modern world.

Early cultures The course of Inuit history is divided into the Pre-Dorset, Dorset, Thule and Historic periods. The Pre-Dorset began 4,000 years ago, when Siberian peoples crossed the Bering Strait into Alaska. Although almost 1,000 years in duration, the period has yielded only a handful of artifacts—mostly harpoon and spear tips that probably combined practical, aesthetic and magical functions. Artifacts from the Dorset culture, which developed from about 600BC, are more sophisticated, though little is known of their purpose. Most are highly expressive, up to about 10cm (4in) high, and made almost exclusively from ivory (wood was virtually nonexistent in polar regions).

NOT ESKIMOS
Inuit means "the people," and is the word now used to describe the people previously known as Eskimos. Eskimo, a word not used by the Inuit themselves, means "an eater of raw meat," and was coined by the Algonquin natives. It was devised as a derogatory term and is still seen as such.

MEAT OR NOTHING
The Inuit diet once consisted entirely of flesh. Everything from ear to eyeball was eaten, usually raw. Choice items included the intestines of seals, dried and plaited, and small birds *en croûte*, in which the birds were stuffed into sealskin and left to putrefy.

A large Inuit sculpture silhouetted by the setting sun at English Bay

No more igloos: a modern Inuit community

Thule culture Inuit culture reached its pinnacle during the Thule era, which began around AD1000 in northern Alaska, spread across Canada and Greenland, and reached eastern Siberia by about the 13th century. Virtually all its exquisitely worked artifacts were female, and took the form of birds, spirits and people imbued with magical and religious properties. Ways of life remained unchanged for centuries, with climate and hunting the primary driving forces. A nomadic habit demanded igloos in winter and skin tents in summer, while transport was by foot, by kayak (*umiaks*) or by sled (*komatik*). Food, tools, clothes and weapons, even heating and cooking oil, had to be culled from the sea, or from roaming herds of caribou and musk ox.

17th to 20th centuries The Historic Period in Inuit culture began in the 17th century, coinciding with the arrival of European whalers, missionaries and fur traders. Inuit behavior changed almost immediately, as some figures were carved specifically for barter. More catastrophic breakdowns of the old order occurred in the 19th century, with the advent of commercial whaling in the north. Local Inuit employed as crew soon fell prey to alcohol, venereal disease and smallpox, scourges that quickly spread through the whole indigenous population.

Traders encouraged Inuit trappers to discard age-old methods of hunting in favor of inland hunting with firearms and metal traps. Missionaries introduced hospitals and schools, but ancient rites and traditional beliefs were lost. Jobs in construction during World War II, together with welfare and housing, had the effect of concentrating the Inuit in permanent settlements, and introduced TV and radio—not to mention alcoholism and lawlessness.

In 1999, the old Northwest Territories were divided into two separate entities. The Eastern Arctic, where the Inuit are concentrated, became Nunavut, meaning "Our Land," and its capital (formerly Frobisher Bay) became Iqaluit. Covering 1.9 million sq km (733,400sq miles), Nunavut has only 27,000 inhabitants. Although it is dependent on Ottawa financially, its government is elected directly by the people. It is hoped that this new political self-determination will help the Inuit find a new and successful way of life.

CRIME
In a society where co-operation was vital to survival, the ultimate Inuit punishment was to be cast off from a nomadic group—a sure sentence of death (the weak and the elderly were also often abandoned when food was scarce). Punishments therefore were usually restricted to "song-duels," in which the injured party would sing a string of insults at the accused, who had to accept this melodic punishment without complaint.

Whales and hunting: two former staples of Inuit life

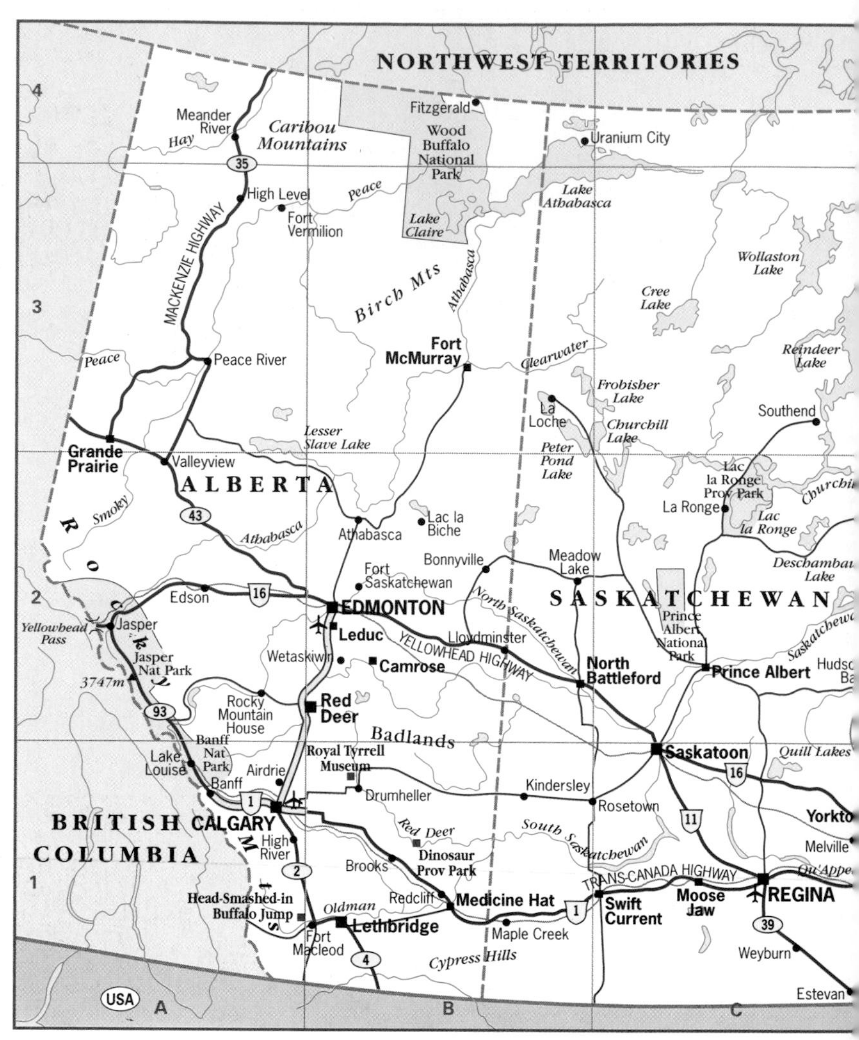

POET'S PRAIRIE

"The Prairie is the High Veldt...plus Hope, Activity and Reward."—Rudyard Kipling, *Letters to the Family* (1907)

Extreme right: Wind generators at Crow's Nest Pass, Alberta
Right: Flax and rapeseed color the Manitoba landscape in early summer

The Prairies

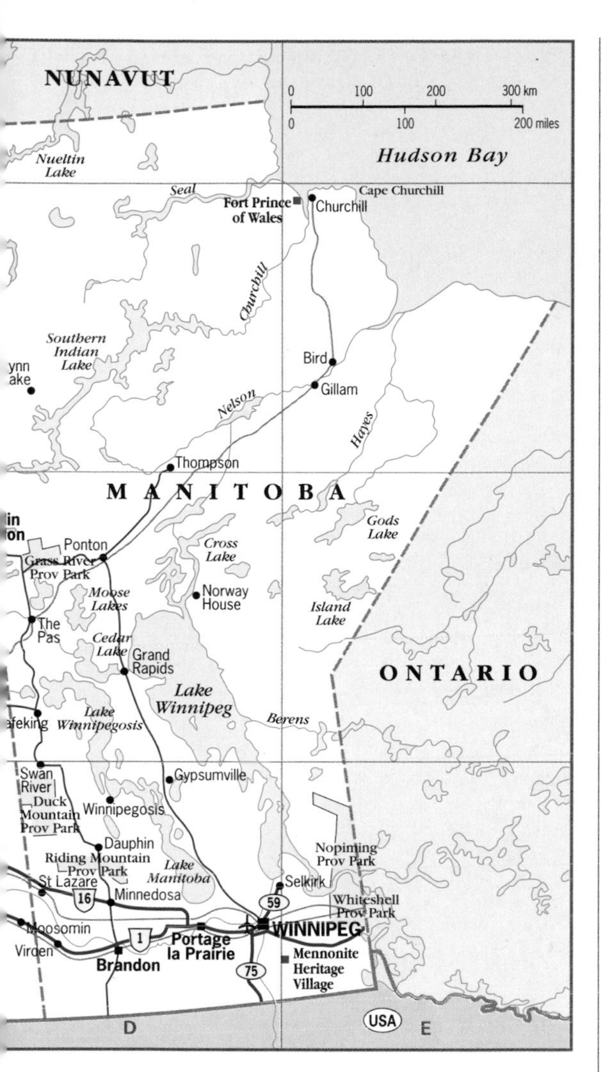

"Why do Canadians cross the Prairies at night?" "Because the view's better." It is an old joke, but one that confirms an image of Canada's heartlands as a place of unrelenting scenic tedium, a region to be hurried through on the way to more exciting cities and landscapes to the east and west. It is a view shared by many Canadians, but one that takes little account of the Prairies' true nature, or of the vast variety of landscapes that patchwork the "Prairie provinces": Manitoba, Saskatchewan and Alberta.

NOT PRAIRIE Prairie—a word of French origin meaning "meadow"—is something of a misnomer, with its connotations of whispering grassland stretching to the horizon in an endless checkerboard of fields. Very little of the Prairies consists of natural grassland. The area of semi-arid grasslands, the region that was once dotted with the buffalo herds of popular imagination, is confined to quite small areas in Saskatchewan and southern Alberta. North

BREAD BASKET
Saskatchewan is said to contain 44 percent of Canada's agricultural land. It produces 60 percent of the country's wheat, or about 2 percent of the entire world's consumption.

FAST RIVER
The province of Saskatchewan takes its name from the Saskatchewan River, whose name is in turn derived from the Cree native word for "the river that runs swiftly."

GREAT SPIRIT
Manitoba takes its name from *manito waba*, an Ojibwan phrase applied to the narrows of Lake Manitoba. Here, the sound of pebbles being crashed against the shore by waves was held to have come from *Manitou*, the "Great Spirit."

GOD-GIVEN WHEAT
"The Lord said 'let there be wheat' and Saskatchewan was born."—Stephen Leacock, *My Discovery of America* (1937)

of these pockets arcs another relatively small ribbon of land, the so-called "wheat-growing crescent." North of this again is a larger crescent of "aspen parkland," a transitional zone of rolling low hills and fertile mixed farming. This, in turn, merges with the largest zone of all—the boreal forest—a vast blanket of trees and muskeg bog that covers over half of the so-called "Prairies."

NOT FLAT Not only are the Prairies not grassy, they are not flat either: they rise in steps from sea level around Hudson Bay to a height of almost 1,200m (4,000ft) near the Rockies. Hills ripple over this gently shelving incline, cut by river valleys and dotted with anomalous landscapes such as the gorges of the Alberta Badlands (see pages 150–151) and the breezy uplands of the Cypress Hills (see pages 146–147). Interest and subtle beauty reside almost everywhere. Vast Prairie skies, for example, blue and overarching, are particularly renowned, as are sunsets and the velvet star-lit skies of the Prairie night (which are often also tinted with the shimmering colors of the Northern Lights). Colors are stark and painted in great swaths across the country, from the blues and yellows of flax and rapeseed to the deep greens and orangey-golds of spring and summer wheat. Towering grain elevators, the "cathedrals of the plains," rise in primary reds and greens above the rippling grasslands, linked by slow-moving freight trains making their heavily laden way across a continent.

BUFFALO AND FURS Before the coming of the Europeans, this land was the domain of the Cree and Blackfoot. Hunters followed the grasslands' herds of buffalo, relying on the animals for food, tools, shelter and clothing. Their first encounter with an outsider was probably with Henry Kelsey, an Englishman who roamed northern Manitoba and Saskatchewan at the end of the 17th century. Thereafter the region was disputed by rival fur traders, its northern wastes exploited by the Hudson's Bay and North West companies for centuries.

The tide of Prairie affairs only began to turn after 1870, the year the new Dominion began to lure thousands of settlers to the region. Not only did this disrupt (not to say destroy) the native way of life, it also led to the Métis rebellions of 1871 and 1885 (see pages 38–39), revolts caused by the erosion of cultural traditions, and by the appropriation of land from the area's many thousands of existing Native Canadian and Métis inhabitants for distribution to the new waves of immigrants.

CHANGE The mass settlement of the Prairies in the 19th century has left its mark in the region's present ethnic mosaic of Scots, Irish, Poles, Ukrainians, Russians, Germans and others (see pages 156–157). Much had to change, however, before any of these groups could happily begin a new life. Land treaties had to be "negotiated" with the native population, rebellions had to be crushed, and law and order had to be established. The last task fell to the North West Mounted Police, forerunners of the famous Mounties (see pages 148–149), whose even-handedness earned the respect of natives and pioneers alike. Then there was the building of the Canadian Pacific Railway, essential to carry settlers and to export wheat and cattle (see pages 40–41). Finally, and perhaps most importantly, there was the task of allocating free land to the new arrivals.

FREE FARMS Land for the taking must have seemed too good to be true to the disenfranchised and dispossessed of Europe. The handout was sanctioned by the Dominion Lands Act of 1872, whose terms allowed each "homesteader" to register a "quarter section" of land 65ha (160 acres). Title deeds were granted if a home was built within three years and a certain proportion of land was cultivated (settlers could then claim further allocations of land). The effect was dramatic. The population in Manitoba increased from 62,000 in 1881 to 153,000 in 1891, 255,000 in 1901 and 461,000 in 1911.

EXPLORING THE PRAIRIES Grasping the vastness of the Prairies is best done from a plane, where the seamless pattern of fields, snaking rivers and lonely, arrow-straight roads unfolds below you for hour after hour. A closer look can be had from a VIA Rail train from Toronto to Edmonton, or from one of the two great roads—the Yellowhead and Trans-Canada highways—that wend their way across the continent's wide-open spaces. Whatever your approach, however, this is a region where you can hope to see only a handful of sights. Calgary is the most interesting city, a key stepping stone for journeys into the Rockies (but worth a day in its own right). Winnipeg comes close behind, thanks mainly to its wonderful selection of museums. Edmonton is less captivating, except during its numerous highly rated summer festivals. Cypress Hills is one of the loveliest landscapes and the tundra of Churchill—with its polar bears—is one of the most exhilarating. The Alberta Badlands are also unmissable, not least for the magnificent dinosaur museum at Drumheller. Native culture is best seen at the wonderfully named Head-Smashed-In Buffalo Jump (see panel), although fascinating fragments of native and pioneer history can be found right across the Prairies—if you have the time and the inclination to pursue them.

BUFFALO JUMPS
For thousands of years, the native people who lived on the Prairies hunted the buffalo by rounding them up into large herds and then stampeding them over cliffs. Once they had plunged to their deaths, the animals were plundered for meat, hides and bones. Such "jumps" existed all over North America, but one of the best-preserved is the Head-Smashed-In Buffalo Jump in southern Alberta (18km/11 miles) northwest of Fort Macleod). Below its 305m (1,000ft) wide cliff lie 10m (30ft) of bones and ash accumulated over the millennia. A magnificent interpretive center is built into the cliff, while the area around can be explored on tours in the company of native guides (tel: 403/553–2731. May–end Aug daily 9–8; Sep–end Apr daily 9–5. *Admission: moderate*).

"Cathedrals of the plains"—grain elevators in Saskatchewan

Calgary owes much of its glittering skyline to the influx of oil money in the 1970s

ALL THE SAME
"These little towns do not look to the passer-by comfortable as homes... there is the difficulty of distinguishing your village from the others."—Rupert Brooke on Prairie towns, *Letters from America, 1913* (1916)

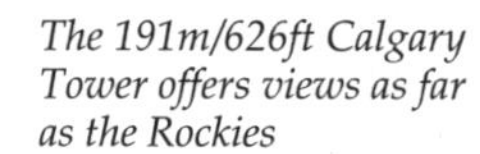

The 191m/626ft Calgary Tower offers views as far as the Rockies

▶▶▶ Calgary *134A1*

Calgary's mirror-sided skyscrapers rise imperiously above the rippling Prairies, a gleaming heart that contrasts beautifully with the homely wooden houses that scatter its wide-flung suburbs. Perfectly situated for visiting the Rockies, just 90 minutes away by car, and well served by roads and international flights, the city makes a far better base for the region than Edmonton, a more downbeat city to the north (see pages 152–153). It offers enough sightseeing to occupy a day or so, not least the Glenbow Museum, one of western Canada's great museums, as well as Prince's Island and the Eau Claire Market.

Oil capital The bend of the Elbow and the Bow rivers was long a favored meeting place for Blackfoot natives, traces of whose culture can be seen in the ancient sites and rock drawings around present-day Calgary. Fur traders occupied the site at the beginning of the 19th century, and in 1875 Fort Calgary was established to stem the flow of illegal whiskey across the border. Greater law and order attracted settlers from Britain and the US, among them American ranchers who left their overgrazed farms for Calgary's virgin pastures. The Canadian Pacific Railway brought in fresh waves of pioneers in 1883. The discovery of oil in 1914 put the city more firmly on the map. Later strikes turned it into a world energy and financial center,

the oil boom of the 1970s bankrolling the city's shiny high-rise center (around 75 percent of the country's oil and natural gas companies have their headquarters here). Falling oil prices in the 1980s brought the city up short, though recession was tempered by the construction jamboree that accompanied the XV Winter Olympics, held in Calgary in 1988.

Downtown The heart of the "Prairie Manhattan" is a well-ordered grid of gleaming high-rise towers, bordered in the north by the Bow River and by the Pacific railway in the south. It is an easy area to explore, and you can cover most distances on foot, though for longer east–west trips be sure to use the free C-Train service (see panel, page 140). The main shopping and pedestrianized area is Stephen Avenue, between 1st Street SE and 4th Street SW. Other large malls such as the Scotia Centre and Toronto Dominion Square are found on 7th Avenue SW. For an overview of downtown, visit the **Calgary Tower**, a 191m (627ft) city landmark whose observation deck offers views as far as the Rockies (9th Avenue SW and Centre Street, tel: 403/266–7171. *Open* mid-Jun to mid-Sep daily 7am–10.30pm; mid-Sep to mid-Jun daily 8am–10pm. *Admission: moderate*). The tower also contains the city's tourist office (see panel, page 140). Across the road lies the excellent Glenbow Museum►► (see page 140).

ARRIVING

Calgary International Airport (tel: 403/265–9555) handles regular nonstop flights from the US, and is also a major hub for domestic flights. The Airport Shuttle Express (tel: 403/531–3909) bus connects to downtown, which lies about 10km (6 miles) to the southwest, and elsewhere on reservation (24-hour service). The main bus terminal is at 850 16th Street SW and at 8th Avenue, about ten minutes' walk from downtown (*Greyhound* tel: 800/661–8747, www.greyhound.ca; *Brewster* tel: 877/791–5500, www.brewster.ca). Note that there are no longer any VIA Rail services to Calgary.

PUBLIC TRANSPORTATION
The C-Train is a modern light railway system that is free on its downtown section along 7th Avenue SW between 10th Street and City Hall at 3rd Street SE. Interchangeable tickets for the C-Train and buses are available from machines at C-Train stations, shops with a "Calgary Transit" sticker, and the Calgary Transit Information Centre at 240 7th Avenue SW (tel: 403/262–1000, www.calgarytransit.com). You can pay on buses if you have the *exact* fare: no change is given.

Other downtown targets include **Devonian Gardens▶▶**, (*Open* daily 9–9. *Admission free*) a latter-day Hanging Gardens of Babylon over an entire floor of the Toronto Dominion Square mall. The 1ha (2.5-acre) indoor site features ponds, waterfalls, walkways, many fully grown trees, and over 20,000 tropical, subtropical and indigenous plants and shrubs. It is especially busy at lunchtime, when shoppers and office workers come here to eat food bought in the adjoining mall (7th Avenue SW, between 2nd and 3rd Streets. *Open* daily 9–9. *Admission free*).

For the low-down on the city's oil and energy industry, call in on the **Energeum**, a small but interesting collection of audiovisual displays in the foyer of the Energy Resources Building (640 5th Avenue SW. *Open* Jun–end Aug, Sun–Fri 10.30–4.30; Sep–end May Mon–Fri 10.30–4.30. *Admission free*). For more general scientific enlightenment, visit the **Calgary Science Centre**, crammed with hands-on displays, and the adjoining **Centennial Planetarium**, which offers popular nightly star shows (701 11th Street and 7th Avenue SW. *Open* daily, tel: 403/221–3700 for hours. *Admission: expensive*).

Glenbow Museum▶▶▶ One of the many windfalls of Calgary's vast oil revenues was the magnificent modern Glenbow Museum (130 9th Avenue, tel: 403/268–4100. *Open* daily 9–5, Thu–Fri until 9. *Admission: expensive*), packed with displays that merit a trip to the city in their own right. Spread over three floors, the museum opens with a section devoted to sacred art, and a gallery dedicated to the painters and paintings of western Canada. The next floor, the museum's heart, traces the history of the region's First Nations, exploring all aspects of native art and culture. Also included are displays exploring the history of the Métis, the North West Mounted Police (the Mounties), the fur trade, the Riel Uprising, ranching, pioneer life and oil and gas exploration. Upstairs lies a vast

INFORMATION
Calgary's Visitor Information Centre and accommodations service is at 220 8th Avenue SW (tel: 403/263–8510 or 0800/661–1678, www.tourismcalgary.com or www.discoveralberta.com.

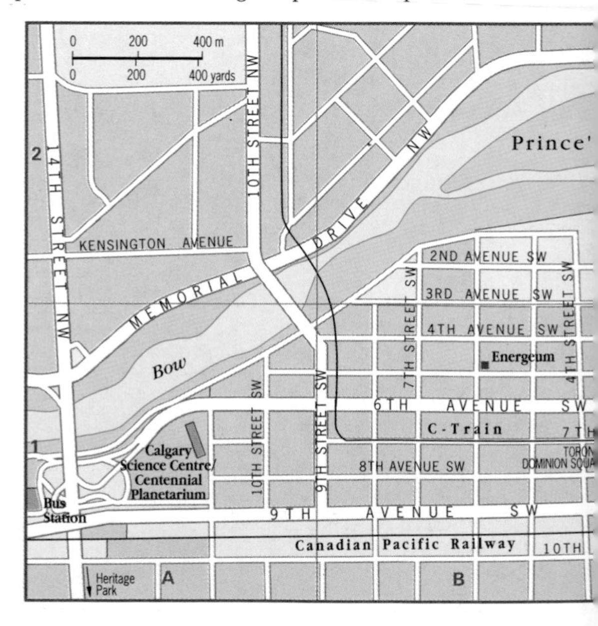

collection of arms and armor, and one of the world's finest collections of gems and minerals.

Prince's Island▶▶▶ A peaceful park on the Bow River, Prince's Island is an oasis of grass and shady nooks that provides a welcome contrast to the granite and mirrored glass of downtown. It is a perfect place to laze, jog or stroll, and lies only a few minutes' walk from the city center. An added bonus is the wonderful **Eau Claire Market▶▶** nearby (2nd Avenue and 2nd Street), a deliberately rather colorful collection of market stalls, restaurants and interesting little shops. The open-plan eating area, ringed with all manner of fast-food vendors, is a good place to watch the world go by.

Fort Calgary▶▶ Built in 1875, Fort Calgary remained in use until 1914, when it was sold to the Canadian Pacific Railway. Neglected for decades, the site has now been restored, and though no more than a few stumps of the original log stockade survive, the area and its adjoining interpretive center offer a compelling rundown of the city's early history. To get there, take the free C-Train to City Hall and walk the five blocks east to the site (750-9th Avenue SE, tel: 403/290–1875. *Open* daily 9–5. *Admission: site, free; center, moderate*).

Calgary Zoo▶▶ This, the biggest zoo in Canada, has made a special effort to answer the criticisms of the animal welfare lobby. As far as possible, the 1,400 animals have been accommodated in their "natural" habitats. Special botanical gardens are located around the site, and there is also a dinosaur-dotted Prehistoric Park. You can reach the zoo by car on Memorial Drive East, by the C-Train, or via walkways along the Bow River (1300 Zoo Road NE, St. George's Island, tel: 403/232–9300. *Open* 9–9; Prehistoric Park Jun–end Sep only. *Admission: expensive*).

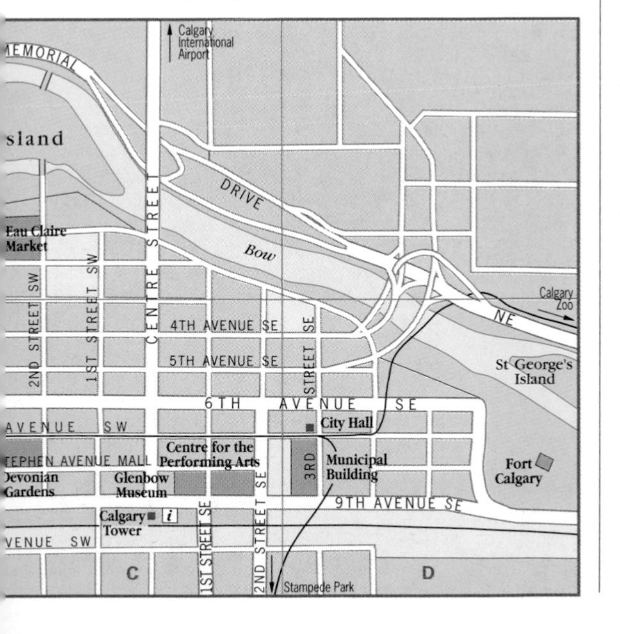

ADDRESSES
Calgary is based around a grid divided into quadrants (NW, NE, SW and SE). The Bow River divides north from south, Centre Street east from west (most of downtown is in SW). Streets run north–south, avenues east–west. The last digits in a sequence refer to the house number: thus 345-6th Avenue SW is on 3rd Street at No. 45, close to the intersection with 6th Avenue, in the SW quadrant of the city. Always check the quadrant carefully.

STILL BUILDING
"They say of Calgary that it's going to look really great when it finally gets uncrated."—Robert Fox, BBC Radio (1981)

CLEAR WATER
Calgary in Gaelic means "clear running water," and took its name from Fort Calgary, which was named after the Scottish birthplace of its first assistant commissioner. The town was granted a formal charter in 1893.

Cattle in Calgary graze on some of the world's finest pasture, producing in turn some of the world's finest steaks. Where cattle roam and steaks sizzle, real-life cowboys cannot be far behind: Calgary is home to the Stampede, a huge fair with the world's largest rodeo at its core.

CHUCK-WAGON RACING
Chuck-wagon races are run in heats, each heat consisting of four teams of four-horse wagons and their outriders. Before starting the contest, teams have to load the wagon with tent poles and a box or barrel intended to symbolize a cooking stove. They then race a figure eight course and finish with a single circuit of Stampede Park's 800m (2,600ft) track.

Top: Chuck-wagon racing
Below: They start them young in cow-town Calgary.

Annual orgy Cattle nibble contentedly on the surrounding Prairie, and filets mignons sizzle on grills, but, wandering around Calgary's gleaming downtown area, it is hard to reconcile the high-rise and staid streets with the city's reputation as Canada's "cowboy town" par excellence.

Come here during ten days in July, however, when the city holds its annual Stampede, and the scene is very different. Then blue jeans and bolo ties are the clothes of choice, finished off with white Stetsons and hand-tooled leather boots. Country-and-western music is the soundtrack, a backdrop for conversations in which everyone adopts suitably antiquated Wild West speech. Staid Calgary suddenly finds the party spirit, and for days hotels are full and the streets are swinging.

Real McCoy Towns the length and breadth of Canada exploit often spurious commemorative occasions as an excuse to dress up and draw in the tourists. Calgary's moments of summer madness undoubtedly have a theatrical edge, and certainly keep the local Chamber of Commerce happy. Yet there is absolutely nothing bogus about the Stampede's thrills and spills, nor any ignoring the fiercely competitive nature of its many events. Most of the cowboys (and girls) are the real thing, drawn here from across North America by the rodeo's status—it is the world's largest—and by the substantial prize money involved (more than $500,000).

Show time The whole thing—the brainchild of an entrepreneur named Guy Weadick—began in 1912. A prize jackpot of $16,000 (at that time a colossal sum) was offered to attract competitors. Spectators were tempted in by an opening ceremony starring 2,000 Native Americans in full ceremonial splendor, and several pistol-toting members of Pancho Villa's original bandit gang. Around 14,000 people turned up to the inaugural ceremony, whose emphasis on the big and the brash has been continued in today's similarly over-the-top opening parades.

Cowboy games Not for nothing is Calgary's Stampede considered the roughest fair of its kind in North America. Injuries may be few and far between in some of its more innocuous segments, but in many of the others competitors can be seen leaving the arena on a hastily trundled stretcher.

By far the most spectacular events are the chuck-wagon races (see panel), which are competitions billed as the

Riding a bull at the annual Calgary Stampede

"World Championships" of this particular "sport." Calgary cowboys claim to have invented this absurdly dangerous form of racing in the 1923 Stampede. Other fiercely contested activities include roping calves, milking wild cows, wrestling steers, riding buffalo, tackling cattle and the more usual business of lassoing and staying on a bucking bronco.

After hours Festivities continue long after the last steer has been wrestled groundward. Locals indulge in impromptu cook-outs (beans and "white hatter stew" are the culinary staples), and all manner of informal partying erupts on the streets. Bars, restaurants and nightclubs across town are more lively than usual, and numerous cast-of-thousands cabarets are staged to keep people in the party mood. Come dawn it is time to start all over again, with the traditional outdoor breakfast of bacon and pancakes washed down by hot coffee.

Most of the action takes place in Stampede Park, in the city's southeastern corner, home to the show venues, bars, restaurants, amusement rides and several large outdoor stages. Do not expect to turn up and join the party, however, as tickets for the Stampede's big events sell out fast; a degree of forward planning is essential (see panel).

JOINING IN

Simply being in Calgary during the Stampede is fun, but if you plan to stay in the city be certain to reserve accommodations well in advance (see the panel on page 140 for details of Calgary's tourist office). Tickets for the main show events go quickly, and retail at anything between $5 and $50. For ticket order forms, advance sales and information visit www.calgarystampede.com.

INFORMATION
Churchill's Visitor Information Bureau (tel: 204/675–2022 or 888/389–2327) is located just across from the VIA Rail train station in the center of town (tel: 800/561–8630). There is also a Parks Canada Visitor Centre at the Bayport Plaza Building (tel: 204/675–8863).

GETTING THERE
Churchill is not accessible by road. Air Canada and smaller airlines fly here mainly from Winnipeg, and there is a rail service (tel: 800/561–8630, www.viarail.ca) from Winnipeg (five weekly in summer, three weekly in winter). The flat, open tundra en route makes the latter one of Canada's more fascinating train rides.

►► Churchill

135E3

It is a fact of Canadian sightseeing that rewards often only come after long journeys. Nowhere is this more true than in Churchill, an isolated outpost perched on the rocky and unforgiving coast of Hudson Bay. On its own the town is not somewhere you would visit, partly because it is hundreds of miles from anywhere, partly because there is little in the way of conventional sights. Nor is it particularly pretty—like most northern communities, it looks battered. Ever-increasing numbers of travelers nonetheless flatter the town with their presence, some drawn by the romance of the two-day rail journey it takes to get here (see panel), others by the chance to visit what has been dubbed the "Polar Bear Capital of the World."

Fur outpost When the Danish explorer Jens Munck arrived in 1619, Churchill's site had been home to the Inuit for some 3,000 years. Munck spent just one winter here before moving on, one of countless seafarers who sought in vain for the Northwest Passage (of the explorer's crew of 65, only Munck and two companions survived). Next on the scene was the Hudson's Bay Company, which in 1717 established a fur post here to trade with the Cree and Assiniboine. In the 19th century attempts were made to promote Churchill as a port, the hope being to export some of the Prairie grain then moving through east-coast ports. In the event the hope was forlorn, not least because the town's harbor was frozen solid for nine months of the year. Nonetheless, a railroad was built from Winnipeg in the 1920s to move the grain north.

Polar bears Some of Churchill's myriad tour operators (see panel opposite) will take you out to see some of the region's 200 or more species of birds: the area straddles a major Arctic migration route. Others organize trips to

An inquisitive polar bear

Polar bears come ashore in Churchill when the winter pack-ice begins to break up

see some of the 3,000 beluga whales that congregate around the mouth of the Churchill River between June and September. The vast majority, however, are kept busy satisfying their clients' passion for the region's polar bears. The animals begin to come ashore around June, about the time that the pack-ice on Hudson Bay begins to break up. Once on land, they amble around the town's outskirts, occasionally—and dangerously—wandering up the main street in search of food. They remain ashore until around November, when the hardening ice provides a platform for them to resume their more normal hunting habits.

POLAR BEAR TOURS
Churchill's polar bears can be seen from helicopters, boats or "tundra buggies" depending on your finances and the time of year you visit. Fall is the best season for sightings (Sep–early Nov), - just before Hudson Bay refreezes completely. Contact the tourist office for details of operators, or call Churchill Wilderness Encounter, one of the longer established companies (tel: 204/675–2248 or 800/265–9458).

Eskimo Museum▶▶▶ Missionaries brought schools, hospitals and the Bible to Inuit communities, but they also played a major part in upsetting the social structures and spiritual beliefs that had sustained them for thousands of years (see page 132). Thus it is with mixed feelings that you admire Churchill's excellent Eskimo Museum (242 Vérendrye Street, tel: 204/675–2030. *Open* Jun–end Aug Mon 1–5, Tue–Sat 9–12, 1–5; Sep–end May Mon, Sat 1–4.30. *Admission donation*), whose collection was largely amassed at the beginning of the 20th century by missionary Oblate Fathers of the Mary Immaculate. Among the exhibits are two large hide canoes and a vast range of tools, artifacts and carvings.

Fort Prince of Wales▶▶ The National Historic Site of Fort Prince of Wales was built by the Hudson's Bay Company between 1731 and 1771. It was constructed partly as a successor to an earlier trading post (see opposite), and partly to protect its interests from the depredations of the French. Workers, oxen and horses were specially shipped from England to work on the project, which despite its 40-year duration produced a building that proved virtually indefensible. When French ships appeared in 1782, the fort's commander, Samuel Hearne, was unable to raise a garrison and surrendered without a struggle. The fort—whose cannons were spiked and walls undermined—was never used again.

SEEING THE FORT
Fort Prince of Wales lies across the estuary from Churchill, so to see its bulwarks, barracks and commander's quarters you need to join a guided boat tour. Contact Parks Canada (tel: 204/675–8863) for details. (*Admission: moderate.*)

Drive

The Cypress Hills

A drive along Prairie back roads through the Cypress Hills, an area of pastoral valleys, gentle hills and historic monuments (200km/120 miles).

Long distances are unavoidable in the Prairies, and to see the Cypress Hills, among the prettiest of the region's landscapes, requires a diversion from the most direct Prairie route, the Trans-Canada Highway (Highway 1). The drive starts at **Medicine Hat►►**, whose evocative name comes from the story of a Cree medicine man who lost his hat during a battle. His followers took the loss as a bad omen, lost heart and were slaughtered by their Blackfoot enemies. The battle site took the name *Saamis*, or "medicine man's hat," and was adopted by the pioneer settlement that grew up here in 1882. Rudyard Kipling called the town a place that "has all hell for a basement," a reference to the vast reserves of natural gas beneath the town (some of which power the town's street lighting). Things to see include the City Hall, a startling piece of modern architecture, the Historical Museum and the former Medalta Potteries (a National Historic Site) at nearby **Redcliff**. The last is also known for its flowers and greenhouses, some of which are open to the public.

Some 50km (30 miles) east of Medicine Hat, turn off Highway 1 on to Highway 41. This takes you to the resort center of Elkwater (34km/21 miles) and then to the **Cypress Hills Provincial Park►►►**. The Blackfoot named the area *Ketewius Netumoo*—"the hills that shouldn't be"—after the anomalous collection of peaks and plateaux that rise above the surrounding Prairie. The hills exist thanks to their height, which kept them above the eroding effects of glaciers in the

Left: Fort Walsh, nestled in the heart of Cypress Hills, a reconstruction of the original Mounties' post

last Ice Age. They contain the highest point in Canada between Labrador and the Rockies, an elevation that creates a cooler and moister climate than elsewhere in the Prairies. This in turn provides lush vegetation, beautifully varied terrain and fine habitats for interesting wildlife and wild flowers. The whole effect, in the words of John Palliser, who surveyed the Prairies in 1859, is "a perfect oasis in the desert."

Information on the park, in particular on its drives and trails, can be obtained from the park visitors' center in Elkwater (tel: 403/893–3777). The best of the drives are short diversions off Highway 41. The first runs west to Horseshoe Canyon and **Head of the Mountain▶▶▶**, the latter a tremendous viewpoint whose panorama extends to the Sweet Grass Mountains of Montana. The second heads east to Reesor Lake, from where you can either loop back to Highway 41 or continue eastward to Fort Walsh National Historic Park (see below). The stretch on to Fort Walsh is beautiful, and removes the need for retracing your steps. However, it is part gravel, part tarmacadam, and can be treacherous in wet weather, so be certain to check road conditions with the Elkford park office before setting off.

If you are unable to take the direct road, you will need to backtrack to Highway 1, following it for 88km (55 miles) to the junction at Maple Creek. Here Highway 21 leads south to the Saskatchewan eastern section of the Cypress Hills Provincial Park. This centers on the small, pretty resort of **Loch Leven▶▶**, home to the park administrative office (tel: 306/662–4411). Here you can pick up a road that leads 32km (20 miles) to **Fort Walsh National Historic Park▶▶▶** (tel: 306/662–3590. *Open* mid-May–end Aug daily 9.30–5.30. *Admission: moderate*), an excellent reconstruction of the fort that featured prominently in the Mounties' story (see pages 148–149). Its interpretive displays

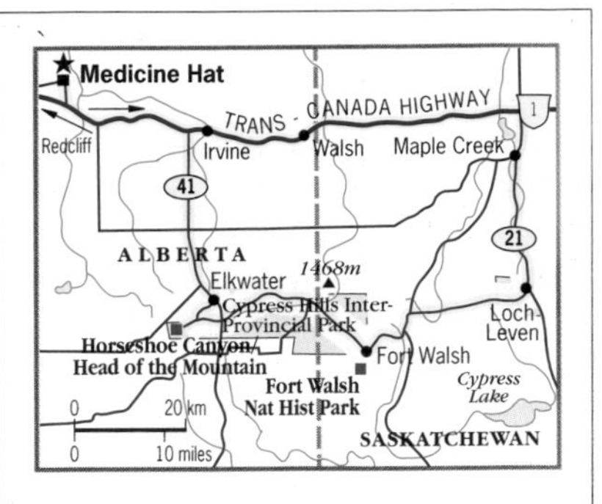

cover the fort's history, the culture of local native tribes and the background to the formation of the North West Mounted Police. Also be sure to see **Farwell's Trading Post▶▶** nearby, one of the infamous "whiskey forts" of the Cypress Hills Massacre (see page 148).

An overnight pitch in the Cypress Hills Provincial Park

Certain characters symbolize an entire city or country for outsiders. Britain has the "bobby," Venice has the gondolier and Canada has the Mountie, the red-uniformed policeman who "always gets his man." A federal bastion of law and order, the Mountie originated in the lawlessness of the old Canadian West.

Top: NWMP camp, Calgary. Right: A recruitment poster

PROTECTION
The Mounties were renowned for their even-handedness. Crowfoot, one of the greatest 19th-century Blackfoot native chieftains, paid the force this tribute: "If the police had not come to the country," he declared, "where would we all be now? Bad men and whiskey were killing us so fast that very few of us indeed would have been left. The police have protected us as the feathers of a bird protect it from the winter."

SITTING BULL
In 1876 Chief Sitting Bull and 5,000 Sioux warriors defeated General George Custer at Little Big Horn in southern Montana. Fearing retaliation from the US authorities, the victors fled to Canada. Inspector James Walsh of the NWMP was given two unenviable tasks: to persuade Sitting Bull to leave the country; and to prevent a full-scale native war (the Sioux were traditional enemies of the Prairies' Cree and Blackfoot tribes). Walsh rode into the vast Sioux camp at Wood Mountain (350km/210 miles east of Fort Walsh) with just six men. His bravery gained the respect—and the eventual departure—of Sitting Bull, who lived out his days, albeit unwillingly, on a native reservation.

Whiskey and whoop-up
The Mounties had fairly slapdash beginnings. Originally christened the North West Mounted Police (NWMP), the force was founded in Ottawa in 1873. Its birth was so inauspicious that it lacked even uniforms, relying instead on a cache of British Army tunics that happened to be at hand (hence the famous red jackets). The task for which it was formed was specific: to bring order to the Canadian West, and to deal with the illicit trade in whiskey that was bringing misery to the Plains natives (see panel). Most of this trade was conducted by US adventurers, who ghosted across the border into Saskatchewan and southern Alberta, an area whose reputation for drunken lawlessness soon earned it the name "Whoop-up Country."

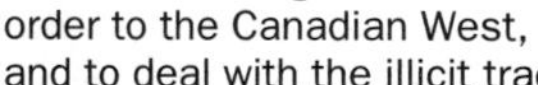

Cypress Hills The whiskey traders brought their wares north in fall, established themselves in a network of log stockades, and then returned south in the spring with furs and hides bartered from the natives. Events at two such stockades, Farwell's and Solomon's—events that became known as the Cypress Hills Massacre—were to be the making of the fledgling force. The precise circumstances of the massacre remain obscure to this day. A gang of Montana wolf-hunters, it appears, was holed up in the stockades. One evening the gang members took against a group of Assiniboine natives, who (they believed) had stolen their horses (the horses were probably taken by the Cree, the Assiniboine's rivals). Addled by drink, the hunters attacked an Assiniboine encampment. Five women were raped and 21 natives killed.

Enforcement When news of the massacre reached Ottawa, Prime Minister Macdonald set about accelerating recruitment of the NWMP. A hastily assembled troop was then dispatched to Fort Whoop-up, the most notorious of

the whiskey stockades (located near present-day Lethbridge). En route, however, the detachment managed to get lost (they had been crossing almost uncharted territory). The traders fled, though honor was restored when the men were eventually arrested. Despite the fact that they were subsequently released for lack of evidence, their arrest earned the respect of the natives, and was instrumental in contributing to the NWMP's long-standing reputation for even-handedness (see panel opposite).

Consolidation By October 1874, the original NWMP troop, exhausted after its epic trek, had established a camp at Fort Macleod. This in turn became the first NWMP post in the Canadian West (taking its name from Colonel James Macleod, its first commander). The post effectively put an end to the whiskey trade, and began a period of consolidation as similar forts were established across the region. Fort Edmonton was built in 1874, Fort Calgary a year later. Men from the latter patrolled 400km (240 miles) north to Edmonton and 161km (100 miles) south to Fort Macleod (giving some idea of the task involved). In 1875 a post was built at Fort Walsh (see page 147), close to Battle Creek, scene of the Cypress Hills Massacre, and one of the most famous meetings in Mountie history (see panel opposite).

The Mounties As time went by, the NWMP increasingly became an arm of the federal government. They extended the reach and authority of the new Confederation, while enforcing its rule as much through the dignity of office as through the force of arms. Their duties were extremely varied, particularly in remote areas, where they were magistrates, law enforcement officers, postmen, even collators of crop reports. In 1920 their country-wide role was recognized when the NWMP was renamed the Royal Canadian Mounted Police—or "Mounties" for short.

ROT-GUT HOOCH
The US whiskey traded with natives to such disastrous effect was notorious for its contents, which in addition to grain spirit were likely to include dye, ink, gunpowder, red peppers, molasses, Jamaican ginger, strychnine and chewing tobacco.

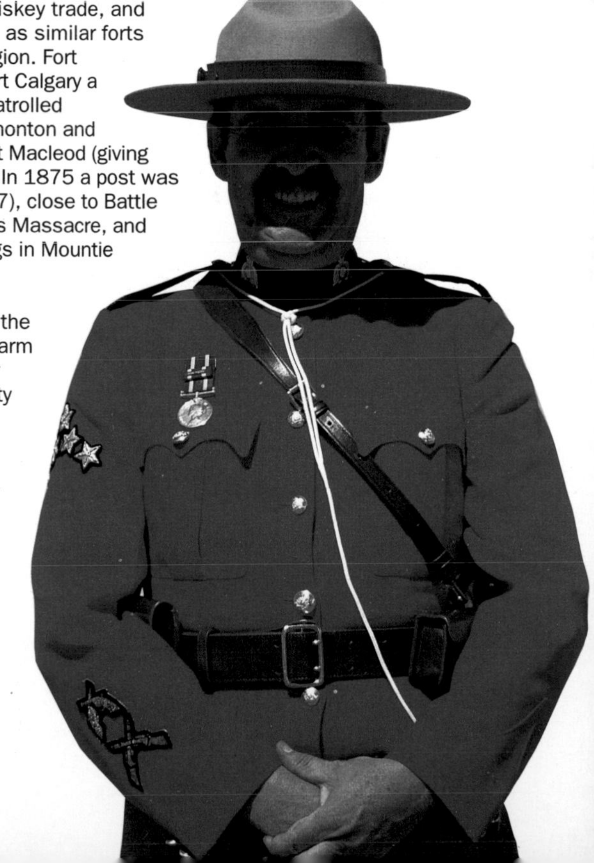

PAINTER'S FAVORITE
The Group of Seven painter A. Y. Jackson (see pages 176–177) was so impressed by the rugged Badlands scenery of the Red Deer River that he called it "the most paintable valley in western Canada."

THEN AND NOW
Although the Alberta Badlands now are bare and almost bone-dry, their appearance 75 million years ago, when countless dinosaurs roamed the region, was one of semi-tropical marshland.The area was a vast inland lake of balmy temperatures and lush vegetation akin to the present-day Florida Everglades.

Lush and verdant in prehistoric times, the landscape around the old mining town of Drumheller is now grey and gloomy

►►► Drumheller and the Badlands *134B1*

The old mining town of Drumheller sits in the Red Deer River valley, the heart of the Alberta Badlands, an extraordinary lunar landscape of bare-rock gorges, windblown bluffs and rambling sun-beaten hills. The town itself amounts to little, but it provides a focus for the Royal Tyrrell Museum of Palaeontology, one of the world's finest museums of natural history. It is also a good point to pick up the so-called Dinosaur Trail, a circular 51km (30-mile) road tour linking several historic sights and numerous viewpoints. Just 140km (87 miles) east of Calgary, the region makes a good day-trip away from the city, though you may need longer if you are visiting Dinosaur Provincial Park (174km/108 miles from Drumheller), home to the best of the Badlands scenery and the source of many of the Tyrrell Museum's dinosaur remains.

Drumheller► In one of Canada's most startling changes of landscape, Alberta's dulcet grasslands suddenly drop away into a gloomy valley that conceals a mess of old mining detritus and the dark little town of Drumheller. If you are simply on the way to the Tyrrell Museum (see below) there is little point in stopping off (unless you need information on the region—see panel opposite), but if you do have an hour to spare here you may want to stop by the **Homestead Antique Museum**, a grab-bag of 4,000 native artifacts and pioneer paraphernalia (off Highway 838, 1km (0.62 miles) northwest of Drumheller, tel:403/823–2600. *Open* Jul–end Aug, daily 9–8; mid-May–end Jun, Sep daily 9–5. *Admission: moderate*).

Royal Tyrrell Museum of Palaeontology►►► Well over half a million visitors a year come to admire this superlative museum, whose exhibits include over 800 fossils, 35 dinosaur skeletons and a huge quantity of superbly presented material on the geological and natural history associated with the dinosaur. Located 6km (4 miles)

Inside the award-winning Tyrrell Museum

northwest of Drumheller, it sits amid some of the baddest of the Badlands scenery, its sleek, modern building beautifully integrated with the surrounding landscape. Inside, the architecture is equally well matched to its purpose, the different levels carefully arranged to suggest the different layers of geological time. After state-of-the-art displays on the evolution of life on earth, plus a primeval garden that aims to replicate the vegetation of 350 million years ago, the museum climaxes with the great central hall of skeletons and life-size dinosaur replicas (*Open* mid-May to early Sep daily 9–9; mid-Sep to mid-Oct daily 10–5; late Oct–early May Tue–Sun 10–5. *Admission: moderate*).

The Dinosaur Trail▶▶ This clearly marked scenic drive initially cuts west from Drumheller along the Red Deer valley, following the line of the glacial melt waters that carved out its course across the Prairies. There are almost 30 recommended stop-offs en route. Make a special point of seeing: **Horsethief** and **Horseshoe canyons**, two viewpoints that look over deeply eroded gorges (the latter features trails around the petrified wood, fossilized oyster beds and dinosaur bones along the canyon floor); the **Hoodoos**, a collection of strange wind-carved rock spires topped with mushroom-like cones; the **Midland Provincial Park**, home to an interpretative center and several trails that explore the region's mining heritage; and the **Atlas Coal Mine** "tipple," a beautiful piece of industrial archeology once used to sort and grade ore.

Dinosaur Provincial Park▶▶ This park, a United Nations Heritage Site, was created in 1955 to curb the enthusiasm of dinosaur diggers (over 300 complete dinosaur skeletons have been found here). Much of the zone is out of bounds, but short, self-guided trails start from the **Field Station of the Tyrrell Museum** (44km/26 miles northwest of Brooks, tel: 403/378–4344. *Open* late May–early Oct daily; Nov–late May Mon–Fri), which also offers bus tours of the park (May–end Oct daily. *Admission: moderate*).

INFORMATION
Drumheller's Chamber of Commerce information point is at 2nd Street West and Riverside Drive (tel: 403/823–1331).

DINOSAUR RUSH
In 1884 the geologist J. B. Tyrrell (after whom the Royal Tyrrell Museum is named) accidentally stumbled across some dinosaur bones amid the scrub and sagebrush of the Alberta Badlands. His discovery unleashed the "great Canadian dinosaur rush," as thousands of genuine and not-so-genuine geologists converged on the Badlands to hack skeletons from the ground. Many of their discoveries are now displayed in museum collections around the world.

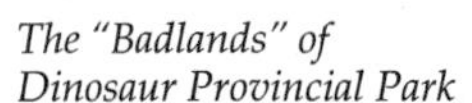

The "Badlands" of Dinosaur Provincial Park

INFORMATION
The Edmonton Tourism Information Centre is downtown in the Shaw Conference Centre at 104, 97th Street and Jasper Avenue (tel: 780/496–8400 or 800/463–4667, www.tourism.ede.org).

ARRIVING
Nonstop international flights from the US and Europe, and most longer domestic flights, use Edmonton's International Airport (tel: 780/890–8382, www.edmonton airports.com), located 32km (20 miles) south of downtown off Highway 2. The Airport Sky Shuttle bus (tel:780/465–8515) runs to the city center, West Edmonton Mall or the university regularly. VIA Rail train services (tel: 780/422–6032, viarail.ca) run to Edmonton from Vancouver, Jasper, Winnipeg and other points east. The station is located north of downtown at 12360 121st Street. Greyhound buses serve Edmonton from many towns and cities (tel: 780/413–8747, www.greyhound.ca). The bus terminal is at 103rd Street and 103rd Avenue.

RAW
"It was the essential rawness of Edmonton that made it seem to conform more to my idea of a new Siberian city than anything else I had seen in Canada... Exciting, perhaps even colourful, but tough; a city I would not like to be unemployed in..."—Alistair Horne, *Canada and the Canadians* (1961)

▶ Edmonton *134B2*

Alberta's provincial capital has just about everything a city needs, from theaters and green space to airports and modern malls. Yet somehow it does little to entice the casual visitor. This may have something to do with its position, which guarantees grim winter climates or its air of being an unfinished frontier town. Only downtown is it more appealing, thanks to the more modern high-rise blocks built with oil money. Unfortunately, the city's most interesting sights are away from the center, including, for many people, the crowd-pulling West Edmonton Mall, the world's largest shopping center.

Downtown▶▶ The ranks of the city's granite and steel skyscrapers fill a tight grid centered on Jasper Avenue, the main street. Bars, shops and restaurants abound here, but sights for visitors are comparatively few. On the third floor of the municipal police station at 9620-103A Street you might take in the often strange exhibits of the **Edmonton Police Museum** (*Open* Mon–Sat 9–3. *Admission free*).

Other downtown sights cluster around the Civic Centre and Sir Winston Churchill Square. Chief of these are the Citadel Theatre, Canada's largest theater complex, and the **Edmonton Art Gallery▶** (*Open* Mon–Wed 10.30–5, Thu–Fri 10.30–8, Sat–Sun, public hols 11–5. *Admission: moderate*), which houses a modern Canadian collection and touring exhibitions. Slightly further afield rises the **Alberta Legislative Building**, a grand structure built in 1912 over the site of the original Fort Edmonton (97th Avenue and 107th Street. Guided tours; tel: 780/427–7362 for hours. *Admission free*).

City environs Edmonton's rather tired **Provincial Museum of Alberta▶** (12845 102nd Avenue, tel: 780/453–9100. *Open* daily 9–5. *Admission: moderate*), should by rights be Alberta's premier museum, but it does not fare well in comparison with Calgary's superior Glenbow Museum (see pages 140–141). It offers only an adequate introduction to the province, and it suffers from being located well out in the western suburbs. To get there take westbound bus 1 or 120 from Jasper Avenue. The **Muttart Conservatory▶▶**, a series of four glass pyramids overlooking the North Saskatchewan River just south of downtown, is a more inspiring building. Three of its pyramids are glorified greenhouses, replicating tropical, temperate and arid habitats; the fourth, a "Show Pavilion," is reserved for special exhibitions (98th Avenue-96a Street. *Open* Mon–Fri 9–6, Sat–Sun 11–6. *Admission: moderate*). Leave time for **Fort Edmonton Park** (*Open* mid-May–end Sep daily, tel: 780/496–8787 for hours. *Admission: expensive*). Set in the ravine of the North Saskatchewan River, this park is a recreation of the city's history. There is an evocative reconstruction of the original Hudson's Bay Company trading post of 1846, and of Jasper Avenue as it looked in 1885, 1905 and 1920. Also excellent is the modern **Edmonton Space and Science Centre ▶▶** in Coronation Park (11211–142nd Street. *Open* Tue–Sun 10–8.30. *Admission: moderate)* with numerous space-and-science related displays.

West Edmonton Mall Few other cities can boast a shopping mall as a tourist attraction, but then no other city in

Reflective Edmonton at night

the world has one to rival the gargantuan West Edmonton Mall (170th Street and 87th Avenue). Some 9 million visitors a year come, most to gawk rather than shop, as the stores are not that exciting. What visitors find is a city within a city, built at a cost of over $1 billion, and stretched over an area the equivalent of 115 football fields. With over 800 stores, 110 restaurants, 19 cinemas and 11 department stores, the complex houses the world's largest indoor amusement park, an 18-hole miniature golf course, a chapel, a bingo hall and an indoor lake with four working submarines. There is also a full-sized replica of Columbus's ship, the *Santa Maria*. The best of the attractions is the huge **World Waterpark** (*Open* all year, Mon–Thu 12–7, Fri, Sat 10–8, Sun 11–6. *Admission: expensive*), a great collection of indoor swimming pools, waterslides and wave pools.

Part of Winnipeg's rejuvenated "Forks" district

ARRIVING
Winnipeg International Airport (tel: 204/987–9400, www.waa.ca) is 6.5km (4 miles) west of downtown, to which it is linked by taxis and the regular Winnipeg Transit shuttle bus. Transcontinental VIA Rail trains and services to and from Churchill arrive at the train station (arrivals and departures, tel: 800/835–3037; reservations, tel: 800/561–8630) on Main Street and Broadway. The bus terminal is at Portage Avenue and Memorial Boulevard.

►► Winnipeg *135D1*

Cities more or less in the middle of nowhere have to make their own entertainment, which is precisely what the "Prairie capital" has done, compensating for its geographical isolation with a thriving cultural life and a healthily diversified economy.

Long known as the "point where the West begins," Winnipeg began life as a Hudson's Bay Company franchise (the company still has its headquarters here), and its pivotal position was reinforced when the rival North West Company established a post here in 1738. Thomas Douglas, the Earl of Selkirk, bought land nearby in 1821, using it to settle Scots who had been forced from their homes by the Highland Clearances. In 1873 Winnipeg was declared a city, and in 1886 it opened its arms to a flood of settlers who came in on the transcontinental railway. Today it is the largest place in Canada between Toronto and Calgary.

For information on the city, visit Winnipeg Tourism, which has an office at 279 Portage Avenue (tel: 204/943–1970, www.tourism.winnipeg.mb.ca), though the best overall information office is the Explore Manitoba Centre in the Forks district (tel: 204/945–3777).

Downtown►► Winnipeg's sightseeing attractions are clustered in several areas: downtown; the "Forks" (to its east); the Centennial Centre and Ukrainian Cultural Centre (to the north); and St. Boniface (an area across the Red River to the east). Downtown offers **Winnipeg Square**, heart of the shopping district, and the **Winnipeg Commodities Exchange** (360 Main Street. *Open* Mon–Fri 9.30–1.15. *Admission free*), where you can see dealers frantically buying and selling wheat, oil and other commodities. It also offers the **Winnipeg Art Gallery►►** (300 Memorial Boulevard and Portage, tel: 204/786–6641.

Open Tue, Thu–Sun 11–5, Wed 11–9. *Admission: moderate*), home to the world's largest collection of Inuit art, and the **Exchange District and Market Square▶▶**, a lively area of bars, restaurants and nightlife in the city's old 19th-century heart.

The Forks▶▶▶ Once a semi-derelict area of warehouses and marshaling yards, the revitalized "Forks" district has been transformed over the last few years into an area that now attracts throngs of enthusiastic visitors.

A visit to the **Explore Manitoba Centre** will give you ideas for exploring the area. The Centre also offers several exhibits on the province as a whole. The site's historical nexus is **The Forks National Historic Site**, which is dotted with plaques outlining the history of the natives and fur traders who first inhabited the "fork" of the Red and Assiniboine rivers.

Other restored railroad buildings house the **Forks Market** and Johnston Terminal, both buzzing areas of bars, street musicians, stores and restaurants. Another contains the dazzling **Manitoba Children's Museum▶▶▶** (*Open* Jun–end Aug Sun–Wed 9.30–4.30, Thu–Sat 9.30–8; Sep–end May Mon–Wed 9.30–5, Thu, Fri 9.30–8, Sat 10–8, Sun 10–5. *Admission: moderate*), whose eclectic mixture of historical, scientific and natural displays should also appeal to adults.

The Centennial Centre Built in 1967 as part of Canada's centennial celebrations, this magnificent complex contains the Manitoba Planetarium and the superb **Manitoba Museum▶▶▶**, whose displays explore both the historical and the geographical aspects of the province. (190 Rupert Avenue, tel: 204/956–2830. *Open* daily 10–5. *Admission: expensive*.) Pride of place goes to the *Nonsuch*, a replica of the ship whose voyage from England in 1668 led to the formation of the Hudson's Bay Company (see pages 168–169). One wing of the museum, which was restored in 1999, houses the Hudson's Bay Company Collection, a hoard of 6,000 artifacts amassed during the company's history and donated to the province by the company's directors. Other eye-catching exhibits include the polar bear diorama in the Arctic–Subarctic Gallery and the full-sized Assiniboine tepee in the Grasslands Gallery. The Planetarium, which offers good, if rather predictable, shows, should be seen in conjunction with the tactile "Touch the Universe" gallery located downstairs, a modern approach, exciting high-tech collection of hands-on scientific displays and exhibits.

ST. BONIFACE

This area of the city was the heart of French Canadian and Métis culture in the early 18th century. Incorporated into Winnipeg just 20 years ago, a quarter of its population still speak French as their first language. Visit St. Boniface Cathedral (avenue de la Cathedral and avenue Tache), rebuilt after a fire in 1968, and the fascinating St. Boniface Museum, a collection of Métis-related artifacts housed in Winnipeg's oldest building (494 avenue Tache. *Open* mid-May to mid-Sep Mon–Fri 9–5, Sat–Sun 10–5; late Sep–early May daily 12–4. *Admission: inexpensive*).

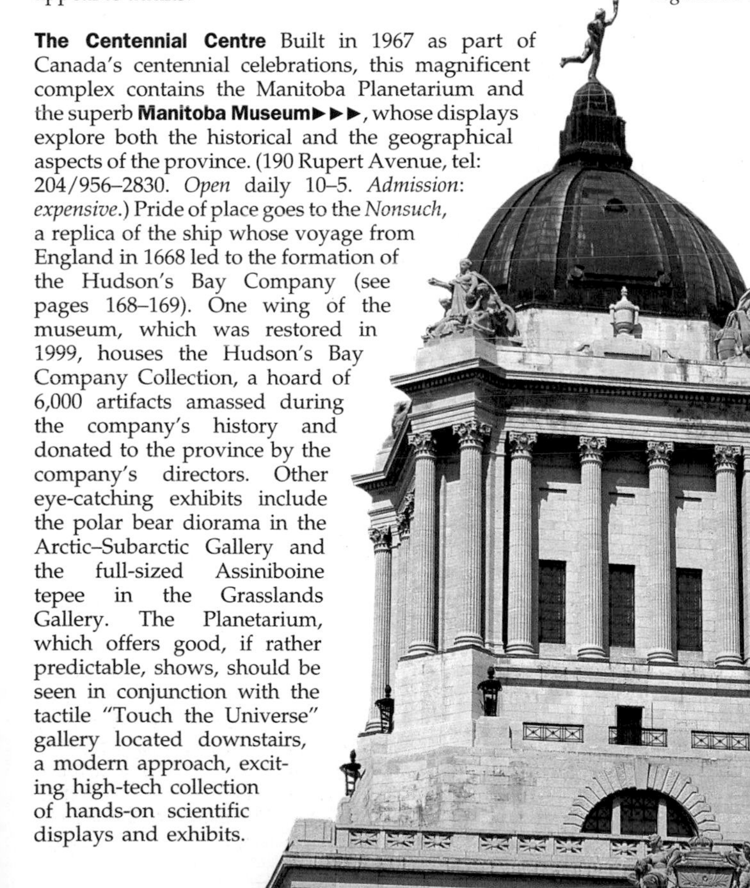

Winnipeg's redoubtable Legislative Building

Among the multi-ethnic mosaic of pioneers who settled the Prairies were three distinct religious groups largely from Russia and eastern Europe. Each of these groups formed strict and fiercely self-contained communities whose way of life, like that of the Amish in the United States, has remained unchanged for centuries.

A Hutterite of the Ewelme colony leads his geese to be fed

IN THE FAMILY
Some 6,000 Hutterites live in central Alberta. So closed are their communities that many are able to trace their families back almost 500 years.

REJECTION
The Hutterite rejection of the modern world is almost total. They refuse to draw pensions or unemployment benefits, and refuse to hold any public office or vote in elections. Their only contact with the outside world is when buying farm supplies, or when acquiring land, something which occasionally causes friction with those living around them.

The Hutterites Of the Prairies' three main religious communities, none has retreated so steadfastly from the modern world, or remained as true to its early utopian ideals, as the Hutterites. An Anabaptist sect founded in the 16th century, the group originated in Moravia and the Tyrol, taking their name from their first leader, Jacob Hutter. After drifting across eastern Europe to Russia, they emigrated to South Dakota in 1870, then north into Canada between 1918 and 1922. The move to Canada was prompted by the Hutterites' pacifist principles, which left them compromised by the threat of military service in the United States.

Today, each Hutterite community consists of around 100 people (about ten families). New offshoot communities are formed when the population reaches about 150. The head of the community is an elected lay preacher, while each household has an elected head, or *wirt*. Work is performed cooperatively, and tasks are rotated by the *wirt* and assigned according to skill and ability. Property is held communally, each family living in simple and almost identical homes. Meals are taken communally, with men and women at separate tables according to age. Children are cared for in nurseries from the age of 18 weeks, and from the age of two are educated for six hours a day in *klein-schul*, or nursery school. Hutterite language is a dialect of German, which is still the language of their church services and provides a strong link with their distant past. Similar anachronisms are reflected in their clothes: dark suits and broad-brimmed hats for the men (who wear beards if they are married); ankle-length dresses and polka-dot headscarfs for the women.

The Mennonites The Mennonites' roots lie in the Netherlands, where the sect was founded at the

Many modern-day Mennonites still follow a way of life similar to their 19th-century ancestors

beginning of the 16th century by Menno Simons. Like many Protestants, they were heavily persecuted for their religious ideals and pacifist convictions. Two arms of the sect now live in Canada, the result of an early split in the movement between the more liberal *Untere*, who came to Manitoba by way of Russia, and the more fundamentalist *Ammanites*, or Pennsylvania Dutch, who fled first to the US and then to Ontario (settling around Kitchener-Waterloo). Today the sect is far larger than the Hutterites, around 175,000. Around 65,000 live in Manitoba, 45,000 in Ontario and the rest in other provinces. Those in Manitoba are more fully integrated into Canadian life, though all are still pacifist. Many of Ontario's Ammanites, by contrast, still spurn cars, telephones and modern machinery, and can often be seen in horse-drawn carts wearing traditional dark costumes.

The Doukhobors The Doukhobors derive not from the Protestant tradition, but from the Russian Orthodox church, whose priests and hierarchical structure they rejected during the 18th century. Their pacifist and communal ideals soon invited official persecution, prompting them to emigrate to Saskatchewan in the 1890s under their leader, Peter Verigin. Unlike other sects, the Doukhobors ran into problems with officialdom in their adopted country. The Canadians insisted that all communal homesteads be declared private property, a demand that led to bitter divisions between those who accepted the government's proposals and those who stuck to their collectivist ideals. The latter went as far as to destroy their "property," even burning their clothes in a show of disdain for worldly goods. Under Verigin they also fled Saskatchewan for British Columbia, leaving behind a more moderate community, who became skilled and prosperous farmers.Today there are around 38,000 Doukhobors in Canada, with 30,000–32,000 in BC.

Cooperation and community living are the heart of Doukhobor society

VILLAGE LIFE

You can experience a taste of Mennonite life at the Mennonite Heritage Village, a period reconstruction with an interpretive center and museum (61km/38 miles southeast of Winnipeg near Steinbach, tel: 204/326–9661 *Open* Jul–end Aug Mon–Sat 10–7, Sun 12–6; May, Jun, Sep Mon–Sat 10–5, Sun 12–5; Oct–end Apr Mon–Fri 10–4. *Admission: moderate*). Genuine Mennonites still live in the area, though few now wear the traditional clothes or work on the old communal farms.

COMMUNITIES

Most Hutterite communities are in central Alberta. You can see their farms around Stettler and Drumheller, and in the Battle and Red Deer river valleys. Hutterites occasionally enter local villages, riding horse-drawn buggies and dressed om their old-fashioned garb.

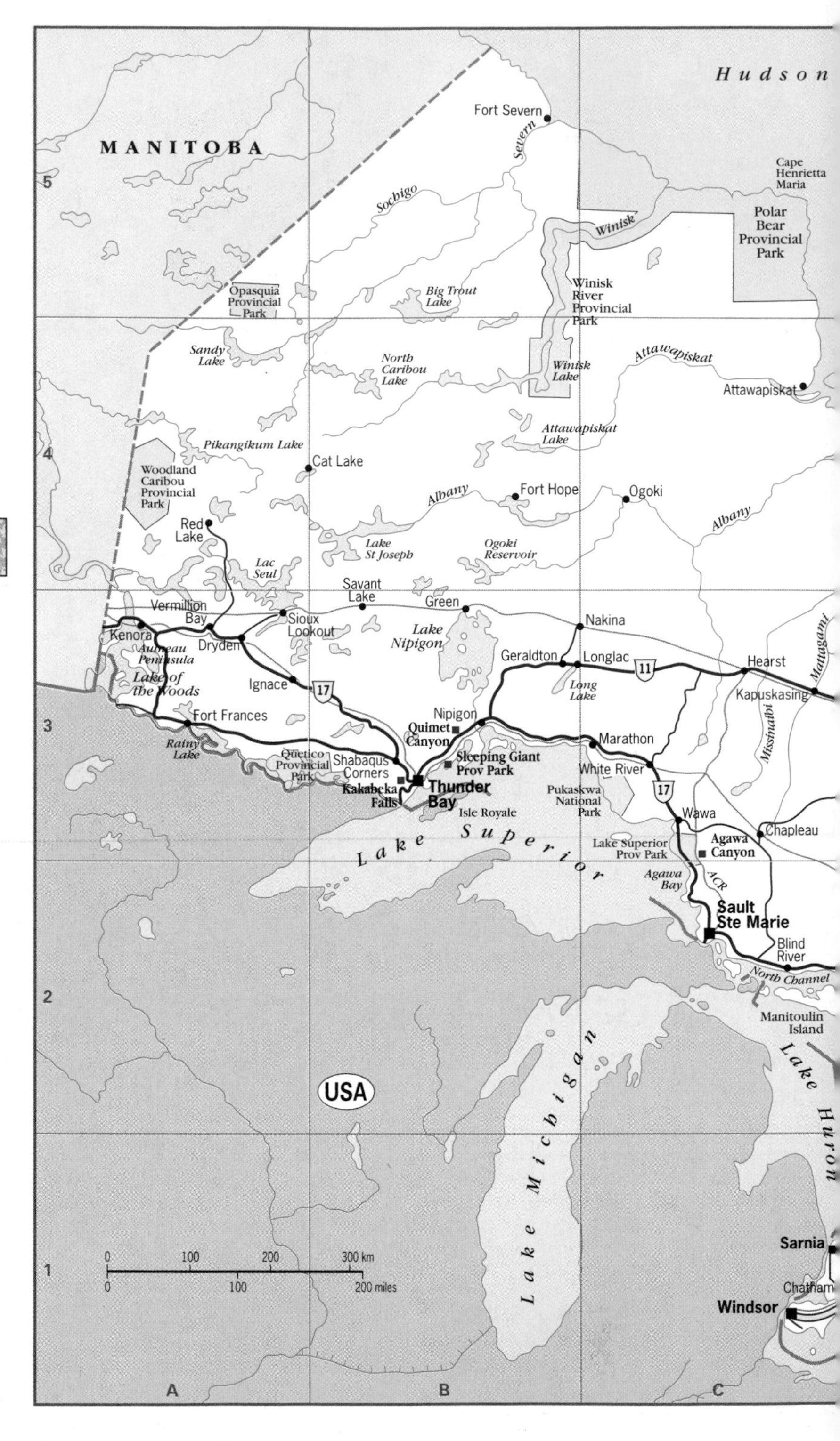
Hudson
MANITOBA
Fort Severn
Severn
Sachigo
Cape Henrietta Maria
Polar Bear Provincial Park
Winisk
Opasquia Provincial Park
Big Trout Lake
Winisk River Provincial Park
Sandy Lake
North Caribou Lake
Winisk Lake
Attawapiskat
Attawapiskat
Attawapiskat Lake
Pikangikum Lake
Cat Lake
Woodland Caribou Provincial Park
Albany
Fort Hope
Ogoki
Albany
Red Lake
Lake St Joseph
Ogoki Reservoir
Lac Seul
Savant Lake
Green
Vermillion Bay
Sioux Lookout
Lake Nipigon
Nakina
Kenora
Aulneau Peninsula
Dryden
Geraldton
Longlac
11
Hearst
Mattagami
Lake of the Woods
Ignace
17
Long Lake
Kapuskasing
Fort Frances
Nipigon
Quimet Canyon
Missinaibi
Rainy Lake
Quetico Provincial Park
Shabaqus Corners
Sleeping Giant Prov Park
Marathon
White River
17
Kakabeka Falls
Thunder Bay
Pukaskwa National Park
Isle Royale
Wawa
Chapleau
Lake Superior
Lake Superior Prov Park
Agawa Canyon
Agawa Bay
ACR
Sault Ste Marie
Blind River
North Channel
Manitoulin Island
Lake Huron
USA
Lake Michigan
Sarnia
Chatham
Windsor
0 100 200 300 km
0 100 200 miles
A
B
C
1
2
3
4
5

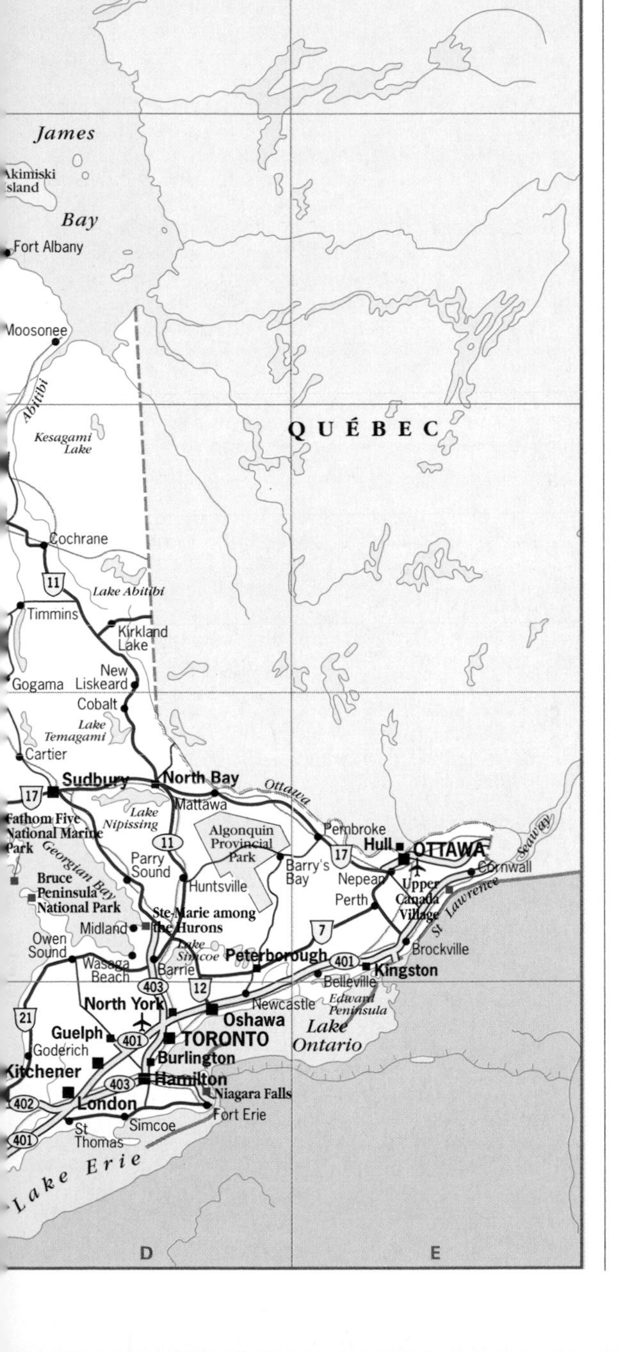
Bay
James
Akimiski
Island
Bay
Fort Albany
Moosonee
Abitibi
Kesagami
Lake
QUÉBEC
Cochrane
11
Lake Abitibi
Timmins
Kirkland
Lake
New
Liskeard
Gogama
Cobalt
Lake
Temagami
Cartier
Sudbury
North Bay
Ottawa
17
Mattawa
Fathom Five
National Marine
Park
Lake
Nipissing
Algonquin
Provincial
Park
Pembroke
Hull
OTTAWA
17
11
Parry
Sound
Barry's
Bay
Georgian Bay
Nepean
Cornwall
Seaway
Bruce
Peninsula
National Park
Huntsville
Upper
Canada
Village
St Lawrence
Perth
Ste-Marie among
the Hurons
Midland
7
Owen
Sound
Wasaga
Beach
Lake
Simcoe
Barrie
Peterborough
401
Kingston
Brockville
403
12
Belleville
North York
Newcastle
Edward
Peninsula
21
Oshawa
Lake
Ontario
Guelph
401
TORONTO
Goderich
Burlington
Kitchener
403
Hamilton
Niagara Falls
402
London
Fort Erie
St
Thomas
Simcoe
401
Lake Erie
D
E

Ontario

▶▶▶ REGION HIGHLIGHTS

BEFORE YOU GO
For information on Ontario call 800/ONTARIO or visit www.ontariotravel.net or www.tourism.gov.on.ca.

BUS AND TRAIN
Voyageur (tel:800/668–4438, www.voyageur.com) provides express bus services in Ontario between Ottawa, Montréal and Toronto. The following rail services operate: Ottawa–Kingston; Cochrane–Moosonee; Sault Ste Marie–Hearst; Toronto–Kingston–Montréal; Toronto–Ottawa; Toronto–Sudbury–Winnipeg–Vancouver. Amtrack connections can be made to Chicago and Buffalo from Toronto.

SECOND LARGEST PROVINCE Ontario is Canada's political, industrial and cultural heartland, its second-largest province, and one of its richest and most populous regions. Wealth and well-being have flowed from its abundant natural resources, rich agricultural land and a strategic position relative to the US that has guaranteed its continued economic growth and national pre-eminence. Ottawa is the country's federal capital, and Toronto is a city in North America's first rank. But while cultural facilities—museums in particular—in these and other cities are unequaled, Ontario's urban spaces lack the grace, and its landscapes the splendor, of those in other provinces.

EXPLORING The region divides neatly into north and south around a line that runs from the Ottawa River to Georgian Bay. North of this line lies a sparsely populated wilderness, a rugged landscape of lake-speckled hills beloved of canoeists and fishermen. Most other visitors confine themselves to the south, beginning trips in Toronto—location of Canada's main hub airport—or following the road and rail routes from western Canada along the shores of lakes Huron and Superior. Toronto forms a platform from which you can visit Niagara Falls, the region's biggest draw, and acts as a staging post for itineraries to Ottawa, Montréal and Québec City. It also lies within striking distance of the province's best scenery, notably the area around Georgian Bay and Lake Huron's Bruce Peninsula, whose towns make pleasant places to stay.

ABORIGINAL PEOPLES Ontario's climate and geography have always determined its settlement patterns. Before the arrival of the Europeans, the colder, more inhospitable north was the home of hardy tribes leading a semi-nomadic existence in the boreal forest. The south, warmer and more fertile, was the domain of the Iroquois and Algonquin, who led a more prosperous and sedentary life (see pages 184–185). Today, their example has been followed by most of Ontario's population, 85 percent of which is concentrated along the province's southern margins, a region that accounts for just 15 percent of its surface area.

BRITAIN AND FRANCE It was with the Iroquois that French explorers and traders first made (largely friendly) contact at the beginning of the 17th century. It was among them, too, that French missionaries first got to work, operating from a base at Sainte-Marie among the Hurons close to modern-day Toronto. This settlement was also to be home to many of the region's newcomers for several years (see page 163). Mission work was to prove a thankless task, however, for in 1650 Sainte-Marie was destroyed and its priests slaughtered. This setback was offset by expansion elsewhere, particularly in the south, where French influence grew apace. In the north, by contrast, it was the British who made the running. Their growing authority was symbolized by the Hudson's Bay Company, created in 1670 (see pages 168–169), whose trading post at Moosonee (established in 1673) is the province's oldest official settlement. Trading activity by either side, however, was no substitute for colonization, and, at the fall of New France in 1759 (see page 33), the number of Europeans across the region's huge expanse was probably little more than 400.

REVOLUTION AND INVASION Numbers of settlers began to increase significantly only following the American Revolution (1775–1783), when an estimated 80,000 of the 1.25 million people who remained loyal to the British Crown swarmed across the border. Some 10,000 of these settled in present-day Ontario. In 1791 the region was formally designated as Upper Canada, to distinguish it from the largely French-speaking Lower Canada—modern-day Québec. Niagara-on-the-Lake was made the capital, later replaced by Toronto.

The US shaped Ontarian history again in 1812, when it sought to invade Canada, encouraged by Britain's apparent preoccupation with Napoleon in Europe. Conquest proved far from easy, and bitter fighting took place around Niagara and on the Great Lakes. After further sporadic battles the Americans were repulsed.

IMMIGRATION Shaken by the invasion attempt, and fearing a repeat performance, Britain sought to bolster Upper Canada through a policy of massive immigration. The offer of free land, coupled with hard economic times at home, saw around 1.5 million Britons emigrate to Upper Canada in the 20 years to 1840. Fresh faces brought fresh ideas, particularly in the political sphere, where the entrenched power of the British governor and his clique—the so-called "Family Compact," named for its closeness—was challenged in 1837 by an armed uprising under William Lyon Mackenzie. Although the revolt was quickly put down, it prompted the British government to reform regional politics. It also spurred the move toward Confederation, led by the Ontarian politician Macdonald and his Québécois counterpart, Cartier. Union was achieved in 1867, and Upper Canada became the province of Ontario.

LAKE LEGACY
Ontario takes its name from an Iroquois native word which has been variously interpreted as meaning "beautiful water," "shining waters" (an allusion to the province's countless lakes), and "rocks standing high beside the water" (perhaps a reference to Niagara Falls).

MINERAL WEALTH
The ancient rocks of the Canadian Shield (see page 12) have yielded immeasurable mineral wealth. Sudbury Basin contains the world's largest deposits of nickel (discovered in 1883); Cobalt has large reserves of silver (discovered in 1903); and the province is also a major producer of gold, copper, iron, zinc and cobalt.

Some 12 million people a year visit Niagara Falls

The red and gold colors of fall in Georgian Bay

INLAND SEAS
The Great Lakes are huge. Rudyard Kipling wrote of them that "Fresh water has no right or call to dip over the horizon, pulling down and pushing up the hulls of big steamers; no right to tread the slow deep-sea dance-step between wrinkled cliffs; nor to roar in on weed and sand beaches between vast headlands that run out for leagues into haze and sea-fog."—*Letters of Travel* (1907)

EERIE AND SOULLESS
"There is something ominous and unnatural about these great lakes... The sea, very properly, will not be allowed in heaven. It has no soul. It is cruel, treacherous, what you will... But these monstrous lakes, which ape the ocean, are not proper to fresh water, or to salt. They have souls, perceptibly and wicked ones."—Rupert Brooke, *Letters from America, 1913* (1916)

▶▶ Lake Huron *158C2*

Bruce Peninsula▶▶ Dividing—and almost cutting off—Georgian Bay from the rest of Lake Huron, the Bruce Peninsula contains a pair of outstanding national parks and a string of interesting little towns and villages. The first of these is sleepy **Owen Sound▶**, visited for the **Tom Thomson Memorial Art Gallery** (*Open* Jul–end Aug Mon–Sat 10–5 (Wed until 9), Sun 12–5; Sep–end Jun Tue–Fri 11–5 (Wed until 9), Sat–Sun 12–5. *Admission: donation*), a modest artistic shrine to the founding father of the Group of Seven (see pages 176–177). Further north lies **Tobermory▶**, a quiet fishing village gathered around Little Tub and Big Tub, its twin harbors. The former houses the National Park Visitor Centre, an essential port of call if you are planning a trip to the peninsula's two parks: the **Fathom Five Marine National Park**, a marine park that embraces 19 uninhabited islands; or the more popular **Bruce Peninsula National Park▶▶**, a patchwork of cliff, beach and forest scenery.

Georgian Bay▶▶▶ So large as to be almost a lake within a lake, Georgian Bay lies at the heart of Lake Huron's sight-seeing temptations. Sainte-Marie among the Hurons is the principal highlight (see opposite), but towns and resorts throughout its vast arc attract locals and visitors alike. The busiest of these is **Wasaga Beach▶**, whose big draw is its 8-mile stretch of sandy white beach. To the east sits the pretty town of **Penetanguishene▶▶**—"place of the rolling white sands"—a former mission station founded in 1639 and abandoned at the same time as Sainte-Marie. Some 7 miles to the northwest lies Awenda Provincial Park, a small paradise of forest, rocky beaches and easy hiking trails. **Midland**, a semi-industrial town down on its luck, is used principally as a base for Sainte-Marie, but is worth an hour for the **Huronia Museum and Huronia Native Village** (Little Lake Park, near King Street, tel: 705/526–2844. *Open* Apr–mid-Oct daily 9–1; mid-Oct–end Mar Mon–Fri 9–5. *Admission: moderate*), both of which explore the history and culture of Georgian Bay's Huron native peoples.

Goderich▶▶ Goderich is the nicest of the generally nondescript towns that are strung out along Lake Huron's eastern shores. Located on a bluff above the lake, it formed the terminus of the Huron Road, a highway built at the beginning of the 19th century to encourage emigration to the area. Elegant, and mazed with tree-lined boulevards, the town is a buzzing summer resort, and is home to the **Huron County Museum**, a collection of pioneer memorabilia from the days of early settlement and the development of Huron County (110 North Street. *Open* Mon–Sat 10–4.30, Sun 1–4.30. *Admission: moderate*); and the fascinating **Huron Historical Jail▶▶**, a bizarre, 150-year-old prison and courthouse (181 Victoria Street. *Open* May–end Dec daily 10–4.30; Jan–end Apr by appointment, tel: 519/524–6971. *Admission: moderate*).

Sainte-Marie among the Hurons▶▶▶ Lying 5km (3 miles) east of Midland on Highway 12, Sainte-Marie among the Hurons (tel: 705/526–7838. *Open* May 21–Oct 10 daily 10–5; May 2–20, Oct 11–28 Mon–Fri 10–5. *Admission: expensive*) is an immaculate reconstruction of the fortified mission that was established among Huron natives by the Jesuits in 1639. Although it was inhabited for only a decade, the settlement contained an estimated 20 percent of all Europeans living in New France up to 1648 (see page 30). Attacks from hostile Iroquois tribes, and the massacre of several priests, brought about its collapse (see panel), a demise hastened by the outbreak of European-imported diseases among the Huron converts.

Before seeing the site, visit the excellent **reception center** and **museum**, which trace the story of the mission. Then move on to the **mission** itself, organized along the lines of a European monastery. Priests and Europeans occupied one section, native converts another. Guides and helpers in costume are on hand to spice up your visit.

TOURIST OFFICES

Goderich 91 Hamilton Street, tel: 519/524–6600, www.town.goderich.on.ca; *Midland* King Street, tel: 705/526–7884, www.southerngeorgianbay.on.com; *Wasaga Beach* Area 1, 550 River Road West, tel:705/429–2247, www.wasagainfo.com.

STICKY END

Five missionaries were martyred by the Iroquois at Sainte-Marie among the Hurons. One, Jean de Brébeuf, had a particularly nasty end. Stripped naked and beaten against a post, he was then covered in boiling water in a mock "baptism" and had a collar of heated axe heads clamped around his neck. Despite his torments the priest preached to his torturers until his tongue and lips were cut out. Impressed by Brébeuf's courage, the Iroquois ate his heart, hoping thereby to acquire some of the dead man's fortitude.

The reconstructed native village at Sainte-Marie among the Hurons

TOURIST OFFICES
Sault Ste-Marie Chamber of Commerce, 334 Bay Street (tel: 705/949–7152, www.ssmcoc.com); *Thunder Bay* Pagoda Building, Water Street and Red River Road (tel: 800/667–8386, www.thunder-bay.on.ca).

BUSY RIVER
The canal and locks at Sault Ste-Marie form one of the world's busiest waterways. Lakers transporting minerals, forestry products, grain, petroleum products and all sorts of other merchandise, pass up and down. In fact, if the locks were open all year (they freeze up in mid-winter), this waterway would handle more tonnage than the Panama Canal.

►► Lake Superior *158B3*

Lake Superior shoreline►► The best of Lake Superior's rugged beauty graces the 230km (140-mile) drive from Sault Ste Marie to Wawa, a tract of the Trans-Canada Highway that passes through predominantly desolate scenery before picking up the granite headlands, coves and bluffs of the lake's wild coastal landscapes. Highlights of the drive include the **Alona Bay** and **Agawa Bay viewpoints►►**, and the 84km (52-mile) section of the road through the **Lake Superior Provincial Park►►**. The park center (tel: 705/856-2284) is located alongside the highway 194km (120 miles) from Sault Ste-Marie.

Sault Ste-Marie►► Sault Ste-Marie—known colloquially as the "Soo"—sits on the St. Mary's River, the waterway that marks the border between Canada and the US and provides a link between lakes Huron and Superior. Its rapids (*sault* in French) were a gathering and trading place for Ojibwa natives from earliest times. In 1669 French Jesuits established a mission here, the germ of a European settlement, now one of Ontario's most important towns.

A pleasant downtown compensates for the eyesores of the town's industrial fringe; its main sight is the **Marie Ermantinger Old Stone House** (831 Queen Street East. *Open* mid-Apr–end Nov daily, tel: 705/759–5443 for hours. *Admission: moderate*). The Georgian-style building was built in 1814 by a prosperous fur trader for his wife, an Ojibwa princess, and is neatly juxtaposed with the **Sault Ste-Marie Museum** opposite, whose displays offer a more generalized account of the town's history (tel: 705/759–7278. *Open* Jun–mid-Oct Mon–Sat 10–6; mid-Oct–end May Tue–Sat 9.30–4.30. *Admission: donation*).

Down on the waterfront, a block to the south, is the museum ship **MS Norgoma** (tel: 705/946–4944 or 800/461–6020. *Tours:* Jun–end Sep daily 10–8. *Admission:*

A train on the Algoma Central Railway, heading toward the Agawa Canyon

Learning first-hand about 350 years of local history at Sault Ste-Marie

moderate). This was the last boat built for passenger service on the Great Lakes. Cruises through the **Soo locks and canals**▶▶—more exhilarating than they sound—depart from the adjacent Norgoma Dock (tel: 705/253–9850. *Open* May–end Oct, two to four trips daily, depending on the season. *Admission: expensive*). The waterway can also be admired from a platform at the southern end of Huron Road. However, most people come to town not for all this, but for the **Algoma Central Railway** (see panel).

Thunder Bay▶ Driving or flying across the Prairies is a sure way to appreciate the sheer scale of their wheat-growing potential. Another is to visit Thunder Bay, once a principal port for Prairie produce, whose colossal grain silos serve as immense monuments to the fertility of the grasslands to the west. Long a pivotal point of commerce (see panel), the modern port marks the westernmost extent of the great 3,200km (2,000-mile) St. Lawrence Seaway. Government policy, however, has been to favor Pacific ports, with the consequence that much of the town's trading pre-eminence has been lost. The result has been an economic downturn, and a rather desperate attempt to promote tourism to compensate. No one could pretend this is a pretty place but its gritty and cosmopolitan atmosphere has an appeal of sorts, and **boat trips**▶▶ round the harbor offer an insight into the port area.

Thunder Bay environs▶▶ Several diversions around Thunder Bay make up for the town's own lack of scenic distinction. Some 30km (20 miles) to the west on the Trans-Canada Highway lie the **Kakabeka Falls**▶▶, a 39m (132ft) cascade that plunges into a narrow gorge. Hydroelectric works sometimes shut the falls down to a trickle, so check with the Thunder Bay tourist office before setting off. Northeast of Thunder Bay is the startling **Quimet Canyon**▶▶, 100m (330ft) deep and 150m (500ft)wide, a huge rocky chasm whose icy and almost barren landscapes can be admired from two platforms perched above its sheer sides. Other impressive landscapes can be found in the **Sleeping Giant Provincial Park**▶, 51km (30 miles) east of Thunder Bay, and along the coastline of **Nipigon Bay**.

ALGOMA CENTRAL RAILWAY (ACR)

Sault Ste-Marie's 500km (300-mile) ACR was built in 1901 to link the town to the forestry resources further north. Today it is still a working railroad, but it is also used for excursions to view the lake, forests and ravines of the Algoma wilderness. The best of the three is the heavily subscribed Agawa Canyon Train Tour (Jun–mid-Oct, daily 8am. Make reservations well in advance), a 366km (227-mile) day trip with a two-hour break to explore the nature trails of the Agawa Canyon).
The Snow Train follows the same route in winter. In summer there is also a two-day Tour of the Line trip which requires an overnight stay in Hearst. For more details contact the ACR, 129 Bay Street, Sault Ste-Marie (tel: 705/946–7300 or 800/242–9287).

FUR EXCHANGE

In Thunder Bay's fur trading days (when it was called Fort William), the town was the key meeting point for Montréal traders, and trappers working for the North West Trading Company. Once a year the trappers would bring in a year's worth of furs from the west, handing them over to the merchants for transport through the Great Lakes to Canada's eastern ports. Fur-laden canoes would congregate here for the six-week "Great Rendezvous" each summer, a period of boisterous celebration re-created each July in Thunder Bay's festival at Old Fort William (16km/10 miles from downtown, tel: 807/473–2344. *Open* mid-Jun–early Sep daily 10–6; late May–mid Jun, early Sep–mid-Oct daily 10–5.

DISAPPOINTMENT
Niagara Falls was long one of North America's favorite honeymoon destinations. This led Oscar Wilde to remark that "Niagara Falls must be the second major disappointment of American married life."

HIGH POINT
Helicopter trips above the falls are operated by Niagara Helicopters Ltd, 3731 Victoria Avenue (tel: 905/357-5672, www.niagarahelicopters.com; very expensive).

NOT WHAT THEY WERE
Before the Niagara River was used for hydroelectric works, around 6 million liters (1.5 million gallons) of water a second cascaded over Niagara Falls. After a US–Canada agreement of 1951 on joint usage, just 3.1 million liters (750,000 gallons) were set aside for the summer spectacle and 1.4 million liters (350,000 gallons) in winter. As a result, the cutback of the falls has dropped from around 1m (3ft) a year to just 30cm (1ft).

SEDUCED BY SOUND
The first European to see Niagara Falls was a Jesuit missionary, Louis Hennepin, in 1678. While traveling on Lake Ontario, he became intrigued by a thunderous sound and followed the Niagara River upstream until he encountered the falls. The reduced flow of water over the falls (see above) means they can no longer be heard from the lake.

▶▶▶ Niagara Falls *159D1*

Niagara Falls are not the biggest or even the highest waterfalls in the world, but with 12 million visitors a year they are undoubtedly the most famous and most visited. The weight of tourist traffic invariably generates considerable commercial nastiness, particularly around the town of Niagara Falls (just north of the falls). While the area around the cascades remains relatively civilized, it can still be more pleasant to visit the area as a day-trip; there are good road and public transport links from most towns in southern Ontario. If you do want to stay, choose the elegant little town of **Niagara-on-the-Lake**, 26km (16 miles) downstream from the Falls.

History Niagara Falls consist of two sets of falls: the **American Falls** (300m/1,000ft wide and 50m/165ft high), so called because they are on the US side of the Niagara River; and the larger and better known **Horseshoe Falls** (800m/2,650ft wide and 50m/165ft high), which are on the Canadian side of the border. Both are young in geological terms, formed when the waters of Lake Erie chiseled out an exit channel toward Lake Ontario at the end of the last ice age. En route the new river fell over a chalk lip—part of the so-called Niagara Escarpment—creating the falls and carving a deep gorge in the process. Over the centuries the falls have cut back upriver, moving some 11km (7 miles) in the last 12,000 years (see panel). In time the water will cut back all the way to Buffalo on Lake Erie, and the falls as they appear today will cease to exist.

River view Having made your way to the falls from Niagara Falls town (home to the nearest bus and train stations), the easiest way to admire the spectacle is from the **Niagara Parkway River Road** (on the west bank of the Niagara River). Most of this area's walkways and viewing platforms are administered by the Niagara Parks Service, which ensures that the worst of the commercial excesses are kept at bay. The flower-filled **Queen Victoria Park** is especially lovely: manicured lawns and tree-lined walkways follow the river bank for about 1km (0.62 miles) to the Rainbow Bridge (a link across the river to the US).

Bird's eye view Two observation towers just off the road provide you with a bird's eye view of the falls: the **Konica Minolta Tower** (www.niagaratower.com. *Open* daily 9–9—later during summer months. *Admission: moderate*) and the slightly superior **Skylon Tower** (5200 Robinson and Murray Hill. *Open* Jun–end Aug, 8am–midnight; Sep–end May daily 11–9. *Admission: expensive*). These towers are among the best places for admiring the falls at night, when the waters are floodlit in alternating red, blue, yellow and white lights. A **helicopter trip** (see panel), the ultimate aerial view, takes you up the gorge below the falls, whisking over "The Whirlpool", where the river doglegs east, and the Whirlpool Rapids, before soaring over the lip of the falls themselves.

First-hand view For the closest possible view, visit **Table Rock House** (tel: 905/354-3631. *Open* daily from 9am. *Admission: moderate*), alongside the Horseshoe Falls (reached by funicular from Portage Road near the Konica

Minolta Tower). Observation platforms provide spray-drenched views; the real point is the tunnels behind the falls for a view through the curtain of water.

For the most exhilarating panorama of all, take **Maid of the Mist boat** (Apr–end Oct daily, approximately every 15 minutes, tel: 905/358–5781 for exact hours. *Admission: expensive*), which nudges almost to the foot of the falls (waterproof clothing is provided). The quay is just below the Rainbow Bridge,and can be reached by funicular from the junction of Clifton Hill and the Niagara Parkway.

The most exciting—and wettest—way to admire the majestic Niagara Falls

The name of the Hudson's Bay Company resonates throughout Canadian history. The remote outposts of this fur-trading concern formed the kernel of countless modern towns and cities, and their representatives ruled vast tracts of the country by proxy for over 200 years.

Radish and Gooseberry Fur trading at the beginning of the 17th century was almost entirely the domain of the French, so it was only fitting—and a trifle ironic—that one of the greatest British-founded companies should have had its roots in the disenchantment of two Frenchmen. Médard Chouart des Groseilliers and Pierre-Esprit Radisson—soon to acquire the nicknames Radish and Gooseberry—had long been frustrated by the exorbitant cost of transporting furs overland to Québec, and by the high taxes they had to pay French administrators on each consignment of furs. In 1661 they reached the southern shores of Hudson Bay, the "inland sea" discovered by Henry Hudson some 50 years earlier, and realized that it might be easier to move furs here than through the convoluted waterways of Montréal and the St. Lawrence.

On returning to Québec with the news, and over 300 canoes of furs, the pair were promptly arrested for trading without a license. Fleeing to the safety of New England, a British colony, they were escorted to London in 1665, where their ideas found more favor with the city's merchants. Several of these, under the guidance of Prince Rupert of Bohemia, cousin of Charles II, then financed the voyage of two ships, the *Eaglet* and the *Nonsuch*, to test the idea. In 1668 the latter returned from the Bay laden with furs. On May 2, 1670, prompted by the expedition's success, Charles II granted a royal

OLDEST COMPANY
The Hudson's Bay Company is the oldest company still trading in North America. It no longer trades in fur, but it is still Canada's largest retailer, and one of the country's biggest real-estate developers.

SHORT CUT
Moving furs through Hudson Bay instead of Montréal cut over 1,500km (930 miles) off the journey to Europe, the main market for Canadian furs.

charter to the "Governor and Company of Adventurers trading into Hudson's Bay": the Hudson's Bay Company (HBC). The new domain, soon christened Rupert's Land, embraced all the land draining into Hudson Bay—an unimaginably vast area (see panel).

Competition The fact that the company's trading posts could be supplied by sea (see panel), and were located in the heart of the finest fur territory, enabled it eventually to triumph over all competition, the keenest of which came from the North West Company. Founded by Montréal merchants in 1783, it became the largest commercial enterprise of its day, harrying the HBC across the "unclaimed" lands of the northwest, and turning its employees—men such as Alexander Mackenzie, Simon Fraser and David Thomson—into some of the greatest explorers of the age (see pages 66–67). In the end the HBC's lower costs won the day, and in 1821 the two companies were merged, though with the HBC remaining the dominant partner. At the same time the British government reconfirmed the company's monopoly, extending it to cover all the lands of the Northwest Territories.

Thriving still The company inevitably played an influential part in the development of these lands, its trading posts becoming the germ of towns across much of western and northern Canada. Indeed, on Vancouver Island in the 1850s, James Douglas was both an HBC employee and the island's governor. Such ties broke down at Confederation, when the Canadian government bought Rupert's Land for £300,000, the largest land deal in history (see page 37). By this time the company's attention was turning from furs to land. As part of the deal it shrewdly negotiated to keep a twentieth of its "fertile lands," and also the areas immediately around its old trading posts—the heart of many present-day towns. As a result, the company still thrives today.

The Hudson's Bay Company relied heavily on native trappers for their furs
Left: The old company flag is raised at Fort Langley

RUPERT'S LAND
Prince Rupert and his merchant colleagues acquired trading and mineral rights to over 7.7 million sq km (3 million sq miles) of territory, which in modern geographical terms included northern Québec and Ontario north of the Laurentian watershed, all of Manitoba, most of Saskatchewan, southern Alberta and a portion of the Northwest Territories.

TRADING POSTS
The Hudson's Bay Company was one of the first "joint-stock" companies. Its shareholders appointed a governor and ruling committee in London, who in turn hired men to deal with the business of shipping and ordering trade goods. The men on the ground, the "factors," or land agents, occupied the trading posts that spread across much of Canada's northern wilderness.

Ottawa's Tulip Festival dates from 1945

ARRIVING
Ottawa International Airport (tel: 613/248–2000, www.ottawa-airport.ca) is 18km (11 miles) south of the city, and is connected to downtown by taxi and the half-hourly Airport/Hotel shuttle bus (tel: 613/260–2359). Long-distance buses arrive at the Voyageur bus terminal (tel: 613/238–5900, www.ottawakiosk.com) in the south of the city at 265 Catherine Street and Kent. The local OC Transport bus 4 runs from there to downtown. The VIA Rail railway station is in the city's southeastern suburbs 5km (3 miles). from downtown at 200 Tremblay Road (tel: 613/244–1660). Bus 95 connects to the center.

NEW NAME
Ottawa takes its name from a native word meaning "a place for buying and selling."

▶▶ Ottawa *159E2*

Ottawa has for years been dubbed one of the dullest cities in North America. Ethnic diversity, investment in culture and the arts and renovation of historic areas have recently done something to liven it up, though for all the cosmetic work and money spent the city remains little more than a pleasantly provincial diversion in comparison to Toronto and Montréal. As the capital of a bilingual country, however, it has made a special effort at integration, linking itself physically and culturally to francophone Hull, a Québécois town across the Ottawa River.

Wilderness Algonquin natives and fur traders used the Ottawa and Rideau rivers as means of transport long before any permanent settlement sprang up at their confluence. Probably the first habitation on the site was raised around 1800 by an American, Philemon Wright, who established a saw mill named Wrightstown on the river bank—he later changed the name to Hull in honor of his parents' British birthplace. Fresh impetus to settlement came with the building of the Rideau Canal in 1826, designed to bypass the dangerous waters of the St. Lawrence and improve links to Lake Ontario. A rowdy construction camp grew up where the canal met the Ottawa River, eventually named Bytown after the Royal Engineers officer in charge of the project.

Westminster By 1850 Bytown was in competition with Toronto, Montréal, and other cities for the role of capital of the "Province of Canada." So intense was the rivalry that the final decision was left to Queen Victoria. Having changed its name in 1854 to try to shake off Bytown's rowdy associations, Ottawa received the royal nod in 1864; legend has it the Queen made her choice simply on the strength of a watercolor she admired of the countryside outside the city. The choice provoked much mirth, not least from the Americans, who joked the city would be safe from attack as any "invaders would inevitably be lost in the woods trying to find it." Civil servants sent to work there were similarly underwhelmed by the city they dubbed "Westminster in the woods," though work has gone on ever since to turn it into a city fit for a capital—a "Washington of the North."

Parliament Hill▶▶ Ottawa's three parliament buildings rise above the city in a successful neo-Gothic pastiche of Britain's Houses of Parliament. Begun in 1860 (but part-restored after a fire in 1916), they were built on land bought from the British military, who had used the site—a high limestone bluff above the Ottawa River—as a barracks during the building of the Rideau Canal. Summer crowds congregate on the front lawn of the "Hill" at 10am for the **Changing of the Guard**, a jamboree preceded by much pageantry, kilt-swirling and bagpipe blowing (late Jun–late Aug daily, weather permitting).

Many of the buildings' Victorian-era interiors are open to guided tours. Make a point of trying to see the lovely old **Library** (behind the complex's so-called Centre Block) and the sumptuous **Senate**, frescoed with scenes from Canada's role in World War I. Things to look out for away from the main buildings include the **Centennial Flame** (close to the entrance gate), lit in 1967 to celebrate 100 years of the Canadian Confederation, and the **Peace Tower**, built in 1927 to honor Canada's war dead: 66,651 in World War I, 44,895 in World War II; the tower can be climbed for a wonderful view of the city (Wellington Street. *Guided tours:* May–end Sep Mon–Fri 9–8, Sat–Sun 9–5; Oct–end Apr, daily 9–4. *Admission free*). Also wander the grounds, which are patrolled by Mounties in full rig, and follow the delightful riverside walk below the Hill.

Upper Town▶▶ Most of Ottawa's more pressing sights cluster in the compact downtown grids south and east of Parliament Hill (known as Upper and Lower Town respectively). Explore these, work your way eastward to the National Gallery, then cross to Hull, and you will have seen the best of downtown. Just west of Parliament Hill lies the country's **Supreme Court** (Kent and Wellington. *Open* Sep–end Apr Mon–Fri

INFORMATION
Ottawa's main tourist office is Canada's Capital Visitor Information Centre, located opposite the Parliament Buildings at 90 Wellington Street (tel: 613/239-5000 or 800/465-1867, www.ottawatourism.ca). Information and help with obtaining accommodation can also be obtained from the Capital Call Centre at 40 Elgin Street (tel: 239/500–5555).

OXIDATION
Copper is widely used across the country for roofing. Over a 10- to 15-year period, new copper oxidizes and turns the distinctive green color that can be seen on buildings such as the Chateau Laurier Hotel in Ottawa, and City Hall in Montréal. The Parliament Buildings were re-coppered in the late 1990s. It will therefore take a few years before they turn green.

The striking, green-roofed Government Building on Parliament Hill before it was recoppered

Taking a boat trip on the Rideau Canal offers a different perspective on downtown Ottawa

OLD COUNTRY
Much of Ontario straddles the Canadian Shield (see page 12), whose rocks—at between 600 million and 3 billion years old—are some of the most ancient in the world.

BUSY PROVINCE
Over 50 percent of all Canada's manufactured goods are made in Ontario.

SKATING COMMUTERS
In winter the Rideau Canal freezes solid and becomes popular with skaters, many of whom use it to get to work.

NO PLACE FOR A CITY
"The nearest lumber camp to the North Pole"—19th-century Toronto writer Goldwyn Smith describing Ottawa

FESTIVALS
Ottawa has even more festivals than most Canadian cities. The most famous is its spring Tulip Festival (mid-May), begun in 1945, when Holland sent 100,000 tulip bulbs because the Dutch royal family took refuge there during World War II, and one of the royal princesses was born there. The flowers create an explosion of color, a spectacle matched by parades, a craft show, concerts and fireworks displays.

9–5; tours, May–end Aug Mon–Fri 9–5. Reservations, tel: 613/995–5361. *Admission free*), housed in a blunt art deco building. Nearby is the Bank of Canada's **Currency Museum** (245 Sparks Street. *Open* May–early Sep Mon–Sat 10.30–5, Sun 1–5; early Sep–end Apr Tue–Sat 10.30–5, Sun 1–5. *Admission free*), whose history of money concentrates mainly on the development of Canadian notes and coins. Displays include coinage from ancient Greece, Rome, China and Byzantium, and examples of the *wampum* (see page 185), Hudson's Bay Company tokens, elephant-hair bracelets, the card money of New France, and even old beaver pelts used as barter. It also has what is claimed to be the world's largest coin.

Just south of the museum stretches the Sparks Street Mall, Canada's first pedestrian mall, a promenade of cafés, shops and department stores. At its eastern end stands Confederation Square, close to the **Château Laurier** (1912), one of the monumental château-style hotels beloved of the big railroad companies that built it.

Nearby is the **National Arts Centre** (1969), an opera hall and arts complex designed by Fred Lebensold (*Open* daily 8am–midnight. *Admission: varies, depending on show*). The center forms the most visible evidence of the considerable federal grants that have been spent to raise Ottawa's cultural profile (money begrudged by other parts of Canada). In truth there is little to raise the pulse beyond the grounds and a slightly dated design, although its café is a good spot for a meal or beverage.

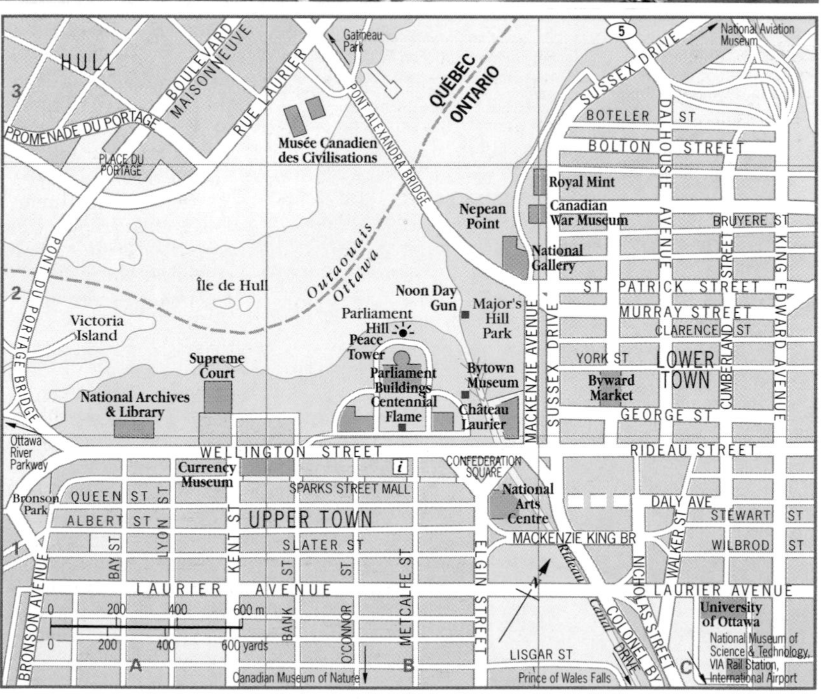
HULL
BOULEVARD MAISONNEUVE
RUE LAURIER
Gatineau Park
PONT ALEXANDRA BRIDGE
QUÉBEC
ONTARIO
5
SUSSEX DRIVE
National Aviation Museum
3
PROMENADE DU PORTAGE
PLACE DU PORTAGE
Musée Canadien des Civilisations
BOTELER ST
BOLTON STREET
DALHOUSIE AVENUE
Royal Mint
Canadian War Museum
Nepean Point
BRUYERE ST
National Gallery
KING EDWARD AVENUE
CUMBERLAND STREET
PONT DU PORTAGE BRIDGE
2
Île de Hull
Outaouais
Ottawa
Noon Day Gun
Major's Hill Park
ST PATRICK STREET
MURRAY STREET
CLARENCE ST
Victoria Island
Parliament Hill
Peace Tower
Supreme Court
Parliament Buildings
Centennial Flame
Bytown Museum
Château Laurier
MACKENZIE AVENUE
SUSSEX DRIVE
YORK ST
LOWER TOWN
Byward Market
National Archives & Library
GEORGE ST
Ottawa River Parkway
WELLINGTON STREET
RIDEAU STREET
Currency Museum
i
CONFEDERATION SQUARE
SPARKS STREET MALL
National Arts Centre
Bronson Park
QUEEN ST
LYON ST
ALBERT ST
UPPER TOWN
DALY AVE
STEWART ST
MACKENZIE KING BR
1
BAY ST
KENT ST
SLATER ST
BANK ST
ST
METCALFE ST
ELGIN STREET
Rideau
WALKER ST
WILBROD ST
NICHOLAS STREET
LAURIER AVENUE
LAURIER AVENUE
0
200
400
600 m
0
200
400
600 yards
BRONSON AVENUE
O'CONNOR
Canal
COLONEL BY DRIVE
University of Ottawa
National Museum of Science & Technology, VIA Rail Station, International Airport
LISGAR ST
A
B
C
Canadian Museum of Nature
Prince of Wales Falls

The stunning modern home of Canada's national art collection

NOON DAY GUN
Ottawa's most famous novelty attraction is the firing of a cannon from Major's Hill Park alongside the National Gallery. The noisy spectacle, begun in 1869 to coordinate postal services, takes place at midday every day except Sunday (to avoid disturbing churchgoers).

CITY DRIVES
Places worth driving to out of Ottawa include Rockcliffe and Sussex Drive (along the Ottawa River; 6km/4 miles); the Ottawa River Parkway (11km/7 miles); Prince of Wales Falls (13km/8 miles), reached on Queen Elizabeth Drive along the west bank of the Rideau Canal (return on Colonel By Drive on the east bank); and the Gatineau Park, a vast wilderness reserve north-west of the city (55km/33-mile round trip).

Lower Town▶▶ Entering the Lower Town takes you across the **Rideau Canal▶**, whose sequence of locks provides an attractive counterpoint to the small gorge cradling the canal. Alongside them on the west bank stands the **Bytown Museum** (*Open* Apr–end Nov, tel: 613/234–4570 for days and hours. *Admission: inexpensive*), housed in the Old Commissariat, Ottawa's oldest stone building (1827). The 3,500 exhibits here are devoted to the building of the canal and the history of the city. A couple of blocks east lies **Byward Market**, a modest outdoor market that has existed on this site since 1846. Restoration of the surrounding area has made this a haven of cafés, bars, galleries and interesting shops. Between the canals and the Château Laurier is the new **Museum of Contemporary Photography▶**, whose 158,000 images are displayed in a series of changing exhibitions (1 Rideau Canal. *Open* May–end Sep daily 10–5, Thu 10–8; Oct–end Apr Wed–Sun 10–5, Thu 10–8. *Admission: inexpensive*). Further north is the **Canadian War Museum▶▶** (tel: 819/776–8600. *Open* May–mid-Oct daily 9–6, Thu 9–9, also Jul–end Sep Thu, Fri 9–9; mid-Oct–end Apr Tue–Sun 9–5, Thu 9–9. *Admission*: *inexpensive*), which explores the history of conflict in Canada and wars involving Canadians: the star exhibit, something billed as "Adolf Hitler's car," actually belonged to Hermann Goering.

National Gallery▶▶▶ Here you'll find the greatest accumulation of Canadian art in the country. The gallery's collection opens with religious art from Québec and Nova Scotia, before moving on to the 19th-century paintings of immigrant artists who received their training in Europe, and the more famous names of Canadian painting: Cornelius Krieghoff, Paul Kane, Emily Carr, Tom Thomson and the Group of Seven (see page 176). Two further highlights are the so-called **Croscup Room**, a salon painted with murals removed intact from the home of a former shipping magnate; and the **Rideau Street Convent Chapel** (1887), a beautiful fan-vaulted chapel dotted with silver and wooden Québécois sculpture. On the upper floor is a solid collection of American and European masterpieces, among them works by El Greco, Rembrandt, Filippino Lippi, Klimt, Picasso, Rothko and Pollock (380 Sussex Drive, tel: 613/990–1985 or 800/318–ARTS. *Open* May–mid-Oct daily 10–5, Thu 10–8; mid-Oct–end Apr Wed–Sun 10–5, Thu 10–8. *Admission: permanent collection, free; special exhibitions, expensive*).

Musée Canadien des Civilisations▶▶▶ No expense has been spared in this magnificent and unmissable museum, from the stunning complex itself—designed to reflect the landscapes at the fringes of the far north and the Canadian Shield—to the polished high-tech presentation of displays dedicated to a comprehensive review of Canadian history. The **Grand Hall** shelters one of the world's largest collections of totem poles, together with several native dwellings whose interiors feature audiovisual accounts of Native Canadian life past and present. **Canada Hall**, by contrast, contains mocked-up historical vignettes, from an Acadian settlement of the earliest French pioneers to a complete 19th-century Ontarian street (100 Laurier Street, Hull, tel: 819/776–7000 or 800/555–5621. *Open* Apr–end Jun, Sep–mid-Oct Fri–Wed 9–6, Thu 9–9; Jul–end Aug Sat–Wed 9–6, Thu–Fri 9–9; mid-Oct–end Apr Tue–Sun 9–5, Thu 9–9. *Admission: expensive*).

Ottawa has national museums to suit all tastes. In addition to those listed above, there is the National Museum of Science and Technology, with its historic automobiles (1867 St. Laurent Boulevard), the Canadian Museum of Nature, with outstanding dinosaur displays (240 McLeod Street) and the National Aviation Museum with its collection of flying machines (11 Aviation Parkway). Contact the Tourist Office for more information (see panel page 171).

VIEWPOINT
One of the best views of Ottawa can be had from Nepean Point, a spot overlooking the Alexander Bridge just west of the National Gallery.

STROLLS
Places to walk in Ottawa include the riverside promenade below Parliament Hill; past the Old Commissariat Building on the west bank of the Rideau Canal; out to the viewpoint at Nepean Point; and around the paths of Major's Hill Park.

UPPER CANADA VILLAGE
This reconstructed pioneer village has been called one of the finest "living-history museums" in North America, and is one of Ontario's major tourist attractions. Two farms, three mills, two hotels, two churches and 25 other buildings cover the 27ha (70-acre) site, which aims to re-create the ambience of a 19th-century Upper Canada Loyalist village. Around 150 "inhabitants" in period dress "live" in the village, some baking bread or making cheese, others stitching quilts or making furniture. The site is 88km (55 miles) south-east of Ottawa, and can be reached on Highways 31 and 2 (Highway 2 East, tel: 800/437–2233 *Open* mid-May to mid-Oct daily 9.30–5. *Admission: expensive*).

The modern interior of the Musée Canadien des Civilisations

Few artists have had such a pronounced effect on a country's self-image as the Group of Seven, a collection of Toronto-based early 20th-century painters who not only forged the first school of Canadian painting, but also altered attitudes to the country's wilderness through their iconoclastic approach to art and landscape.

SELF-EXPRESSION
"Only by fostering our own Canadian art shall we develop ourselves as a people."—A. Y. Jackson, a member of the Group of Seven

MANIFESTO
According to the Group of Seven, wilderness, and in particular the "northland" of Canada, was the real "painters country." "Nature," claimed one, "is the measure of a man's stature." A pioneer spirit, moreover—so apt for a country like Canada—was part of the artist's approach, for art, they claimed, involved "taking to the road" and "risking all for the glory of a great adventure."

Early days Although the Inuit and other Native Canadian peoples had been producing art and artifacts for many thousands of years, the early art of mainstream white and immigrant Canadians remained true to the traditions they had brought with them from Europe. Apart from a few votive pictures and occasional portraits, the majority of early French Canadian paintings were imported into Canada from France. British settlers, notably the watercolorist Thomas Davies, ventured a little further, reflecting something of their feeling for Canada in topographical drawings and idealized ornamental landscapes.

Stylistic debt The debt to conservative European tradition survived until the end of the 19th century, when explorer-painters such as Paul Kane (1810–1871) and William Hind (1833–1889) began to record the landscapes, animals and native cultures of Canada's western wilderness. Landscapes, albeit wildly romantic ones, were also the bread and butter of artists such as Allan Edson (1846–1888) and Lucius O'Brien (1832–1899). Though both were eminent and influential in their time, neither threw off the shackles of European convention.

Tom Thomson The man credited with creating a purely Canadian form of artistic self-expression was Tom Thomson (1877–1917), who began his career as a lowly commercial artist in a Toronto art firm, Grip Ltd. His artistic awakening followed a trip to the Algonquin wilderness north of Toronto in 1912. The visit opened his eyes to the unique beauty of the Canadian countryside,

The Group of Seven painters at Toronto's Arts and Letters Club in 1920

turning him into a rugged outdoorsman in the process. He then began to paint the wilderness, and in doing so created the first truly Canadian school of art.

Tom Thomson's Silver Birches *(1914), painted three years before his death*

Group of Seven Thomson shared his vision with a group of friends, many of whom were fellow employees at Grip Ltd. Several accompanied him on his trips to the wilderness, and were soon inspired by his powerfully naturalistic treatment of the country. Four in particular stood out: A. Y. Jackson, J. E. H. MacDonald, Franklin Carmichael and Lawren Harris. The last of these, who was independently wealthy, built a studio in Toronto in which the five painters could work together (though Thomson often painted alone in a shack in the studio grounds).

World War I, and Thomson's death by drowning in 1917, galvanized the group. The surviving members recruited three fellow artists—Arthur Lismer, Frederick Varley and Frank Johnston—thereby creating the Group of Seven. They held their first joint exhibition in Toronto in 1920.

Reaction Borrowing from Cézanne, the Impressionists, Scandinavian artists and art nouveau, the Group of Seven painted the wilderness in all its terrible beauty. Their colors were often harsh, and their paintings stark, vivid and iconoclastic. Despite their success—they held 40 shows over the next 11 years—their startling works drew initially unfavorable reviews. Many argued that the group portrayed Canada in a relentlessly gloomy light, though by the British Empire Exhibition of 1924, in which they were heavily represented, their works were being described as "the most vital paintings of the century," and the "foundation of what may become one of the greatest schools of landscape painting."

After the Group officially disbanded in 1932, several members formed the similar Canadian Group of Painters the following year. Their influence continued to be felt strongly until the 1950s—too strongly, according to some, who claimed then (and still do) that the Group cast too large a shadow over succeeding generations of painters.

TAMING THE WILD

In the words of the critic Hugh MacLennan, the Group of Seven "made tolerable and beautiful one of the chief sources of the Canadian neurosis—the stark, somber, cold and empty land...".

McMICHAEL COLLECTION

This outstanding collection of works by Tom Thomson and the Group of Seven—essential viewing if you like their paintings—was accumulated privately and bequeathed to Ontario in 1965. It is Canada's greatest collection of the Group's works, and is housed in a suitably rustic collection of log and stone buildings amid 40ha (100 acres) of pastoral open country. The nearest town is Kleinburg, a commuter suburb of Toronto some 40km (25 miles) northwest of downtown off Highway 400 (10365 Islington Avenue, tel: 905/893–1121. *Open* May–end Oct daily; Nov–end Apr Tue–Sun. *Admission: moderate*).

►► Toronto 159D1

In the 17th century, Toronto's site marked the beginning of a "portage" route used by French fur traders heading north (a portage was a point where canoes were carried overland between lakes or rivers). In the middle of the next century it acquired the French-built Fort Rouillé, a fortress that was to prove no match for the British, who captured it in 1759 during the Seven Years War. In 1787 an area of land corresponding to modern-day Toronto was bought from the Missisauga natives for £1,700. Six years later the plot was set aside as the site of a new town by John Graves Simcoe, Lieutenant General of Upper Canada. Simcoe's superiors considered the spot a better bet than Niagara-on-the-Lake, the province's then capital, deemed too close to America. The site still left much to be desired: "better calculated for a frog pond," observed Simcoe, "than for the residence of human beings."

INFORMATION
The main office of Tourism Toronto is on the fifth floor of the Queen's Quay complex at 207 Queen's Quay West (tel: 416/203–2600 or 800/449–2514, www.torontotourism.com).

Muddy York By 1812 the settlement—now known as York—was still little more than a village, its miserably damp situation having earned it the nickname "Muddy York." By 1834, however, a respectable 10,000 people lived in the city, and York was renamed Toronto (a native word meaning "meeting place"). For the rest of the 19th century, the city enjoyed a series of liberal but stolid administrations, a dour period that laid the foundations of Toronto's present reputation for financial probity (the city has the fourth-largest stock exchange in North America). Industry, wealth and population grew apace in the 20th century, but only during the last 20 or so years has Toronto come into its own. Suburbs have mushroomed, industry has boomed and the population has exploded, fueled by immigration from every corner of the globe. Other cities may be prettier, but few match Toronto's rich cultural life: its theater, opera and ballet are some of the best in the country.

AMERICAN LOOK
"There is a Yankee look about the place...a pushing, business-like, smart appearance."—Charles Mackay, *Life and Liberty in America* (1859)

A young citizen of Toronto takes the weight of the world on his shoulders

Harbourfront►►► Three million people a year now visit Toronto's previously dispiriting waterfront district. Over the last few years, the area has been transformed into a dynamic complex of walkways, shops, cafés, marinas, arts centers, fashionable apartments and breezy open spaces. Things to make a special point of seeing in the area, which stretches for more than 2km (1.2 miles) west of Yonge Street, include the **Power Plant**, just west of Queen's Quay (*Open* hours variable. *Admission: moderate*), an exhibition space for the contemporary arts housed in a converted power station. To get here, either walk from Union Station, or take the LRT to Queen's Quay Station (see panel, page 181).

Toronto Islands►►► The Harbourfront is also the point to pick up **boat trips** around the harbor and the (least expensive) ferries to the Toronto Islands 730m (800 yards) offshore (actually one island with four different names: Centre, Ward's, Algonquin and Hanlan's Point). Both the boats and the ferries offer unmissable views of Toronto's fabled **skyline►►►**, though the visit to the islands would

The CN Tower and Toronto's city skyline are best seen from a boat trip on Lake Ontario

be worth making even without the breathtaking panorama. All four islets are given over to parks, gardens and playgrounds, and all have plenty of outlets where you can rent canoes, rowboats and bikes (there are no cars). There are also sandy beaches, though Lake Ontario is of dubious cleanliness; the best are on the west side of Hanlan's, the southeast of Ward's and the southern edge of Centre. Boat tours leave from the foot of York and Yonge from May to late October, while ferries depart from close by at the foot of Bay (three per hour). For more information and details contact Mariposa Cruises (tel: 416/203–0178 or 800/976–2442).

Fort York► About 1km (half a mile) west of Harbourfront lies the stronghold of Fort York. Begun in 1793, the fortress was built to bolster British power in the region, but was captured by the Americans and destroyed in 1813. The present buildings date from 1815, and include eight log and stone structures ranging from the old powder room to the former Officers' Quarters (Toronto's oldest residential building). Free guided tours are available, backed up by interpretative material on the fort and on 19th-century Canadian history (100 Garrison Road off Fleet Street, tel: 416/338–3888. *Open* mid-May–early Sep daily 10–5; early Sep–mid-May Mon–Fri 10–4, Sat–Sun 10–5. *Admission: moderate*).

CN Tower►►► Most visitors to Toronto rush lemming-like to join the line for the biggest attraction in the city, the CN Tower, which at 553m (1,815ft) is the world's highest free-standing building. Built in 1976 by Canadian National Railways (CN), it was designed to carry TV and radio transmission masts, and to provide microwave facilities for CN telecommunications. Visitors are ferried up the CN Tower in four, stomach-churning elevators on the *outside* of the building, with just a glass front between you and free-fall. First stop are the Look Out level galleries (335m/1,100ft), the circular platform that interrupts the tower's minaret-like profile about two-thirds of the way

ARRIVAL

Toronto's main Lester B. Pearson International Airport (*terminals 1 and 2* tel: 416/247–7678; *terminal 3* 416/776–1690, is 25km (15 miles) northwest of downtown. The Airport Express (tel: 905/564–3232 or 800/387–6787) bus runs to and from downtown from all three terminals, and there are shuttle services to the subway. The city bus terminal (tel: 416/393–7900) is at 610 Bay Street, close to Dundas Street. Amtrak and VIA Rail trains arrive at Union Station (65 Front Street, tel: 416/366–8411).

CN TOWER STATISTICS

Begun 1972, finished 1976. Cost: $57 million. Height: 553m (1,815ft). Stairs: 1,760. Weight: equivalent to 23,500 elephants. Elevators: 4. Speed of elevators: 365m (1,200ft) a minute, equivalent to the rate of ascent of a jet at take-off. Movement of tower in storms: shaft 25cm (10in); summit 2.5m (8ft). Number of storms in Toronto: 60–80 a year.

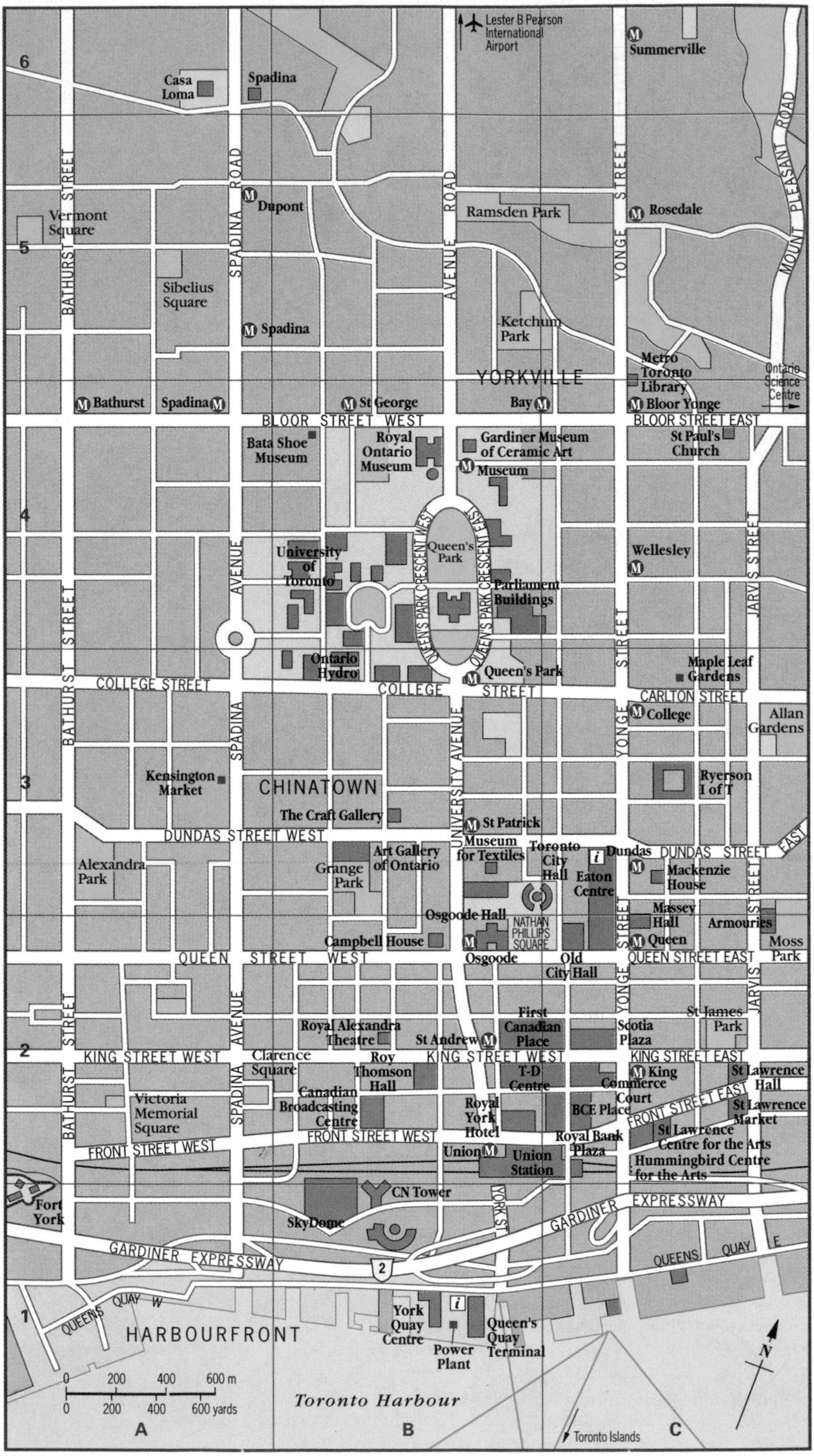

Lester B Pearson International Airport
Summerville
Casa Loma
Spadina
Spadina Road
Bathurst Street
Dupont
Vermont Square
Avenue Road
Ramsden Park
Rosedale
Yonge Street
Mount Pleasant Road
Sibelius Square
Spadina
Ketchum Park
Metro Toronto Library
Yorkville
Ontario Science Centre
Bathurst
Spadina
St George
Bay
Bloor Yonge
Bloor Street West
Bloor Street East
Bata Shoe Museum
Royal Ontario Museum
Gardiner Museum of Ceramic Art
Museum
St Paul's Church
Queen's Park
Queen's Park Crescent West
Queen's Park Crescent East
University of Toronto
Spadina Avenue
Wellesley
Jarvis Street
Parliament Buildings
Ontario Hydro
Queen's Park
Maple Leaf Gardens
College Street
Carlton Street
College
Allan Gardens
University Avenue
Kensington Market
Chinatown
Ryerson I of T
The Craft Gallery
St Patrick
Dundas Street West
Museum for Textiles
Toronto City Hall
Dundas
Dundas Street East
Alexandra Park
Art Gallery of Ontario
Grange Park
Eaton Centre
Mackenzie House
Osgoode Hall
Nathan Phillips Square
Massey Hall
Armouries
Campbell House
Queen
Moss Park
Queen Street West
Osgoode
Old City Hall
Queen Street East
First Canadian Place
St James Park
Royal Alexandra Theatre
St Andrew
Scotia Plaza
King Street West
Clarence Square
Roy Thomson Hall
King Street East
King
St Lawrence Hall
T-D Centre
Commerce Court
Victoria Memorial Square
Canadian Broadcasting Centre
Royal York Hotel
BCE Place
Front Street East
St Lawrence Market
Front Street West
Royal Bank Plaza
St Lawrence Centre for the Arts
Union
Union Station
Hummingbird Centre for the Arts
CN Tower
York St
Fort York
SkyDome
Gardiner Expressway
Queens Quay E
2
Queens Quay W
Harbourfront
York Quay Centre
Power Plant
Queen's Quay Terminal
0 200 400 600 m
0 200 400 600 yards
Toronto Harbour
Toronto Islands
N
A B C
1 2 3 4 5 6

The SkyDome's retractable roof opens to reveal the 553m (1,815ft) CN Tower

up. The galleries are seven stories high, and has an outdoor observation deck on Level 2 and a more reassuring indoor deck on Level 3 (it also boasts the world's largest revolving restaurant). The views are awe-inspiring, extending on clear days to the misty spray rising from Niagara Falls (120km/70 miles distant). For a few dollars more you can ride the elevators to the tiny Sky Pod (446m/1,464ft), the world's highest public observation gallery (301 Front Street West, tel: 86–TOWER. *Open* Sun–Thu 9.30am–10pm, Fri–Sat 9.30am–10.30pm. *Admission: expensive; additional charge for Space Deck*). Weekends, and the hours from 11am to 4pm, see the tower at its most crowded.

Art Gallery of Ontario (AGO)►►► In 1900 the AGO was a gallery without a home and without a collection. Today it is one of the greatest art galleries in North America, its prestige having been further enhanced by a stunning $50 million renovation in 1992. Its collection divides into three, beginning with the **European Collection**, whose assortment of Old Masters, Impressionists and 20th-century movements includes works by Pieter Bruegel, Tintoretto, Rembrandt, Franz Hals, Gainsborough, Renoir, Monet, Picasso, Gauguin, Dégas and Van Gogh (more modern works are included in the gallery's airy new wings). The upper floor's **Canadian Collection** is predictably strong, in both its accumulation of contemporary works and its attention to the country's earlier artists. Toronto's Group of Seven painters are much in evidence, in particular Tom Thomson, their founding father, whose *West Wind* (1917)—perhaps the most famous Canadian painting of all—hangs

PUBLIC TRANSPORTATION
The Toronto Transit Commission, or TTC, runs an integrated transport system of buses, trolley buses, a two-line, 60-station subway and a light railway (tel: 416/393–4000 or 416/393–4636 for fares, routes and timetables, www.city.toronto.on.ca/ttc). Tickets and tokens are available from subway stations and stores bearing TTC stickers. You can pay on buses, but must have the exact fare. An unlimited travel Day Pass is valid for one person Mon–Fri after 9.30am, all day Saturday and for two people on Sunday. Tickets and tokens are valid for one complete ride across the system. If you change from one form of transportation to another, obtain a free paper transfer ticket, available from bus drivers or machines in the subway.

SKYDOME
The 52,000-seat home of the Toronto Blue Jays baseball team has become one of the city's best-known landmarks. The only stadium in the world with a fully retractable roof—its great dome takes 20 minutes to slide into place, and covers some 3ha (8 acres) of playing field and seating—the arena also claims the world's largest video replay screen. You can see inside the stadium by watching a game or by attending one of the arena's many concerts and miscellaneous events or by taking a tour (*Open* daily, tours every 45 minutes, tel: 416/341–2770 for details. *Admission: expensive*).

Figures by Henry Moore in the Art Gallery of Ontario

here (see pages 176–177). The gallery concludes with the **Henry Moore Sculpture Centre**, opened by Moore himself in 1974, which houses the world's largest public collection of the sculptor's works. Among the 300 exhibits are five major bronzes, 15 large casts, 200 woodcuts and 60 drawings (317 Dundas Street West, tel: 416/979–6648. *Open* call for current times and charges or visit www.ago.net.

Royal Ontario Museum (ROM)►►► The birth of the ROM was somewhat inauspicious: it opened in 1912 on the very day that the *Titanic* sank. Today it is dubbed "Canada's single greatest cultural asset," and, with the completion of more than two decades of renovation by the end of 2000, it will be the second-largest museum in North America (after New York's Metropolitan Museum of Art). Its 6 million exhibits embrace virtually every branch of fine and applied arts, the sciences, natural history and archeology.

By far the most important of these is the world-renowned **Far East Collection**, the greatest such collection outside China (displayed on the museum's first level). Spanning nearly 4,000 years from the Shang Dynasty (1523BC) to the formation of the Republic in 1912, it is particularly renowned for its finely carved tomb retinues, and for the famous ceramic figurine of Yen Lo Wang, King of the Underworld. Equally lauded is the 17th-century **Ming Tomb**, the only such complete tomb in the West.

Life sciences dominate the second level of the museum, where the most captivating sections are the **Dinosaur Gallery**, which has a collection of skeletons from Alberta's Badlands (see pages 150–151); the **Evolution Gallery**, which brings alive Darwin's evolutionary theories; the **Bat Cave**, a spookily interactive display with 4,000 artificial and freeze-dried bats; and the **European Musical Instruments Gallery**, with more than 1,200 beautiful instruments. Other sections are devoted to Canadian history and heritage, in particular the country's native peoples (100 Queens Park, tel: 416/586–5549 or 800/461–3333. *Open* Mon–Thu, Sat–Sun 10–6, *Admission: expensive; free* Fri 4.30–9.30).

While you could easily spend hours amid the museum's exhibits, be sure to visit the **Gardiner Museum of Ceramic**

BATA SHOE MUSEUM
This appealing collection of historic footwear is housed in a fascinating building designed by Raymond Moriyama (327 Bloor Street West. *Open* Tue–Sat 10–5, Thu until 8, Sun 12–5. *Admission: moderate*).

YORKVILLE
Just north of Bloor Street west of Yonge lies a fashionable and popular part of the city known as Yorkville. Extending along Yorkville Avenue as far as Avenue Road, the area encompasses Cumberland Avenue and numerous little laneways and interconnections, all lined with boutiques, restaurants and expensive condominiums.

Art, located across the street from the ROM (111 Queen's Park, tel: 416/586–8080. *Open* call for times *Admission: expensive*). Left to the city by a wealthy businessman, the gallery contains a magnificent collection of ceramics from across the world. Its 4,000-year span is divided into pre-Columbian pottery, Italian majolica, English delftware and 18th-century European porcelain.

Hands-on and interactive displays attract over a million visitors a year to the **Ontario Science Centre** located about 11km (7 miles) from downtown. The 700 exhibits explore the history of technology and a wealth of more contemporary scientific developments. To get there, take the Yonge Street subway to Eglinton and transfer to an Eglinton East bus, disembarking at Don Mills Road, or take the Bloor subway to Pape and transfer to the Don Mills bus. (770 Don Mills Road, tel: 416/696–3127. *Open* daily 10–5. *Admission: expensive*).

Casa Loma►► Some way from downtown, but well worth the trip, is the wonderfully bizarre Casa Loma (1 Austin Terrace on Spadina Avenue; Dupont subway station, tel: 416/923–1171. *Open* daily 9.30–5. *Admission: expensive*). This castellated mansion, a pastiche of a medieval castle, provides a measure of architectural contrast from the city's high-rises. It was built between 1911 and 1914 by Sir Henry Pellatt, a self-made millionaire whose fortune came from harnessing the hydroelectric potential of the Niagara Falls to heat and light much of Ontario. He spent round $3 million on the house's 60 rooms, 38 bathrooms, a private telephone system, a library of 100,000 books, secret tunnels, a pipe organ and a Great Hall capable of accommodating 2,000 people. The folly eventually passed to the city in lieu of unpaid taxes, Pellatt having been humbled by business failings and the expense of paying the house's army of servants. Today it is a museum, with maps and free, taped itineraries to guide you around the labyrinth of eccentric rooms.

MARKET STROLL
Toronto is full of distinct ethnic enclaves, and countless nationalities come to shop in the warren of tiny stores and raucous market stalls just north of Dundas between Spadina and Augusta, an area known as Kensington Market. After a visit you might take in Bellevue Square, a lovely little park nearby.

CHINATOWN
Of all Toronto's energetic ethnic neighborhoods, Chinatown's collection of shops, markets and restaurants is one of the most colorful. It is concentrated along Dundas between Bay and Spadina, Spadina as far as King, and along surrounding streets.

Research work in the Royal Ontario Museum

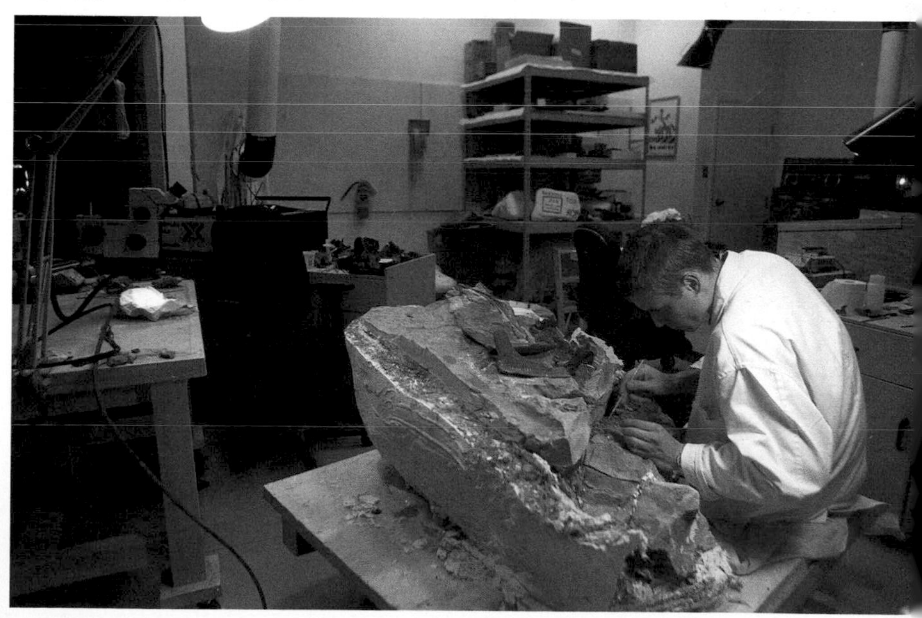

Some of Canada's best-known Native Canadian tribes once lived in southern Ontario's fertile lowlands. Most belonged to the so-called Woodland tribes, a group of semi-nomadic clans whose way of life was markedly different from that of the country's other important tribes.

NATIVE LANGUAGES
Canada has more than 50 different native languages and dialects, each of which belongs to one of ten basic linguistic groups. Of these, the most important is that of the Algonquin (60 percent), followed by the Athabasca, Iroquois, Salish, Wakasha, Tsimischian, Sioux, Kootenai, Haida and Tlingit.

This beautiful Huron screen, which dates from 1840, is embroidered with elk hair

Sedentary life The cultures and lifestyles of native peoples were largely determined by the weather and by what lay at hand in the way of food, tools, shelter, weapons and clothing. In the balmy climate and teeming woodlands of southern Ontario, they found an agricultural abundance that allowed a way of life whose cultural and artistic sophistication rivaled that of tribes in the Pacific Northwest. Two major groups bloomed in the region: the Algonquin and the Iroquois. While each had its own language, ways of life in both groups were broadly similar.

Living Both lived in scattered woodland communities, the population in individual villages often numbering several hundred. Settlements were chosen for their proximity to water, rich soils and forest resources, all widely available in the Ontario lowlands. People usually lived in longhouses in palisaded villages, though certain Algonquin tribes opted instead for circular domed huts. Each house supported several families and had its own hearth and sleeping platform. Food consisted largely of beans, squash and corn—the so-called "three sisters" of the Woodland diet. Crops were rarely rotated, however, so as land became exhausted tribes were forced to seek pastures new. Otherwise life was mainly sedentary, though tribes would also hunt from birch-bark canoes in summer, and trap in the woods in winter using snowshoes and toboggans.

Women rule One of the main things that set the Iroquois apart from the Algonquin was their adherence to a matriarchal structure (that of the Algonquin was patriarchal). Descent was matrilineal, clans being divided into matriarchal hierarchies with a female elder at their head. Women ruled individual longhouses, though "rule" in Woodland tribes tended to be consensual rather than authoritarian. When a man married, he married outside his clan, and left his home to live in the longhouse of his wife. Chieftains, or *sachems*, however, were always male, and came from clans of traditional *sachem* caste. At the same time they were selected by a tribe's female elders, and then confirmed by an intertribal council.

War and religion The Iroquois were also unique in being the only aboriginal people to believe in two Great Spirits—Good and Evil—and in using the leisure time afforded by ample supplies of winter

An Iroquois attack on a settlers' stockade on the Ottawa River

food to wage war. To do this they organized a confederacy of Iroquois tribes, the so-called Five Nations—which rather confusingly consisted of six tribes (the Mohawk, Onondaga, Seneca, Cayuga, Oneida and Tuscarora). In addition to picking on the Algonquin, the alliance fought against the French, and against the Hurons (France's allies in the fur trade), a fellow Iroquois-speaking tribe outside the Iroquois confederacy (see page 31). Though the alliance was primarily a martial one, the Five Nations also had their own system of "currency," the *wampum*, which was used for ceremony and trade.

Arts Iroquois culture was producing distinctive artifacts as early as 900–1600BC, and was characterized by symbolically patterned pottery and intricately decorated stone and clay pipes used in the ritual smoking of tobacco. Later, Huron art developed a personalized approach, individual self-expression becoming as important as tribal self-expression. Huron embroidery was particularly prized, and consisted of flower motifs and elk-hair weaving, usually worked on a black leather background (such motifs were eventually replaced by the colored beads introduced by European traders). Equally distinctive were the Iroquois "False Masks," or "False Faces," wooden masks with metal eyes and human hair that were used in healing ceremonies or to ward off disease and evil spirits.

NATIVE POPULATIONS
Canada's last full census (1996) recorded 799,010 people of aboriginal descent (out of a total population of 28.5 million). Of these, 554,290 belonged to native groups such as the Iroquois (as opposed to the Inuit, or people of mixed race such as the Métis). Most owe allegiance to one of the 576 so-called native "bands," and around 70 percent live on reservations on their "own" land.

NATIVE HOMES
The distribution of native populations by province varies enormously across Canada. In the Northwest Territories and Nunavut they comprise 61 percent of the population; in the Yukon 20 percent; in Manitoba and Saskatchewan 11 percent; and in Prince Edward Island just 0.7 percent.

ONE OF A KIND Québec may be North America's most singular region. Almost 80 percent of the province's 7.3 million population are of French extraction. As a result, the region's manners, morals, customs—even its food and physical appearance—are thoroughly French. The Gallic association is proudly held, its roots going back to the days when Québec formed the heart of French North America (see pages 28–33). Québec *was* Canada in its early days, and its status is a key to the country's development over centuries. More recently the issue of separatism has dominated the region, a potential schism with the rest of Canada that threatens to tear the country apart (see pages 22–24). Few of these tensions touch casual visitors, however, who can enjoy not only all the French culture and cuisine but also two of Canada's most dynamic and ancient cities, Québec and Montréal.

ARRIVING The two metropolises attract the attention of most visitors. Both are served by numerous domestic and international airlines and by rail connections to Toronto and the US Amtrak network. Most approaches by road bring you to Montréal, the larger and more cosmopolitan of the two cities (nearly half of all Québécois live in the metropolitan area). Fast roads then link to Québec on the north shore of the St. Lawrence by way of Trois Rivières. Slower roads run along the southern shore, a good way of exploring the rural countryside of L'Estrie (see page 195). Beyond Québec roads are a little slower, but generally more scenic. One of the prettiest is the highway along the Charlevoix Coast (see pages 210–211), a route that opens up possibilities of exploring the region's interior landscapes. Like most routes in the province, however, it is one that compels you to retrace your steps. Most roads end at the edge of the northern wilderness that covers most of Québec. The only exceptions are those that take you into New Brunswick and the Maritimes, and even then you have to turn back eventually (unless you drive south into the US).

GASPÉSIE Outside the cities, Québec's most appealing feature is the Gaspésie, the long peninsula that curves along the St. Lawrence's southern shores. Poor and half-deserted for centuries, the region is now a popular destination for vacations, luring visitors with its combination of pretty villages and superlative coastal landscapes. The peninsula is some 550km (330 miles) long, however, so should not be treated lightly. You need to spend a few days here, allowing time to detour from the coast to explore the interior, a mountainous wilderness containing one of the province's highest points (the 1,268m/4,159-ft Mont Jacques Cartier). This and other peaks form part of the Appalachians, whose finest tracts are protected by the outstanding Parc de la Gaspésie and the Parc National de Forillon. The region's southern reaches are less alluring, but road routes here will take you on to New Brunswick and Nova Scotia, or allow you to loop back to Québec by way of Edmundston.

ABORIGINAL PEOPLES Québec's Native Canadian question adds another dimension to the already complicated problems associated with the province's ever-imminent

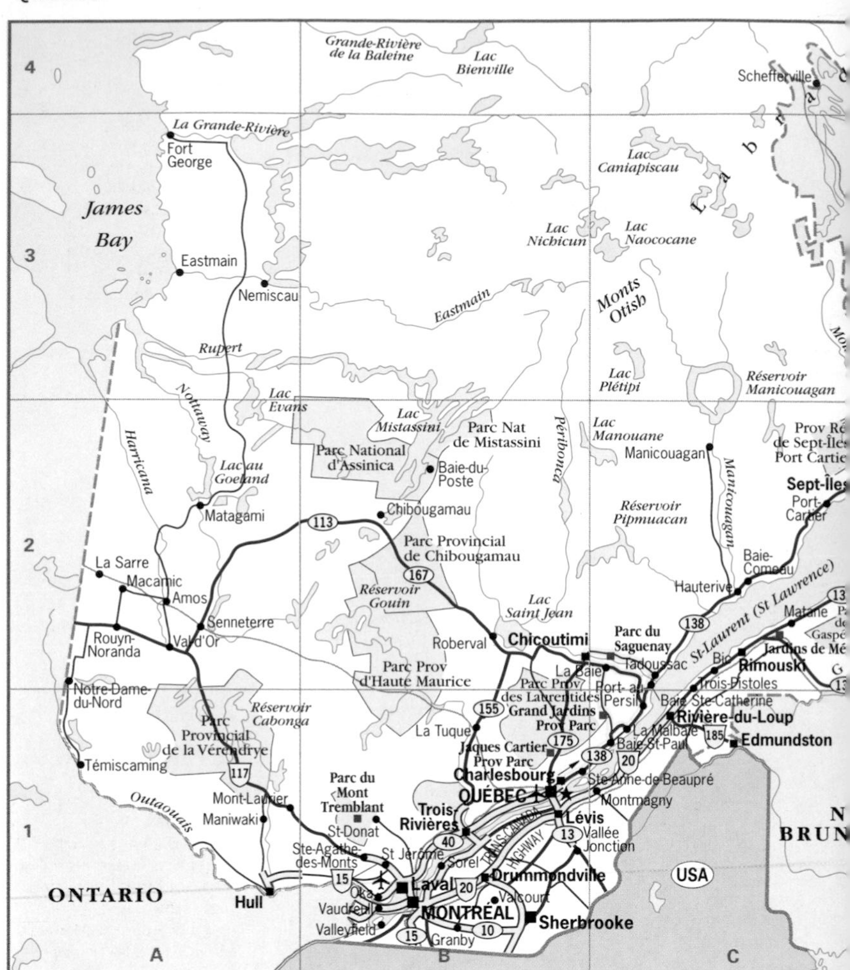

REGION HIGHLIGHTS

Baie-St.-Paul *page 210*

Boat trips *page 211*

Île Bonaventure *page 193*

Jardins de Métis *page 190*

Montréal *pages 196–202*

Parc National de Forillon *pages 191–192*

Percé *page 193*

Québec *pages 203–209*

Page 186: The glorious colors of fall in the Laurentides
Page 187: Detail, Place d'Armes, Québec City

divorce from Canada (see pages 22–24). Disputes over land rights affect most of the country's native populations, but here the land issue is bound up in a potential three-way struggle between state, province and aboriginal peoples. At least eleven native peoples inhabit Québec—among them the Huron, Cree and Mohawk—and virtually all of them lean toward the English-speaking minority. Until recently most spoke English rather than French, and many harbor anti-French sentiments that date back to the earliest days of New France (see page 31).

Draft bills drawn up in anticipation of any split from Canada have always stressed the rights of Québec's English-speakers, as well as underlining the possibility of limited autonomy for native groups. At the same time, it has always been the provincial line that native lands would remain part of any future Québécois state. Native Canadian leaders, however, argue that the destiny of their land is for them to decide, and not for Québec to dictate. The vast majority wish land—in name at least—to remain Canadian.

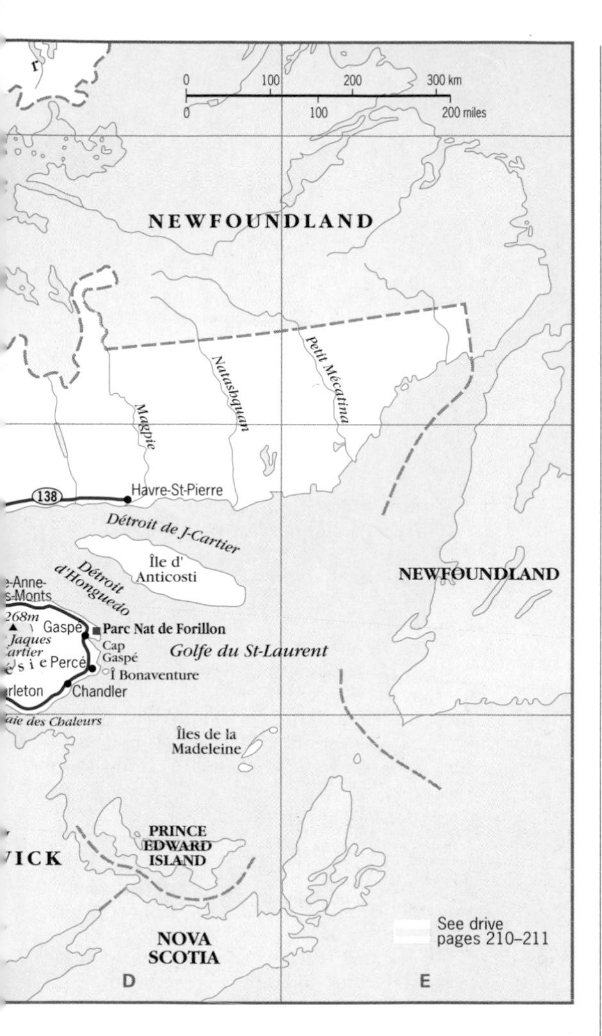

CONFLICT The territory in question is more than a few threadbare reserves. Native Canadian lands cover almost a third of the province. They are rich in lumber and other primary resources, with the rivers essential to Québec's long-held dream of hydroelectric self-sufficiency. Peacefully filed land claims have recently given way to a more high-profile militancy. Pitched street battles between Mohawks and Montréal police in 1990 made world headlines, while the Hurons have fought a long-running legal battle to retain hunting rights to certain areas. Around James Bay the Cree successfully fought plans for hydroelectric works that would have flooded an area of land larger than Germany. The issues are vital: Without native land Québécois independence is a non-starter, since Québec's economy is founded on mining, water-power and forestry, the last accounting in some years for more than a third of Canada's total output of pulp and paper, and half of its exports of newsprint—20 percent of all world production. Canada also has a lot to lose: Québec occupies a sixth of its territory—some 1.65 million sq km (635,000sq miles).

TIMELY REMOVAL
It is barely more than a decade since a lintel reading *Les Portes de sauvage* above a portal in Québec's National Assembly—redolent of ancient prejudices against Canada's aboriginal peoples—was altered to the less inflammatory *Les portes de la Famille Amerindienne.*

WHEN TO GO
Québec suffers extreme variations of climate. Winters are bitterly cold, especially in the north (Montréal's January temperatures range between –14°C/8°F and –6°C/22°F). Snowfall is high, though winter skies are often bright and sunny. Spring is short, merging into summer in June. Summer temperatures—and often humidity—are usually high (Montréal's July average is 26°C/79°F). Fall is prolonged, its colors and the region's "Indian summers" (in October and early November) making this a good time to visit.

EARLIEST AMERICANS
"Americans south of the Canadian border forget, or never knew...that the French were the first Westerners."—Alistair Cooke, *Alistair Cooke's America* (1973)

The Métis Gardens, created from the proceeds of the Canadian Pacific Railway

NATIVE NAME
The Gaspé Peninsula takes its name from *gaspeg*, a native word meaning "where the land ends."

TEARS IN THE TREES
The name of Anse-Pleureuse on the Gaspé's northern coast means the "Crying Cove." It is associated with several morbid legends, some of which ascribe the sound of the wind in its trees to the wail of lost children, while others attribute it to the moans of a murder victim or the ghostly cries of shipwrecked mariners. Curiously, the nearby village of Rivière-la-Madeleine has a similar spirit of the winds, the *braillard de Madeleine*—the "howling of Madeleine."

▶▶▶ Gaspésie (Gaspé Peninsula) *188C2*

Jardins de Métis▶▶▶ After a string of relatively undistinguished towns—Rivière-du-Loup, Trois-Pistoles, Bic and Rimouski—the Gaspé's first essential port of call is the beautiful Jardins de Métis (near Grand-Métis, tel:418/775–2222. *Open* Jun–mid-Oct daily 8.30–6. *Admission: expensive*). The seven ornamental gardens were the handiwork of Elsie Reford, who was left the surrounding estate in 1919 by her uncle, Lord Mount Stephen (1829–1921), the first president of the Canadian Pacific Railway. Stephen had been drawn to the region by its salmon fishing (some of the world's best) but by 1928 his non-angler niece had transformed the estate into an English-style garden, a remarkable achievement given the region's rocky coast and brutish climate (temperatures can touch –40°C/–40°F in winter). Among the gardens' 500 native and exotic species are plants not normally seen this far north, while spring's late arrival, in June, means that flowers that would normally be over further south bloom alongside late-flowering species. At the heart of the estate lies the Stephen family mansion, some of whose apartments are open to guided tours (*Open* as gardens above). Note that the nearby little village of **Métis-sur-Mer▶▶**, the region's oldest resort, has several fine beaches and a medley of attractive old buildings.

Parc de la Gaspésie▶▶ Highway 132 becomes increasingly rugged and more dramatic beyond the semi-industrial town of Matane, its improving coastal scenery matched by the increasing grandeur of the mountains inland. Highway 195 strikes into the interior from Matane, running 34km (23 miles) to the **Réserve Faunique de Matane▶** tel:418/797–5214. *Admission: inexpensive)*, a nature reserve best known for its herds of moose and fish-filled lakes and rivers. For a more striking touch of wilderness, however, it is worth saving your detour from Highway 132 for the **Parc**

de la Gaspésie, reached on the 39km (24-mile) diversion south from Sainte-Anne-des-Montes on Highway 299. The twisting road provides superb views of the Chic-Choc Mountains, culminating in a breathtaking ravine beneath the pinnacles of Mont Albert. Here you will find the park's Reception and Interpretation Centre (tel: 418/763–7811 *Open* early Jun–late Sep daily 8–8. *Admission: inexpensive*), with information, among other things, on the park's 250km (150 miles) of trails. Three of the best walks lead to the summit of Mont Albert, whose slopes are noted for over 150 species of alpine flowers. You might glimpse the park's moose, caribou and Virginia deer herds. This is the only place in Québec where these species can be seen together.

Parc National de Forillon►►► The road along the Gaspé's northern coast is spectacular thus far—alternately hugging the shore and perching on knife-edge clifftops—but beyond Mont-St-Pierre it becomes grander still, culminating in the Forillon National Park, the Appalachians' last gasp, a majestic 240sq km (96sq mile) park of wildlife and dramatically varied landscapes. Offshore, huge numbers of seals, porpoises and some 12 species of whale, notably the pilot whale, can be seen (whale-watching trips are available from Grande-Grave). Over 200 species of migrating and resident birds also visit the park. Guillemots, herring gulls and double-crested cormorants nest on the limestone cliffs of the park's northern fringe, a fantastic coastline with pebble beaches and sandy bays and home to rare alpine flora and marine wildlife. Inland, the park has plenty of trails and forest, the domain of bears, moose and beavers.

From the practical point of view, the park can be seen by following the loop created by highways 132 and 197, and by following a couple of the roads that lead off them.

BUSY PENINSULA
The Gaspé is hardly a well-kept secret, its well-deserved reputation drawing in numerous summer visitors. It is therefore essential to reserve accommodations in the more popular towns and villages.

VIGNEAUX
Although big, modern boats have largely replaced the Gaspé's old wooden fishing ketches, it is still possible—especially around the village of Cloridorme—to see the traditional outdoor trellis tables, or *vigneaux*, once used to split, salt and dry cod.

Coastal landscape in the Forillon National Park

NAVAL BASE
On the road west of Capaux-Os, on the southern edge of the Forillon Peninsula, stands Fort Péninsule, the ruins of a coastal battery used in World War II as a defense against the German U-boats that once prowled up the St. Lawrence. The fort was also used to defend the town of Gaspé, which—with Shelburne in Nova Scotia—was earmarked as the base for the British Navy in the event of a German invasion of Britain.

BAIE DES CHALEURS
This large bay fringes the Gaspé's southern shores, a gentler and more cultivated region with larger towns. Beyond Percé, however, resorts such as Bonaventure and Carleton are still worth a stop, and make quieter accommodation bases than the peninsula's more famous towns.

Traditional homestead on the Gaspé Peninsula

Among the latter, the best is the secondary road to Anse-aux-Sauvages, where you can pick up a superlative short trail to the viewpoint at **Cap Gaspé▶▶**, the park's easternmost point (a 90-minute round hike). A little to the north (near Cap-des-Rosiers) another road leads to the Cap Bon Ami area, where a short beach walk provides glorious views of **Cap Bon Ami▶▶▶** and its limestone cliffs. The park interpretative center (*Open* Jun–mid-Oct daily 9–8/9. *Admission: moderate*), a good place to start a visit, is close to the village of Cap-des-Rosiers, and there are two park information centers, one on the northern side at L'Anse-au-Griffon, the other to the south at Penouille (tel: 418/368–5505, www.pc.gc.ca for information).

Gaspé▶ The peninsula's main town is an anticlimax after the Forillon's scenic fireworks, a somewhat dispersed settlement scattered over the hills of the York Rivière. As a place of pilgrimage, however, particularly for French-Canadians, it is almost unequaled. It was here, in July 1534, that the French explorer Jacques Cartier first set foot in North America, planting a wooden cross carved with the escutcheon of Francois I to claim the new land for the king (he remained here just 11 days). The legendary cross was recalled in 1934 by the stone **Croix de Gaspé**, erected near the Hôtel de Ville (Town Hall) as part of the celebrations to commemorate the landing's fourth centennial.

The town's **Cathédrale▶▶**, which was begun at the same time as the Croix de Gaspé was erected, is a bizarre all-wood building (North America's only wooden cathedral) whose intimidating exterior gives way to a more pleasing interior of wood and stained glass. One window and a fresco inside were presented by France in 1934 in memory of Cartier's voyage. **The Musée de la Gaspésie▶▶**, which is located just to the east of the town center (80

boulevard Gaspé. *Open* late Jun–early Sep daily 9–7; early Sep–mid-Dec and mid-Jan–late Jun Tue–Fri 9–5, Sat–Sun 1–5. *Admission: inexpensive*) is a punchy museum devoted to the history and folklore of the Gaspé, Cartier's voyage and Québec's Anglo-French question. In the museum grounds stands a monument to Cartier, made up of six impressive bronzes (1976) with bas-reliefs on one face and accounts of Cartier's voyage on the other.

Percé▶▶▶ If Gaspé is disappointing, the next major stop on the peninsula more than makes amends. The town of Percé is preceded by another stunning 75km (46-mile) section of Highway 132. The scenery becomes especially beautiful beyond Belle-Anse, where views open up across the bay to Percé, and in the final descent to Percé itself, where a "Belvédère" offers superb views of the Grande-Coupe hills, the Pic de l'Aurore, and the town below; at this point you should also walk the short path to **Cap Barre▶▶▶**, which offers further tremendous seascapes.

Percé was once the peninsula's main fishing port. Now it is a thriving tourist town, full of shops, galleries and excellent restaurants. Despite the number of visitors, the town manages to retain its charm, particularly off-season. Most people enjoy the beauty, walk the boardwalks along the beach and take a picture of the famous **Rocher Percé▶▶▶**, a 100m (330ft) high offshore rock pierced (*percé*) at one end by a large hole. It is best seen from Mont Joli, the headland just west of the town center.

Just inland, the scenery is equally impressive, especially on the 20km (12-mile) path to the viewpoint summit (320m/1,050ft) of **Mont-Ste-Anne▶▶** accessed from the church on avenue de l'Eglise; or on the 3km (2-mile) "Route des Failles" drive to the Auberge de Gargantua, where a 1.6km (1-mile) trail leads to the gorge the **Grande Crevasse**. Less strenuous is **Île Bonaventure▶▶▶**, a cliff-edged island and nature reserve (see panel) and the **Centre d'interprétation faunique** (tel: 418/782–2240. *Open* Jun–mid-Oct daily 9–5. *Admission inexpensive*), that delves into the geology, history and wildlife of the Percé region.

Île Bonaventure has the world's largest gannet colony (over 50,000 birds)

ÎLE BONAVENTURE

Île Bonaventure lies just off Percé, and provides a sanctuary to a huge variety and number of birds. Ferries from the wharf on Percé's south beach (Jun–mid-Oct, *Admission expensive*) make the 3.5km (2.2-mile) run daily at regular intervals (tel: 418/782–2750). Until 6pm you can disembark and follow nature trails for a closer look at the birds, but be sure to check and reserve your return passage.

PARC DE MIGUASHA

This little peninsular park, now a UNESCO World Heritage Site, just 20km (12 miles) west of Carleton, has cliffs riddled with fossils over 400 million years old, including 24 species of fish. The museum and interpretive center (tel: 418/794–2475. *Open* Jun–end Aug, daily 9–6; Sep–end Oct, daily 9–5. *Admission moderate*), offers guided walks along the fossil-rich beach.

Traditional wooden houses in the Laurentides, a few kilometers from Montréal

TOURIST INFORMATION
Tel: 450/436–8532 or 800/561–6673, www.laurentides.com.

MOVING MOUNTAINS
Mont Tremblant derives its name from the natives' belief that it was inhabited by spirits that were capable of moving mountains.

KING OF THE NORTH
As late as 1870 the Laurentians were barely populated, and those few settlers who had put down roots were gradually moving on to take up jobs in the US. Events were turned around by Curé Antonie Labelle, who became pastor of St-Jérôme in 1868. From here he devoted himself to attracting pioneers to the region, working tirelessly to establish 20 new parishes. He even managed to persuade the government to route the Québec–Montréal railroad through his home town.

▶▶ Laurentides (Laurentians) *188B1*

In theory, the rolling, wooded hills of the Laurentians extend across Québec from Ottawa to the Saguenay on the north side of the St. Lawrence. In truth—at least as far as most Québécois are concerned—the region is confined to the more easily accessible swath of hills, lakes and valleys immediately north of Montréal between St-Jérôme and the Parc du Mont Tremblant. This area has become a playground for city-dwellers, packed as it is with watersport facilities, hiking trails, lively resorts, vibrant nightlife, fine restaurants, and—above all—ultramodern ski resorts.

One of the area's two segments, **Les Basses Laurentides (Lower Laurentians)**, starts virtually on Montréal's doorstep. The main highlights are the remains of two seigneuries, **La Seigneurie de Terrebonne▶▶** and **La Seigneurie du Lac-des-Deux-Montagnes▶**, remnants of the 17th-century land concessions that dominated Québec's early settlement history (see page 32). In the seigneurie of Terrebonne, a number of restored buildings of the period can be visited (20 minutes' drive north of Montréal on Île-des-Moulins, Terrebonne. *Open* Jul–end Aug daily 9–6). In Saint-Eustache (40 minutes' drive northwest of Montréal), a former seigneurial manor house (now City Hall) and seigneurial mill can be visited (tel: 450/974–5166 for opening times). Saint-Eustache was also partially the scene of the "Revolte des Patriotes," a failed but famous uprising against British rule in 1837. Nearby on Lac-des-Deux-Montagnes, the town of Oka is worth visiting with its venerable Trappist monastery.

Highways 15 and 117, both scenic roads, bring you to **Les Hautes Laurentides (Upper Laurentians)**, a recreational center for weary Montréalers. Ski resorts dot the region, particularly beyond St-Sauveur-des-Monts; some respite from the swish of skis and clank of lifts is available at busy **Ste-Agathe-des-Monts▶▶**, the region's largest town. From here you can explore the quieter and wilder areas to the north, particularly those of the Parc du Mont Tremblant (see panel), one of Québec's best-loved provincial parks.

▶ L'Estrie (Eastern Townships) *186B1*

This region of great rural charm hugs the US border, fringing New York State and New England to the south and east. It was settled after the American Revolution, when the British offered land to exiled Loyalists to the east and west of Montréal (see pages 34–35). The so-called Western Townships have long been absorbed into Ontario, but in the east the Eastern Townships label has stuck, though Montréalers, confusingly, know them simply as the "Townships" or "Cantons de l'Est." *L'Estrie* is a recent invention, concocted from *est* (east) and *patrie* (homeland).

The area has long been a cottage and summer resort retreat, though over the last few years a certain amount of development has put tourism on a more commercial footing with new ski resorts very much to the fore. Elsewhere, however, the region retains its pastoral allure, with its lake-filled valleys, quaint villages and wooded hills (the foothills of the Appalachians). Visitors come here year-round, but particularly in the fall, when the leaves are turning, and in very early spring, when there is a chance to sample some of Canada's famous maple syrup (see panel).

Granby▶, some 80km (50 miles) from Montréal, is the region's "gateway;" thereafter, the best way to see the region is to explore the back roads off highways 10, 55 and 243. The town is known for its zoo, the **Jardin Zoologique** (525 rue St.-Hubert. *Open* Jul–end Aug daily 10–7; mid-May–end Jun, early Sep daily 10–6; mid-Sep to mid-Oct Sat–Sun 10–6. *Admission: expensive*). Other worthwhile villages include **Magog▶▶**, a lakeside base that is ideal for excursions to the 1912 Benedictine monastery of **St-Benoît-du-Lac**, famous for its cheeses, and the superb viewpoint atop nearby Mont-Orford, accessible by chair-lift in summer. Many people also visit **Valcourt▶▶**, just to the west, mainly to see the **museum** dedicated to the inventor of the snowmobile, Joseph Armand Bombardier (1001 avenue J. A. Bombardier. *Open* May–end Aug daily 10–5; Sep–end Apr Tue–Sun 10–5. *Admission: moderate*).

Canadian favorite—delicious maple syrup

MAPLE SYRUP
Around 90 percent of Canada's annual 4.5 million liters (1.1 million gallons) of maple syrup is produced in rural areas of Québec such as L'Estrie. Although the syrup has been known to native peoples for centuries, the first recorded European mention is made in 1706. Trees were tapped each spring, to allow the sap to flow from a diagonal cut into a hollowed-out trunk. Once the sap was collected, it was boiled down in a copper kettle over a fire and the resulting sugar formed into cakes for later use. Modern methods are more sophisticated, but plenty of small wooden "sugar shacks" (*cabanes à sucre*) survive. Families use them for "sugaring off" ceremonies, when hot syrup is poured onto clean snow and the resulting "taffy" (*tires*) is eaten.

FRENCH SPIRIT
"There is nowhere in the world where the spirit of France works so movingly as it does in the Province of Québec."—André Malraux quoted by Mordecai Richler, *Québec Oui, Ottawa Non* (1964)

ARRIVING BY AIR
Montréal's major international airport is Montréal–Trudeau, 22km (13 miles) southwest of the city (tel: 514/394–7377). Aérobus (tel: 514/931–9002 or 800/465–1213) operates a shuttle every 30 minutes (5am–11pm) from the airport to the main bus station (Station Centrale Berri) and the Station Aérobus (777 rue de la Gauchetière Ouest).

ARRIVING BY BUS AND TRAIN
Montréal's bus station is Station centrale des autobus at 505 boulevard de Maisonneuve Est (tel: 514/842–2281). It is linked directly to the Berri-UQAM Métro station. The VIA Rail train station (Gare Centrale) is on rue de la Gauchetière, below the La Reine Elizabeth hotel (VIA Rail tel: 888/842–7245, www.viarail.ca). The nearest Métro is Bonaventure.

Part of Montréal's Ville Souterraine

►►► Montréal *186B1*

Situated in the heart of the St. Lawrence River, on one of over 230 small islands, Montréal is Canada's second-biggest city, the world's second-largest French-speaking city (after Paris), and one of the most cosmopolitan and exciting places to visit in Canada. Its streets are a vibrant mix of the old and new, juxtaposing skyscrapers with an old quarter that contains more historic buildings than any other city in North America. Museums, churches and galleries abound, and there are plenty of parks, a rejuvenated harbor area, and bars, cafés and multiethnic restaurants galore.

History Jacques Cartier claimed Montréal for King François I of France in 1535. Its site at the time was occupied by Hochelaga, a native village of some 1,000 people. The tribe's leaders took Cartier to the hill behind the settlement, where the summit so impressed the explorer that he christened it *un mont réal*, a "royal mountain" (though other stories suggest the name was coined simply to honor the French king). The area was then probably not visited until 1603, when Samuel de Champlain established a trading post here known as Place Royale. In 1642 it was visited again, this time by the god-fearing Paul Chomedey de Maisonneuve. He established a mission, Ville-Marie de Mont-Réal, which became the germ of the present city.

By 1672 de Maisonneuve's settlement probably numbered about 1,500 people. In time it became a trading center, and a base for explorers and trappers pushing inland to the Great Lakes, Ohio and the Mississippi River valley. At the arrival of the British in 1759 the city had a population of 5,000, and was contained within walls that corresponded more or less to the area of Vieux-Montréal (see below). Immigration and Loyalist refugees further boosted its population, greatly stimulating the city's booming fur trade. In 1783 the trade was consolidated further by the formation of the North West Company, a great rival of the Hudson's Bay Company. By the time of Confederation in 1867, Montréal had emerged as Canada's leading city.

In the second half of the 20th century, Montréal's former financial prominence was challenged by Toronto, which has gone on to become the economic linchpin of Canada. In addition, Québec government's separatist policies precipitated a drift of English-speaking businesses away from Montréal. The Port of Montréal has, however, undergone a renaissance, and is now considered the premier port for handling containerized transport in Eastern North America.

Orientation Montréal extends over a large island (51km/30 miles by 16km/10 miles), but the city's central core is a far smaller area that divides conveniently into three: **Vieux–Montréal** is the heart of the old city, and runs along the St. Lawrence River; **Mont Royal** is the large hill that rises up behind the city center; and **downtown** is an area of high-rises, malls and older buildings that lies roughly between Vieux-Montréal and Mont Royal. Further out lie the impressive facilities built for the 1976 Olympics. Distances between the areas are too great for all but the keenest walkers, but within the districts you should be able to wander easily between sights.

Downtown from the Parc du Mont-Royal

Montréal's excellent Métro is on hand for longer trips (see panel opposite), and when the weather is bad you can take to the famous Ville Souterraine, or Underground City, to stroll between sights (see panel, page 199).

Place-d'Armes▶▶ This square is one of two possible starting points for a tour of Vieux-Montréal (the other is Place Jacques-Cartier). In 1644 it was the site of a pitched battle between natives and missionaries. Paul Chomedey de Maisonneuve, who is commemorated by a statue at its center, is said to have personally killed the native chieftain on this spot. The piazza's north side is dominated by the **Banque de Montréal▶** (129 rue St-Jacques. *Open* Mon–Fri 10–4. *Admission free*), built in 1847 as the headquarters of Canada's oldest bank (founded in 1817), with interior fittings dating from 1905, and a small museum.

To the south rises the **Basilique Notre-Dame▶▶▶** (116 rue Notre-Dame Ouest. *Open* late Jun–early Sep daily 7am–8pm; late Sep–late Jun daily 7–6. *Admission: moderate*), a Catholic church built in 1829, and easily recognized by its two towers, Temperance and Perseverance. In the westerly tower is one of North America's largest bells, the 12-ton Gros Bourdon, reputedly audible 25km (15 miles) away. The church's sumptuous interior includes a blue vault, fine wooden carving and delicate French stained glass.

GETTING AROUND

Montréal is justly proud of its magnificent 65-station Métro. It has four color-coded routes, with signs that indicate the direction of trains by stating their terminus destination. Tickets can be bought singly or in a six-ticket *carnet*. A free transfer ticket, or *correspondance*, is available from station dispensers, allowing rides to be completed on buses up to a time limit of one hour. You can also use it to transfer from bus to Métro.

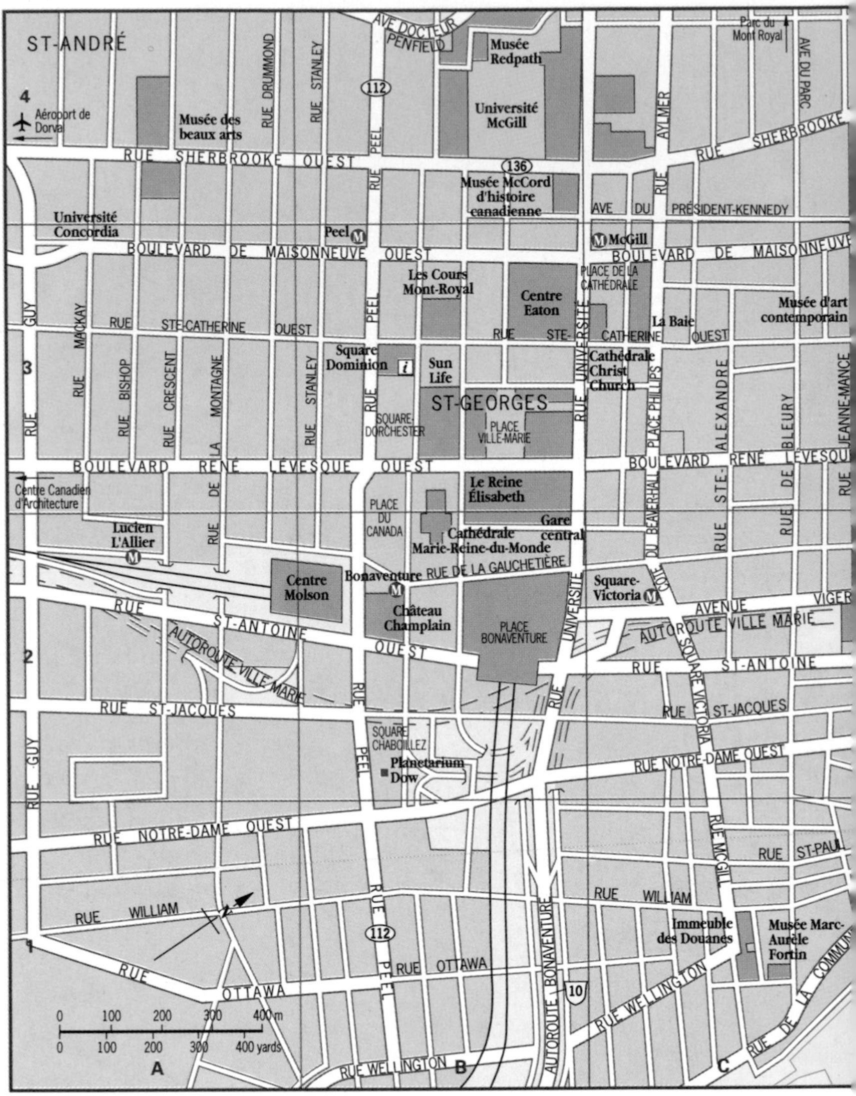

BOAT TRIPS
Cruises of Montréal's harbor depart in summer from the Vieux-Port area (tel: 514/849–9952, www.bateau-mouche.com), and also from Jacques Cartier Pier. The nearest Métro is Champ-de-Mars. The Jet Boat makes more exhilarating but expensive trips from Clock tower Pier up through the Lachine Rapids (tel: 514/284–9607, www.jetboatingmontreal.com).

Nearby lies the **Séminaire de Saint-Sulpice►**, Montréal's oldest building (1685–1715). It was built for the Sulpician order (founded in Paris in 1641). The order's main job was training men for the priesthood, but it became involved in recruiting men and missionaries to colonize New France, and, as the driving force behind de Maisonneuve's mission, a prime mover in the birth of Montréal. The order retained property rights to much of the city until as late as 1854, and continues to occupy the building (which is closed to the public). Note the clock above the main door, the oldest public timepiece in North America (pre-1710).

Château Ramezay►► Moving east along rue Notre-Dame, Montréal's oldest street, brings you to another cluster of city monuments. On the left stands the **Old**

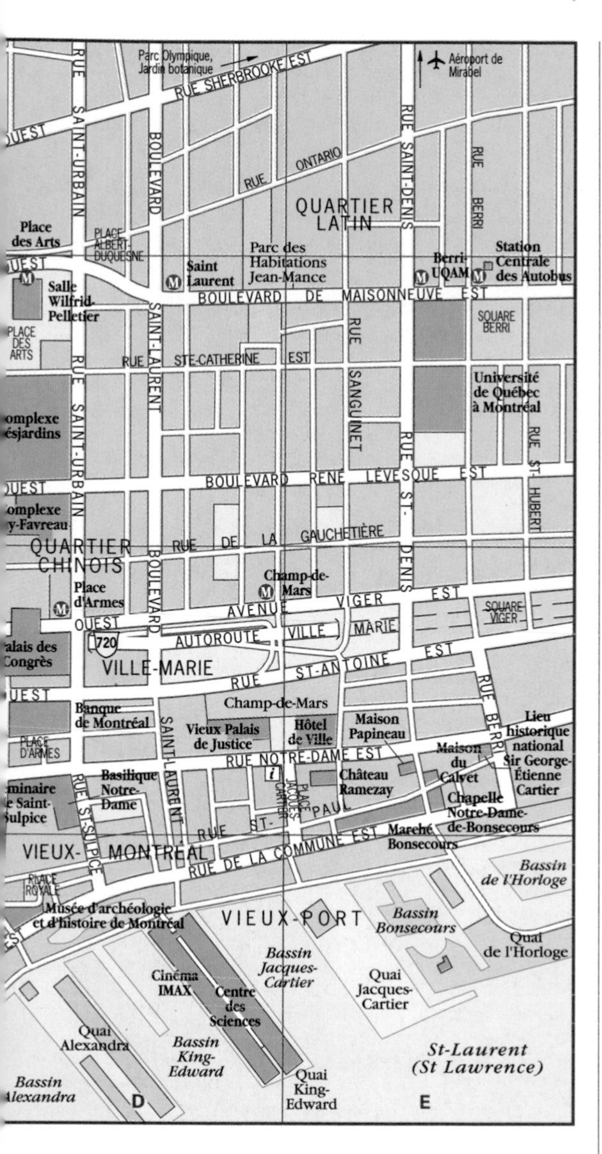

Courthouse, built by the British in 1857; beyond it is the 1878 **Hôtel de Ville (City Hall)**, from whose balcony the late French president Charles de Gaulle delivered his famous *Vive le Québec libre* speech in 1967. Across the street is one of North America's oldest buildings, **Château Ramezay** (280 rue Notre-Dame Est, tel: 514/861–3708. *Open* Jun–end Sep daily 10–6; Oct–end May Tue–Sun, 10–4.30. *Admission: moderate*). Built in 1705 by Claude de Ramezay, Governor of Montréal, in 1755 it became the headquarters of the Compagnie des Indes, which long held a monopoly on beaver pelts exported from the city. In 1763 it was sold to the British, but was later the headquarters of the American forces, opposed to the British, who briefly occupied the city in 1775. Fine period rooms house a museum telling the history of the city and château.

TOURIST INFORMATION
Montréal's main downtown Tourisme-Québec tourist office is Infotouriste on the north corner of Metcalf and Square-Dorchester at 1255 rue Peel (tel: 514/873–2015 or 877/266–5687, www.bonjourquebec.com or www.tourism-montreal.org). The nearest Métro stop is Peel. The office will find accommodations free of charge. There is a smaller office in Vieux-Montréal at 174 rue Notre-Dame Est, on the corner of Place Jacques-Cartier (tel: 514/873–2015) and summer-only kiosk on quai Jacques Cartier.

VILLE SOUTERRAINE
Montréal's humid summers and icy winters have led to the development of the so-called "Underground City," an ever-expanding maze of passages that allow Montréalers to shop, go to work and visit museums, cinemas and theaters without ever setting foot on the city's streets above. The network began in the 1960s with the opening of the Place Ville-Marie complex, and now it extends over almost 30km (20 miles).

RUE SHERBROOKE
This street takes its name from Sir John Sherbrooke, Governor General of Canada 1816–1818. It is estimated that between 1870 and 1920 the few thousand people living on or just off this street near the rue Crescent owned around 70 percent of Canada's wealth. This earned the area the title of the "Golden Square Mile." Today its former exclusivity is symbolized by the grand Ritz-Carlton Hotel and numerous expensive galleries and shops.

PARC DU MONT-ROYAL
The unmissable hill above the city has been jealously guarded as a city park since it was bought in 1875 for the then-vast sum of $1 million. Frederick Law Olmsted, the landscape architect responsible for New York's Central Park and San Francisco's Golden Gate Park, was commissioned to do the landscaping. Walking, relaxing and enjoying the views here are a highlight of any trip to the city.

PARC OLYMPIQUE
The scale and splendor of Montréal's 1976 Olympic complex are extraordinarily impressive. Guided tours are available around the main stadium, and it is possible to take an exhilarating ride up the stadium's 168m (554ft) "inclined" tower for some astounding views (tel: 514/ 252–8687. *Open* late Jun–early Sep daily 9–7; early Sep–late Jun daily 9–5. *Admission: expensive*). The nearest Métro stations are Viau and Pie IX.

Houses in Vieux-Montréal, the heart of the old city

Place Jacques-Cartier▶▶▶ Vieux-Montréal's second focal point is the heart of the old city's summer social and cultural life. Its flanks are lined with cafés, shops and restaurants, and its open spaces filled with milling tourists, horse-drawn buggies and raucous street performers. In 1804 the square was opened as the city's main market, but today only a handful of flower stalls hark back to its original function. At its western end, the site of the old Silver Dollar Saloon (1811) now houses an Infotouriste office (see panel, page 199). The statue on the square's column (1809) is of Admiral Nelson, a surprising incumbent given Montréal's strong francophone tradition. The statue was erected after Nelson's victory at Trafalgar, and was paid for with money raised from a general collection to which the Sulpician Fathers of the Notre-Dame Basilica (who were persecuted in France by Napoleon) contributed heavily. A little street off the square's southern side, rue St-Amable, is known for its numerous street artists and caricaturists.

Lieu historique Sir George-Étienne Cartier▶▶ This pair of adjoining houses formed the home and offices of Sir George Étienne Cartier, one of the founding fathers of the Confederation (see pages 36–37). Québécois separatists these days see Cartier, once considered an all-Canadian hero, as something of a traitor to the cause. As a result, the displays in the house, decorated and furnished as it would have looked in Cartier's day, are somewhat politic in their choice of subject matter. Most deal with Cartier's pivotal role in the transcontinental railroad rather than his efforts at creating a united Canada (458 rue Notre-Dame Est. *Open* late May–end Aug daily 10–6; Sep–late May Wed–Sun 10–12, 1–5. *Admission: moderate*).

Chapelle Notre-Dame-de-Bonsecours▶▶▶ Barely a block west of Cartier's former home stands Montréal's loveliest little church. The first wooden chapel on the site was built in 1657, and has been replaced three times since. The present structure dates from 1772, though the rear tower and statue of the Virgin were added in the 19th century. Be sure to climb the main tower, or *Monument*, for some lovely views. The church became known as the sailors' church, hence the ship-shaped votive offerings inside. Behind the chapel, there is an interesting museum devoted to Marguerite Bourgeois, who founded the church and Montréal's first school after joining de Maisonneuve in his original mission. Canonized in 1982, she became Canada's first female saint. The museum also explains the work of the Congregation of Notre-Dame, the teaching order founded by Marguerite Bourgeois. (*Open* May–end Oct Tue–Sun 10–5.30; Nov–end Apr Tue–Sun 11–3.30. *Admission: chapel, free; museum, inexpensive.*) Next to the chapel stands the elegant Marché Bonsecours (1854), which began life as a market and subsequently housed municipal offices. Renovation in the 1990s turned the main floor into a series of designer shops and other handicrafts all made locally. There are exhibition galleries on the second floor. (*Open* daily 10–5.)

Vieux-Port▶▶ Montréal's former half derelict Old Port area has been completely transformed. Today a linear park runs

The interior of the basilique Notre-Dame is one of the most beautiful in the city

for several kilometers/miles along the waterfront, offering fine views of city and river, and there is a wide variety of activities summer and winter. The Quai King Edward has an an interactive science and technology museum,the **Centres ds Sciences** (tel: 514/496–4724. *Open* daily 10–5. *Admission: expensive).*

Musée d'archéologie et d'histoire de Montréal▶▶ This superlative museum complex, opened in 1989, illustrates the development of Montréal. It has been built around excavations that have revealed traces of the city's earliest incarnations, including parts of its first Catholic cemetery. Sleek galleries present a high-tech picture of how the city began life as a meeting place, and of its transformation from a mission post to one of North America's great trading cities (350 Place Royale, tel: 514/872–9150. *Open* late Jun–early Sep Tue–Fri 10–6, Sat–Sun 11–6; early Sep–late Jun Tue–Fri 10–5, Sat–Sun 11–5. *Admission: expensive*).

Place Ville-Marie▶▶ This square is located in the heart of downtown Montréal. Around its open spaces lie several other large squares and skyscraper ensembles, notably Place du Canada, Square-Dorchester and Canada's largest commercial building, Place Bonaventure. Also here are some of the main entrances to the malls and walkways of the Ville Souterraine. **Square-Dorchester▶** was a Catholic cemetery until 1870 (there are still bodies beneath the concrete), but later became the heart of the 20th-century city, a role it relinquished gradually during the process of urbanization. Today it is home to the Infotouriste building (see panel, page 199). **Place du Canada▶▶** is best known for the **Cathédrale Marie-Reine-du-Monde** (1894), commissioned in 1870 to reassert the role of Catholicism in the new Dominion and designed as a small-scale copy of St. Peter's in Rome. Opposite it stands the Sun Life Building (1914), Montréal's first skyscraper and for 25 years the tallest building in the British Empire.

THE "BUZZ"

The "Main," the name given to boulevard St.-Laurent, the street that traditionally separated the French and British districts of the city, is the center of all that's hip in Montréal. The bohemian streets on and around it—especially the ten or so blocks north of rue Sherbrooke—are full of cafés, galleries, restaurants, bookstores and secondhand stores: they are also home to many of Montréal's painters, writers and poets. Particularly good for strolling down are the rue Ste-Catherine; rue Prince Arthur; Square St-Louis; and the Latin Quarter, located around rue St-Denis.

Aboriginal carving, one of 700,000 artifacts held by the Musée McCord

BIÔDOME
Designed to stage Olympic cycling events in 1976, the magnificent globe-shaped Velodrome now houses a deservedly popular environmental museum and was renamed "Biôdome" to signal its new role. (4777 avenue Pierre-de-Coubertin, Parc Olympique, tel: 514/868–3000. *Open* late Jun–early Sep daily 9–7; early Sep–late Jun Tue–Sun 9–5 *Admission: expensive.*)

JARDIN BOTANIQUE
In summer free shuttle buses run from the Parc Olympique to this fine 72ha (180-acre) garden, which contains over 30 different types of ornamental garden—Alpine, Chinese, Japanese, annuals, perennials, poisonous, monastery and so on (4101 rue Sherbrooke Est, tel: 514/872–1400; Métro station Pie IX. *Open* late Jun–early Sep daily 9–6; early Sep–end Oct 9–9; Nov–late Jun 9–5. *Admission: moderate*).

Rue Ste-Catherine▶▶ Montréal's main shopping street is the site of most of the city's department stores—La Baie, Ogilvy and Simons—as well as a host of other high-quality stores and middling-to-good restaurants. (Montréal's grandest shop, Holt Renfrew, lies just to the north on rue Sherbrooke.) There is also the neo-Gothic **Anglican Christ Church Cathedral** (1857–1859). Inside, behind the altar, lies a fine carved stone reredos, and the famous Coventry Cross, forged from nails recovered from the wreckage of the English city of Coventry's bombed cathedral. Farther north up the street lies the modern **Place-des-Arts▶**, Montréal's main theater complex, also home to the **Musée d'art contemporain▶** (185 rue Ste-Catherine Ouest, tel: 514/847–6226. *Open* Tue, Thu–Sun 11–6, Wed 11–9. *Admission: moderate*), a gallery of modern works by Québécois, Canadian and international artists.

Musée McCord▶▶▶ This outstanding museum lies close to **McGill University**, one of Canada's most prestigious seats of higher education, endowed in 1813 by James McGill, a wealthy Scottish fur trader. The museum also has Scottish links; its collection is built around a private collection accumulated by the Irish-Scot McCord family in the 19th century. The displays concentrate on Canada's social history, with textiles, native cultures and costumes (over 10,000 pieces), and the development of Montréal's fur trade and the North West Company. Equally outstanding is the museum's **Notman Photographic Archive**, a collection of 700,000 prints and period photographs (690 rue Sherbrooke Ouest, tel: 514/398–7100. *Open* Tue–Fri 10–6, Sat–Sun 10–5, Mon and hols 10–6 summer only. *Admission: moderate*).

Musée des beaux-arts▶▶▶ Canada's oldest museum (opened in 1862), more than does justice to its excellent collection of Canadian, European and international paintings and fine arts. The national collection traces the evolution of the country's art from the pictures and artifacts of New France through to the works of Paul Kane, Cornelius Krieghoff and the Group of Seven. The European collection includes canvases by El Greco, Rembrandt, Breugel, Gainsborough and others, many donated by wealthy merchants during Montréal's days of financial glory. Other exhibits include silverware, furniture and porcelain, together with native and Inuit artifacts, sculptures by Henry Moore and decorative and applied arts from Africa and the Far East (1379 rue Sherbrooke Ouest, tel:514/285–1600. *Open* Tue, Thu–Sun 11–6; Wed 11–9. *Admission free; temporary exhibits, expensive*).

Centre Canadien d'architecture▶▶ This sleek monument to the architectural profession, opened in 1989, has quickly become one of downtown's big attractions. Behind its gargantuan and windowless facade lies an older building, the beautiful Shaughnessy mansion, with its art nouveau Devoncore conservatory, skilfully incorporated into the complex. Changing exhibitions display prints, plans, drawings and models dedicated to individual architects and different schools of architecture (1920 rue Baile, tel: 514/939–7026. *Open* Jun–end Sep Tue–Wed, Fri–Sun 11–6, Thu 11–9; Oct–end May Wed, Fri 11–5, Thu 11–8, Sat–Sun 11–5. *Admission: moderate; free* Thu 11–8).

►►► Québec City (Québec) *188B1*

Canada's oldest city is also one of its most beautiful. Cobbled lanes, old houses and ancient churches tumble from an enormous rocky promontory—the "Gibraltar of North America"—which perches picturesquely above the St. Lawrence River. It is also North America's only walled city, whose great fortifications form a protective embrace around the Haute Ville, or Upper Town (the old harbor area below is known as the Basse Ville, or Lower Town).

As capital of French-speaking Québec, the city's atmosphere is unfailingly French, from the deliberately Gallic appearance of its civic and religious architecture to the coffee, *baguette* and croissant of your *petit déjeuner*. It is also a relaxed and provincial city, easy and pleasant to explore on foot, and full of superlative restaurants, quaint shops, relaxed nightlife and charming cafés.

French capital Iroquois natives were the first to inhabit the heights above the St. Lawrence—an area they called *Kebec*, which means "a place where the waters narrow."

INFORMATION
Québec has several tourist offices: the most central is the Maison du Tourisme de Québec, opposite the Château Frontenac at 12 rue Ste-Anne, Place d'Armes (tel: 418/649–2608 or 800/363–7777, www.bonjourquebec.com). Another is found at 835 avenue Wilfrid Laurier (tel: 418/641–6290, www.quebecregion.com).

Eating out in Québec's charming Basse Ville

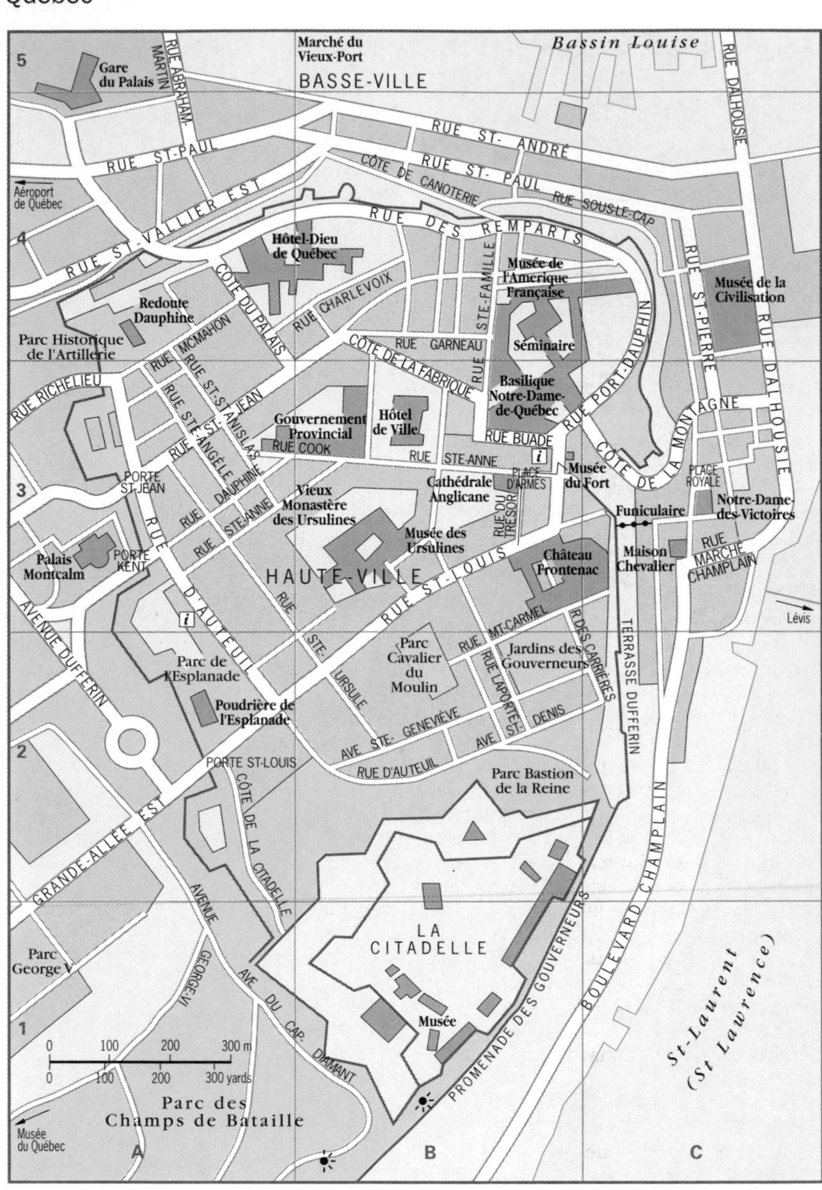

MOTHER CITY

"Québec...ranks by herself among those Mother-cities of whom none can say, 'This reminds me.'"—Rudyard Kipling, *Letters to the Family* (1907)

Jacques Cartier, who spent a winter here in 1535, named the site's rocky promontory Cap aux Diamants, in expectation of the mineral wealth that he hoped to find in the new land. In 1608, Samuel de Champlain established a settlement here—a humble fur post that would eventually become capital of all France's far-flung North American territories.

Skirmishes with Britain punctuated the city's early years, culminating in the battle that was to change the course of Canadian history. In the summer of 1759 a British force of 40 ships, 2,000 cannon and 10,000 men under the command of 31-year-old General James Wolfe,

The Château Frontenac Hotel was built on the site of the palace of Québec's former French governors

bombarded the city for two months. On the evening of September 15, in a plan that even Wolfe described as "desperate," 5,000 British troops silently scaled the heights around the city. Next morning the French, under the Marquis Louis Joseph de Montcalm, found their opponents drawn up just 1.5km (1 mile) from their lines. Disorganized and bewildered, the French engaged in a brief but bloody battle during the course of which Wolfe was killed and Montcalm was mortally injured. Twenty minutes later the British were victorious.

The city continued to prosper under its new masters, becoming capital of Upper Canada in 1840. In the first half of the 20th century, however, stagnation followed the collapse of its lumber and shipbuilding industries, as accessible timber supplies were exhausted. Recently it has found a new lease of life, becoming once more a vibrant symbol of French-Canadian aspirations.

Place d'Armes▶▶▶ This busy, pleasant square (Arms Square) forms the heart of Québec's upper town. On its southern flank, at 1 rue des Carrières, rises the grandiose **Château Frontenac▶▶▶**, a Gallic pastiche of towers, turrets and steeply pitched roof that is the city's principal landmark. Built for the Canadian Pacific Railway in 1892, the hotel occupies the site of the Château St-Louis, former home of the French colonial governors (of whom one, the Comte de Frontenac, gave it his name).

To the south stretch the pretty **Jardins des Gouverneurs▶**, graced by a joint monument to Wolfe and Montcalm and the **Terrasse Dufferin▶▶▶**, an unmissable promenade with superb views of the St. Lawrence and the lower part of Vieux-Québec.

On the square's northeastern corner sits the **Musée du Fort▶▶** (10 rue Ste-Anne, tel: 418/692–1759. *Open* Apr–end Oct daily 10–5; Nov–end Mar Thu–Sun 11–5.

ARRIVING
Domestic and international flights arrive at Québec City International Airport in Sainte-Foy, 19km (12 miles) west of the city center. VIA Rail trains (418/692–3940) from Montréal arrive in the Basse-Ville at the Gare du Palais (tel: 418/524–4161). Services from the Maritimes arrive in Lévis across the St. Lawrence (see panel, page 207) at the Gare du Lévis (tel: 800/835–3037).

Québec's many peaceful corners offer momentary respite from the rigors of sightseeing

GETTING AROUND
Almost all of Québec City can be seen on foot. For longer excursions (see panels, pages 207 and 209) use CTCUQ buses (tel: 418/627–2511). Tickets bought on the bus (exact fare only) are around 50¢ more expensive than pre-bought tickets, which are available (with day passes) from numerous shops and newspaper stands around the city. Taxi firms include Taxi Coop (tel: 418/525–5191), or Taxi Québec (tel: 418/525–8123).

NOBLE AND IMMORTAL
"Is there any city in the world that stands so nobly as Québec?... Québec is as refreshing and definite after the other cities of this continent, as an immortal among stockbrokers... You are in a foreign land..."—Rupert Brooke, *Letters from America, 1913* (1916)

Admission: moderate), which is worth a visit for its sole exhibit, a large scale-model of Québec as it might have appeared around 1750. The six battles fought in and around the city are also illustrated with the aid of a 30-minute interpretive program.

A block to the west of the square runs the rue du Trésor, once the spot where early settlers paid taxes to the French Treasury. Today it is a prettified street wedged with artists touting for portrait trade.

Séminaire (Seminary)▶▶ This large complex of religious and former university buildings was founded in 1663 by François-Xavier de Laval-Montmorency, first bishop of Québec. Intended as a training ground for priests, it also became the main seat of learning in New France and the germ of the city's present Université Laval, Canada's first francophone university (founded in 1852).

A small area of the complex can be seen on guided tours around the **Musée de l'Amerique Française▶** (Welcome Pavilion, 2 Côte de la Fabrique, tel: 418/692–2843. *Open* Jul–end Sep daily 10–5; Oct–end Jun Tue–Sun 10–5. *Admission: moderate*), a three-section collection accumulated over the centuries by the seminary's bishops and academics. Look for Joshua Reynolds' portrait *General Wolfe*, a fine assortment of scientific instruments and the outstanding examples of Québécois gold- and silverware. The building's most beguiling parts are the imposing staircase (1880), the flagstoned kitchen and refectory, and the chapel built for Jean Oliver Briand, bishop of the city from 1766 to 1784, which retains its beautifully carved wooden interior (1785).

Within the seminary grounds stands the **Basilique Notre-Dame de Québec▶** (tel: 418/694–0665. *Open* daily 7.30–4.30. *Admission free*), church to the longest-established parish north of Mexico. It was built in 1647, but badly damaged by fire in 1922. The main altar lamp was a gift from Louis XIV, while the crypt contains over 900 bodies, among them the remains of Samuel de Champlain—though no one is quite sure which body is which.

Hôtel-Dieu de Québec▶▶ The Hôtel-Dieu was founded by an order of Augustinian nuns from Dieppe in 1637. The oldest hospital in North America, it has existed on this site since 1639, and is still inhabited by the Augustinians. Its small museum contains some fascinating paintings. Among them is the earliest known picture of Québec—as the background to a portrait of Cardinal Richelieu and his niece, patrons of the hospital—and the grisly *Martyrdom of the Jesuits*, which portrays the deaths and tortures suffered by Jesuit missionaries at Sainte-Marie among the Hurons (see panel, page 163). Other displays include early and frighteningly crude surgical instruments, period furniture, metalware and various *objets d'art* that over the years have been donated to the hospital by grateful patients (32 rue Charlevoix. *Open* Tue–Sat 9.30–12, 1.30–5, Sun 1.30–5. *Admission: donation*).

Parc Historique de l'Artillerie (Artillery Park)▶▶ A short detour west from the Hôtel-Dieu brings you to Artillery Park, a collection of buildings and fortifications begun by the French at the beginning of the 18th century. They were built for a British attack from the Saint-Charles River, an attack that proved unforthcoming. The British later expanded the site, which was eventually used by the Canadians as a foundry and armaments factory during the two world wars. To make sense of the park, it is a good idea to visit the excellent visitors' center, which contains a venerable model of how Québec appeared in 1808. Then wander around key buildings such as the **Redoute Dauphine**, variously used as the French barracks and the British officers' mess. (Corner of rue St-Jean and rue d'Auteuil, tel: 418/648–4205. *Open* Apr–mid-Oct daily 10–5. *Admission: inexpensive.*)

Cathédrale Anglicane (Holy Trinity Anglican Cathedral)►►► Québec's Anglican cathedral was the first such cathedral to be consecrated outside the United Kingdom (in 1804). Modeled closely on London's church of St. Martin-in-the-Fields, it was built on the orders of King George III of Great Britain, replacing an earlier church that was given to the Récollet Fathers (early Franciscan missionaries) by the King of France. Britain provided many of the building's material treasures: the silver was presented by George III, for example, while wood for the pews came from the King's Windsor forests. The *pièce de resistance*, however, is the French **bishop's throne**, reputedly carved from an elm under which de Champlain sat to meet Huron and Iroquois natives. Look out for the little gold bars on the balcony, which are markers denoting pews for the exclusive use of British monarchs. (Corner of rue Ste-Anne and rue des Jardins, tel:418/692–2193. *Open* May–end Jun daily 9–6; Jul–end Aug daily 9–8; Sep–mid-Oct daily 10–4. Free guided tours.)

Vieux Monastère des Ursulines (Ursuline Convent)►►► The original convent on this site was founded in 1639 by a group of Ursuline nuns who gloried in the name of the "Amazons of God in Canada." Designed initially to

AUTHOR'S VIEW
"The old world rises in the midst of the new... The St. Lawrence shines at your left...and beyond it...on its promontory, sits the ancient town, belted with its hoary wall and crowned with its granite citadel."—Henry James, *Portraits of Places* (1883)

EXCURSION TO LÉVIS
Regular ferries leave Québec's Place Royale for the pleasant old town of Lévis, 15 minutes away across the St. Lawrence. Most people make the trip purely for the lovely views back across the water to Québec (the return trip is free if you stay on the ferry), but it is well worth climbing to Lévis's "Terrasse" for an even more dramatic panorama of the city.

Dusk falls over Vieux-Québec and the Ursuline Convent

STROLLS
Much of Québec's old port area has been a trifle over-renovated, but the rambunctious market stalls of the Marché du Vieux-Port along the old basin recall the area's more colorful past (daily from 8am). Rue St-André, close by, forms the heart of the city's antiques trade, and is also the hub of a warehouse district of bars, galleries, little shops and interesting restaurants.

OLD HOUSES
Rue St-Jean and rue St-Louis are both renowned for their restaurants, but the latter also has some of the city's oldest and loveliest houses. Watch in particular for Maison Maillou (No. 17), completed in 1753; the 1649 Maison Kent (No. 25), once home to the Duke of Kent, Queen Victoria's father (and the place where Québec surrendered to the British in 1759); and the Maison Jacquet (1677) at No. 34, a famous but somewhat touristy restaurant, Aux Anciens Canadiens.

provide a Christian education for native girls, it later expanded its brief to provide a grounding for daughters of French settlers, making it the first girls' school in North America. Marie de l'Incarnation, its first Mother Superior, worked hard among the region's tribes, compiling the first dictionaries of the Iroquois and Algonquin languages. Long revered (and beatified in 1980), she is entombed in a chapel adjoining the main church, whose lovely interior glows with a succession of early 18th-century altars. The interesting little museum vividly evokes the hardships of early convent life, and also contains a macabre clutch of relics, among them the skull and a single bone of the Marquis de Montcalm (Chapel: rue du Parloir. *Admission free*. Museum: 12 rue Donnacona, tel: 418/694–0694. *Open* May–end Sep Tue–Sat 10–12, 1.30–5, Sun 1–5; Oct–end Apr Tue–Sun 1–4.30. *Admission: moderate*).

La Citadelle►►►Built between 1820 and 1852 on the orders of the Duke of Wellington, who was anxious about possible American raids, the star-shaped linchpin of Québec's magnificent defenses sits atop the highest point of Cap aux Diamants (Côte de la Citadelle, tel: 418/694–2815. *Open* Apr–mid-May daily 10–4; mid-May to mid-Jun daily 9–5; mid-Jun–end Aug daily 9–6; Sep daily 9–4; Oct daily 10–3. Guided tours only; Nov–May groups by reservation only. *Admission: moderate*). The Citadel's bastions and earthworks cover 16ha (40 acres) and enclose a complex of 25 buildings. Canada's only fully francophone regiment, the Royal 22ième Régiment, founded at the beginning of World War I, is still based here. A small museum occupies one of the many restored buildings, but most people come here to see either the **Changing of the Guard** (mid-Jun–end Aug daily 10am) or the **Beating of the Retreat** (Jul–end Aug: contact visitor center for schedule).

Parc des Champs de Bataille ►► The open meadows of the Battlefields Park are the same Plains of Abraham on which British and French troops clashed in the summer of 1759 (the Plains took their name from Abraham Martin, the first pilot of the St. Lawrence River in 1620). Fine views and shady walkways make this a pleasant area to wander, and occasional interpretative boards are on hand to explain the stages of the 1759 battle. For an overview of the area, visit one of the park's two **Martello towers**, built between 1805 and 1812 in anticipation of US attack. (Access the park on foot via Promenade des Gouverneurs. Martello Tower: *Open* summer months, daily 10–5.30. *Admission inexpensive.*)

Musée de Québec►► Québec's premier art gallery occupies a building in the grounds of Battlefields Park, an enjoyable but longish walk from downtown (take bus 11 to Place Montcalm if you do not want the exercise). A superb summary of Canadian art from the 17th century to the present day, its 18,000-piece collection traces the developments from Church-sponsored art of the early days to

A statue of Louis XIV in the Place Royale

Martial music at the Citadelle, the linchpin of Québec's magnificent defenses

modern movements such as Montréal's "Automatistes" (1 Place Montcalm, tel: 418/643–2150. *Open* Jun–early Sep 10–5.45, Wed 10–9; early Sep–end May Tue, Thu–Sun 11–5.45, Wed 11–9. *Admission: moderate*).

Place Royale▶▶▶ Countless steps, or the *funiculaire,* from Place d'Armes lead to the Basse Ville (Lower Town), whose nexus is Place Royale, the site where de Champlain established his first settlement in 1608 (reputedly a single farm and storage shed). While religious, military and administrative functions eventually moved to the Haute Ville, the Lower Town and its port remained the city's commercial heart and are home to its oldest buildings and narrowest streets. A dingy area until the 1970s, when restoration began in earnest, it is now an attractive, if occasionally over-prettified, medley of old houses and intriguing nooks and crannies. The finest beneficiary of the renovation work has been the church of **Notre-Dame-des- Victoires** (1688), named after two naval victories over the British in 1690 and 1711. Ironically, the church was almost completely destroyed during the British bombardment of 1759.

Musée de la Civilisation▶▶▶ This striking, award-winning museum (the city's finest), designed by Moshie Safdie in 1988, is skilfully incorporated into three older buildings, including the building occupied by the First Bank of Québec. The museum's innovative and dynamic architectural exterior, which consists of stone quarried in the province, is complemented by state-of-the-art displays of the culture and history of Canada and Québec. Its four permanent sections are: "Memories" (an exploration of the life of Québec and its settlers over almost four centuries); "Messages" (the history of communication); "La Barque" (a 250-year-old boat found on the museum's site); and "Objects of Civilization" (a constantly changing selection of the museum's collection of historical artifacts). The museum also hosts temporary exhibitions. (85 rue Dalhousie, tel: 418/643–2158. *Open* Jun 24–early Sep daily 10–7; early Sep–Jun 23 Tue–Sun 10–5. *Admission: moderate.*)

EXCURSION TO MONTMORENCY FALLS

These magnificent 83m (272ft) waterfalls (9km/5.5 miles northeast of the city) remain a majestic sight, despite their rather overenthusiastic development for tourists, and the fact that they have been slightly tamed by various hydroelectric works. To reach them by public transportation, take bus 50 (for top of falls) or 53 (for bottom) from Beauport terminus. Get to Beauport by Métro bus 800 from Place d'Youville. (*Admission: expensive.*)

Drive

The Côte de Charlevoix (Charlevoix Coast)

See map on pages 188–189.

A drive along the beautiful village-studded coastline between Québec and Tadoussac, gateway to the stunning Parc du Saguenay (225km/140 miles).

Much of this drive follows highways 138 and 362, tracing a route along the St. Lawrence's northern shore that takes in farming country and sleepy villages dating back to the earliest days of 17th-century French settlement. The roads also weave through woods and rocky headlands, occasionally climbing the cliff-tops to give wonderful views of the Côte de Charlevoix, a coast that takes its name from the Jesuit historian François-Xavier de Charlevoix.

The drive begins in Québec (take Highway 40 to Courville or Highway 138 to escape the city), passing the **Montmorency Falls▶▶▶** (see panel, page 209) before reaching **Ste-Anne-de-Beaupré▶**, a religious shrine visited by almost 2 million pilgrims a year. As early as 1665 "paralytics" here were reported to "walk, the blind recover their sight and the sick, whatever their malady, to recover their health." At Beaupré, 15km (9 miles) beyond, take Highway 138 to see the **Chutes Ste-Anne▶▶**, where a short forest walk leads to the 74m (243ft) St. Anne's Falls.

The drive's best scenery begins in earnest at **Baie-St-Paul▶▶▶**, a village whose beautiful setting, narrow streets and 200-year-old houses have long made it a favorite with artists and visitors. An enticing village to explore, it is also a good place to spend the night, especially if you also want to see the nearby **Île aux Coudres▶▶**, a timeless (and popular) little island served by a panoramic circular road (24km/14 miles). The island can be reached in 15 minutes by ferry from St-Joseph-de-la-Rive (on Highway 362).

Moving on, the road passes **Pointe-au-Pic**, a long-standing resort known for the Manoir Richelieu (1920s), one of the region's finest hotels. At La Malbaie, just beyond, a detour takes

The interior of Ste-Anne-de-Beaupré, a major point of pilgrimage

you to one of the region's scenic highlights, the **Parc Regional des Hautes-Gorges-de-la-Rivière-Malbaie▶▶**, a breathtaking series of 700m (2,300ft) deep gorges (Canada's deepest outside the Rockies). To reach them, take Highway 138 to St-Aimé-des-Lacs and then follow the magnificent (but unpaved) 30km (20-mile) forest road.

Back on the coast road, **Cap-à-l'Aigle** and the much-visited **Port-au-Persil▶▶** herald a more rugged section of coastline, both villages providing eye-catching views of the St. Lawrence. **Baie-Ste-Catherine▶▶**, almost at the end of the drive, is a well-known center for **whale-watching▶▶▶**, with opportunities to spot the whales from boats or—more occasionally—from the viewpoint above Halte Cotière de Pointe-Noire. Highway 138 crosses the Saguenay River by way of a free 24-hour ferry, taking you to the beautifully situated town of **Tadoussac▶▶**, another whale-watching center. An excellent base, it provides a springboard for exploring the Saguenay National Park, which is best seen by

Tadoussac: Once a fur-trading center, now a whale-watching base

taking a boat trip along the magnificent Saguenay fjord.

Rather than retracing your steps at Tadoussac, the drive's conclusion, you should follow Highway 172 along the Saguenay River to **Chicoutimi▶**. This 125km (77-mile) drive offers occasional stunning views of the Parc du Saguenay, which was created to protect one of the world's largest fjords (see above). Chicoutimi, like Tadoussac, offers **boat trips▶▶▶** along the fjord (which is also accessible from Highway 172).

From here you can choose between two equally good options for returning to Québec. One is to take Highway 170 along the river's southern shore, returning to St-Siméon, an 129km (80-mile) trip that rewards you with more views of the fjord and its superb surroundings. The second is to take Highway 381 to Baie-St-Paul, a route that passes through more glorious country, and repeats less of your outward trip on the return to Québec.

Whatever primal fascination draws people to whales (and drew hunters in the past), there is no denying the attraction of the world's largest mammals, nor the thrill of watching them close up, an experience that can be enjoyed by joining tours at several key points on Canada's Pacific and Atlantic coasts.

THE PACIFIC
On the Pacific coast the best place to watch whales is on Vancouver Island, from Victoria, Telegraph Cove (near Port McNeill) or from Tofino and Ucluelet in the Pacific Rim National Park. All these centers (and others mentioned here) have companies that offer whale-watching trips.

THE ST. LAWRENCE
Whale-watching trips in Québec on the St. Lawrence and Saguenay fjord depart from Baie-Ste-Catherine, Tadoussac and Rivière du Loup.

Ritual slaughter Whales have not always been the object of environmentally friendly onlookers. The Inuit have been hunting the creatures for centuries, seeking the oil, blubber and bone upon which their survival rested. Natives of the West Coast have also been great hunters, in particular Vancouver Island's Nuu-Chah-Nulth, whose whale-hunts assumed a ritualistic element. Before being allowed to hunt, men first had to learn how to handle fragile cedar canoes. Then they underwent a period of purification that included bathing, fasting and sexual abstinence. They might also visit shrines in the forest, honoring the image of a whale surrounded by skulls or human corpses. Some carved statues of past whalers, invoking the dead to help them, or to save them from the hunt by beaching dead whales on local beaches.

New hunters European whalers observed no such niceties. Foreign hunters began to probe Arctic waters around 1818. Most prowled the eastern Arctic, searching the ice-strewn waters of the Davis Strait for bowhead whales. As more and more ships were lost, however—entombed and then crushed in the Arctic ice—the viability of whaling in the region was called into question. The solution was to establish semi-permanent whaling stations, and employ the Inuit and their methods to hunt the whales. The system proved so successful that by the 1880s the survival of the Arctic bowhead was on a knife-edge.

The sight that makes the waiting worthwhile

Waiting for whales in the St. Lawrence near Tadoussac

Disease It was not only the whales, however, that began to feel the impact of the outside world. The Inuit, too, were susceptible to the consequences, which became most marked after the arrival of American whalers in the 1890s: European diseases, already widespread, began to ravage the native population. As early as 1858 a Scottish whaler, William Penny, noted that Baffin Island's population was a mere 350, compared with the over 1,000 of a decade earlier. A report on one community in the 1920s found that a third of the Inuit population had died from influenza in just 14 years. In Coppermine, in 1931, 19 out of 100 Inuit were diagnosed as having tuberculosis.

Atlantic Today the waters around Canada's shores offer some of the world's finest whale-watching opportunities. Both the Atlantic and Pacific coasts sit astride major migration routes, their waters rich in food and their shorelines full of the sheltered bays used by whales to rest and feed. On the Atlantic, where the Saguenay joins the St. Lawrence River, the shrimp and capelin of the region's shallow waters attract blue, finback, humpback and beluga whales. Farther north, off New Brunswick, Nova Scotia and Newfoundland, the same types, together with minke and right whales, can be seen.

Pacific On the Pacific coast, California gray whales and orcas (also called "killer" whales) can often be seen during their migrations, which at up to 8,000km (5,000 miles), are longer than those of any other mammal. The journey takes the grays from their breeding and calving lagoons in Baja (Mexico) to the summer feeding grounds of the Bering and Chukchi seas (off Siberia). Mating takes place in Mexican waters in December, after which the males immediately head north (at a cruising speed of only two to four knots). They are followed by the females and their young in February (grays have one offspring, and a gestation period of 13 months). By March and April they have reached Vancouver Island, where some of the estimated 19,000 animals making the trip occasionally break off and spend the summer in Canadian waters. In September and early October they appear again, this time heading home for the winter.

THE ATLANTIC
In Newfoundland from Trinity and elsewhere on the Bonavista Peninsula companies run whale-watching trips. Key points in Nova Scotia include Brier Island and Long Island (Tiverton). In New Brunswick boats leave from St. Andrews and the islands of Deer and Grand Manan.

WIVES AND WHALES
While whalers of the Pacific Northwest's Nuu-Chah-Nulth tribes were out hunting, their wives were expected to lie perfectly still at home in the hope that the whales would become equally docile.

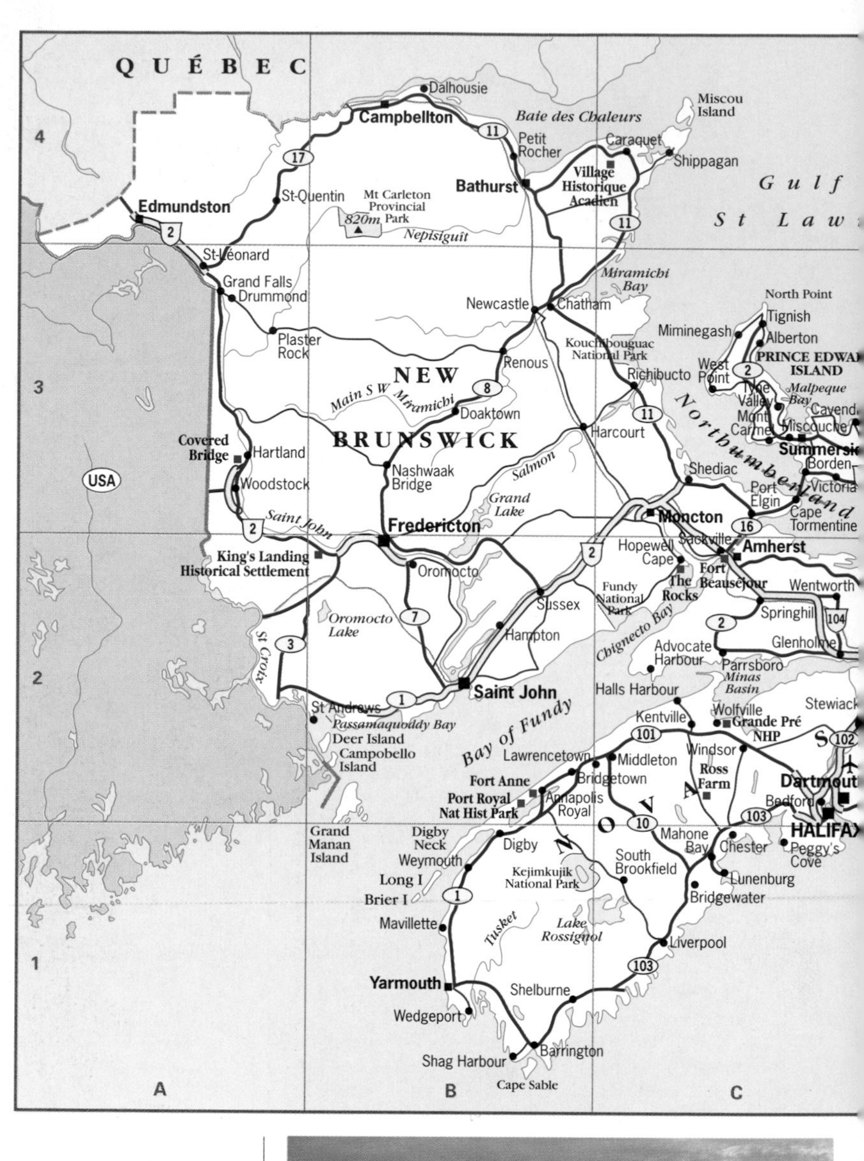

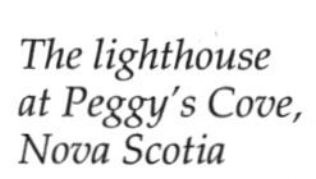

The lighthouse at Peggy's Cove, Nova Scotia

The Maritime Provinces

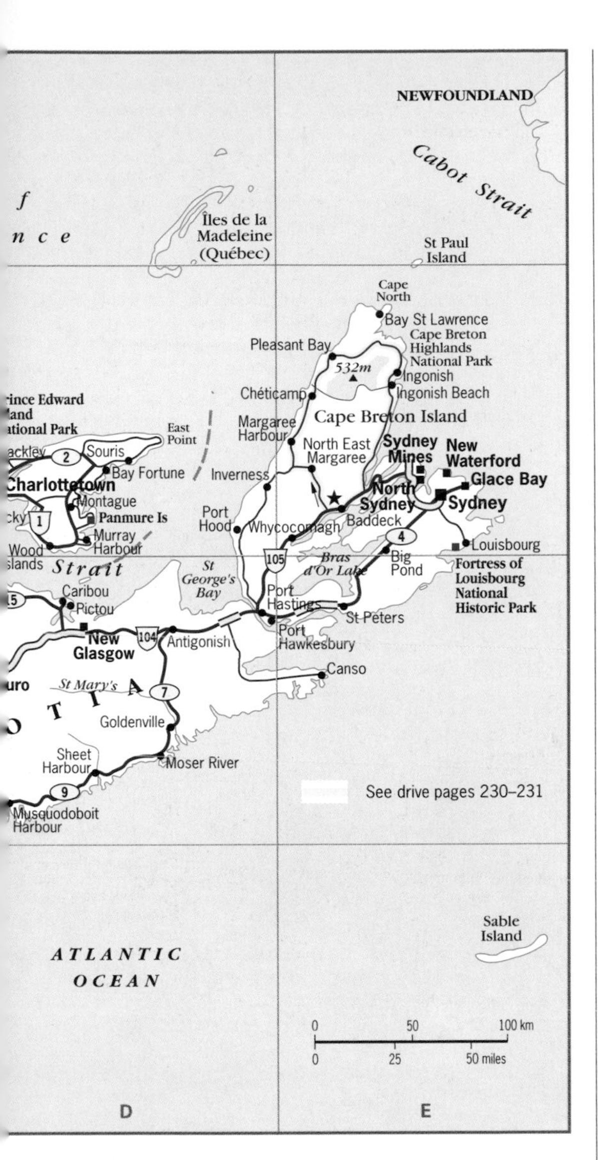

SEASCAPES The Maritimes—Nova Scotia, New Brunswick and Prince Edward Island—are Canada's smallest provinces. Most visitors come here to enjoy their beautiful coastlines, or to revel in their pristine countryside and unspoilt fishing villages. Cuisine is also a major draw—lobsters, oysters and all manner of fish feature on local menus—while cultural and artistic life is a rich tapestry of the traditions introduced by the area's French, Scottish, Irish and other European settlers.

EXPLORING THE MARITIMES Few places are easy to explore in Canada, with its vast distances and wild landscapes. In the Maritimes the problems are greater than usual. They are peripheral to the rest of the country, their forested interiors are intractable, and their rambling

REGION HIGHLIGHTS

WHEN TO GO
With the sea their constant companion, the Maritimes are often damp and breezy. Dense fogs are a possibility throughout the year (August and September are the clearest), and winter blasts of Arctic air usher in blizzards and freezing conditions. Average summer temperatures are a healthy 17–18°C (63–66°F), and the region is far less humid than Ontario or Québec. Fall is also popular, with the leaves of the area's many woods and forests turning.

CLOSE TO THE SEA
The sea, as the Maritimes' name suggests, is a constant factor of life in the region. Nowhere in any of the three provinces is more than 160km (100 miles) from the ocean, and most places are less than 50km (30 miles) from the coast.

coastlines can make progress by car laborious. The best option is to fly to one or more of the provincial centers and then rent a car. This means using Halifax, Fredericton or Charlottetown as bases, though even these main points of entry are still a considerable distance from one of the region's highlights, Cape Breton Island (part of Nova Scotia). Driving routes come into New Brunswick from Québec and the Gaspé Peninsula (and thus on to Nova Scotia and Prince Edward Island).

HIGHLIGHTS It takes some time to decipher the ins and outs of the baffling coastline and decide which of a multitude of villages to include on your itinerary. Therefore, it is worth knowing some of the region's highlights, and planning a trip around these. Prince Edward Island (PEI), the smallest of the provinces, is the place to visit for a quintessential view of the region's timeless and unspoiled villages and landscapes. Its size, and three marked drives, also make it an easy place to get to grips with.

Cape Breton Island, part of Nova Scotia, and Fundy National Park in New Brunswick (NB), offer the finest landscapes, while Halifax, Annapolis and Charlottetown are the most invigorating cities. Of the many historical remnants, the old French fort at Louisbourg stands out, closely followed by Fort Beauséjour (NB) and the Village Historique Acadien.

NOVA SCOTIA Before the advent of Europeans, the Maritimes were the domain of the Micmacs and Malecites, Algonquin-speaking natives of the eastern Woodland group of tribes (see pages 184–185). John Cabot was probably the first outsider to land in the region, though he may have been preceded by Basque fishermen and Viking explorers (Newfoundland, which likes to keep the Vikings to itself, bitterly disputes the latter). Various attempts were made at settlement before the foundation of Port Royal in 1605, a fur post established by Samuel de Champlain on the southern shores of the Bay of Fundy. In 1613 this fell to the British, and in 1621 King James I granted the region to Sir William Alexander, a fellow Scot. The charter called for the foundation of a "New Scotland,"or *Nova Scotia*, as the region was called in the document's original Latin.

Alexander's settlement was short-lived, and in 1632 James's son, King Charles I, returned the region to France through the treaty of St-Germain-en-Laye. The French re-established Port Royal, and named their new colony Acadie. At the Treaty of Utrecht in 1737, however, the area returned to the British, except for Prince Edward Island and Cape Breton Island, which were ceded to the French. Britain's victory in the Seven Years War saw it consolidate its position, partly through the shameful deportation of thousands of French "Acadian" settlers (see page 225). Immigration from Ireland, England and Scotland followed, an influx bolstered by a flood of Loyalist exiles after the American Revolution. The surge in population led to an administrative shake-up, with the break-up of Nova Scotia and the creation of the provinces of Prince Edward Island in 1769 and New Brunswick in 1784.

SHIPBUILDING Like many parts of the Maritimes, Nova Scotia then enjoyed a period of economic boom. Agriculture prospered, shipbuilding flourished and fishing brought in huge revenues. The region's forests, especially in New Brunswick, had long supplied the British Navy with masts for its ships. During the 19th century they provided lumber for brigs, barques, schooners and clippers that became famed throughout the world. In time Halifax became the British Navy's principal North Atlantic base. By the end of the century the region was the wealthiest in Canada. The advent of steam, and the use of steel hulls, ended the boom, however. The Maritimes failed to adapt and, if it were not for tourism, the provinces would be back where they started—reliant on fishing, agriculture and forestry.

PRETTIEST PLACE
"I have traveled the globe. I have seen the Canadian and American Rockies, the Andes and the Alps, and the Highlands of Scotland: but for simple beauty Cape Breton outrivals them all."—Alexander Graham Bell, inventor and long-time Cape Breton resident.

SPUD ISLAND Prince Edward Island was claimed for France in 1535 by Jacques Cartier, who described the island as "the fairest that may possibly be seen." However, the Île-St-Jean, as it became known, was not settled until some 200 years later, when French Acadians founded the village of Port La Joie near the site of present-day Charlottetown. Most were expelled in 1758 when the island fell to the British, who divided the land into plots and awarded it to English landlords in the hope that they would promote settlement. The hope was largely forlorn, and years of injustice were to result from the award. Its effects were removed only by the Land Purchase Act of 1875, when freehold rights were compulsorily extended to thousands of tenant farmers. Economic hardship continued to blight the island, however, leaving it largely reliant on fishing and potatoes: a reliance that earned it the dismissive nickname "Spud Island." These days tourism has eased the situation slightly, though unemployment and rural depopulation continue to be a problem.

BLUE WITH COLD
The Maritimes are often battered by appalling weather. In the 18th century Nova Scotian settlers earned the nickname "Bluenoses" for their ability to withstand the bitter winter cold.

Halifax and its citadel, built on the orders of the Duke of Wellington

FISH—AND MORE FISH
The Maritimes have been hit by the same problems of over-fishing as Newfoundland (see pages 242–243). At the same time fish and shellfish remain the province's culinary staples. New Brunswick is known for its sardines and Atlantic salmon, Malpeque (PEI) for its oysters, and Nova Scotia for its swordfish. All three provinces have bluefin tuna and lobsters, the latter often raised in special offshore pounds to meet high year-round demand.

TOURIST OFFICES
Fredericton City Hall, 397 Queen Street and York (tel: 506/460–2129 or 888/888–4768, www.fredericton.ca); *Moncton* City Hall, 655 Main Street (tel: 506/853-3590, www.gomoncton.com); *Saint John* One Market Square, King Street (tel: 506/658–2990, www.tourismsaintjohn.com); Tourism New Brunswick (tel: 800/561–0123, www.tourismnewbrunswick.ca).

FREDERICTON'S FROG
The prize exhibit in Fredericton's York-Sunbury Museum is the so-called "Coleman Frog." The gigantic specimen, which weighs in at around 20kg (44 lb), was reputedly discovered in nearby Killarney Lake by a 19th-century hotelier, Fred Coleman. Fred claimed to have fed the frog beer and buttermilk in his bar, and then preserved it for posterity on its demise. Many believe the frog is not all it seems...

New Brunswick

▶▶▶ Fort Beauséjour *214C2*

This old French fort stands close to the border between New Brunswick and Nova Scotia, offering beautiful views over an arm of Chignecto Bay. The area was first settled by the French, who named it the "Beau Bassin," but passed to the British following the 1713 Treaty of Utrecht. Thereafter the region formed the border between British Nova Scotia and French Acadia. The British built Fort Lawrence to defend their side of the border, prompting the French to construct Beauséjour in 1750 to protect theirs. Five years later the redoubt fell to the British, who refortified the site to guard against Acadian reprisals. Later it was used as a defensive outpost against possible American attack. It remained in service until 1835, and became a National Historic Site in 1925.

Today the site preserves many of the original earthworks and fortifications, and boasts a charming **museum** that explores the history of the fort and Acadian culture (Aulac, 55km (33 miles) south of Monckton, tel: 506/364–5080. *Open* Jun–mid-Oct daily 9–5. *Admission: inexpensive*).

▶▶▶ Fredericton *214B2*

New Brunswick's provincial capital—the so-called "City of Stately Elms"—evolved from the French settlement of Point Ste-Anne, established around 1732, and sprang more fully to life with the arrival of Loyalist exiles in 1783. It was made capital the following year (in preference to Saint John), taking its name from British King George III's second son. Today it is restrained and genteel, and many of its citizens are employed by the government and city university.

A "stilted" settlement on Grand Manan Island

Most sights lie within downtown's shady environs, starting with the **Historic Garrison District**, a park-like area between Queen Street and the Saint John River. Within the complex, the site of the former British garrison, sits the **York-Sunbury Museum▶▶** (*Open* early Jun–end Aug daily 10–5; May–early Jun Tue–Sat 1–4; Sep–mid-Dec Tue–Sat 12–5. *Admission: inexpensive*), an interesting and eclectic hodgepodge of artifacts and city memorabilia. The restored **Guard House** and **Soldiers' Barracks** (*Open* Jun–end Sep daily 10–6. *Admission free*) present a glimpse of 19th-century military life, and in summer a Changing of the Guard ceremony takes place twice daily in Officers' Square.

On **The Green▶▶**, an attractive riverside park to the south, lies the excellent **Beaverbrook Art Gallery▶▶▶**, where you'll find paintings by Dali, Hogarth, Turner, Gainsborough, Bacon and Reynolds, and Canadian works by Emily Carr, Cornelius Krieghoff and the Group of Seven (tel: 506/458–0970. *Open* daily 9–5.30, Thu 9–9. *Admission: moderate*). Also make time to see **Christ Church Cathedral** (1853), (tel: 506/450–8500), a fine piece of neo-Gothic architecture, and the imposing **Legislative Assembly▶▶** (*Open* daily 9–4; for tours tel: 506/453–2527), famed for its impressively decorated interior.

▶▶ Fundy Islands *214B2*

Three main destinations stand out in this archipelago of islands, which lie scattered across the Bay of Fundy between Maine and southwestern New Brunswick. The first is **Deer Island▶**, which is reached by ferry from Letete on Passamaquoddy Bay (beware of lines for ferries on weekends and during holidays). This is an enjoyable voyage that takes you between numerous smaller islets.

LORD BEAVERBROOK

William Maxwell Aitken was born in Ontario in 1879, but moved to New Brunswick at an early age. By 1910, already a successful businessman, he traveled to England, entered politics, and was made Lord Beaverbrook in 1917 (taking his title from a small New Brunswick town). He formed Beaverbrook Newspapers, became an immensely wealthy press baron, and served in key posts in Winston Churchill's War Cabinet during World War II. He retained a sentimental attachment to New Brunswick all his life, and helped to endow Fredericton's art gallery, theater and university. His UK newspaper, the *Daily Express*, has continued to flourish since his death in 1964.

SEAWEED SPECIALTY
Dulse is a form of edible seaweed found in much of New Brunswick. The pinky-purple fronds—soft or leathery depending on age—are picked at low tide and then dried in the sun for about five hours. Experienced pickers can gather around 60kg (130 lb) at a time. It can be eaten raw, toasted over a flame or powdered to add to soups, chowders and casseroles. The delicacy is rich in iron and iodine, but its smell—once sniffed—is never forgotten, and its powerful taste is best described as "acquired."

The population is just 800, and there is only one hotel, so, although the interior is pretty, most people explore the island's couple of roads and then pick up a ferry to **Campobello Island▶▶▶**.

This oasis of sandy beaches and wooded coves was a favorite of Franklin D. Roosevelt, who vacationed here regularly until he was struck by polio contracted while swimming in the Bay of Fundy. This American connection ensures the island is constantly thronged in summer (there is a bridge link to Lubec, Maine). Most people make for **Roosevelt's "cottage"**—a 34-room mansion that has been transformed into a museum devoted to the former president (Roosevelt Park Road, tel: 506/752–2922. *Open* mid-May to mid-Oct daily 10–6. *Admission free*).

The largest of the three main islands, **Grand Manan▶**, is reached by ferry from Blacks Harbour, a terminal just west of Letete on Passamaquoddy Bay (the crossing takes two hours). More rugged than its neighbors, Grand Manan is known for its cliffs, its dulse (see panel), its whale-watching trips and its 230 species of birds. Tourist information is available in the museum at Grand Harbour, the island's main settlement.

▶▶▶ Fundy National Park *214C2*

This outstandingly beautiful but modestly sized park protects some 207sq m (80sq miles) of the Bay of Fundy, including an 13km (8-mile) stretch of spectacular coastal scenery backing on to the park's wooded and river-cut uplands. It can be approached from Moncton to the east on Highway 114, which bisects the park, or from Saint John and Highway 114 from the west. Two visitor information centers straddle Highway 114, one on the park's eastern side close to the hamlet of **Alma**, the other about 20km (12 miles) to the west at **Wolfe Lake**. Both have details of the

Fundy is one of the Maritimes' most beautiful national parks

park's many hikes (along trails totaling some 100km/60 miles); most are comfortable day or half-day walks.

Specific things to visit in the area include Alma's vast **beach**, where you can see at first hand the scope of the area's famous tidal reach (see panel); **Herring Cove**, where there are fine views and a path down to the cove's pool-flecked shoreline (11km/7 miles) from the eastern park entrance); and **Point Wolfe**, a pretty cove reached via a 10km (6-mile) side-road off Highway 114. Beachcombers will find the park a treasure trove, while birdwatchers stand a chance of seeing many of the region's 215 species of bird.

▶ Moncton *214C3*

Moncton is a fairly nondescript place that owes its modicum of fame to its **tidal bore** (see panel), which these days is not the rampaging wall of water it once was (the silting up of the river has been primarily responsible for its taming). Contact the tourist office for times of the tide (see panel, page 218), and at the appointed hour make for Bore View Park, the best place from which to view the spectacle. The town is also the self-proclaimed capital of Acadie, the French-speaking corner of New Brunswick (see pages 224–225). German and Dutch settlers from Pennsylvania were the region's first settlers, but were joined by the Acadians after the Deportations of the 1750s. Today around a third of the town's population is French-speaking.

Acadian culture is celebrated and remembered in the ephemera-packed **Acadian Museum▶▶**, nearly 3km (2 miles) north of downtown on the campus of Moncton University (Clément Cormier Building, Moncton University. *Open* Mon–Fri 10-5, Sat–Sun 1–5. Closed Mon Sep–end Jun. *Admission: inexpensive*). A sillier, but vastly more popular, outing is take your car to **Magnetic Hill**, where a famous optical illusion deceives you into thinking that you are facing "uphill"—when you release the brake, you move forward! (Magnetic Hill is located off Route 2.)

▶▶ Passamaquoddy Bay *214B2*

A journey to New Brunswick's southwestern corner requires a major diversion from the main transprovincial highways, but it is one that is worth making for the Fundy Islands (see pages 219–220), and for the attractive villages and rural byways that ring Passamaquoddy Bay. The area was the first to be settled by Samuel de Champlain, "Father of New France," at the end of his pioneering 1605 voyage (see page 30), though the site, on the St. Croix River, is now just across the US border in Maine. Full-scale settlement was established in 1783 with the influx of Loyalist exiles.

St. Andrews▶▶▶ is the bay's main focus. It is a quaint little resort town of elegant old houses and quiet tree-lined streets (280 of the town's 550 buildings date from before 1880). Self-guided walking tours take you through the best of the heritage buildings. Special points of interest include the Court House, Greenock Church and **Blockhouse Historic Site▶▶** (Joe's Point Road, tel: 506/529–4270. *Open* Jun–end Aug daily 9–8; early Sep daily 9–5. *Admission free)*, the only surviving example of 14 wooden defensive posts built to protect the New Brunswick border against American attack. Also worth seeing are the **Huntsman**

TIDAL BORE

Much is made of New Brunswick's tidal bore. Normally the ebb and flow of tides is barely noticeable, but in V-shaped bays such as the Bay of Fundy where the inlet narrows sharply—the tide can be "squeezed" as it rushes toward the bay's head and its tributary rivers, producing a wave, or bore. The height between high and low tide, or its tidal flow, can be over 19m (60ft), the highest in the world; in the open sea it is just 80cm (32in).

HOPEWELL CAPE

Near this little village (35km/22 miles south of Moncton) lies the Rocks Provincial Park, a coastal refuge created to protect a strange but beautiful collection of wind- and sea-sculpted rocks and cliffs. At high tide the 15m (50ft) high stacks are like little islands, but at low tide they appear as tree-covered giant "flower-pots."

FIDDLEHEAD

A "fiddlehead" is the unopened frond of an ostrich fern, a delicacy that is picked in early May from New Brunswick's woods and riverbanks. The region's Malecite natives have prized the shoots as food and medicine for centuries. Today they are picked commercially and frozen, and are so well known that they have almost become the province's unofficial symbol.

The pristine scenery of the Saint John River valley

TOURIST INFORMATION
For information in St. Andrews, contact the Welcome Center at 46 Reed Avenue (tel: 506/529–3555, www.town.standrews.nb.ca).

VILLAGE HISTORIQUE ACADIEN
This reconstructed and beautifully situated pioneer village consists of 24 original buildings brought here from elsewhere in New Brunswick (only the church is a copy). It is designed to resemble the type of village settled by Acadians after the Deportations (see page 225). As in similar "living" museums, the staff wear period costume and practice various rural crafts (11km/7 miles west of Caraquet, tel: 506/726–2600. *Open* Jun–end Aug daily 10–6; Sep, daily 10–5. *Admisssion: expensive*).

Traditional Acadian rug-making and embroidery skills are practiced to this day in much of the Maritimes

Aquarium and Museum▶ (Brandy Cove Road, tel: 506/529–1202. *Open* Jul–end Aug daily 10–5.30; May–end Jun daily 10–4.30. *Admission: moderate*), which is devoted to marine displays, and the **Ross Memorial Museum▶▶** (188 Montague Street, tel: 506/529–5124. *Open* late Jun–early Oct Mon–Sat 10–4.30. *Admission: donation*), an Aladdin's cave of rugs, porcelain and period furniture.

▶ Saint John *214B2*

Saint John, the "Loyalist City," has always been New Brunswick's commercial center, leaving the job of government to Fredericton. In the 19th century the city was dubbed the "Liverpool of America," so rich had it become through trade and shipbuilding. Wood from the region's limitless forests having been the key to its success, its prosperity disappeared almost overnight with the advent of steel ships. Economic well-being has only recently returned following massive investment in container and deep-water port facilities.

Many people are here to pick up ferries to Digby on Nova Scotia (see panel, page 226), or they are simply passing through while driving from Passamaquoddy Bay to the west. The dispersed and scrappy outskirts hardly augur well, and though the downtown core is better looking, the town is not rich in diversions. The best area to explore is the **Market Slip▶▶▶**, the heart of the old harbor, which is now full of cafés, restaurants and shops. Here you will find **Barbour's General Store▶▶** (*Open* mid-Jun to mid-Sep daily 9–6; mid-Jun–end Aug 9–7. *Admission free*), a museum crammed with the produce you might have found in a 19th-century shop: look for the 300 or more "cure-all or kill-alls." Five minutes up King Street, downtown's main thoroughfare, lies **Loyalist House▶▶** (120 Union Street, tel: 506/652–3590. *Open* Jul–end Aug, daily 10–5; Jun, Sep Mon–Fri 10–5. *Admission: inexpensive*), built in 1810 for a wealthy merchant family, and today restored. Be sure to browse in the colorful **City Market▶▶** near King's Square, Canada's oldest public market.

Nearby, in Market Square, stands the **New Brunswick Museum▶** (277 Douglas Avenue, tel: 506/643–2349. *Open*

Mon–Wed 9–5, Thu 9–9, Sat 10–5, Sun and hols 12–5. *Admission: moderate*), the province's main museum of history and culture. Nearby lie the much-touted **Reversing Falls Rapids▶**, where tidal effects create rapids that change direction depending on the direction of the tide. The effect, when it happens (check tide times), is interesting, but the viewing area cannot be called a pretty one. The nearby **Carleton Martello Tower▶** (*Open* Jun– end Oct, daily10–6. *Admission: inexpensive*), built in 1814 as a defense against American invasion, and offering good views of the town, as does the **Fort Howe Lookout▶▶**, perched on a rocky cliff just west of downtown.

▶▶ Saint John River Valley *214B2*

New Brunswick's natives called the Saint John *Oo-lahs-took*—"the goodly river"—glowing testimony to its lush countryside and the rich soils. It still lives up to its name, yielding an abundance of agricultural produce (notably potatoes), and offering an array of landscapes that range from the near-mountainous terrain of the north to the maple and pine-forested farming land further south.

The province's main artery, the Trans-Canada Highway, follows the river's course, making the drive from Québec to Fredericton a good way to enjoy Saint John's attractions. **Edmundston**, an industrial town, is not one of the sights, but things pick up further on when you come to **Saint Leonard▶**, known for its famous Madawaska weavers, whose work and looms can be admired in workshops around the village. Just to the south of Saint Leonard are the **Grand Falls▶▶▶**, Edmundston's mighty 66ft waterfalls. **Drummond** is the start of potato country, while at **Hartland** you'll find the world's longest wooden **covered bridge▶▶** (see panel). Pretty **Woodstock▶▶** contains several elegant old houses. The valley's highlight, however, is the sublimely situated **King's Landing Historic Settlement▶▶▶** (30km (20 miles) west of Fredericton. *Open* Jun–mid-Oct daily 10–5. *Admission: expensive*), a reconstructed 19th-century British Loyalist village.

COVERED BRIDGES
Wood-covered bridges—also known as "wishing" or "kissing" bridges—are found across much of Québec and New Brunswick. In the past, uncovered bridges crumbled after a few years in Canada's harsh climate. A wooden roof and sides allowed bridges to survive for as long as 80 years, with the additional benefit that horses were not frightened by the sight of rushing water beneath them. The bridges had to be "high enough and wide enough to take a load of hay."

The world's longest covered bridge is in Hartland

Acadia, or Acadie, was the name given to the areas of present-day Maine, Nova Scotia and New Brunswick, settled by French pioneers in the 17th century. Descendants of those pioneers inhabit parts of these regions still, continuing a way of life that has been interrupted over the centuries by persecution and deportation.

THE NAME
"Acadia" may derive from the Micmac native word *akade*, meaning abundance, a reference to the region's fertile land and bountiful sea. Or it may have been coined by European fishermen, who looked on its beautiful pastoral pastures and recalled the *Arcadia* of Classical Greece, a region of bucolic rural tranquility.

Top: Acadian House, Cheticamp
Right: Samuel de Champlain

WHERE ARE THEY NOW?
The quaint farms, timeless villages and characteristic *joie de vivre* of the Acadians are today found mainly around Edmundston, along the Saint John River, along the border of New Brunswick and Maine, on New Brunswick's Atlantic coast between Moncton and the Gaspésie (notably around the Acadian Peninsula), on the Îles de la Madeleine, on Cape Breton Island's southwest coast and in the western reaches of Prince Edward Island.

Early days The first Acadian settlement was founded in 1604 by Pierre Sieur de Monts and Samuel de Champlain. After sailing from France, the pair built a stockade in an obscure spot on Docher's Island on the St. Croix estuary (a part of the Bay of Fundy now in Maine). Countless settlers died in the harsh winter that followed, prompting the ill-nourished survivors to found Port Royal, a village on the more sheltered coast of present-day Nova Scotia.

First forty The richer pickings of the St. Lawrence soon tempted de Champlain to move on, starting a flow of colonists to Québec that would marginalize French settlement in the Maritimes (Acadie) for centuries to come. In 1613 Port Royal was captured by British settlers from Virginia, and in 1614 it was abandoned, probably remaining empty for about 20 years while under British control. In 1632 the region was returned to the French by treaty; in the same year 40 settlers from western France refounded Port Royal on the site of present-day Annapolis Royal.

Settlement Some historians believe a handful of settlers from the first Port Royal may have struggled on through the British occupation. Others accept these 40 "pilgrim fathers" as the first Acadians, a group that was soon joined by a steady stream of French settlers. Most of these colonized the Annapolis Valley, spreading across present-day Nova Scotia as far as the Chignecto Isthmus (the neck of landing linking Nova Scotia and New Brunswick). Over the next few years Acadie was attacked by the New England colonies, and title to the land passed back and forth between France and Britain. The Acadians, however, settled into a gentle farming life that paid little heed to the wider political struggle.

Loyalty All this changed in 1713, when the Treaty of Utrecht awarded mainland Nova Scotia to the British. It also offered the Acadians an unenviable choice: either swear an oath of allegiance to Britain or leave British territory for Cape Breton Island (which was still French). Few wanted to leave Nova Scotia's rich farming land, but fewer still wished to swear an oath that might force them to bear arms against fellow Frenchmen. In the end they agreed to take an oath if they could be exempt from military service, a request that was accepted by the new British governor largely because the Acadians were the only people who could supply the colony with food.

Showdown Come the Seven Years War, this cozy arrangement fell apart. First the building of Louisbourg, a French fort on Cape Breton Island, threatened Nova Scotia. Secondly, a surprise French attack on Grand Pré in 1747, when almost 100 British soldiers were killed, aroused suspicions of Acadian complicity. Thirdly, the foundation of Halifax in 1749 meant the colony could be supplied without Acadian assistance. Attitudes hardened accordingly and, as war approached, Nova Scotia's governor, Charles Lawrence, issued an ultimatum: swear an unqualified oath of allegiance or leave. In August 1755, when the Acadians refused, he issued his infamous Deportation Order.

Deported Over the next eight years some 14,600 people were deported. Few were allowed any choice as to their place of exile. About half wound up in the American colonies, where the British hoped they would pose little threat amid the English-speaking majority. Few were well received. The rest went to France and New Brunswick, or Québec and Prince Edward Island.

By 1780, with peace between Britain and France, many had returned to Nova Scotia to find British settlers working their land. As a result, most moved west to New Brunswick, where the majority of their descendants live to this day.

Acadian cultural traditions have flourished for centuries

RUTHLESS
The deportation of the Acadians underlined the vigor with which British colonial policy was at times pursued. Governor Lawrence, who ordered the expatriation, wrote to an officer involved ordering him to "proceed with the most vigorous measures possible not only in compelling them to embark, but in depriving those who should escape of all means of shelter or support, by burning their houses and destroying everything that may afford them the means of subsistence in the country."

CAJUN ROOTS
Many Acadians deported during the French and Indian War were sent to the American colonies. Few found a welcome. Almost the only place they established a foothold was in Louisiana. In 1785 their colony there was joined by over 1,500 Acadian refugees who had previously escaped to France. These were the forebears of the state's Cajuns, whose name is a corruption of *Acadiens.*

ARRIVING BY AIR
Foreign and domestic airlines fly to Halifax International Airport (tel:902/873–1223, www.hiaa.ca), which is connected by taxi and Airbus shuttle buses (tel: 902/873–2091 to downtown Halifax, 40km/25 miles away to the southwest). Domestic carriers also fly to Sydney Airport on Cape Breton Island.

FERRIES
In the US, two linked companies sail from Maine to Yarmouth, a port on Nova Scotia's western coast: Bay Ferries from Bar Harbour (tel: 902/566–3838 or 888/249–7245, www.nfl-bay.com) and Prince of Fundy Cruises from Portland (tel: 800/341–7540). Bay Ferries (902/566–3838 or 800/565–0201) also operates from Saint John (NB) to Digby near Annapolis Royal. Northumberland Ferries operates from Caribou to Wood Islands (PEI); Marine Atlantic (tel: 800/341–7981, www.marine-atlantic.ca) operates to Newfoundland from North Sydney, Cape Breton Island.

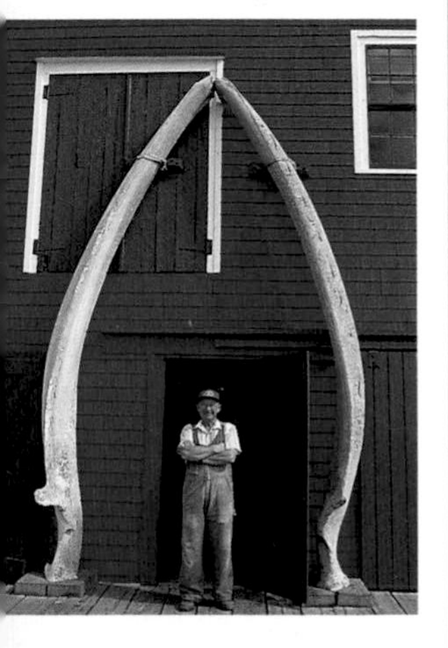

A novel Nova Scotian threshold

Nova Scotia

►► Annapolis Valley *214B2*

This pastoral farming region in northern Nova Scotia was the cradle of permanent European settlement in Canada. At its heart lies **Annapolis Royal►►**, close to the site of an outpost founded by Samuel de Champlain in 1605, and thus the longest-established town in the country (see page 224). The post has been recreated at the beautifully executed **Port Royal Historic Site►►►** (10km/6 miles west of Annapolis Royal. *Open* mid-May to mid-Oct daily 9–6; mid-Oct to mid-May by appointment. *Admission: inexpensive*). Annapolis itself is likable, with a pleasant boardwalk promenade and easygoing air. See **Fort Anne►►**, the remains of an 18th-century French fort (*Open* site, daily. Museum, mid-May to mid-Oct daily; mid-Oct to mid-May Mon–Fri by appointment), and the **Royal Historic Gardens**, a swath of variously "themed" gardens (441 Upper St. George Street. *Open* daily. Tours, mid-May to mid-Oct daily 8–dusk. *Admission: moderate*).

Moving up the valley, a former stronghold of Acadian culture, you pass endless orchards, dairy farms and many tranquil villages. All make this an enjoyable drive, interspersed with pleasant towns such as Bridgetown, Middleton and Lawrencetown. Perhaps the nicest spot is Wolfville, thanks to its proximity to the **Grand Pré National Historic Park►** (tel: 902/542–3631. *Open* mid-May to mid-Oct daily 9–6. *Admission free*), a modest park-cum-museum recalling the vicissitudes of Acadian fortunes.

►► Atlantic Coast *214C1*

Nova Scotia's wild southern coast is one of rugged beaches and breezy granite coves, providing a fine contrast to the pastoral inland countryside of the Annapolis Valley to the north. Easily explored from Halifax, it can be included in a circular itinerary that heads inland from Liverpool (on Highway 8), skirts the **Kejimkujik National Park**—which provides a taste of Nova Scotia's imposing interior wilderness—and then follows the Annapolis Valley before looping back to Halifax. Villages en route have plenty of charming bed-and-breakfast accommodations, as well as some of the province's best restaurants, with lobster and chowder well to the fore.

The coast's undoubted highlight is **Peggy's Cove►►►**, probably the most painted and photographed village in eastern Canada. Founded in 1811, it is a little fishing community of clapboard houses and shacks raised on stilts above the water. Although tourists swarm here, the village's charm remains miraculously unsullied. Indian Bay, **Chester►►** and their surrounding villages are also pretty places, especially Chester, which is full of frame houses and leafy boulevards. It attracts plenty of US visitors, and it is a favored retirement town for wealthier Canadians. Some 24km (14 miles) to the north lies **Ross Farm►►** (New Ross, tel: 902/689–2210. *Open* May–end Oct daily 9.30–5.30; Nov–end Apr Wed–Sun 9.30–4.30. *Admission: moderate*), a "living" museum of 19th-century agricultural life. **Mahone Bay►►** is equally prosperous, its wealth, like that of many local towns, having been founded on ship-building and the dubious antics of 18th-century privateers (see panel, page 229).

Peggy's Cove: photographers and artists never fail to succumb to its charms

Lunenburg▶▶▶ has lovely old houses and the superlative **Fisheries Museum of the Atlantic** (*Open* daily 9.30–5.30; also Jul–end Aug Tue–Sat until 9pm. *Admission: expensive, free mid–Oct–end Apr*). The water-front building, part of an old fish-processing plant, is Nova Scotia's principal maritime museum, and features an aquarium, model ships, real ships (moored outside), and numerous displays. Sailing ship *Bluenose II* makes popular two-hour cruises twice daily from the museum (tel: 902/634–4794). The town has a marked European atmosphere, having been founded by German and Swiss settlers in 1753.

▶▶▶ Halifax *214C2*

Nova Scotia's capital combines the services and outlook of a city with the charm and intimacy of a breezy coastal town. Founded in 1749 around one of the world's finest harbors, its original purpose was to counter the threat of the French fortress at Louisbourg (see page 229). Since then its role has been primarily militaristic. It was the Royal Navy's principal North Atlantic base, and became one of the main departure points for Britain-bound convoys during World War II. Today offices have replaced some of the old brothel-lined wharves of yesteryear, yet the downtown and harborfront areas retain their allure.

The main sight is the hilltop **Citadel▶▶▶**, begun in 1828 on the orders of the Duke of Wellington (*Open* Jul–end Aug daily 9–6; mid-May, Jun, Sep and Oct daily 9–5; Nov–mid-May grounds only 9–dusk. *Admission: grounds, free; citadel, inexpensive*). As you climb up to it, notice the four-sided **Town Clock** (1803), the city's symbol. It was commissioned by Edward, Duke of York, Queen Victoria's fastidious father, to ensure soldiers and sailors had no excuse for tardiness. In the star-shaped fortress you can clamber over the ramparts, enjoying fine views of the city, and browse among the military exhibits of the Army Museum. West of the citadel, you might visit the **Nova Scotia Museum of Natural History▶▶**, which delves into the region's geology, culture and natural history (1747 Summer Street, tel: 902/424–3563. *Open* Jun–mid-Oct

TOURIST INFORMATION
For information on the province as a whole, visit the Nova Scotia Visitor Information Centre, located on the waterfront at Old Red Store, Historic Properties (tel: 902/424–5000 or 800/565–0000, www.novascotia.com). The International Visitors' Centre at 1595 Barrington Street (tel: 902/490–5946) serves the Halifax area.

BUSES AND TRAINS
VIA Rail trains connect Halifax's Terminal Road station (tel: 800/561–3949, www.viarail.ca) with Montréal via Truro, Moncton and Saint John. Long-haul Acadian Lines buses leave from 6040 Almon Street (tel: 902/454–9321) for Annapolis Royal, Charlottetown, Fredericton, Liverpool, Moncton, Montréal and Sydney.

Mon–Sat 9.30–5.30, Wed 9.30–8, Sun 1–5.30; mid-Oct–May Tue–Sat 9.30–5, Wed 9.30–8, Sun 1–5. *Admission: moderate*). In downtown, parts of the old harbor and warehouse district, known as the **Historic Properties▶▶▶**, have been restored and turned into a pleasant pedestrian area of shops, cafés and restaurants. A similar area, **Brewery Market▶▶**, lies to the south on Water Street. Other rewarding areas to explore on foot include the Public Gardens, **Grand Parade** (Halifax's elegant main square), and the Old Burying Ground, the city's eerie first cemetery. Downtown's main indoor attractions are **Province House▶** (1726 Hollis Street, tel: 902/424–4661. *Open* Mon–Fri 9–4; Jul–end Aug Mon–Fri 9–5, Sat, Sun 10–4. Guided tours. *Admission free*), the graceful Georgian home of the provincial legislature; the **Maritime Museum of the Atlantic▶▶** (1675 Lower Water Street. *Open* May–end Oct Mon–Sat 9.30–5.30, (Tue until 8pm), Sun 9.30–5.30 (1–5.30, May, Oct); Nov–end Apr Tue 9.30–8, Wed–Sat 9.30–5, Sun 1–5. *Admission: inexpensive)*, which explores the region's proud seafaring traditions; and the **Art Gallery of Nova Scotia▶**, whose collection includes several fine works by the Group of Seven painters (1723 Hollis Street. *Open* Fri–Wed 10–5, Thu 10–9. *Admission: moderate*).

▶▶▶ Louisbourg 215E2

The ruined coastal **fortress of Louisbourg** is one of the greatest surviving monuments to French colonial ambitions in North America. Built on Cape Breton Island's eastern shore in 1719, it was designed to guard the Atlantic approaches to Québec and the St. Lawrence, and to reassert some of the imperial authority lost six years earlier to Britain in the Treaty of Utrecht. Its site extended over 40ha (100 acres), an area that enclosed a huge star-shaped fortress, a vast harbor—the largest north of Boston—and an entire village designed to supply and man the garrison (the largest in North America). The total cost was about $250 million at today's prices.

Even then the fortress was a failure. The boggy ground made building difficult, living conditions caused mutinies among the men, and corruption among French officials saw construction funds diverted into bureaucrats' pockets. Worse still, it was overlooked by numerous hillocks, while advances in artillery technique rendered the necessity for its high stone walls all but obsolete. In all it faced only two attacks, and on both occasions it surrendered. In 1745, before it was properly finished, it was sacked by 4,000 New Englanders (but later returned to the French by treaty), and in 1758 it was captured and razed by James Wolfe en route to Québec (see page 33).

Today over $30 million has been ploughed into restoring the fortress. A reception center on site provides historical background, while within the fortress's Cyclopean walls around 50 buildings have so far been rebuilt. Some have genuine 18th-century interiors, while others feature historical exhibits. All marvelously evoke the scale and grandeur of the fortress, an effect complemented by the 200 or more costumed "inhabitants," who act as guides. (The fortress is located 2km/1.5 miles from Louisbourg village, 34km/21 miles south of Sydney, tel: 902/733–2280. *Open* Jul–end Aug, daily 9–5; May, Jun, Sep and Oct daily 9.30–5. *Admission: expensive.*)

Opposite: The parish church of Mahone Bay

BIG BANG
In 1917 Halifax experienced the world's largest man-made explosion prior to the detonation of the first atomic bomb. It was caused by the collision of a Belgian relief ship and a French munitions boat bound for the Flanders battlefields. The latter was loaded with 250,000kg (550,000 lb) of TNT. Over 1,400 people were killed instantly and 600 died later of their wounds. Some 900 were injured and 199 blinded. All of northern Halifax was obliterated, while windows were shattered in Truro over 100km (60 miles) away. All that was found of the French ship was a cannon and a half-ton lump of anchor that came to rest 4km (2.5 miles) away.

PRIVATEERS
Privateering was a form of legalized piracy much favored by Nova Scotians (and others) in the second half of the 18th century. Local ships attacked French, Spanish and Yankee boats off their shores, often plundering as far afield as New England and the French Caribbean. Captains had to obtain a license from the British authorities in Halifax—the raids had official blessing—and take all booty to the city's Vice Admiral for confirmation that it was "legal." Profits from the "trade" were enormous.

Drive

The Cabot Trail

Alexander Graham Bell

See map on pages 214–215.

A drive that takes in the coast and beautiful mountain scenery of northern Cape Breton Island (286km/177 miles).

This journey has often been called the most beautiful drive in eastern North America. The road takes its name from the explorer John Cabot, who was, reputedly, the first to make landfall on Cape Breton Island, which he happened upon in 1497 while voyaging in search of a route to Asia. The Cabot Trail traverses some of the most stunning and varied scenery in Canada. After wending its way through idyllic farming land, it follows a dramatic coast, cresting cliffs, coves and headlands, before going inland to cross the mountains and forests of the Cape Breton Highlands National Park.

Most people follow the drive clockwise from **Baddeck►►**, a busy tourist resort on the Bras d'Or Lake, an inland arm of the sea that almost cuts Cape Breton in two. Baddeck is a pleasant town, best known for its association with the inventor Alexander Graham Bell (1847–1922), who spent many summers here and is buried close to his former home, Beinn Breagh (which is still privately owned by Bell's family). Visitors flock to the waterfront **Alexander Graham Bell Museum►►►** (Chebucto Road. *Open* Jun daily 9–6; Jul–mid-Oct daily 8.30–6. *Admission: moderate*), whose various displays run the gamut of Bell's genius, with exhibits and models that explore his interest in the telephone, aviation, medicine,

In the Cape Breton National Park

work with the deaf, animal husbandry and marine engineering.

From Baddeck the road picks up the verdant Middle and Margaree valleys. The latter boasts some of Canada's best salmon fishing, a blessing that is celebrated in a museum in the village of **North East Margaree▶▶**. The Salmon Museum (tel: 902/248–2551. *Open* mid-Jun to mid-Oct daily 9–5. *Admission: inexpensive*) details the life of the Atlantic salmon and features displays of rods, hooks, jigs and *flambeaux* (beacons for night fishing).

North of the Margaree you enter Acadian country (villages to the south are mostly Scottish, while those in the valley itself are predominantly Irish). **Chéticamp▶**, a fishing village, is the center of the island's French-speaking culture. It is best known for its rugs and "hooked" mats, which can be seen in the appealing **Les Trois Pignons** museum (15584 Cabot Trail Hury, tel: 902/224–2642. *Open* Jul–end Aug daily 8–7; May, Jun, Sep–mid-Oct daily 9–5. *Admission inexpensive*). The village, like many in the region, is also known for its summer whale-watching tours. Contact Whale Cruisers Ltd (tel: 902/224–3376).

North of Chéticamp the drive enters the sublime **Cape Breton Highlands National Park▶▶▶**, the park "where the mountains meet the sea." Magnificent views abound, particularly as you climb from the coast to French Mountain (459m/1,505ft) and drop toward the aptly named Pleasant Bay. Close to the latter, and just off the road, stands the **Lone Shieling▶**, a reconstructed crofter's cottage that was built to symbolize Cape Breton's links with the Scottish Highlands, former home of many of the island's first settlers. Further west, near Big Intervale, the delicate **Beulach Ban▶▶** waterfalls tumble through lovely wooded country. At South Harbour, make the little detour north to **Bay St. Lawrence▶▶**, a beguiling fishing village, stopping off en route at Sugarloaf Beach, the spot at which John Cabot is supposed to have landed.

There are around 30 marked trails in the park, most starting from trail-heads on the road. One of the most popular is the Skyline Loop just north of Chéticamp. For full details of park highlights, contact the park reception centers at Chéticamp (tel: 902/224–2306) or Ingonish Beach (tel: 902/285–2535).

Verdant pasture and idyllic homesteads line much of the Cabot Trail

Near Ingonish Beach, at the park's eastern entrance, the Cabot Trail loses the atmosphere of solitude that characterizes its early stages, passing more developed little resorts such as **Ingonish▶▶**. The trail begins to head south along the so-called **Gaelic Coast**, named in honor of its first settlers' Scottish roots. These are further celebrated in South Gut St. Ann's **Gaelic College**, North America's only college dedicated to Gaelic arts and culture, and in a campus museum devoted to tartan, bag-piping, dancing and the like.

Picture perfect: Green Gables House at Cavendish

Prince Edward Island

In a country packed with idyllic rural countryside, few places in Canada present as pretty a pastoral picture as Prince Edward Island (PEI). Canada's smallest province, the island is a colorful patchwork of peaceful rolling hills, rich red soils, pristine coastlines, bucolic villages, sandy beaches and verdant farms (the island's nickname is "Million Acre Farm"). It was also the birthplace of Lucy Maud Montgomery's literary creation, Anne of Green Gables, whose pig-tailed countenance—ever-present in much of the island—seems thoroughly at one with the province's wholesome image.

The best way to explore Prince Edward Island is to visit Charlottetown, the only town of any size, and then follow one or more of the three scenic drives specially laid out by the provincial government (see pages 233–234).

GETTING THERE
Charlottetown is connected by air to most eastern Canadian cities. Access to Prince Edward Island is via the Confederation Bridge from New Brunswick (see panel, opposite). Northumberland Ferries (tel: 902/566–3838 or 800/565–0201, www.nfl-bay.com) operate between Caribou (Nova Scotia) and Wood Islands, 61km (39 miles) east of Charlottetown (75 minutes). Public transportation is thin on the ground, but many companies in Charlottetown offer organized bus, boat, walking and cycling tours of the island.

►► Charlottetown *215D3*

Charlottetown is every bit as elegant and urbane as the woman after whom it was named (the British King George III's wife), with tree-lined streets, leafy squares and clapboard houses. Its most famous sight is **Province House►**, a sandstone building that played host to the "Fathers of Confederation" in 1864 (see page 37). The room where the meeting took place, now something of a national shrine, has been restored to its 19th-century appearance (Richmond and Great George streets, tel: 902/566–7626. *Open* Jul–end Aug daily 8.30–6; Jun daily 8.30–5; Sep–mid-Oct daily 8.30–5; mid-Oct–end May Mon–Fri 9–5. *Admission free*).

Almost next door lies the **Confederation Centre of the Arts►**, a blunt concrete eyesore built in 1964 to commemorate the centennial of the Confederation meeting. Every Canadian citizen paid $15 toward its construction, and contributes to its upkeep to this day. Inside are a small museum, art gallery, café, library and 1,100-seat theater. (Queen Street. *Open* for hours and information tel: 902/566–1267 or 800/565–0278. *Admission free.*) A trio of churches nearby, **St. Paul's, St. Dunstan's** and **St. Peter's**, are worth a glance, though for the most part Charlottetown is best enjoyed by walking at random. The recently restored harborfront is a good area to stroll, as are Victoria Park, which overlooks the town, and the old quarters around King Street and Water Street.

►►► Blue Heron Drive *214C3*

Named after the bird that migrates to PEI, this 191km (120-mile) drive explores the center of the island (known as Queen's County), linking fine beaches, little fishing villages and some glorious coastal and interior scenery. It also brings you to Anne of Green Gables country, a region centered on Cavendish, whose touristy trappings are somewhat at odds with the rest of the island.

The best of the coastal landscapes are to be found in **Prince Edward Island National Park►►►**, a 40km (25-mile) sliver of the northern coast filled with woodland and seafront trails, silvery strands of sand where you can picnic and swim, and a kaleidoscope of superlative cliff, dune and seashore scenery. Park visitor centers are located at Brackley and **Cavendish**, the latter famous for its fine beach and crowd-pulling **Green Gables House** (*Open* May–end Oct daily 9–5; Jul–end Aug daily 9–8. *Admission: moderate*). The pretty wooden farmhouse was once home to the cousins of Lucy Maud Montgomery, who used it as the setting for her novel *Anne of Green Gables* (1908), a tale that pulls in devotees to Cavendish from all corners of the globe.

Other worthwhile stop-offs on the drive include New London, Montgomery's birthplace; Victoria, a picturesque fishing village; York, which has a reconstructed pioneer settlement; Malpeque, known for its oysters and its gardens; Rustico Island, summer home to hundreds of great blue herons; and Rocky Point, close to a Mi'kmaq reserve and the original site of Port La Joie (see page 217).

►► Kings Byway Drive *215D3*

This 375km (232-mile) drive circles the eastern part of PEI, known as Kings County, starting from Charlottetown and looping through quiet farms, tranquil fishing villages, tiny woodlands and timeless countryside. It probably requires one or two overnight stops, pauses you could make at one of the many homely farm guest houses en route.

One of the drive's key halts lies a few miles from Charlottetown. The **Orwell Corner Historic Village►►►** is a living-history museum which re-creates a farm as it would have been while in the hands of Scottish and Irish settlers in the 19th century (tel: 902/651–8510. *Open* Jul–early Sep daily 9–4.30; May–end Jun Mon–Fri 9–4.30; early Sep–early Oct Sun–Fri 9–4.30. *Admission: moderate*). In nearby Belfast, **St. John's Church►►**, which was built by settlers from the Isle of Skye in 1823, is particularly pretty.

INFORMATION
Details and maps of PEI's three marked drives can be obtained from any of the island's tourist offices. The main provincial office is in Charlettetown at 178 Water Street (tel: 902/368–4444, www.peiplay.com). Charlottetown's office is in the City Hall at Queen Street and Kent (tel: 902/566–5548, www.visitcharlottetown.com).

COLORFUL ISLAND
A Mi'kmaq native legend tells how the god Glooscap colored all the world's loveliest places, and then dipped a brush in every color of his celestial palette to create Abegweit, his favorite island—present-day Prince Edward Island.

IRISH MOSS
Irish moss is the common name for two types of red algae, a seaweed that yields carrageenin, an emulsifier used in wine, soups, icecream, toothpaste and cough medicine. Almost half the world's supply comes from PEI, where it is raked from the beaches after violent storms.

CONFEDERATION BRIDGE
Confederation Bridge (1997), which crosses the Northumberland Strait from Cape Jourimain, New Brunswick, to Borden-Carleton, PEI is, at 13km (8 miles) long, the longest over-saltwater bridge in the world. Tolls are in effect on the bridge for cars leaving the island (very expensive), and there are regular shuttle buses for cyclists (you cannot bike across the bridge).

OYSTERS GALORE
Around 10 million oysters a year are harvested from Malpeque Bay in the west of Prince Edward Island.

Glorious pastoral countryside has earned Prince Edward Island the nickname "Million Acre Farm"

POTATO HEAVEN
Prince Edward Island's first potato, the common white, or Irish potato, was introduced by settlers at the end of the 18th century. Now the province produces over 90 percent of Canada's potatoes. The island's temperate climate and sandy red soils are ideal for growing them, and support over 30 different potato varieties. Seed potatoes from the island have been used to start crops in 18 countries.

LADY SLIPPER DRIVE
This drive is named after the lady's slipper orchid, the province's floral emblem, the route being marked with a red flower in a red frame on a white background. The flower is known locally as the "moccasin flower" or "whippoorwill's shoe" and thrives in the acidic soils of the island's shady woodlands. It can take 12 years to reach maturity and often dies if its flowers are picked.

Moving round to the island's east coast you encounter a host of half-forgotten fishing villages, many of them little gems, most notably Murray Harbour, Montague and **Bay Fortune▶▶**. At **Milltown Cross** you can visit a bird sanctuary and a deer and buffalo paddock, while Gaspereaux's **Panmure Island** is graced with one of the region's finest white-sand beaches. **Souris** is a vital stop along the route, mainly because of its nearby **Basin Head Fisheries Museum▶▶▶**, an interesting and beautifully located museum that explores the lives and history of PEI's inshore fishermen (tel: 902/357–7233. *Open* Jul–end Aug daily 9–5). Bird- and seal-watching boat tours are available from several local centers.

▶▶ Lady Slipper Drive *214C3*

This is the least busy of PEI's three drives (287km/178 miles), taking in the tiny villages, sandstone cliffs, fertile meadows and white-sand beaches of the island's western extreme. It is a region known for its oysters and Irish moss (see panel, page 233), for its potatoes—half PEI's vast production comes from here—and as an area where the Acadian-influenced way of life has barely altered in 200 years.

The first stop is **Summerside▶**, PEI's second town, a potato port that was once known for its silver foxes, bred

for fur. For background information on the fur trade, and for details of self-guided walking tours around the town, visit the **International Fox Museum** (286 Fitzroy Street. *Open* mid-Jun–end Sep, tel: 902/436–2400 for times. *Admission: donation*).

Just to the west, in **Miscouche**, lies the drive's highlight, the **Acadian Museum of Prince Edward Island▶▶▶**, which traces the history of the island's 15,000-strong Acadian population. Its evocative displays include reconstructed buildings—church, store, school, forge and village hall—and tools, utensils, furniture and old *objets d'art*. (*Open* Jul–end Aug daily 9.30–7; May, Sep daily 9.30–5; Oct–end Apr Mon–Fri 9.30–5, Sun 1–4. *Admission: inexpensive.*)

Other high points include the **Green Park Shipbuilding Museum** at Port Hill (tel: 902/831–4947. *Open* Jun–end Sep, daily 10–5. *Admission: inexpensive*), the **Irish Moss Interpretative Centre** at Miminegash (*Open* Jun–end Sep daily 10–7. *Admission: inexpensive*) and the **Acadian Pioneer Village** at Mont-Carmel (*Open* Jun–end Sep daily 9–7. *Admission: inexpensive*). Among the villages you should aim for are Alberton, where Jacques Cartier first landed; Tignish, a *bona fide* Acadian community (known for its monstrosity of a church); friendly little West Point (visit its old lighthouse); and Tyne Valley, reputed to have some of the best oysters in the province.

SAND AND SEA
PEI has some of the warmest sea water north of Florida, and some of eastern Canada's best beaches. Among the finest are Bothwell Beach (near Souris); Greenwich (near St. Peter's Bay); Cedar Dunes (near West Point); and Brackley Beach in Prince Edward Island National Park.

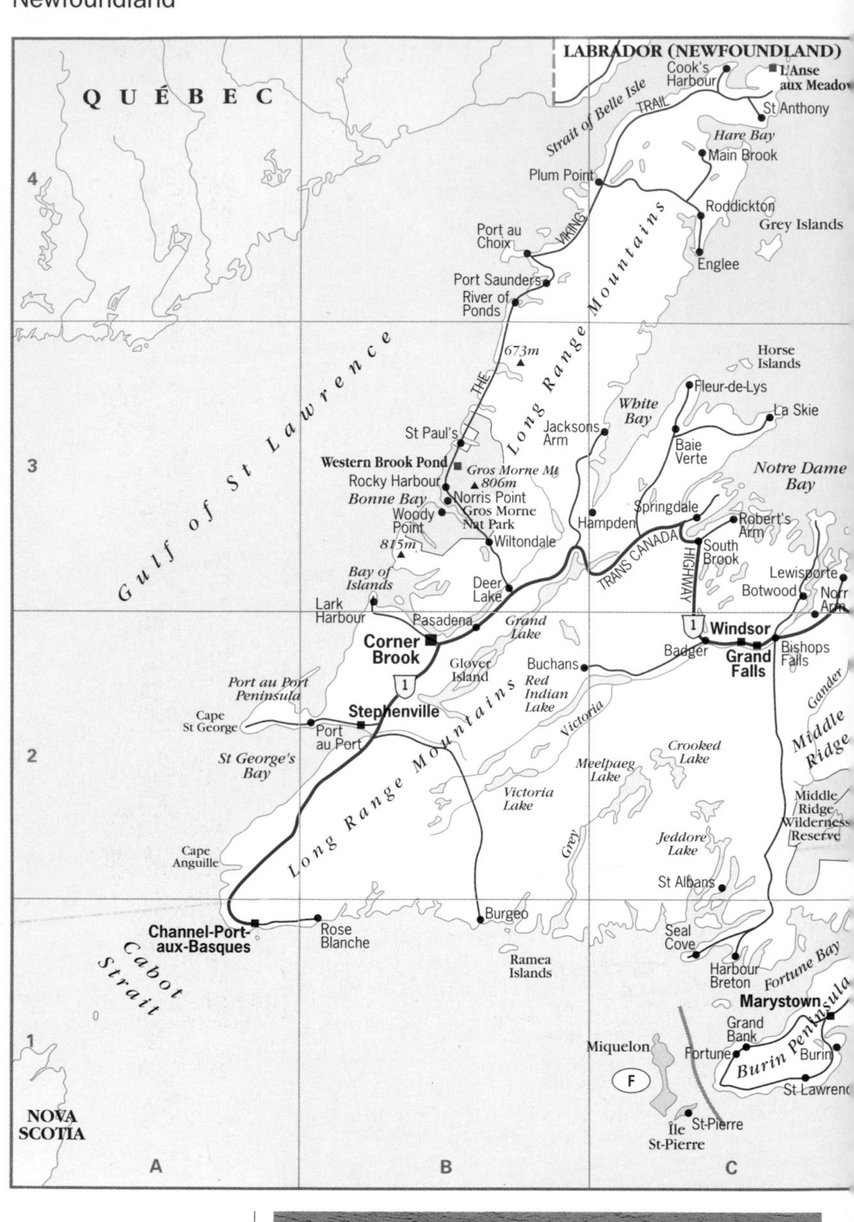

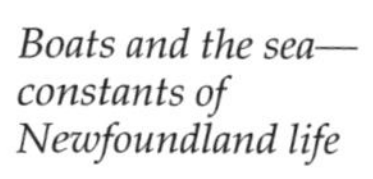

Boats and the sea—constants of Newfoundland life

Newfoundland

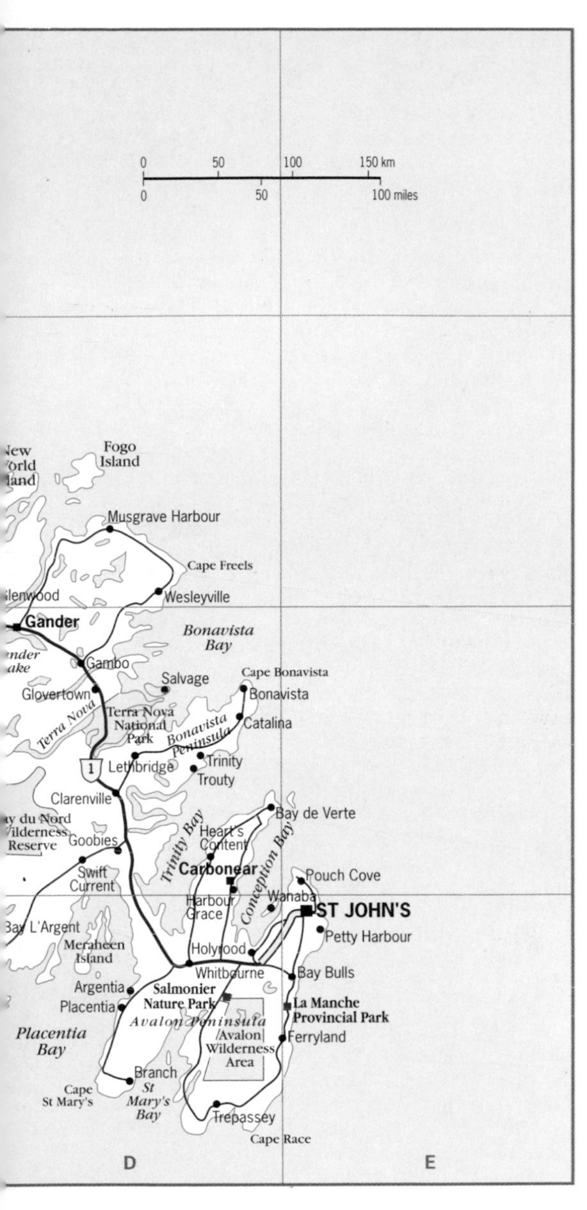

ISLAND OUTPOST Newfoundland has always excited strong reactions, perhaps because of its uncompromising terrain and atrocious weather, perhaps because of its insular and distinctive people, the so-called "Newfies," butt of a thousand jokes, a group that has fought a long battle for survival against a maverick sea and unforgiving land. Visitors to this corner of Canada, which is remote and inhospitable even by Canadian standards, have a hard time of it: much is inaccessible, the weather is poor, museums are few, and hotels—where they exist—often little more than adequate. At the same time it can also be a land of surprises and rewards, especially for the more

REGION HIGHLIGHTS

ARRIVING BY SEA
Marine Atlantic operates a year-round car ferry from North Sydney (Nova Scotia) to Port-aux-Basques on the western side of Newfoundland (900km/540 miles from St. John's). The crossing takes 5–5½ hours, depending on the weather. The company runs a second service (late Jun–mid Sep) from North Sydney to Argentia on the eastern side of the island (131km/81 miles southwest of St. John's). Reservations for car passengers are essential (tel: 800/341–7981. www.marine-atlantic.ca).

LANGUAGE
Two Canadian provinces have their own dictionaries: Prince Edward Island's has 873 entries, Newfoundland's has over 5,000 (most of them related to fish, scenery and weather). Accents and dialects, all of them marked, vary from one part of the island to another, drawing on a mixture of Irish, Dorset, Devon and Cornish idioms that have not been heard in their home countries since the 17th century. Scholars claim that parts of Newfoundland speech are as close as the modern world gets to the language of Shakespeare.

adventurous, or for those who want to enjoy a unique and all but unspoiled corner of North America.

CONTINENT'S CRADLE Newfoundland's lonely shores may well have been the first part of North America ever seen by Europeans. Long before Columbus's voyage of 1492, 6th-century Irish sailors may have trawled the province's waters, followed 200 years later by fishermen from England and the Basque country (chronicles tell of these men crossing the "western sea" to the "Isle of Brasil"). Before that, over a period of at least 6,000 years, the land was home to the Beothucks, natives of the Woodland group of tribes (see pages 184–185). Around AD 1000 they were joined by the Vikings, traces of whose settlements were found during excavations at L'Anse aux Meadows in the 1960s (see page 246–247). More Europeans drifted west following the voyage in 1497 of John Cabot, whose tales of the region's fish-rich waters attracted flotillas of seasonal fishermen from Britain, Spain, France and Portugal.

FISH FREE-FOR-ALL By the 16th century men were swarming to Newfoundland, sailing from Europe in the spring and returning with holds full of dried, salted cod in autumn. Permanent settlement was actively discouraged by the British West Country merchants who dominated the trade (and feared competition from a resident population). A few dissenters jumped ship, however: the so-called "Masterless Men," indentured sailors who preferred the freedom of Newfoundland's coves and cliffs to a slave-like apprenticeship on the high seas.

FISHING ADMIRALS In 1583, partly to ward off the French, Elizabeth I was declared sovereign of Newfoundland and the island became England's first-ever "colony." However, in practice the Crown exercised little control, a fact tacitly recognized in a charter granted by Charles I in 1634. This passed authority for enforcing law and order in any harbor to the first ship's captain to enter it in any season. This arrangement survived for almost 150 years.

A BRITISH COLONY British attitudes to the region's settlement began to change with the encroachment of the French, who in 1662 had established a colony at Plaisance (Placentia). Their presence led to skirmishes that continued until the 1713 Treaty of Utrecht, which awarded Newfoundland to Britain (though France retained fishing rights on the northwest coast, the so-called "French Shore," until 1904). Settlement restrictions were then relaxed, bringing in thousands of predominantly Irish and English settlers (30,000 by 1790). In 1824 the island became an official British colony.

PART OF CANADA In 1855 Newfoundland became a self-governing dominion. Five years later it declined to join the new Canadian Confederation. A change of heart followed the Depression of the 1930s, when Newfoundland's export-led economy collapsed. World War II brought renewed prosperity, and this in turn paved the way for two referenda on union with Canada. On March 31, 1949, Newfoundland entered the Canadian fold, some 52 percent of its population—a majority of 7,000—having voted for confederation.

GETTING AROUND A car is essential if you are really going to explore Newfoundland. If you are without one, look into DRL Coach Lines (tel: 888/263–1854, www.drlgroup.com) which run daily along the Trans-Canada Highway (Highway 1), the island's main road and principal lifeline. The highway bisects Newfoundland from west to east, connecting Port-aux-Basques with the capital, St. John's, in 15 hours (see panel opposite). Otherwise, transportation services are restricted to the minibuses that link a handful of the island's "outports," the tiny settlements that characterize Newfoundland's lonely coastline.

EXPLORING NEWFOUNDLAND Newfoundland is three times the size of New Brunswick, Nova Scotia, and Prince Edward Island combined, but has far fewer sights. Scenery consists mostly of low and occasionally forested hills; not for nothing is Newfoundland's nicknamed "The Rock." Things are more exciting in the west, where the Long Range Mountains, a continuation of the Appalachians, straggle up to a height of 814m (2,669ft); distances on this part of the island are immense, however, and you are a long way from St. John's, the island's pleasant capital and natural focus. In the west, in addition to some of the island's finest scenery, is the much-visited Viking village at L'Anse aux Meadows (see page 247).

If Newfoundland's interior is occasionally bland, its 10,000km (6,000-mile) coastline is almost continually appealing. The best areas are protected by the Gros Morne and Terra Nova national parks, but all over the island tortuous roads wind past quaint collections of clapboard houses perched precariously above the shore. Elsewhere, such as on the Avalon, Burin, and Bonavista peninsulas, breakers crash against wild beaches, winds blow over blustery headlands, and boat trips provide a first-hand taste of Newfoundland's compelling maritime experience.

PLACE-NAMES
Something of the Newfoundlanders' sense of humor can be gleaned from what they call their settlements. Here's a selection: Joe Batt's Arm, Jerry's Nose, Heart's Content, Heart's Desire, Cuckold Cove, Come by Chance, Happy Adventure, Little Heart's Ease, Famish Gut, Useless Bay, Stinking Cove, Witless Bay and Blow Me Down.

ARRIVING BY AIR
Most US, European and Canadian carriers fly to St. John's, but as planes are vital for covering the vast distances in Newfoundland there are other airports at Gander, St. Antony, Stephenville and Deer Lake. The last is particularly useful if you are visiting Gros Morne National Park.

Decline in the fishing industry has led to hardship in Newfoundland's traditional coastal villages, or "outports"

PIRATE
Peter Easton, a former British Royal Navy veteran, took to piracy in 1604. Six years later he based himself at Harbour Grace, his fleet manned by 5,000 Newfoundland fishermen . In 1613 he turned to the Mediterranean, bought a palace in France, became a marquis, and died one of the world's richest men. The Customs House built on the site of his former fort at Harbour Grace is now a museum (tel: 709/596–5465. *Open* Jun–end Sep daily 11–1, 1.30–5. *Admission: moderate*).

FIRST CABLE
In 1866, the *Great Eastern* arrived in Heart's Content, having laid 4,447km (2,757) miles of copper cable across the Atlantic (the longest ever made). Four previous attempts had failed. The old Cable Station is now a museum (tel: 709/583–2160. *Open* mid-Jun to mid-Oct, daily 10–5.30. *Admission: inexpensive*).

The Avalon Peninsula meets the sea at Cape St. Mary's

►► Avalon Peninsula 237D1

The easternmost part of Newfoundland, Avalon Peninsula is a four-pronged isthmus connected by a narrow strip of land to the rest of the island. Its proximity to St. John's makes it one of the easily accessible parts of the province. Heading north, Highway 30 leads to **Logy Bay**, passing the **Ocean Sciences Centre►►** where you can watch seals and other marine animals at close quarters (Marine Lab Road, tel: 709/737–3706. *Open* Jun–early Sep daily 10–5; Apr–end May, Sep–end Nov Sun 1–5. Guided tours, daily every 30 minutes. *Admission: moderate*). **Pouch Cove►►**, a lovely village on the northern edge of Conception Bay, was settled in 1611, its dangerously narrow harbor deliberately chosen to discourage ships searching for illegal settlers. Driving south on Highway 21 along Conception Bay you pass more old villages, before arriving in **Holyrood**.

Here you can double back to St. John's, or follow Highway 70 to **Harbour Grace►►**, the prettiest of the many appealing villages dotted around Conception Bay. It was settled in 1550, and fortified by the pirate Peter Easton (see panel). Another fascinating village, **Heart's Content►►**, lies to the west, known for its role in the laying of the first transatlantic cable (see panel).

South of St. John's lie some of the oldest and most traditional settlements in the province, notably **Petty Harbour**, **La Manche**, **Brigus South**, Bay Bulls and Ferryland (some are now evocatively deserted). These, and the area's wild coast, can be explored from Highway 10. Stop off at **Salmonier Nature Park►►** (Highway 90. *Open* Jun–early Sep daily 10–6; early Sep–mid-Oct daily 10–4. *Admission inexpensive*) to see its moose, beavers and caribou.

The highlights of the peninsula's southwestern corner are **Placentia►►**, the old capital of French Newfoundland, and Cape St. Mary's Ecological Reserve (tel: 709/277–1666. *Open* mid–Jun to mid-Sep daily 8–7. *Admission moderate)* that protects the world's second-largest gannet colony.

The Bonavista Peninsula, John Cabot's first glimpse of North America in 1497

►► Bonavista Peninsula *237D2*

The best-known of Newfoundland's many peninsulas occupies a special place in the island's mythology, for it was here that John Cabot is said to have first glimpsed the Americas in 1497. Its name reputedly comes from Cabot's observation—he was an Italian by birth—that here was a *buona vista*, a "beautiful view." Its rocky margins are flecked with attractive bays, while the village of **Trinity►►►** is one of the loveliest spots in the entire province.

Trinity comes into view 74km (46 miles) off the main highway (see panel). This narrow-streeted web of clapboard houses, edged around a hill-backed and picture-perfect bay, is one of the island's oldest settlements, and the site of the island's first "Court of Admiralty" (held in June 1615), when Sir Richard Whitbourne was sent from England to settle disputes between resident fishermen and their migratory counterparts. Among its many old buildings are the church of **St. Paul's**, whose wooden ceiling, similar to an upturned boat, owes much to the skills of the village's early shipwrights. Almost opposite stands the 1,000-exhibit **Trinity Museum** (tel: 709/464–3599. *Open* mid-Jun to mid-Sep daily 10–6. *Admission: moderate*), built in 1880. Its displays range from shoe- and barrel-making to whale-catching and ancient model boats.

Highway 239 just south of Trinity leads to **Trouty**, an evocative and rock-bound little hamlet, and then continues north to **Bonavista►**, the peninsula's dispersed 400-year-old main town. Drop in at the modest Bonavista Museum on Church Street, whose historical exhibits have been gathered by local people, and wander around the collection of historic buildings known as the **Mockbeggar Property** (tel: 709/468–7300 or 800/563–6363. *Open* mid-Jun–early Oct daily 10–5.30. *Admission: moderate*). About 5km (3 miles) north lies **Cape Bonavista►►►**, a beautiful and desolate seascape, capped by the restored **Bonavista Lighthouse** (*Open* mid-Jun to mid-Oct daily. *Admission: moderate*).

GETTING THERE

The Bonavista Peninsula can be seen from Highway 230, a road known as the "Discovery Trail," which strikes north from the Trans-Canada Highway (Highway 1) at Clarenville, 190km (119 miles) west of St. John's. It is 119km (68 miles) from here to the tip of the peninsula at Cape Bonavista. If you are without transportation, Newhook's Transportation (tel: 709/227–2552 or 709/726–4876) run a taxi service to Trinity and other Bonavista villages.

SCREECHING

The Newfie's favorite traditional tipple is "screech," a lethal hooch once conjured from the swill in old casks of rum. Although now (mostly) made under government supervision, it remains a rough-and-ready drink. People having their first encounter with the brew can attend a "screeching-in" ceremony (sometimes held in civic halls), where tradition requires you to swallow a piece of raw fish after your first taste.

TIME WARP

In an aberration that seems only appropriate given Newfoundland's unique outlook, the province has its own bizarre time zone: half an hour in advance of the Atlantic Standard Time observed by the Maritime Provinces (one and half hours ahead of Eastern Standard Time).

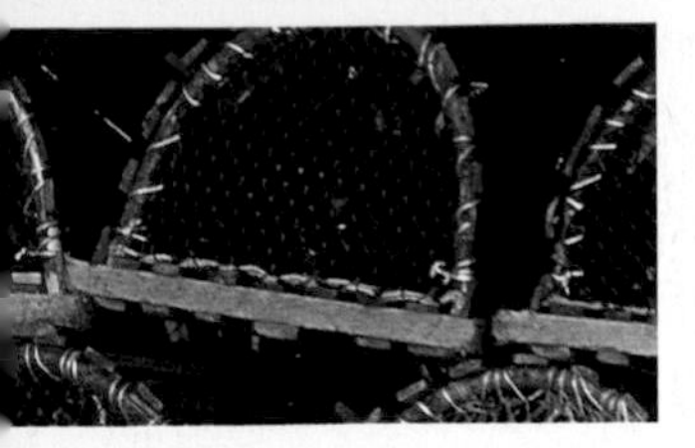

Fishing, like forestry, is fundamental to the well-being of many Canadian regions, but nowhere has it been more vital than in Newfoundland. After five centuries of almost unrivaled bounty, however, the once-teeming waters of the Grand Banks are virtually empty, their overfished stocks the subject of bitter international dispute.

FISH GALORE
Newfoundland's fishing good fortune stemmed from the "banks," vast shallow-watered extensions of the continental shelf that lie off the province's southern and eastern shores. The largest of these are the Grand Banks, situated where the Labrador Current meets the Gulf Stream. The former's cold water sinks under the warmer Gulf Stream waters, stirring up the seabed's plankton which then rise to the surface, attracting the shoals of fish once associated with the region.

Inspecting a catch at St. John's

Fishy tales King Henry VII of England, who had been expecting gold, spices and riches beyond the dreams of avarice, was singularly unimpressed with the fishy tales brought back by John Cabot after his transatlantic voyage of 1497 (the voyager received £10 for his troubles). Europe's fishermen, though, took rather more note of the mariner's reports, which stated that Newfoundland's seas were "swarming with fish, which can be taken not only with the net, but in baskets let down with a stone." Within a few years the Grand Banks (see panel) were being trawled by British, French, Spanish and Portuguese fishermen, whose migratory voyages (out in spring, back in fall) netted vast stocks of cod, turbot and halibut for the tables of Europe.

Fish for all Once settlement took hold in Newfoundland, fishing methods remained unchanged for hundreds of years. Trawlers still arrived from abroad, but in the days before refrigeration were limited to the stocks they could salt on board or dry on the island's traditional wooden "flakes." Local fishermen operated from small boats, their methods varying from season to season. Most business was done during the summer "capelin run," when the capelin, a tiny fish, swam ashore to spawn, drawing the cod, their main predator, in their wake. Large square nets scooped up the cod, which were then taken to be dressed and salted in Newfoundland's 700 or more "outports."

Hook, line and sinker At other times of the year, fish were caught by "longlining," which is a traditional method using lines payed out from a boat. These lines were attached in turn to smaller lines with baited hooks, or "jigging," the fish being snared either by the bait or the bobbing lead "jiggers" on the water. As markets became more voracious, however, and stocks a little more scarce, "gill-netting" was adopted. With this method a net—weighted to hold it on the sea bed—was suspended from floats on the surface. More recently still, "longliners" were introduced, boats that used gill-netting and longlining, but which could stay at sea for several days.

Empty seas Stocks of fish were so immense, and the Grand Banks so bountiful, that it seemed inconceivable that the fish would ever run out. In 1992, however, the inconceivable occurred, and northern cod stocks all but vanished. These days it is fashionable to blame

foreign fleets for the loss, particularly the Spanish and Portuguese—who certainly played their part—but the Newfoundlanders themselves have also over-fished their waters for years. The introduction of freezer ships in the 1930s started the rot, and this was compounded by the move from Newfoundland's more traditional offshore methods. In the past, fishing was done from "dories," small flat-bottomed boats that were launched from the decks of schooners only when the shoals of fish had been located. Since 1945 the dories' place has been taken by longliners, draggers and trawlers, and recently by the new breed of supertrawler, which locates fish by satellite and sonar.

Fishing future After the 1992 disaster the Government of Canada imposed a two-year moratorium on cod fishing. In 1994 marine scientists discovered that cod stocks were still not being replenished, raising the prospect that an indefinite ban might be necessary. Over 40,000 Newfoundland fishery workers lost their jobs. In 1994 the yellowtail and flounder also vanished from the seas and had to be protected by a moratorium. Since that time, the situation has improved. Ground fish stocks are beginning to recover, albeit at a slow rate. The yellowtail and flounder fishery reopened in 1998, and the Government of Canada hopes to reopen the other fisheries in the next few years.

FISHY DISHES
"Fish" in Newfoundland always means cod; other fish are referred to by name (lobster, mackerel, salmon, herring, capelin, turbot, squid, scallops and shrimp can all still be caught). In serving cod, locals have had centuries to fathom new variations on a theme. "Specialties" include brewis (cod stew and hardtack) and cod tongues (sliced and fried).

FOREIGN VESSELS
The problem of foreign vessels fishing the Grand Banks is now subject to much tighter international monitoring and enforcement measures. Whether they work, however, is another matter.

The twilight of the Newfoundland fishing industry?

GETTING THERE
The 230km (140-mile) Burin Peninsula is served by Highway 210, which leaves the Trans-Canada Highway at Goobies, 160km (100 miles) west of St. John's.

GETTING TO ST.-PIERRE
Flights to the islands operate from St. John's. Contact Air St-Pierre (www.airsaintpierre.com). Two ferry companies operate daily crossings (70 minutes) from Fortune (mid-Jun–late Sep): SPM Tours (tel: 709/832–0429), and Lakes Travel (tel: 709/832–2006). Reservations for cars are essential.

INFORMATION
The Office du Tourisme on St-Pierre is at Place Général du Gaulle (tel: 877/277–7765, www.st-pierre-et-miquelon.com). Among other things, it provides details of the numerous island tours and boat trips available from the town.

WALKING
Gros Morne National Park offers several excellent hikes in addition to the easy stroll to Western Brook Pond (see text). The most popular, the James Callahan Trail, starts 7km (4 miles) east of Rocky Harbour on Highway 430 and climbs to the summit of Gros Morne Mountain. Some 4km (2.5 miles) west of Woody Point you will find the trailhead for the Tablelands Hiking Trail (4km/2.5 miles), a loop through tundra-like terrain; 8km (5 miles) beyond is the Green Gardens Trail (9km/5.5 miles), which loops through a variety of marine landscapes. Rocky Harbour's information center has full details of these and other hikes.

►► Burin Peninsula *236C1*

Although the Burin Peninsula has its scenic moments and no shortage of fishing villages, most people are here to visit **St-Pierre et Miquelon►►►**, a tiny archipelago at its tip that constitutes the only French colony in North America.

Highway 210 picks up the peninsula some 50km (30 miles) beyond Goobies (see panel), the start of only intermittently interesting country as the road follows the Burin's central plateau. For the real highlights, you need to follow side-roads to some of the outports *en route*, places such as Bay l'Argent, Little Bay East, Rushoon, Baine Harbour, the outstanding **Beau Bois**, **Little Bay** and **John the Bay**, and **Swift Current** (the last is known for its broad beaches and the stunning scenery around Piper's Hole River).

The first major town on the highway is **Marystown►**, whose shipyards once produced the bulk of the trawlers that fished off Newfoundland. Beyond lies Grand Bank, whose **Provincial Seaman's Museum►►►** (Marine Drive tel: 709/832–1484. *Open* May–end Oct daily 9–5. *Admission inexpensive*) offers a fascinating account of fishing and fishermen on the Grand Banks. Just beyond lies **Fortune**, a somnolent little terminal for ferries to the islands of St-Pierre et Miquelon (see panel).

St-Pierre itself is no joke: you need passports to enter and the local currency is the euro (though Canadian dollars are widely accepted). First claimed for France by Cartier in 1536, the area was left to the French by the British in 1763, as a foothold for their fishing fleet. In 1976 it became a fully fledged French *département*, returning a member to the Senate and a *deputé* to the French parliament. The main town (also known as St-Pierre) has a thoroughly European flavor, with some wonderful shops and exquisite French restaurants, and though there's little to see—bar the cathedral and a small museum—it is a delightful place to spend a couple of days.

►►► Gros Morne National Park *236B3*

Gros Morne takes its name from the French for "big bleak hill," a less-than-flattering summary of one of the finest assortment of landscapes in eastern Canada. Immense fjords cut into the park's mountainous interior, their sheer-cliffed sides rising to craggy peaks and impressively forested plateaux. Much of the scenery—and the abundant marine wildlife—is best seen from a boat (trips are available at several centers), but highways 430 and 431 also offer snatches of the region's grandest landscapes. Gros Morne's occasionally tundra-like terrain is unique for species of flora and fauna usually only found much further north, including the Arctic hare, Arctic tern, bear, lynx and Newfoundland caribou.

In the south, the twisting watery arms of **Bonne Bay►►►**, the park's largest fjord, can be seen on a circular drive from Wiltondale or from the pretty village of **Rocky Harbour►►**. The latter, with its information center (tel: 709/458–2417), makes the best place to start (and stay) in the park. It lies 11km (7 miles) north of **Norris Point**, where boat tours are offered on Bonne Bay (contact Ocean View Motel, tel: 709/458–2730). From Woody Point on the opposite shore, Highway 431 skirts the fjord's South Arm, passing through lake-dotted country under the looming bulk of Gros Morne Mountain, the park's highest point

(806km/2,644ft). At Wiltondale (34km/21 miles), Highway 430 swings north along East Arm, running for another immensely beautiful 38km (23 miles) back to Rocky Harbour. From here you should drive north toward St. Paul's (36km/22 miles) on a breezy stretch of coastal road that weaves past cliffs, sandy beaches, wind-battered dwarf forests (known locally as "tuckamores") and a string of fishing villages. Shortly before St. Paul's, watch for the access point to **Western Brook Pond▶▶▶**, a majestic glacial lake framed by towering mountain cliffs. An easy 40-minute stroll over boardwalks leads from the access point to the lake edge, where you should take a **boat trip▶▶▶** (*Open* Jul–Aug three trips daily; Jun, Sep–mid-Oct one trip daily. Contact Ocean View Motel in Rocky Harbour, tel: 709/458–2730. *Admission: expensive*) to enjoy the grandeur of the "pond's" higher reaches.

Gros Morne's deceptively barren landscapes are a haven for tundra species of flora and fauna usually found much further north

Almost 1,000 years ago, the Vikings established a settlement in North America referred to in the ancient Icelandic sagas as Vinland. Argument over the location of this possibly mythical land raged until the 1960s, when a settlement was found at Newfoundland's L'Anse aux Meadows.

WINE-LAND

The vagaries of Old Norse had long allowed experts to assume that the *Vin* of Vinland, Leif Eriksson's first North American settlement, meant that it had to be located in an area where grapes could grow. Until the discoveries at L'Anse aux Meadows, this led scholars to claim that the settlement was somewhere on the south-eastern coast of the US However, no ships could have sailed so far south in the time-scale described in the Icelandic sagas.

New lands By the end of the 9th century, overpopulation was forcing Viking pioneers to abandon Scandinavia to explore and colonize parts of Iceland and Greenland. Exploits from the period are recounted in two Icelandic epics, the *Graenlendinga* and *Eirick* sagas, the latter an account of the travails of Erik the Red, a Norse hothead banished from Scandinavia for murder in AD982. Part of his three-year exile was spent exploring the shores of Greenland, where he established two colonies. In AD986 a settler from one of these colonies was blown off-course, and in the teeth of a gale glimpsed a previously unknown shore (see page 28). Erik's son, Leif Eriksson, set sail for the new land in AD995, tempted by the tales of its abundant timber, a vital commodity on Greenland's treeless shores. In time he landed at a fertile spot he called Vinland, where he remained for a year—the first European to set foot in North America.

Discovery Almost 1,000 years later, a Viking settlement was found in Newfoundland by Helge and Anne Stine Ingstad, a pair of Norwegian explorers whose reading of the Icelandic sagas had led them on an obsessive search for Vinland. In 1960 they were guided by a local to an unremarkable collection of ridges and grassy burrows at Epaves Bay (Newfoundland), a site that excavations between 1961 and 1968 revealed to be a Norse settlement built around the year AD1000.

Turf and timber Viking buildings at L'Anse aux Meadows

Boats have changed little in almost 1,000 years

Iron Finds at the site included the foundations of seven turf and timber buildings (similar to Viking sod houses discovered in Iceland), cooking pits, bones, peat, charcoal, an oil lamp and the floorboard of a Norse boat. More exciting still was the discovery of a soapstone flywheel (used for spinning wool), the oldest European household article ever found in North America (and identical to artifacts found at Viking sites in Iceland, Greenland and Scandinavia). The most crucial find of all, however, was the remains of a smithy, and with it a stone anvil, nails and pieces of bog-iron. All were evidence of iron-working, an art then unknown to North America's native cultures.

The argument The Ingstads' discovery was unquestionably a Viking settlement; to date it is the only such authenticated site in North America. What is less certain is whether it is the Vinland of the *Eirick* and *Graenlendinga* sagas, a debate that has kept archeologists at loggerheads for almost 40 years. The sagas themselves give only the vaguest clues as to the settlement's location, narrative details having been mangled in the telling over the years (the oral tradition prevailed for centuries before the sagas were written down). This has left experts to argue over linguistic niceties, some contending that *Vin* was a word meaning fertile (which could apply to Newfoundland) others that it referred to wine or grapes, which could not (see panel opposite).

The site The doubts do not deter the thousands of visitors that come each year to L'Anse aux Meadows, a windswept headland at the tip of Newfoundland's Great Northern Peninsula. A UNESCO World Heritage Site, the area is under the care of the Canadian Parks Service, whose excellent Interpretation Centre (tel: 709/623–2601 or 623–2608. *Open* Jun 10–Sep 5 daily 9–8; Jun 1–10 and Sep 6–Oct 10 daily 9–5. *Admission*: *moderate–expensive*) presents audiovisual displays on the Vikings, and exhibits some of the objects found at the site. A few minutes' walk away is a series of mounds—all that remains of the original village since the site was returned to its natural state after excavation—and three reconstructed sod houses: a longhouse, a workshop and an animal shed, complete with burning fires and sheepskins to add a touch of verisimilitude.

GETTING THERE

L'Anse aux Meadows is about as far from civilization as it is possible to get in Newfoundland (which is saying something). It lies near the northern end of Highway 430, some 450km (280 miles) from Deer Lake on the Trans-Canada Highway. Gros Morne National Park is also on this road, so a trip to the park and settlement can easily be combined (see pages 244–245). You can also fly regularly (schedule varies with time of year) to St. Antony, the nearest town, from elsewhere in Newfoundland, and from several eastern Canadian cities. There is a thrice-weekly Viking Express bus (tel: 709/634–4710) from Deer Lake.

Radio pioneer Guglielmo Marconi

ARRIVING AND INFORMATION
St. John's airport is 6km (4 miles) northwest of the city center. Its summer-only information desk (tel: 709/772–0011, www.stjohnsairport.com) is complemented by the city tourist office at 348 Water Street (tel: 709/576–8106, www.stjohns.ca).

WATER STREET
This is one of the oldest streets in North America. In 1627 it was known simply as the "lower path," but was already the social and commercial heart of St. John's, a role its bars, shops and restaurants fulfil to this day. The War Memorial (1924) at its eastern end marks the spot on which Sir Humphrey Gilbert claimed the colony for Queen Elizabeth I of England in 1583.

►► St. John's *237E1*

Newfoundland's capital and the oldest "European" town in North America occupies a magnificent site, spread over the rocky slopes of one of the world's finest natural harbors. Ships enter its sheltered nook via the "Narrows," a 200m (650ft) wide passage guarded by a series of cliffs that rise to Signal Hill, the loftiest of the town's various panoramic lookouts. Fires over the centuries have devastated many of St. John's older buildings, but traditional flat-topped wooden houses still straggle up and down many of its steep narrow streets.

Downtown►► The **Newfoundland Museum** provides the perfect introduction to St. John's and its province, with displays on Beothuck and Inuit culture, sealing, fishing, shipwrecks and other maritime subjects (285 Duckworth Street, tel 709/729–2329. *Open* Jun–mid-Oct daily 9.30–4.45; mid-Oct–end May Tue–Fri 9–4.45, Sat 9.30–4.45, Sun 12–4.45. *Admission: inexpensive*). Opposite is the **Anglican Cathedral** (1849), an outstanding example of North American neo-Gothic architecture. Almost as impressive is the **Roman Catholic Cathedral** (1842–1890), a city landmark on Military Road. Both cathedrals are dedicated to St. John the Baptist, after the legend that John Cabot landed on Newfoundland on the saint's feast day. Other venerable buildings in downtown St. John's include the Colonial Building (1850), Government House (1830), Commissariat House (1821) and the church of St. Thomas (1836).

St. John's harbor from the Queen's Battery

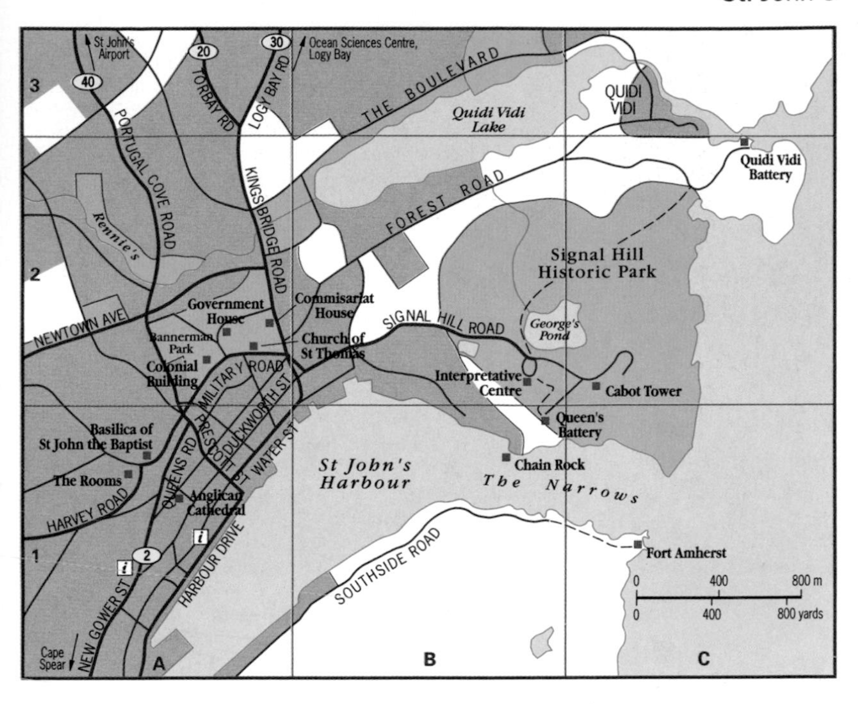

Signal Hill Historic Park▶▶▶ After taking in the harbor's local color, follow Harbour Drive past "The Battery," a little fishing settlement, and continue up the well-worn path that leads to Signal Hill Historic Park. The cliff-edged defensive bastion closes the northern arm of St. John's harbor, its present ruined defenses dating from 1812. The site was used to "signal" the approach of enemy vessels, or the arrival of friendly merchant ships. It was also here in 1901 that Guglielmo Marconi made history by receiving the first long-distance wireless transmission: a letter "S" in Morse code from Poldhu, 2,700km (1,600 miles) away in Cornwall, UK St. John's was also the spot from which Alcock and Browne launched the first nonstop transatlantic flight in 1901. The views are fantastic, and there is an interpretative center for background on the site's points of historical interest (tel: 709/772–5367. *Open* mid-Jun–end Aug daily 8.30–8; Sep–mid-Jun daily 8.30–4.30. *Admission: mid-May–end Oct, inexpensive; Nov–mid-May, free*).

Also here is the **Queen's Battery**, fortifications that look over the harbor. Down below you should be able to see the so-called Chain Rock, a white-painted pillar from which a chain was stretched across the Narrows to exclude enemy ships. At the park's highest point looms the **Cabot Tower** (*Open* summer, 8.30am–4pm; winter, 9–5. *Admission free*), built in 1898–1900 to celebrate Queen Victoria's Diamond Jubilee and the 400th anniversary of Cabot's landing. Returning to downtown, detour to **Quidi Vidi▶▶**, a pretty fishing hamlet just to the north (paths lead down here from the park). The old **Quidi Vidi Battery** (tel: 709/729–2977. *Open* mid-Jun to mid-Oct daily 10–5.30. *Admission: inexpensive*), another defensive outpost, has been restored to its 1812 appearance; to the east the paths around Quidi Vidi Lake are popular with walkers and joggers.

CAPE SPEAR POINT

Highway 11 leads 11km (7 miles) south of St. John's to Cape Spear Point, which, at a longitude of 52° 37' 24", is the most easterly point in North America. Views from here are magnificent, and it is sometimes possible to see whales feeding at the foot of the surrounding cliffs. The nearby Cape Spear Lighthouse (1835), Newfoundland's oldest, is also worth a visit. (*Open:* mid-Jun–mid-Oct daily 10–6. *Admission: inexpensive.*)

RED INDIANS

The term "red indian," or "redskin," is thought to have been brought back to Europe by John Cabot in 1497. The explorer coined the phrase after encountering Newfoundland's Beothuck natives, who used red ocher to decorate their bodies.

Explore the back roads to make the most of Terra Nova National Park

►► Terra Nova National Park *237D2*

Terra Nova National Park, which gathers around the indented shores of Bonavista Bay, is easy to see in conjunction with the Bonavista Peninsula just to the east (see page 241). The Trans-Canada Highway (Highway 1) cuts through the park, but to make the most of the area's hidden nooks and crannies you should aim to explore the back roads. Landscapes aside, other highlights include boat tours, whale-watching trips (see panel) and any number of hiking and nature trails. The park also has plenty of moose, bears and foxes, and over 350 species of plant, including several rare bog orchids.

For the low-down on these and other attractions, make for the park's **Visitor Information Centre** (tel: 709/533–2801), located about 20km (12 miles) north of the park's southern entrance close to Newman Sound fjord. Most of the park's shops and services are here, though **Glovertown**, makes an equally good base. You might take the short trail (1.6km/1 mile) along the Sound from this point, or drive out to a couple of outstanding viewpoints: the best is probably **Bluehill Pond Lookout►►**, a fire tower that offers a panorama over the park. There is a summer intepretative centre at Saltons off the Trans-Canada Highway.

Off the Trans-Canada the best diversion is Highway 310, which strikes off along the **Eastport Peninsula►►** from the park's northern boundary. At its easternmost tip, the village of **Salvage►** is one of Newfoundland's oldest outports, and with outstanding coastal scenery. The village's **Fishermen's Museum** (tel: 709/ 677–2414. *Open* mid-Jun to mid-Sep daily 9.30–7.30) delves into the area's fishing- dominated past, and it is possible to find excellent home-cured capelin and salmon in local restaurants.

Close by lies **Sandy Cove►**, which is one of the province's loveliest beaches (though the water is too cold for all but the bravest bathers), and the popular little stopovers of Eastport and Happy Adventure, where fresh lobster figures on local menus.

ALL AT SEA
Boat trips at Newman Sound are organized by Ocean Watch (tel: 709/533–6024. *Open* mid-May–end Oct), whose excursions offer the chance to fish and to spot the pilot, minke and humpback whales that inhabit the area's inshore waters. Farther off shore you might also see killer whales, bay and harp seals, dolphins and squid.

ICEBERG COUNTRY
The cold waters of the Labrador Current wash the shores of the Terra Nova Park, bringing with them icebergs from the frozen floes to the north during the early days of summer.

Travel Facts

Arriving

Entry formalities

Citizens and legal residents of the United States do not need a passport or a visa to enter Canada, but proof of citizenship (a birth certificate, valid passport or voter registration card) and proof of identity are essential. Naturalized US residents should carry their naturalization certificate or Green Card. US residents entering Canada from a third country must have a valid passport, naturalization certificate or Green Card. For fees, documentation and other information, contact the **Office of Passport Services** (tel: 202/647–4000, www.travel.state.gov/passport).

While traveling, keep one photocopy of your data page separate from your wallet and leave another copy with someone at home. If you lose your passport, promptly call the nearest embassy or consulate, and the local police; having the data page can speed replacement.

UK, other European Union and most British Commonwealth citizens need only a full passport to enter Canada. Visas are not necessary for stays of under six months. Visitors may be required to show a return ticket out of Canada, and prove they have sufficient funds to travel. The length of stay is usually the duration of your holiday (the maximum is three months). Visitors may have to complete a waiver form, which requires details of where you will be traveling and staying (write 'touring' if you are unsure).

By air

Toronto, Canada's busiest airport, is the country's main east-coast hub; Vancouver, the second biggest, is the main west-coast hub; Calgary is the best placed for the Canadian Rockies. Montréal is another major hub, and international flights also serve the smaller centers of Ottawa, Edmonton and Halifax.

US carriers serving Canada include **American** (tel: 800/433–7300); **Continental** (tel: 800/525–0280); **Delta** (tel: 800/221–1212); **Northwest** (tel: 800/225–2525); **United** (tel: 800/241–6522).

Flying time to Toronto is 1½ hours from New York and Chicago, and 4½ hours from Los Angeles. To Vancouver: 5½ hours from Montréal, 4 hours from Chicago, and 2½ hours from Los Angeles. To Calgary: 5½ hours from New York, 3½ hours from Toronto, and 4 hours from Los Angeles.

Air Canada has an extensive network of internal and international flights

The least-expensive airfares from the major airlines are priced for round-trip travel and are subject to restrictions. You must usually book in advance and buy the ticket within 24 hours, and you may have to stay over a Saturday night. Contact a number of airlines, and when you find a good price, reserve it on the spot—the same fare on the same flight may not be available the next day.

Journey times from London are roughly 8 hours to Toronto, 8 and a half to Calgary and 9½ to Vancouver. Return flights, with following winds, can be anything up to an hour quicker. Most non-stop flights operate from London's Heathrow and Gatwick airports. More limited non-stop services are also available from Birmingham, Manchester and Glasgow. Air Canada has the most flights from Heathrow, and serves a good deal more destinations than its competitors, especially during peak periods.

By car

There are 13 main road routes across the US–Canada border, most of these hooking up with the Trans-Canada Highway within a few kilometers. The busiest crossings are Niagara Falls and Detroit–Windsor, though all routes become busy in summer and during public holidays. Entry procedures for US citizens are easy.

Fuel is cheaper in the US, so fill up before crossing the border. Also ensure your car has registration documents and full insurance cover. Confirm the current minimum coverage in Canada with your insurer. It can vary from province to province. US drivers should ask insurers for the Canadian Non-Resident InterProvincial Motor Vehicle Liability Card. This is accepted as guarantee of responsibility across Canada. Mention to US rental companies if you intend to take rental cars into Canada (see page 261), and obtain a letter authorizing usage if you are borrowing a car not registered in your name.

By train

There are four daily transborder connections between Amtrak, the US rail network and VIA Rail, its Canadian counterpart. Note that prices are often higher than equivalent journeys made by bus or plane, and that journeys are usually quicker by bus or car. The *Maple Leaf* train runs between New York and Toronto via Buffalo and Niagara Falls (12 hours); the *Adirondack* plies between New York and Montréal via Albany (10 hours), with some connections to Washington DC (19 hours); the *Empire* runs from New York to Niagara Falls via Syracuse and Buffalo (14 hours). A fourth crossing, from Eugene to Vancouver, via Seattle, the *Cascade,* runs once daily (4 hours). Be certain to reserve seats and sleepers well in advance. For further information, contact Amtrak, tel: 800/872–7245, www.amtrak.com.

Customs

The following limits apply to goods brought into Canada duty-free:

- 200 cigarettes, 50 cigars or 400 grams of tobacco
- 1 liter bottle of wine or spirits or 24 35ml cans or bottles of beer
- gifts up to the value of $60

Duty-free limits for visitors returning to the US from Canada are as follows:

- 200 cigarettes and 100 non-Cuban cigars
- 1 liter of spirits (if you are aged over 21), provided the beverage laws of the state through which you re-enter the US allow it
- Antiques and works of art more than 100 years old
- $400 worth of foreign goods

Duty-free limits for visitors returning to the UK are as follows:

- 200 cigarettes or 100 cigarillos, or 50 cigars, or 250g of tobacco
- 1 litre of spirits or 2 litres of fortified wine or sparkling wine
- 2 litres of still table wine
- 60ml of perfume and 250ml of toilette water
- gifts, souvenirs and other goods up to a value of £145.

Travel insurance

It is recommended that you take out fully comprehensive travel insurance before traveling to Canada.

Essential facts

Climate

Weather across Canada is immensely varied. Areas near the coasts, or the Great Lakes, generally have milder winters and cooler summers than the interior. Summer can be pleasantly warm across the whole country, though snow flurries are not unknown in the north during August. Winters are bitterly cold in many regions, though Canadian towns and cities are used to the cold and are well equipped to deal with extremes.

British Columbia and the west have mild winters and summers, with often heavy rainfall in fall and winter. Certain areas of the southwest, however, such as the Okanagan, enjoy hot and dry summers. The Rockies and Prairie provinces have good short summers and long severe winters, the former interspersed with sudden storms, the latter with driving blizzards. Québec and Ontario enjoy long gentle springs (April to June), but hot and often unpleasantly humid summers; winters are cold and damp in Ontario, drier and colder in Québec. Other parts of eastern Canada and the Maritimes experience more distinct seasons, with short snowy winters, mild springs, warm summers and long falls, though weather in these regions can be some of the most unpredictable in the country.

When to go

July and August offer the best weather, but they are also the busiest months to visit as well as the most

VANCOUVER

October–March

May–August

inches 12 10 8 6 4 2 0

°F 90 80 70 60 50 40 32

J F M A M J J A S O N D

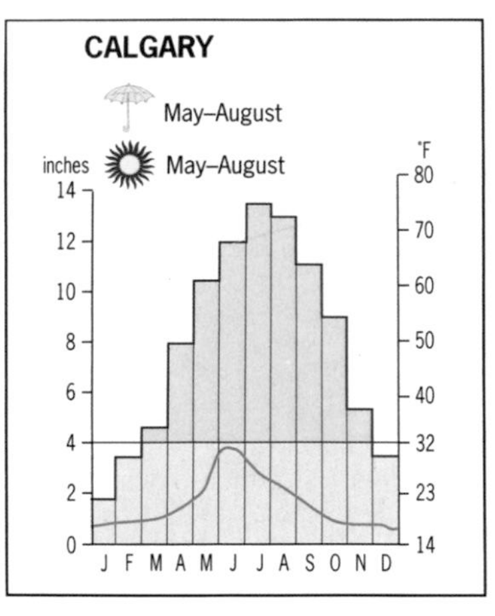

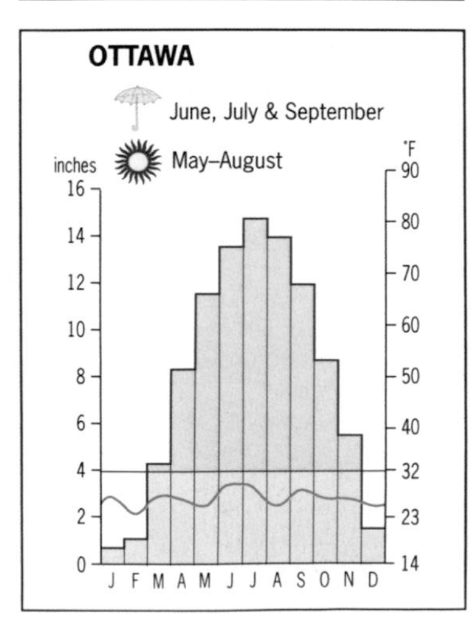

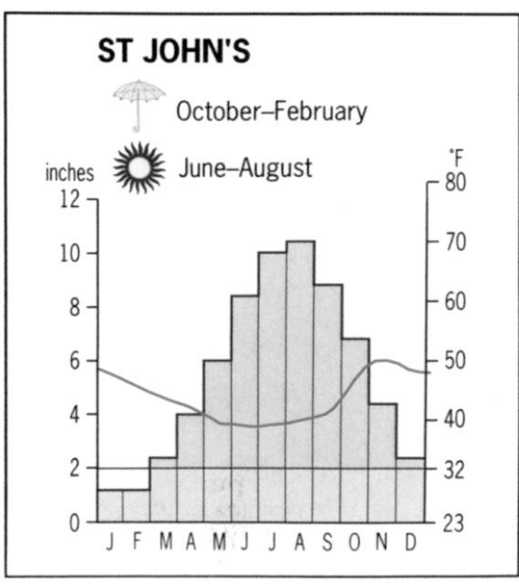

expensive. Summer is the best time to see the Rockies, though all mountain areas are also busy with skiers between the months of December and March. The Prairies are at their best in the summer. It is also the only feasible time to visit the Yukon and the far north of the country.

Early fall and late spring offer the chance to avoid the rains and the worst of the crowds in British Columbia. Spring is a good time to enjoy eastern Canada, though in certain areas snow can remain on the ground until April and May. Fall is also popular in the east, particularly in Québec and New Brunswick. Remember that many sites, hotels and campsites, especially outside the cities, open only between Victoria Day (mid-May) and Labor Day (early September).

National holidays

Banks, schools and government offices close on:
New Year's Day (January 1), Good Friday; Easter Monday, Victoria Day (Monday before May 25), Canada Day (July 1), Labor Day (first Monday in September), Thanksgiving (second Monday in October), Remembrance Day (November 11), Christmas Day (December 25), Boxing Day (December 26).

Provincial holidays

Banks, schools and government offices close on the following provincial holidays, which if movable are usually observed on a Monday to make a long weekend:
Alberta—Heritage Day (first week in August)
British Columbia—British Columbia Day (first week in August)
New Brunswick—New Brunswick Day (first week in August)
Newfoundland and **Labrador**—St. Patrick's Day (March 17), St. George's Day (late April), Discovery Day (next to last Monday in June), Memorial Day (first week in July) and Orangeman's Day (third week in July)
Manitoba, Northwest Territories, Ontario and **Saskatchewan**—Civic Holiday (first week in August)
Québec—St. Jean Baptiste Day (June 24)
Yukon—Discovery Day (mid-August).

Time differences

Canada is divided into six time zones: Newfoundland Standard Time (NST); Atlantic Standard Time (AST); Eastern Standard Time (EST); Central Standard Time (CST); Mountain Standard Time (MST); and Pacific Standard Time (PST). The time difference between the two most eastern zones (NST and AST) is only half an hour, so the overall time difference between the east and west coasts is 4½ hours. NST is 1½ hours ahead of EST; AST is one hour ahead, and so on to PST (British Columbia and the Yukon), which is three hours behind EST.

NST is 3½ hours behind Greenwich Mean Time (GMT) in the UK; AST is 4 hours behind, and so on to PST (British Columbia and the Yukon), which is 8 hours behind GMT.

Daylight Saving Time

Daylight Saving Time (Canadian Summer Time) is observed all over Canada except for Saskatchewan and the northeastern corner of British Columbia. Clocks are moved forward one hour on the first Sunday of April, and they are moved back one hour on the last Sunday in October.

Arctic Circle: Land of "white nights" in the endless days of summer

Where to stay

Canada's accommodations are varied, reasonably priced, and usually of a high standard. See pages 272–278 for recommendations to suit your requirements, or try one of the chains listed here.

Hotels

Canadian hotels can be divided into three basic types.

At the bottom of the barrel are the cheerless hotels above bars in towns and city centers. Often, these date from the days when it was difficult to run a bar without having a restaurant or hotel attached. Although centrally located, rooms are usually run-down, and may be on top of a bar with pounding live music.

At the other extreme is a range of top-class city and resort hotels, where standards are the equal of any in Europe. Mid-range chain hotel rooms are easy to reserve and have the benefit that you know the quality and type of accommodations available in advance. Hotels belonging to any of the following chains should prove to be reliable options:

- **Best Western International,** tel: 800/780–7234, www.bestwestern.com
- **Fairmont,** tel: 800/441–1414, www.fairmont.com
- **Delta Hotels,** tel: city hotels: 877/814–7706; resort hotels: 888/778–5050, www.deltahotels.com
- **Holiday Inns,** tel: 877/465–4329, www.holiday-inn.com
- **Renaissance Hotels,** tel: 800/HOTELS–1, www.marriott.com
- **Sheraton,** tel: 888/625–5144, www.sheraton.com
- **Travelodge,** tel: 800/578–7878, www.travelodge.com
- **Westin Hotels,** tel: 888/625–5144, www.westin.com

Canada has no national government rating system for hotels, but many provinces rate their accommodations.

Motels

Motels provide reliable and mid-priced accommodations on highways

The Banff Springs, a great "railway hotel"

outside towns and cities. Standards are high, and you can expect a good bed, private bathroom, TV and phone in most rooms. Some also have family rooms, kitchenettes, saunas and swimming pools.

Bed-and-breakfast
Bed-and-breakfast or "guest house" accommodations can now be found in most Canadian towns, cities and rural backwaters. Many cities have central reservation services, though tourist offices usually carry extensive listings. Rooms do not always have private bathrooms, and breakfast can vary from "continental" (a roll and coffee) to the full cooked breakfast. Rooms may vary within an establishment, and some places are a long way from town and city centers. So, check carefully on a B&B's location, and facilities offered.

Hostels
Canada has some 80 youth hostels affiliated to Hosteling International (H.I.)—the new name for the International Youth Hostel Federation—and many more independent "mini-hostels" or "homes." Most HI hostels are open to members and non-members alike, though preference is given to members.

Hostels are often impressive modern affairs, with cafeterias, credit-card reservations and long opening hours. Many offer private rooms as well as single-sex dormitories. Most cities also have a YMCA and YWCA (or a "Y"), offering a choice of good-quality dorm, single, double or family rooms.

Some YWCAs will accept only women and children or men as part of a mixed couple. Tourist offices will advise on the nearest hostels (see pages 269–270).

Booking
It is vital to reserve accommodations well in advance if you are visiting popular areas during July and August. At other times it is a good idea to call a few days in advance to secure a room. Remember that large areas of the country are remote, which means a long drive if your chosen hotel of is full when you arrive.

To make a reservation, simply give a credit-card number over the phone; if you then change your mind, be sure to cancel in good time, as the hotel is perfectly within its rights to charge a night's fee to your card.

If you know you may be arriving late, inform the desk, as many hotels—especially in busy areas—hold reservations only until 4pm or 6pm. Also confirm check-in times, as rooms in some hotels may not be available until mid- or late afternoon.

Some popular areas, notably Banff and Jasper in the Rockies, have tourist agencies that will find you a room for a small fee. B&B agencies are also common, though most tourist offices will be happy to help find accommodations free of charge.

Prices and discounts
Aside from the quaint hotels of Québec, Canada's accommodations more closely resemble those of the United States than of Europe. Prices and listings are obtainable in advance from provincial and local tourist offices (see pages 269–270), though listed prices do not usually include the sales and room taxes levied by most provinces (see page 267), which can add between 5 and 12 percent.

Bed-and-breakfast rates vary according to the facilities; don't be bashful about asking to see a room before making a choice.

If you are traveling with children, or in a group, ask about a "Family Plan," where children under a certain age sharing their parents' room stay free; be sure to ask about the cut-off age. Most places will also introduce a third single bed into a double room for an additional charge of between $5 and $20. If you are traveling alone, check whether there is an extra charge for single room occupancy.

Hotels and motels also offer numerous off-season midweek deals, or give special discounts for extended stays. City hotels aimed primarily at business travelers may offer lower weekend rates, and most places, except for the skiing resorts, have hefty price reductions in winter.
For accommodations for those with disabilities, check with the specialist organizations on page 268.

Getting around

By air

Air Canada has a network of domestic routes serving more than 125 destinations. They are complemented by numerous smaller low-cost airlines that cover the most obscure corners of the far north and elsewhere. These include **Air North** (Northern Canada and Alaska); **West Jet** (major cities); **Jetsgo** (major cities); and **Air Canada Jazz** and **Tango** (low-cost). Air Canada has links with smaller companies, allowing them to offer integrated routing and ticketing arrangements. Smoking is banned on all internal flights in Canada.

- **Air Canada,** tel: 888/247–2262, (US); 08711 220 1111(UK) www.aircanada.com
- **Air North,** tel: 800/661–0407, www.flyairnorth.com
- **Air Canada Jazz,** tel: 888/247–2262, www.flyjazz.ca
- **Jetsgo,** tel: 866/440–0441, www.jetsgo.net
- **Tango,** tel: 800/315–1390, www.flytango.com
- **West Jet,** tel: 888/WEST-JET, www.westjet.com

Tickets and passes Flying in Canada is fairly expensive, though airlines offer a variety of discounted tickets (as well as student, youth and senior-citizen discounts), so inquire about these before you leave.

By train

Most passenger services in Canada are operated by VIA Rail (see box this page). Rail travel is often slower and more expensive than the equivalent journey by bus, though VIA Rail does provide comfort and service. As a result, traveling by train can be a pleasant way of seeing the country.

- **Services** Winnipeg–Edmonton–Jasper–Van-couver; Winnipeg–Churchill; Jasper–Prince George–Prince Rupert; Victoria–Courtenay (Vancouver Island); Toronto–Winnipeg; Toronto–Ottawa–Montréal– Québec City; Montréal–Halifax.
- **Classes** "Silver and Blue" is a first-class service on trans-Canada trains offering, among other things, exclusive use of the famous domed sightseeing carriages. Second class in Canada is known as "coach" or "comfort."
- **Sleepers** "Section" class offers seats that become curtained bunks at night. "Roomettes" are private single sleepers with toilet and folding bed; "bedrooms" are single apartments that cost about twice as much as roomettes. Reclining "Dayniter" seats are also available on many night trains.
- **Reservations** Reserve seats whenever possible, certainly for the trans-Canada service (Toronto–Vancouver) and the scenic lines in western Canada. Reservations are obligatory for first-class seats, all sleeping-car accommodations, and the Dayniter services in Ontario, Québec and the Maritime Provinces.
- **Reductions** Discounts of 10 percent are available to senior citizens aged over 60. Children between 2 and 11 travel half price. Reductions of up to 40 percent on coach-class fares are often available (except during weekends and peak periods), if you reserve in advance.
- **Rail passes** The Canrailpass (obtainable from VIA Rail stations and agents) is available to all visitors. It allows 12 days of comfort-class travel within a 30-day period; sleeping cars sell out very early and must be reserved at least a month in advance during the high season (Jun 1–Sep 30). The pass is not valid during the Christmas period (Dec 15–Jan 5). The Canrailpass must be purchased prior to arrival in Canada; for more information, contact VIA Rail (see box below).

- **VIA Rail Canada,** tel: 888/842–7245, www.viarail.com
- **Rocky Mountain Railtours,** tel: 877/460–3200, www.skymtnrail.com

- **Private companies** Rocky Mountain Railtours run expensive but popular chartered trains (Jun–end Sep) along the famous Calgary–Banff–Vancouver route through the Rockies (now closed to VIA Rail services). It is best to reserve the trip as part of a package (see box opposite). Other private lines include the Polar Bear Express (Cochrane to Moosonee) and Ontario's Algoma Central Railway (Hearst to Sault Ste-Marie).

> • Tickets and bookings for VIA Rail and Rocky Mountain Railtours can be obtained in the UK through Leisurail, PO Box 5, 12 Coningsby Road, Peterborough PE3 8XP (tel: 0870-7500 222).

By bus

The bus is an essential form of transportation in Canada, especially if you want to visit out-of-the-way towns that do not have airports or rail lines. Two major companies, together with a host of provincial firms, provide a network of bus routes throughout Canada. In the east, the main company is **Voyageur** (tel: 800/668–4438, www.voyageur.com); in the west, it is **Greyhound** (tel: 800/661–8747, www.greyhound.ca). In the United States, you can contact Greyhound, on tel: 800/231–2222.

By ferry

Toll-free ferries form part of the highway system in much of Canada, providing vital links in the country's road network. Elsewhere, ferries offer connections to islands on the country's east and west coasts.

The main west-coast company, with almost 50 ports of call, is the British Columbia Ferry Corporation, better known as **BC Ferries** (tel: 888/223–3779 or 250/386–3431, www.bcferries.com). Its key services operate between the BC mainland and Vancouver Island; between Vancouver Island and Prince Rupert (which also known as the "Inside Passage"); and between Prince Rupert and the Queen Charlotte Islands.

Easy ticketing

Some ferries on the east coast are run by **Marine Atlantic** (tel: 902/794–5254 or 800/341–7981, www.marine-atlantic.ca). They operate between Nova Scotia and Newfoundland.

Tour organizations

If you would rather leave the planning to someone else, visit Canada as part of an organized tour. There are plenty available and in addition to the standard group sightseeing tours, include adventure trips and cycling, cultural, dogsledding, fishing, golf, health, horseback riding, educational, skiing, train and walking tours. The **National Tour Association**, 546 E. Main Street, Lexington, KY40508 (tel: 606/226–4444 or 800/682–8886, www.ntalonline.com), and **United States Tour Operators Association**, 275 Madison Avenue, Suite 2014, New York, NY10016 (tel: 212/599–6599, www.ustoa.com), can provide lists of member operators and information on how to reserve tours.

Roads are few and far between in Canada's remote back country

Driving

Documents

Full US and UK driver's licenses are valid for driving in Canada, though drivers must be over 21. The International Driving License is also valid, but it should be accompanied by your own driving license. Spot fines can be levied for failure to carry your license while driving. Proof of full insurance coverage against injury, death or damage is required. You should confirm minimum Canadian coverage with your insurer.

Roads

Canada's roads are generally excellent, though they are scarce, and may have a gravel or dirt surface in remote areas. Expressways and highways link major towns; "secondary highways" are usually single-lane roads between smaller towns and villages; "tertiary" roads are minor paved roads; and "gravel" highways are unpaved or asphalt-topped roads (these are often used for logging). All roads are numbered, and most are clearly marked. Distances are shown in kilometers; speed limits are in kph.

Rules of the road

- Drive on the right. On multiple-lane expressways outside built-up areas, it is possible to pass on the left or right.
- At crossroads without traffic lights in built-up areas, priority is given to the first car to arrive, and to the right-hand car if two cars arrive at the same time.
- Right-turn-on-red is permitted if there is no traffic from the left, except in Québec. You must first come to a complete stop at the intersection.
- Flashing yellow lights are a sign to slow down and often indicate a place where accidents tend to occur.
- The use of infant and child seats and seat belts is mandatory in all provinces and territories.
- Some provinces insist on the use of headlights for periods after dawn and before sunset. In the Yukon, headlights must be used at all times.
- Speed limits vary slightly between provinces, but the uniform top speed on expressways is 100kph (62mph); 90kph (56mph) on the Trans-Canada and Yellowhead highways; 80kph (50mph) on most rural roads; and between 40 and 60kph (25–37mph) in urban areas. Speed limits are rigidly enforced, with fines for violations.
- It is illegal to overtake yellow/ orange school buses (from either direction) that are stopped with their warning lights flashing.
- Driving under the influence of alcohol is a serious offense; alcohol in a car must be carried unopened in the trunk.
- Parking is forbidden on sidewalks, near traffic lights, within 5m (16ft) of a fire hydrant, and within 15m (50ft) of railroad crossings.
- Hitchhiking is illegal in some places.

Car breakdowns

If your car breaks down, try to ensure it will not block traffic. Raise the hood and tie a white cloth to the driver's side to indicate that help is required. Emergency phones are found at the side of most major roads. Canada's main towing agency is the **Canadian Automobile**

Association (CAA), with offices in most major towns and cities. Its central office is at 1145 Hunt Club Road, Suite 200, Ottawa, Ontario K1V 0Y3 (tel: 613/247–0117, www.caa.com). Its emergency number is 800/CAA–HELP. Members of the AA, AAA, and other affiliated national motoring organizations, receive free assistance from the CAA on presentation of a membership card.

Car rental

Cars can be rented on presentation of a driver's license, which usually needs to have been held for at least a year. Discounts of between 15 and 30 percent are possible with advance booking. Look out for hidden charges, notably GST and provincial taxes (see page 267). A "drop-off" charge, often equivalent to a week's rental, may be levied if you rent the car in one town and leave it in another. Collision or Loss Damage Waiver, an insurance against accident or damage, is worth considering. Check to see whether unlimited mileage is included, or whether an additional charge cuts in after a set daily mileage. Many companies now rent cellular phones, which can add to your sense of security, especially if you are traveling in remote areas. Note that many firms will not rent cars for use on gravel roads. All rental firms require either a large cash deposit or a credit-card number before renting a vehicle. Drivers must be over 21, and under 25s may incur higher insurance premiums.

Wilderness driving

Driving in wilderness areas or on gravel and logging roads requires special care. Fuel stations in remote areas can often be hours apart, so fill your tank at every opportunity and carry spare cans of gasoline. In cold or potentially bad weather—which in mountain areas can strike at any time—carry spare food, warm clothes, a good tool kit, a tow-rope and a shovel. If your car gets caught in drifting snow *do not* run your engine (you may asphyxiate on trapped exhaust fumes). In rural areas, look out for logging trucks and large animals. On gravel roads, have a spare tire (preferably two), and special protective grilles for your headlights and possibly windshields.

Gravel roads require extra care, but traverse beautiful scenery

Communications

Media

Canada has two national newspapers—*The Globe and Mail*, a quality full-size paper published in Toronto (but with a so-called "National" edition), and the *National Post*. Most large cities have their own papers, notably the *Toronto Star*, *Calgary Herald* and *Vancouver Sun*, though news is invariably parochial, something that is still more true of the country's many small-town newspapers. Canada also has its own news magazine, the weekly *Maclean's*. UK and other European newspapers are difficult to find, but larger newsagents often have copies of Sunday papers a few days after publication.

Canada's television, apart from innumerable local stations and the Canadian Broadcasting Corporation (CBC), remains all but indistinguishable from that of the United States. Most hotels and motels have TVs, with cable, satellite and pay-per-view TV options.

CBC provides the best of the country's radio broadcasting, which otherwise tends to be a bland mixture of music, chat and small-town stations.

Mail

- **Post offices** These are often found inside shops, department stores and rail stations, so be on the look-out for "Canada Post" signs (www.canadapost.ca).
- **Opening hours** Post offices are usually open Mon–Fri 8.30–5.30, though a few also open on Sat 9–noon.
- **Stamps** Post offices, newsstands, hotel vending machines, train stations, bus terminals, airports and many other retail outlets, sell stamps.
- **Postal rates** For postcards and letters, current prices are: 48¢ plus tax, within Canada; 65¢ plus tax, to the US; 1.25¢ plus tax overseas. These are prone to change and tax additions.
- **Poste restante** Letters sent poste restante should be sent c/o "General Delivery," Main Post Office, followed by the name of the town and province. Mark a pickup date if known; otherwise letters will be kept for a maximum of 15 days, after which they will be returned to the sender. Take some form of government-issued ID when collecting mail. Letters sent for pickup in hotels should be marked "Guest Mail."
- **Intelpost** This service allows you to send documents or photographs via satellite to many Canadian, American and European destinations. The service is available at main postal facilites in Canada, and is paid for in cash.

Telephones

- **Public phones** Call boxes and public phones are widely available. Local calls cost 25¢. For calls outside an area code, and for some longer-distance calls within an area code, you need to prefix your dialed number with 1. This puts you through to an operator who will tell you how much money is required before your call is connected. Thereafter you need to have plenty of 5¢, 10¢ and 25¢ coins ready to feed the phone. Prepaid phonecards, which are especially

Mailboxes come in all shapes and sizes

convenient for making long-distance calls, can be purchased at tourist offices and many other outlets.

- **Long-distance and international calls** The number of 25¢ coins needed for these calls means that it makes sense to use your phone-company charge card, or to find one of the increasingly common public phones that accepts credit cards. See the box on the right-hand side of this page for international codes. Calls to the US are dialed direct.
- **Direct-dial phones**, with calls charged directly to your bill, are common in better hotels and motels. Elsewhere an operator may reply and ask for a room number to which the call is to be charged. In either case hotels levy a surcharge.
- **Toll-free numbers** Many organizations have these free numbers, which can be recognized by their 800 and other 888, 866 or similar prefixes. Some operate only within a province, others anywhere in Canada, and a few anywhere in North America.
- **Collect calls (reverse calls)** can be made by dialing 0 for the operator.
- **Information** The nationwide number is 411.
- **To call UK** Dial 001, then 44, then the full area code and the number.

Canada's provincial codes

- **Alberta:** South 403
North 780
- **British Columbia** 604 and 250
- **Manitoba** 204
- **New Brunswick** 506
- **Newfoundland** 709
- **Nova Scotia and Prince Edward Island** 902
- **Ontario**: Toronto region 905
Central & NE 705
SW peninsula 519
Ottawa region 613
Northwest 807
- **Québec**: Montréal 450
City 514
North 819
East 418
- **Saskatchewan** 306
- **Yukon, Nunavut and the Northwest Territories** 867

International codes

- **Australia** 011 61
- **Germany** 011 49
- **Ireland** 011 353
- **New Zealand** 011 64
- **South Africa** 011 27
- **UK** 011 44

Canada's telephone numbering system matches that of the US. To call abroad from Canada, dial the country code, the area code, and the number required.

A crime-free zone: The Sun Yat-Sen Temple in Vancouver's Chinatown

Emergencies

Crime and police

For the most part, Canada is crime-free. Be cautious at night in larger cities. Also avoid leaving luggage or valuables in cars, do not carry around large quantities of cash, and keep passports and credit cards in a pouch or belt. Avoid parks, rail stations and other noncommercial areas after dark, and leave jewelry and other valuables in a hotel safe.

If you are the victim of a crime, call the police (tel: 911). The Royal Canadian Mounted Police (RCMP) are Canada's main police force, though Ontario and Québec have their own provincial forces. Ensure the crime is recorded if you intend to make future insurance claims. Also make a note of the crime reference number in police records.

If you lose your passport, report the loss to the police and contact your nearest embassy or consulate (see below).

US Embassy

490 Sussex Drive, Ottawa
(tel: 613/238–5335.
www.usembassycanada.gov)

US consulates

- **Montréal** 1155 rue St-Alexandre (tel: 514/398–9695)
- **Toronto** Consulate General of the United States, 360 University Avenue, just north of Queen Street, M56 1S4 (tel: 416/595–1700)
- **Vancouver** 1095 W. Pender Street (tel: 604/685–4311)

UK embassies and consulates

- **Montréal** 1000 de la Gauchetiere West, Suite 4200 (tel: 514/866-5863)
- **Ottawa** British High Commission, 80 Elgin Street (tel: 613/237-1530)
- **Toronto** 777 Bay Street, Suite 2800 (tel: 416/593-1290)
- **Vancouver** Suite 800, 1111 Melville Street (tel: 604/683-4421)

There are also consulates in Calagary, Halifax and Québec City.

Health insurance

Canada's health service is excellent, but foreigners on vacation have to pay for any treatment they require, so check your insurance coverage before your visit. If you become sick, you will be treated and charged later; in some provinces there is a surcharge of up to 30 percent for treatment of nonresidents.

Doctors and dentists

If you need a doctor or dentist, first consult your hotel. Otherwise look in the Yellow Pages. Ambulance and other emergency services are usually found listed on the inside cover of phone directories. Remember that you will have to pay for a house call and any treatment. Keep all receipts and paperwork for claims.

Pharmacies

Most over-the-counter medicines can be bought at drugstores. If you need a prescription medication, most towns and cities have at least one 24-hour pharmacy. Bring your prescription with you if you need to renew medication.

Health

Canada's main health hazards are associated with the outdoors.

Check tap water at campsites (some is only good for washing) and in the backcountry boil water for at least 10 minutes to guard against *Giardi lamblia* ("beaver fever"). This parasite thrives in warm water, so hot springs are a potential breeding ground. Symptoms, which include vomiting and stomach cramps, can appear up to a week after infection.

Lyme disease is also increasingly common. It is caused by bites from woodland ticks carrying *Lyme borreliosis*. Signs of infection include a distinctive bull's-eye-like rash and flu-like symptoms. It is spreading in wooded areas of southern Canada, so ask tourist offices about its local prevalence. Tick repellents are available, and you can reduce the risk of bites by wearing thick socks, long trousers tucked into your socks, and long-sleeved shirts when you hike. Check your body nightly for ticks.

Country areas, particularly in southern Ontario and Québec, also contain clumps of poison ivy. Park and forest visitor centers can provide information. Creams and ointments to treat the blisters and sores are widely available.

Less unpleasant, but equally irritating, are the blackflies and mosquitoes, found in northern areas between April and October. Repellent creams with DEET make reasonably effective deterrents, and bites can be soothed with antihistamine cream.

Beware of too much sun—wear a hat and use a good sun-block—and equip yourself with suitable boots, protective clothing and extra food.

Emergency telephone numbers

The countrywide telephone number for police, fire and ambulance services is **911**, though in more remote areas you may have to call **0** for the operator, who will then put you through to the service required.

In the case of a car breakdown, first notify the police and then call the Canadian Automobile Association (CAA). The nationwide number for its towing and repair service is **800/CAA-HELP**.

Vaccinations

Vaccinations are not necessary unless you are traveling from a known infected area. Check current requirements if you are traveling from the Far East, South America, Africa or the Middle East.

You shouldn't pick up any nasty ailments in Victoria's renowned Butchart Gardens

Other information

Addresses
Most Canadian towns are arranged around a grid of streets (running one way) and avenues (running the other). Some are further divided into quadrants (NW, NE, SE and SW), or into north and south or east and west of downtown. Streets and avenues may be numbered, named, or both. Addresses refer you to a house number, a block (formed by the intersection of a street and avenue), and sometimes a sector of the town or city. House numbers are the last numbers of a sequence, street or block numbers the first. Numbering of blocks is usually made from the center of downtown outward. Thus 830-Fourth Avenue S.W. is house number 30 on 8th Street close to the intersection with Fourth Avenue (in the SW corner of the city). 830-Fourth Avenue NW would be a long way from this address, so it is vital to take careful note of sectors.

Electricity
Current in Canada is 110 volts AC (60Hz), and standard North American two-flat-prong sockets are used. For UK visitors, plug adaptors will be required for appliances such as shavers, hair dryers and musical equipment and should match these sockets.

Etiquette
Canadian morals and manners are similar to those in the US and Britain, though you should be sensitive to the more traditional ways of rural areas.

It is also vital to respect the customs of the aboriginal peoples, who are increasingly asserting their rights and distinct cultural identities. It is an insult, for example, to address an Inuit as an "Eskimo," or a Native or aboriginal Canadian as an "Indian." In the French-speaking parts of Canada, notably Québec, you should also be prepared to acknowledge French as the first, sometimes only, language.

Many Canadians still smoke, but smoking in public places is increasingly frowned upon or in many cases, forbidden.

Money matters
The units of Canadian currency are the cent (¢) and the dollar ($1 = 100¢). Notes are printed in English and French in the following dollar denominations: 5, 10, 20, 50, 100, 500, 1,000. Coins are issued in denominations of 1¢ (a "penny" or "sou"); 5¢ (a "nickel" or "cinq sous"); 10¢ (a dime); 25¢ (a "quarter" or "vingt-cinq sous"). The $1 coin is known as a "loony," and the $2 coin is called a "twony." US dollars are widely accepted but check the exchange rate.

Foreign exchange
There are relatively few places to exchange currency in Canada away from resorts and big cities. Exchange facilities can usually be found in large hotels, airports and train stations, but rates are often poor and commission fees high. Banks offering exchange facilities are surprisingly rare, and many charge a fee. The best way to carry money is in the form of traveler's checks, which if made out in Canadian dollars can be used as cash in most shops, restaurants and garages across the country (change is given in cash). American Express or Visa checks are the most common. Any amount of Canadian or foreign currency can be exchanged, or brought into, or out of, the country.

ATMs
You can use your bank card at Canadian ATMs to withdraw money from an account and get cash advances on a credit-card account.

Credit cards
It is virtually essential to have at least one credit card when traveling in Canada. Giving a credit-card number is usually the only way to reserve hotel rooms in advance. Cards can also be used for cash advances, to pay for theater and sports events, to rent skis, buy groceries, to prepay for hotel rooms, and for renting a car. Many rental companies and hotel chains will *only* deal with cardholders so they are more useful than traveler's checks in most places. Visa, MasterCard, Diners Club and American Express are the most common cards.

General sales tax
A general sales tax (GST) of 7 percent is levied on most transactions, including hotel and restaurant bills, but excluding basic food purchases. It is added to bills, and so is not a "hidden cost." Visitors are eligible for a GST rebate on most goods taken out of Canada within 60 days (but not food, drink, tobacco, car and RV rental charges, and other transportation expenses). More significantly, you can claim a GST rebate on all accommodations costs over $100 if you apply within a maximum one-month period. Claim forms are available from airports, stores and hotels, and from any Canadian embassy. All receipts must be enclosed with the forms, which should be returned within 60 days of leaving Canada.

Provincial taxes
In addition to GST, all provinces except Alberta, Yukon Territory and the Northwest Territories, levy provincial sales taxes of 5–12 percent on restaurant meals and most goods bought in shops. Québec, Manitoba, Nova Scotia and Newfoundland offer a rebate to visitors along the lines of the GST rebate; for information, contact provincial tourist offices (see pages 269–270).

Most provinces also charge a tax on hotel rooms, so this too should be factored into accommodations charges (which are listed without tax).

Opening times
- **Stores** Mon–Sat, about 9–5.30, though stores are increasingly staying open later in the evening. Many retail stores stay open extra late on Thursday and Friday evenings.
- **Shopping malls** Longer hours than stores, usually about 7.30–9pm.
- **24-hour shopping** Most towns have round-the-clock pharmacies and stores, such as Mac's or 7Eleven, and Dépanneurs in Québec.
- **Banks** Mon–Fri 10–3; extended hours (10–5 or 6) on certain days, usually Thursday or Friday.
- **Post offices** Mon–Fri 8.30–5.30, and occasionally Sat 9–noon.

Edmonton's vast West Edmonton Mall is the largest shopping complex in the world

- **Restaurants** Noon–11pm, longer on weekends. Diner-type establishments and restaurants in small towns and villages, close earlier (8–9.30pm).
- **Museums and galleries** Store hours usually apply, though they may have limited Sunday, seasonal, and public holiday opening. Big-city museums often have late opening one evening a week.
- **Seasonal opening** Many tourist sites, museums, parks, tourist offices, resort hotels, campsites, motels and B&Bs open seasonally, typically from Victoria Day (in mid-May) to Labor Day (early Sep) or Canadian Thanksgiving (mid-Oct). This is especially true in more remote areas.
- **Sunday opening** Most stores in malls and downtown shopping areas will open between 11 and 5 or noon and 5.

Tipping
Service is rarely added to the check, and even in the most humble diners and restaurants, it is usual to leave around 15 percent of the total check (waiting staff rely heavily on tips). Drinks are often brought to tables in bars, and here, too, bar staff should always be tipped. Barbers, hairdressers and taxi drivers should be tipped around 15 percent.

CONVERSION CHARTS

FROM	TO	MULTIPLY BY
Inches	Centimeters	2.54
Centimeters	Inches	0.3937
Feet	Meters	0.3048
Meters	Feet	3.2810
Yards	Meters	0.9144
Meters	Yards	1.0940
Miles	Kilometers	1.6090
Kilometers	Miles	0.6214
Acres	Hectares	0.4047
Hectares	Acres	2.4710
Gallons	Liters	4.5460
Liters	Gallons	0.2200
Ounces	Grams	28.35
Grams	Ounces	0.0353
Pounds	Grams	453.6
Grams	Pounds	0.0022
Pounds	Kilograms	0.4536
Kilograms	Pounds	2.205
Tons	Tonnes	0.9058
Tonnes	Tons	1.104

MEN'S SUITS

US	36	38	40	42	44	46	48
UK	36	38	40	42	44	46	48
Rest of Europe	46	48	50	52	54	56	58

DRESS SIZES

US	6	8	10	12	14	16
UK	8	10	12	14	16	18
France	36	38	40	42	44	46
Italy	38	40	42	44	46	48
Rest of Europe	34	36	38	40	42	44

MEN'S SHIRTS

US	14	14.5	15	15.5	16	16.5	17
UK	14	14.5	15	15.5	16	16.5	17
Rest of Europe	36	37	38	39/40	41	42	43

MEN'S SHOES

US	8	8.5	9.5	10.5	11.5	12
UK	7	7.5	8.5	9.5	10.5	11
Rest of Europe	41	42	43	44	45	46

WOMEN'S SHOES

US	6	6.5	7	7.5	8	8.5
UK	4.5	5	5.5	6	6.5	7
Rest of Europe	38	38	39	39	40	41

Visitors with disabilities

All public buildings have wheelchair access and special toilets. Curbs in most cities and large towns are dropped to meet the needs of wheelchair users. Difficulties may still be encountered on public transportation, though buses are increasingly being adapted to accommodate wheelchairs.

VIA Rail trains can accommodate wheelchairs of up to 114kg (250 lb), and measuring no more than 81 by 182cm (32 by 72in), but they require 48 hours' notice (the Québec–Windsor corridor requires 24 hours). Hotels in the Best Western and Journey's End chains have full wheelchair access, and Holiday Inn hotels provide special suites for guests with disabilities. Provincial tourist offices (see pages 269–270) can usually provide details of other suitable hotels.

The following agencies in the US and Canada provide information on tour operators, special guides and other aspects of traveling abroad for visitors with disabilities:

- **Mobility International,** (tel: 541/343–1284, www.miusa.org)
- **Access-Able,** (www.access-able.com)
- **SATH,** (tel: 212/447–7284, www.sath.org)
- **Wheels Up,** (tel: 888/38–WHEELS, www.wheelsup.com)
- **Canadian Paraplegic Assocation,** (tel: 617/723–1033, www.canparaplegic.org)

In the UK:

- **Royal Association for Disability and Rehabilitation (RADAR),** (tel: 020-7250 3222, www.radar.org.uk)
- **Tripscope,** (tel: 08457 585 641, www.tripscope.org.uk; outside UK +44 117 939 7782
- **Holiday Care Service,** (tel: 0845 124 9971, www.holidaycare.org.uk; outside UK +44 208 760 0072)

Tourist offices

Few tourist offices in the world are as efficient or as well-stocked as those in Canada. Offices (also called "Visitor centers" or "info centers") dispense information on a huge range of activities. They will provide details of accommodations, but don't make specific recommendations. Rural offices can advise on anything from hikes and fishing permits to whale-watching and chartering planes for backcountry exploration.

Smaller offices are usually open mid-May to early September, though they often open in July and August from 9am to 9pm and from 9am to 5 or 6pm for the rest of the summer. Small information kiosks at airports and train stations, and on city streets, complement the main tourist office. National parks and major tourist sights often have their own visitors' centers.

Provincial tourist offices

The offices listed below are good sources of information, and, if you contact them before you leave, can provide help and background material on every aspect of your trip.

- **Alberta** Alberta Tourism, PO.Box 2500, Edmonton, Alberta T5J 2Z4 (tel: 780/427–4321 or 800/661–8888, www.explorealberta.com)

Tourist offices throughout Canada have information on a wide range of sports and outdoor activities

- **British Columbia** Tourism British Columbia, Parliament Buildings, Victoria, British Columbia V8V 1X4 (tel: 250/387–1642 or 800/663–6000, www.hellobc.com)
- **Manitoba** Travel Manitoba, 7th Floor, 155 Carlton Street, Winnipeg, Manitoba R3C 3H8 (tel: 204/945-3777 or 800/665–0040, www.travelmanitoba.com
- **Nunavut,** Nunavut Tourism, PO Box 1450, Iqaluit, Nunavut, X0A 0H0 (tel: 866/NUNAVUT, www.nunavuttourism.com)
- **New Brunswick** Tourism New Brunswick, PO Box 6000, Fredericton, New Brunswick E3B 5H1 (tel: 506/753–3876 or 800/561–0123, www.tourismnbcanada.com)
- **Newfoundland and Labrador** Tourism Newfoundland and Labrador , PO Box 8730, St.-John's, Newfoundland A1B 4K2 (tel: 709/729–2830 or 800/563–6353, www.gov.nf.ca/tourism)
- **Northwest Territories**, NWT Arctic Tourism, PO Box 610, Yellowknife, Northwest Territories X1A 2N5 (tel: 867/873–7200 or 800/661–0788, www.nwttravel.nt.ca)
- **Nova Scotia** Nova Scotia Tourism, PO Box 456, Halifax, Nova Scotia B3J 2R5 (tel: 902/424–5000 or 800/565–0000, www.explorens.com)

The sun sets over the waters of Mahone Bay in Nova Scotia

- **Ontario** Ontario Travel, Queens Park, Toronto, Ontario M7A 2E5 (tel: 416/314–0944 or 800/668–2746, www.tourism.gov.on.ca)
- **Prince Edward Island** Tourism P.E.I., PO Box 940E, Charlottetown, Prince Edward Island C1A 7M5 (tel: 902/629–2400 or 888/734–7529, www.peiplay.com)
- **Québec** Tourisme Québec, PO Box 979, Montréal, Québec G1R 2B5 (tel: 514/873–2015 or 800/363–7777, www.tourisme-quebec.org)
- **Saskatchewan** Tourism Saskatchewan, 500–1900 Albert Street, Regina, Saskatchewan S4P 3V7 (tel: 306/787–2300 or 877/237–2273, www.sasktourism.com)
- **Yukon** Tourism Yukon, PO Box 2703, Whitehorse, Yukon Y1A 2C6 (tel: 867/667–5340 www.touryukon.com)

Further reading

History

Pierre Berton: *Klondike: The Last Great Goldrush*; *The Last Spike* (a history of the transcontinental railroad); *The Arctic Grail* (an account of the search for the Northwest Passage); *Flames Across the Frontier* (a history of US–Canada relations)

Kenneth McNaught: *The Penguin History of Canada*

Peter C. Newman: *Caesars of the Wilderness* (award-winning account of the Hudson's Bay Company)

George Woodcock: *A Social History of Canada*

Travel and culture

Hugh Brody: *Maps and Dreams* (account of the Beaver natives of northwest Canada)

Barry Lopez: *Arctic Dreams* (extraordinary and award-winning book on all aspects of the far north)

Duncan Pryde: *Nununga: Ten Years of Eskimo Life*

Dennis Reid: *A Concise History of Canadian Painting*

The Milepost, pub. Northwest Books (an encyclopaedic guide to northern roads)

Literature

Margaret Atwood: *Alias Grace*, *Surfacing*, *Cat's Eye* and *Lady Oracle* (four novels with a Canadian setting; many of Atwood's short stories provide local color)

Leonard Cohen: *Poems 1956–1968*; *Beautiful Losers* (a novel)

Grey Owl: *Pilgrims of the Wild*; *Tales of an Empty Cabin*; *The Men of the Last Frontier*

E. Annie Proulx: *The Shipping News* (Pulitzer prize-winning novel set in contemporary Newfoundland)

Robert Service: *The Best of Robert Service* (gold-rush ballads)

Accommodations & Restaurants

ACCOMMODATIONS

The hotels listed below are divided into three price categories:

- **budget** ($) under $100 double room
- **moderate** ($$) $100–150 double room
- **expensive** ($$$) over $150 double room

Toll-free numbers (prefixed by 800 or 888) are given where applicable; however, there are often restrictions on the areas from which they can be used (see page 263).

BRITISH COLUMBIA

Telephone code 250 (Vancouver, 604).

Kootenays

Ainsworth Hot Springs Resort ($$)
Ainsworth Hot Springs (Highway 31) tel: 229–4212 or 800/668–1171 www.hotnaturally.com
Pleasant lakeside chalets convenient for Kaslo, Nelson and the rest of the Kootenays.

Heritage Inn ($$)
422 Vernon Street, Nelson tel: 352–5331 www.heritageinn.org
A central, four-story heritage property dating from 1898 with pleasant period-feel rooms.

Kaslo Motel ($)
330 D Avenue, Kaslo tel: 353–2431 www.kaslomotel.com
Kaslo has many accommodations dotted around the lake, but this simple and adequate motel is the best option in the village itself.

Okanagan

Lake Okanagan Resort ($$$)
2751 Westside Road, Kelowna tel: 769–3511 or 800/663–3273 www.lakeokanagan.com
Self-contained lakeside resort with swimming, tennis, golf and riding. All rooms have rental facilities. The renovated "Lakeside Terrace" rooms are the best.

Willow Inn ($)
235 Queensway, Kelowna tel: 762–2122
Virtually the only downtown accommodations in Kelowna. Pleasant, reasonably priced.

Skeena Valley

Inn on the Harbour ($$)
720 1st Avenue, Prince Rupert tel: 624–9107 or 800/663–8155
Central, amiable motel; rooms with a sea view are a delight.

Parkside Resort ($$)
101 11th Avenue East, Prince Rupert tel: 624–9131. www.parksiderestort motel.com
A comfortable if slightly colorful-looking resort hotel, in a pleasant setting about 1km (half a mile) from downtown.

Vancouver

Buchan Hotel ($)
1906 Haro Street tel: 685–5354 or 800/668–6654 www.buchanhotel.com
A no-smoking hotel, close to Stanley Park (15 minutes' walk to central downtown). About half the 60 rooms have private bathrooms.

Greenbriar Hotel ($$)
1393 Robson Street at Broughton tel: 604–4558 or 888/355–5888 www.greenbriarhotel.com
On Robson between Stanley Park and downtown. Rooms and family suites, many with kitchen facilities.

Hotel Vancouver ($$$)
900 West Georgia Street tel: 684–3131 or 800/441–1414 www.fairmont.com
Traditional, old "château-style" building. One of the best-known top hotels.

Kingston Hotel ($)
757 Richards Street tel: 684–9024 or 888/713–3304 www.kingstonhotelvancouver.com
Popular, clean and welcoming. Some rooms have a private bathroom, but most have basin and shared bathrooms at the end of the corridor. Reservations essential.

Sandman Hotel Downtown ($)
180 West Georgia Street tel: 681–2211 or 800/726–3626 www.sandman.ca
A large and reliable chain hotel a few blocks east of the main downtown core.

Sutton Place Hotel ($$$)
845 Burrard Street tel: 682–5511
Large but still intimate luxury hotel.

Sylvia Hotel ($$)
1154 Gilford Street tel: 681–9321 www.sylviahotel.com
Extremely popular, waterfront hotel, a short walk from most sights. Call well ahead.

Wells Gray Provincial Park

Jasper Way Inn ($)
Dutch Lake, Clearwater tel: 674–3345
Only about a kilometer west of the main highway, this quiet motel overlooks Dutch Lake.

VANCOUVER ISLAND

The Vancouver Island telephone code is 250.

Pacific Rim National Park

Canadian Princess ($$)
The Boat Basin, 1943 Peninsula Road, Ucluelet tel: 726–7771 or 800/663–7090 www.canadianprincess.com
This hotel's simple rooms (shared bathrooms) have been converted from the 34 berths of a former survey ship. There are plainer rooms on shore in the adjoining resort.

Tofino Swell Lodge ($$)
341 Olsen Road tel: 725–3274
Perhaps the best of the many "cottage resorts" dotted to the south of Tofino village.

Victoria

Cherry Bank Hotel ($)
825 Burdett Avenue tel: 385–5380
Popular old-style hotel with breakfast included. A few minutes from the Inner Harbour.

Empress Hotel ($$$)
721 Government Street tel: 250/384–8111 or 800/441–1414 www.fairmont.com
The grand old dame of Victoria has been thoroughly renovated by Canadian Pacific, and it really is *the* place to stay if you can afford it.

James Bay Inn ($$)
270 Government and Toronto tel: 384–7151 www.jamesbayinn.bc.ca
Competes with the Cherry Bank Hotel as Victoria's best low-cost option. The building was the former home of painter Emily Carr.

Ocean Pointe Resort Hotel ($$$)
45 Songhees Road tel: 250/360–2999 or 800/667–4677 www.oprhotel.com
Splendid, very luxurious resort overlooking the Inner Harbour.

THE ROCKIES

The telephone code for Banff is 403, for Jasper 780. The code for Yoho and Kootenay parks is 250.

Banff Townsite

Banff Springs Hotel ($$$)
Spray Avenue tel: 762–2211 or 800/441–1414 www.fairmont.com
Built in 1888, this immensely impressive, castellated, Gothic monster is one of the most famous hotels in Canada. Most of the hotel's 770 rooms have good views, but some are small, and at busy time things can get a little hectic.

Bumper's Inn ($$)
Banff Avenue and Marmot Crescent tel: 762–3386 or 800/661–3518
This motel lies away from the town center, but with 39 rooms there is a good chance that you will find space here when other places are full.

Castle Mountain ($$–$$$)
Bow Valley Parkway/Highway 1a tel: 762–3868 www.castlemountain.com
Located just east of Kootenay park on the scenic road linking Banff and Lake Louise. Several categories of cabin-style accommodations, all with kitchenettes and open fires.

Elkhorn Lodge ($$)
124 Spray Avenue tel: 762–2299 www.elkhornbanff.ca
A small eight-room hotel in the quieter southern part of town across the Bow River.

Red Carpet Inn ($$)
425 Banff Avenue tel: 762–4184 or 800/563–4609
Clean and simple rooms.

Rimrock Resort ($$$)
Mountain Avenue tel: 762–3356 or 800/661–1587 www.rimrockresort.com
This hotel gives the Banff Springs a run for its money. It's not central—it is up by the Sulphur Mountain gondola—but it does have superb views and top-quality rooms.

Y Mountain Lodge ($)
102 Spray Avenue tel:762–3560 www.ywca-banff.ab.ca
Very clean, modern YWCA hostel with dorm rooms or good-value singles and double.

Icefields Parkway

Columbia Icefield Chalet ($$$)
Icefields Parkway at the Athabaska Glacier tel: 780/852–6550
A good place to stop between Banff and Jasper. About half the total 32 rooms have spectacular views of the Athabaska Glacier.

Num-Ti-Jah Lodge ($$–$$$)
45km (25 miles) north of Lake Louise on the Icefields Parkway tel: 403/522–2167 www.num-ti-jah.com
Historic lodge in lovely setting on the shores of Bow Lake overlooking the Bow Glacier; simple, rather rustic accommodations.

Jasper Townsite

Alpine Village ($–$$)
Highway 93a, 1.6km (1 mile) south of Jasper tel: 852–3285 Open: Apr–end Oct www.alpinevillagejasper.com
Various cabin-type chalets with beamed ceilings, fireplaces and other rustic features. Many cabins have fine mountain views.

Becker's Chalets ($$)
Highway 93, 5km (3 miles) south of Jasper tel: 852–3779 Open: May–end Oct www.beckerschalets.com
Over 100 excellent new cabins, many with kitchenettes and wood-burning stoves.

Château Jasper ($$$)
96 Giekie Street tel: 852–5644 or 800/661–9323 www.charletonresorts.com
This motel-like place has a noted restaurant.

Jasper Park Lodge ($$$)
Off Highway 16, 4km (2.5 miles) northeast of Jasper tel: 852–3301 or 800/441–1414 www.jasperparklodge.com
The town's top resort hotel is a village-like collection of rooms, cabins and sports facilities. Rooms are modern to rustic.

Whistlers Inn ($$)
105 Miette Avenue tel: 852–3361
Central motel almost opposite the train station.

Kootenay National Park

Alpen Motel ($)
Highway 93, 5022 Western Park Gate tel: 347–9823 www.alpenmotel.com
One of the closest hotels to the western entrance to the park; it is also close to Radium Hot Springs.

The Chalet Europe ($$)
5063 Madsen Road, Radium Hot Springs tel: 347–9305 www.chaleteurope.com
Better than most Radium motels, mainly because it occupies a lofty position above the town, The Chalet has plain but adequate rooms, each with small kitchenette.

The Radium Resort ($$)
8100 Golf Course Road, 9.5km (6 miles) south of the hot springs tel: 347–9311 www.radiumresort.com
Radium Hot Springs, just west of the park, has some 30 motels, though the nicest places to stay are out of town on the approach road to the hot springs and park entrance. This resort is one of the biggest and best in the area.

Lake Louise

Château Lake Louise ($$$)
Lake Louise tel: 522–3511 or 800/441–1414 www.fairmont.com
This famous hotel, overlooking Lake Louise, is almost without equal. However, despite its 513 rooms it can suffer from the sheer number of guests and visitors that flock to the lake.
Deer Lodge ($$)
Lake Louise Drive tel: 522–3747 or 800/661–1595 www.crmr.com
One of two lodges on the 5km (3-mile) road between Lake Louise and the village below.
Lake Louise Inn ($$)
Lake Louise Village tel: 522–3791 or 800/661–9237 www.lakelouiseinn.com
The most reasonable of the hotels in the village, with many rooms of differing standards and sizes, some with self-catering facilities.
Moraine Lake Lodge ($$$)
Moraine Lake tel: 522–3733 www.morainelake.com Open: May– end Oct
Award-winning cabins and the matchless scenery of Moraine Lake, make this one of the loveliest hotels in the Rockies.
Post Hotel ($$$)
Lake Louise Village tel: 522–3989 or 800/661–1586 www.posthotel.com
The best of the hotels in Lake Louise Village.

Yoho National Park

Cathedral Mountain Chalets ($$)
Off Highway 1, 4km (2.5 miles) east of Field tel: 343–6442 www.cathedral mountain.com Open: May–end Oct
One of two reasonably priced options on or just off the Trans-Canada Highway (Highway 1).
Emerald Lake Lodge ($$$)
Emerald Lake tel: 343–6321 or 800/663–6336 www.crmr.com
Not quite as grand as the Canadian Pacific Railway's other creations (the Banff Springs and Château Lake Louise), but this is still the place to stay if you are doing the Rockies in style.
Kicking Horse Lodge ($$)
100 Centre Street, Field tel: 343–6303 or 800/659–4944 www.kickinghorselodge.net
The only accommodations in Field apart from B&Bs, the park's one settlement of any size.
Lake O'Hara Lodge ($$$)
Lake O'Hara tel: 343–6418
One of the finest locations in the Rockies, and certainly the best spot in Yoho as a base for walking. Reservations must be made well in advance. Out of season (May and Oct–end Jan), tel: 403/678–4110 www.lakeohara.com
West Louise Lodge ($$)
Highway 1, 11km (7 miles) west of Lake Louise tel: 343–6311 or 800/258–7669
Just inside the park's eastern boundary, and one of two popular lodges on or just off the Trans-Canada Highway.

YUKON

The telephone code for the Yukon is 867.

Dawson City

Downtown Hotel ($$)
2nd Avenue and Queen tel: 993–5346 www.downtown.yk.net
One of the best of the town's selection of old wood-fronted hotels.
Klondike Kate's Cabins ($)
3rd Avenue and King tel: 993–6527 www.klondikekates.com
Hostels aside, this is the town's premier budget choice—simple but clean and warm.
Westmark Dawson ($$$)
5th Avenue and Harper tel: 993–5542 www.westmarkhotels.com
The town's leading hotel is one of the top-of-the-range Westmark chain: comfortable and spacious, but prone to takeover by tour groups.

Whitehorse

Edgewater Hotel ($$)
101 Main Street tel: 667–2572 or 877/484–3334 www.edgewaterhotel.yk.ca
Probably the best of Whitehorse's mid- range accommodations.
High Country Inn ($)
4051 4th Avenue tel: 667–4471 www.highcountryinn.yk.ca
A reliable and relaxed hotel at the western end of town. Also has a popular bar/restaurant.
Stratford Motel ($)
401 Jarvis Street tel: 667–4243
Another good and amiable, inexpensive choice.

THE PRAIRIES

Calgary

Hawthorn Hotel and Suites ($$)
618-5th Avenue SW tel: 263–0520 or 800/661–1592 www.hawthorncalgary.com
This downtown hotel has over 300 rooms with a choice of studio, one- or two-room apartments, all of them with kitchenettes.
The Palliser ($$$)
133 9th Avenue SW tel: 403/262–1234 or 800/441–1414 www.fairmont.com
Calgary's oldest top hotel, recently renovated.
Sandman Hotel ($$)
888-7th Avenue SW tel: 403/237–8626 or 800/726–3626 www.sandman.ca
Big, reliable, high-rise, mid-price hotel, convenient for the free C-Train section of the downtown transit system.

Churchill

Churchill Motel ($$)
152 Kelsey Boulevard tel: 204/675–8853
There is little to choose between Churchill's unprepossessing hotels: all are functional but heavily booked at most times of the year.

Seaport Hotel ($$)
299 Kelsey Boulevard tel: 204/675–8807
One of the town's newer hotels.

Drumheller

Badlands Motel ($)
On Dinosaur Trail tel: 403/823–5155
Comfortable log cabins, 1km (half-mile) out of town on the road to the Royal Tyrrell Museum.

Drumheller Inn ($$)
100 South Railway Avenue tel: 403/823–8400
On a bluff above the town, this is the best of the handful of Drumheller hotels.

Edmonton

Edmonton House Suite Hotel ($$)
10205-100th Street tel: 780/420–4000 or 800/661–6562 www.edmontonhouse.com
An odd tower-like building, with good rooms and well-equipped kitchens. There is an in-house general store and free shuttle bus service to the West Edmonton Mall.

Inn on Seventh ($$)
10001-107th Street tel: 780/429–2861 or 800/661–7327 www.innon7th.com
A central, more than adequate high-rise hotel: the best mid-price option in Edmonton.

Hotel Macdonald ($$$)
10065 100th Street tel: 780/424–5181 or 800/441–1414 www.fairmont.com
This central, renovated, Canadian Pacific hotel offers views of the North Saskatchewan River.

Winnipeg

Gordon Downtowner ($)
330 Kennedy Street tel: 204/943–5581 www.downtowner.mb.ca
The nicest inexpensive option in the city, close to the Portage Place Mall.

Delta ($$)
350 St Mary Avenue tel: 204/942–0551 or 800/227–7663 www.deltahotels.com
Alongside the Convention Centre, this is the city's largest hotel.

Hotel Fort Garry ($$$)
222 Broadway tel: 204/942–8251 or 800/665–8088 www.fortgarryhotel.com
Winnipeg's old railway hotel (built in 1913) has been restored to its former glory and is once again one of the city's favorite places to stay.

ONTARIO

Niagara-on-the-Lake

Charles Inn ($)
209 Queen Street, Niagara-on-the-Lake tel: 905/468–4588 www.charlesinn.ca
One of the less expensive of the many B&Bs and several chic, pleasantly traditional hotels.

Prince of Wales ($$$)
6 Picton Street, Niagara-on-the-Lake tel: 905/468–3246 or 888/669–5566 www.vintageinns.com
A well-regarded traditional hotel close to the center of town.

Queen's Landing ($$)
Melville and Byron, Niagara-on-the-Lake tel: 905/468–2195 www.vintageinns.com
Views from this tasteful hotel are excellent, and some rooms are furnished with antiques and have fireplaces; others have Jacuzzis.

Ottawa

Capital Hill Hotel and Suites ($$)
88 Albert Street tel: 613/235–1413 or 800/463–7705 www.capitalhill.com
Nicely appointed comfortable rooms in a great location three blocks from Parliament.

Château Laurier ($$$)
1 Rideau Street tel: 613/241–1414 or 800/441–1414 www.fairmont.com
This hotel, built in 1916, is an Ottawa institution. Its mock castle exterior conceals more than 400 spacious rooms, and though less obviously chic than more modern luxury hotels, it remains the place to stay in the city.

Doral Inn ($)
486 Albert Street tel: 613/230–8055 www.doralinn.com
This restored inn, just five minutes from the Parliament Buildings, dates from 1879 and retains some of its old-fashioned atmosphere.

Lord Elgin Hotel ($$)
100 Elgin Street tel: 613/235–3333 or 800/267–4298 www.lordelginhotel.ca
This venerable city landmark is good value given the high quality of the hotel.

Toronto

Delta Chelsea Inn ($$)
33 Gerrard Street West tel: 416/595–1975 www.deltachelsea.com
Close to the Eaton Centre, but some way from a subway station, this is Toronto's biggest hotel; its 1,600 rooms are good and the facilities are excellent. It is popular with tour groups and conventions, so make reservations.

Four Seasons Hotel ($$$)
21 Avenue Road tel: 416/964–0411 or 800/268–6282 www.fourseasons.com
Attached to the Renaissance Court complex on the edge of Yorkville, and close to the ROM, the University of Toronto, restaurants and stores.

Metropolitan Hotel Toronto ($$$)
108 Chestnut Street near Nathan Phillips Square tel: 416/977–5000 or 800/668–6600 www.metropolitan.com
This is an extremely central, well run, fairly new hotel with 522 rooms over 16 floors.

Quality Hotels ($)
280 Bloor Street West/111 Lombard Street near Queen and Jarvis tel: 416/968–0010 or 800/228–5151 www.choicehotels.ca
This hotel is part of a reliable budget chain that has two reasonably central downtown locations.

Royal York Hotel ($$$)
100 Front Street West
tel: 416/368–2511 or 800/441–1414
www.fairmont.com
The largest hotel in the British Empire when it opened in 1927—it has 1,408 (recently refurbished) rooms—this Toronto landmark is one of the most famous of Canada's traditional "railway" hotels.
Westin Harbour Castle Hotel ($$$)
1 Harbour Square tel: 416/869–1600 or 800/927–8461 www.westin.com
This large hotel (it has 980 rooms) has a superb site on the waterfront. Its rooms offer great views of either the city or Lake Ontario.
Windsor Arms Hotel ($$$)
18 St. Thomas Street
tel: 416/971–9666 or 877/999–2767
www.windsorarmshotel.com
Just south of Bloor Street, and close to Yorkville, the University and the ROM, this is the place for the person who wants to be pampered but who hates big chain hotels. The once fashionable Courtyard Cafe has re-opened in its lovely atrium.

QUÉBEC

Montréal

Auberge du Vieux-Port ($$)
97 rue de la Commune est
tel: 514/876–0081 or 888/660–7678
www.aubergeduvieuxport.com
This charming, small hotel in a renovated 19th-century warehouse in Old Montréal is convenient for local restaurants and nightlife.
Le Château Champlain ($$)
1 Place du Canada tel: 514/878–9000 or 800/200–5909 www.marriotthotels.com
Vast arched windows on this skyscraper hotel in the heart of downtown make it a city landmark (known as the "cheese grater"). It has around 600 airy, elegant rooms.
Château Versailles ($$)
1659 rue Sherbrooke Ouest
tel: 514/933–3611 or 888/933–8111
www.versailleshotels.com
Charm and a central location make this one of the city's most popular mid-range hotels, so you'll need to reserve rooms several weeks in advance.
Hotel Inter-Continental Montréal ($$$)
360 rue St-Antoine Ouest tel: 514/987–9900 or 800/361–3600
www.intercontinental.com
This must be first choice in the luxury range if you want to be in Vieux-Montréal.
Hôtel Le St-André ($$)
1285 rue St-André tel: 514/849–7070
This hotel is a good 61-room budget option, and it's close to the heart of some of the city's trendiest districts.
Hôtel Omni ($$$)
1050 rue Sherbrooke Ouest
tel: 514/284–1110 or 800/843–6664
www.omnihotels.com
Probably the best of Montréal's many luxury hotels. Service is outstanding, though at the prices charged most business is corporate.
Ritz-Carlton Montréal ($$$)
1228 rue Sherbrooke Ouest
tel: 514/842–4212 or 800/363–0366
www.ritzcarlton.com
Comfort, luxury and high-quality service in a venerable European-type upscale hotel.

Québec

Auberge du Quartier ($$)
170 Grand Allée Ouest tel: 418/525–9726 www.aubergeduquartier.com
A friendly, family-run 13-room hotel about 20 minutes' walk west of the old city. Continental breakfast.
Auberge Saint-Antoine ($$$)
10 rue Saint-Antoine tel: 418/692–2211 or 888/692–2211 www.saint-antoine.com
Close to Place Royale in the Basse-Ville, this is a charming and elegantly appointed small hotel (30 rooms). Reserve well in advance.
Auberge Saint-Louis ($)
48 rue St-Louis tel 418/692–2424
This is perhaps the best-located budget choice. Rooms are small, and most have a shared bathroom, but the service is good.
Château Bonne Entente ($$$)
3400 chemin Ste-Foy, Sainte-Foy
tel: 418/653–5221 or 800/463–4390
A smart resort hotel set in extensive grounds about 20 minutes' drive from the old city.
Château Frontenac ($$$)
1 rue des Carrières tel: 418/692–3861 or 800/441–1414 www.fairmont.com
Québec's most famous hotel and single most famous building. Reservation essential.
L'Hôtel du Capitole ($$$)
972 rue St-Jean tel: 418/694–4040
www.lecapitole.com
A former theater and cinema that was converted in 1992 into a slightly glitzy but still high-quality 40-room hotel.
Hôtel Loews Le Concorde ($$$)
1225 Place Montcalm tel: 418/647–2222 or 800/463–5256 in Canada, 800/23LOEWS from the US
www.loewshotels.com
This large modern hotel, with revolving restaurant at the top, and fine views over the Old City and the famous Chateau, gives the Chateau Frontenac a run for its money. Better to stay in it that have a view of it.
Manoir d'Auteuil ($$$)
49 rue d'Auteuil tel: 418/694–1173
If the size of the large top-price hotels is off-putting, this lavishly appointed 16-room establishment is the ideal alternative.
Manoir des Remparts ($)
3.5 des Remparts tel: 418/692–2056
www.manoirdesramparts.com
This hotel on the northern fringe of Vieux-Québec has good, clean rooms, some with fine river views; private or shared bathrooms.

THE MARITIME PROVINCES

New Brunswick

Algonquin Resort ($$$)
184 Aldophus Street, St. Andrews
tel: 506/529–8823 or 800/441–1414
www.fairmont.com
This is an outstanding mock Tudor resort belonging to the Canadian Pacific group.

Carriage House Inn ($$)
230 University Avenue, Fredericton
tel: 506/452–9924 or 800/267–6068
This Queen Anne-style heritage house has just 10 rooms, so reservations are essential. The breakfasts are good.

Hotel Beauséjour ($$$)
750 Main Street, Moncton
tel: 506/854–4344 or 800/268–1133
www.deltahotels.com
This is Moncton's top hotel.

Parkerhouse Inn ($$)
71 Sydney Street, Saint John
tel: 506/652–5054
This is a nine-room hotel in a three-story Victorian town house.

Seaside Beach Resort ($$)
339 Water Street, St. Andrews
tel: 506/529–3846
www.seaside.nb.ca
This resort has homely wooden housekeeping units on the waterfront, each with a large wooden deck offering great views of Passamaquoddy Bay sunsets.

Sheraton Inn ($$$)
225 Woodstock Road, Fredericton
tel: 506/457–7000 or 800/325–3535
www.sheraton.com
This new hotel is the city's first choice of the top-price options.

Nova Scotia

Boscawen Inn ($$)
150 Cumberland Street, Lunenburg
tel: 902/634–3325
This old 1888 mansion has 17 elegant rooms, some of which have views of the harbor. Closed Nov–end Apr.

Halliburton House Inn ($$)
5184 Morris Street, Halifax tel: 902/420–0658 www.halliburton.ns.ca
This is a well-restored historic house in downtown Halifax.

Hotel Halifax ($$$)
1990 Barrington Street, Halifax
tel: 902/425–6700or 800/268–1133
www.deltahotels.com
This historic hotel is regarded as one of the town's best.

Kaulbach House Historic Inn ($$)
75 Pelham Street, Lunenburg tel: 902/634–8818
www.kaulbachhouse.com
One of the town's many historic houses that double as hotels and B&Bs in this lovely town, this one, built around 1880, overlooks the harbor. It has eight no-smoking rooms.

Keltic Lodge ($$$)
Middle Head Peninsula, Ingonish Beach
tel: 902/285–2880 or 800/564–0444
www.signaturerestorts.com
Superbly located on a narrow peninsula extending into the ocean from the Cabot Trail on Cape Breton island, this hotel has magnificent views, good food and famous golf course.

Louisbourg Fortress Inn ($$)
7464 Main Street, Louisbourg
tel: 902/733–2844
A good base from which to visit the nearby Louisbourg fortress.

Queen Anne Inn ($)
494 Upper Saint George Street, Annapolis Royal tel: 902/532–7850 or 877/536–0403 www.queenanneinn.ns.ca
This is a restored 1865 mansion with 10 pleasant rooms.

Waverley Inn ($$)
1266 Barrington Street, Halifax
tel: 902/423–9346 www.waverleyinn.com
Oscar Wilde and P.T. Barnum were guests at this likable 32-room inn.

Prince Edward Island

The Charlottetown ($$$)
75 Kent Street and Pownal, Charlottetown
tel: 902/894–7371 www.rodd-hotels.ca
This five-story, redbrick Georgian hotel full of charm and old-world grandeur is located just two blocks from the center of town.

Duchess of Kent Inn ($$)
218 Kent Street, Charlottetown
tel: 902/566–5826
www.duchessofkentinn.ca
This Victorian turreted house in central Charlottetown has four rooms and three suites.

Gulf View Cottages ($$)
near North Rustico, PEI National Park
tel: 902/963–2052
www.gulfviewcottages.com
One of only a handful of accommodations in the PEI National Park, Gulf View has twelve two-bedroom cottages with sea view.

Inn at Bay Fortune ($$$)
Highway 310, Bay Fortune, Souris
tel: 902/687–3745
www.innatbayfortune.com Open: mid-May–mid-Oct
A gem of a hotel, and winner of many awards, this is a great place for a treat and retreat.

Island's End Motel ($)
Highway 12, 6.5km (4 miles) north of Tignish tel: 902/882–3554
www.islandsendmotel.com
A possible stop-off on the island's Lady Slipper Drive.

West Point Lighthouse ($$)
West Point, Lady Slipper Drive
tel: 902/859–3605
www.westpointlighthouse.com
Open: Jun–end Sep
A still-functioning (automatic) lighthouse, with nine rooms, this is a quirky and unusual place to stay.

NEWFOUNDLAND

Best Western Travellers Inn ($$)
199 Kenmount Road near Avalon Mall, St. John's tel: 709/722–5540 or 800/261–5540
A 91-room motel; 5km (3 miles) from downtown.
Compton House B&B ($$–$$$)
26 Waterford Bridge Road, St. John's tel: 709/739–5789
This restored, historic property, 2km (1 mile) west of downtown, has just six rooms.
Hotel Newfoundland ($$$)
Cavendish Square, St. John's tel: 709/726–4980 or 800/441–1414 www.fairmont.com
Not the grandest in the city, but this 300-room hotel is certainly the most historic.
Ocean View Motel ($)
Rocky Harbour tel: 709/458–2730 www.oceanviewmotel.com
This 44-room base is ideal for exploring Gros Morne National Park. It also offers boat trips (see pages 244–245).

Prescott Inn ($)
19 Military Road, St. John's tel: 709/753–7733 or 888/263–3786 www.prescottinn.nf.ca
This eight-roomed well-placed B&B is the city's most popular and welcoming.
Quality Hotel Harbourview ($$$)
2 Hill O'Chips, St. John's tel: 709/754–7788 or 800/228–5151 www.choicehotels.ca
A large 161-room motel in a reliable chain with perfect downtown location and sea views.
Terra Nova Golf Resort ($$)
Port Blandford, Clode Sound tel: 709/543–2525
A rustic base for the Terra Nova National Park. Closed Nov–end Apr.
Valhalla Lodge B&B ($)
P.O. Box 265, L'Anse aux Meadows tel: 709/623–2018; 896–5476 in winter Open mid-May–end Oct
One of the few accommodations convenient for the Viking village at L'Anse aux Meadows.
Village Inn ($–$$)
Taverner's Path, Trinity tel: 709/464–3269 www.oceancontact.com
Just 12 rooms close to the "Discovery Trail," making reservations essential.

RESTAURANTS

The restaurants listed below are divided into three price categories.

- **budget** ($ = up to $25)
- **moderate** ($$ = $25–$40)
- **expensive** ($$$ = over $40)

Telephone numbers are given where reservations are recommended.

BRITISH COLUMBIA

Kootenays

Main Street Diner ($)
616 Baker Street, Nelson tel: 250/354–4848
This place, in a central location, has far better food than its name suggests.
Treehouse Restaurant ($)
419 Front Street, Kaslo tel: 250/353–2955
This welcoming, homey restaurant has good food, and the air of a village social center.

Okanagan

De Montreuil ($$$)
368 Bernard Avenue, Kelowna tel: 250/860–5508
Widely considered the best in the Okanagan.
Earl's ($–$$)
211 Bernard Avenue, Kelowna tel: 250/763–3121
A good, downtown cove for ribs, seafood, steaks and other staples in a nice setting. Another branch of this popular and reliable mid-range chain is at the corner of highways 6 and 97, Vernon (tel: 250/542–3370).
The Italian Kitchen ($)
2916 30th Avenue, Vernon tel: 250/558–7899
This is a reliable choice for a good Italian meal or snack in central Vernon.
O'Keefe Ranch Restaurant ($–$$)
North of Vernon on Highway 97 tel: 250/542–2178
You'll find good home cooking with a Western flavor, and outdoor barbecue in season, on the historic O'Keefe Ranch (see page 56).

Skeena Valley

Green Apple ($)
301 McBride, Prince Rupert tel: 250/627–1666
This little shack is a town institution, renowned for its fish and chips.
Smile's Seafood Café ($)
113 Cow Bay Road, Prince Rupert tel: 250/624–3072
This café has been serving up mouthwatering seafood since 1934; and it's still popular.

Vancouver

Bishop's ($$$)
2183 West 4th Avenue, near Yew Street tel: 604/738–2025
One of Vancouver's best restaurants; superb contemporary food; reservations essential.
Blue Water Café ($$)
1095 Hamilton Street tel: 604/688–8078
The Yaletown district buzzes with restaurants, cafés and bars. This large restaurant is one the best, serving fish and seafood in relaxed setting.
La Bodega ($)
1277 Howe near Davie tel: 604/684–8814

This lively and popular bar offers tapas and other Spanish food.

Bridges ($$)
1696 Duranleau, Granville Island
tel: 604/687–4400
Popular, busy and good for a drink or a meal, Bridges has a restaurant (upstairs), plus a bar and informal bistro (the best option).

Brothers Restaurant ($–$$)
1 Water Street, in Gastown
tel: 604/683–9124
Franciscan "monks" serve excellent food in an old monastery setting in the heart of Gastown.

"C" ($$$)
1600 Howe Street tel: 604/681–1164
This very elegant and creative Chinese restaurant has a fresh seafood bar with seafood tartare and sashimi.

Cloud 9 ($$$)
1400 Robson Street, tel: 604/218–6146
If there is one place where you should eat in a revolving restaurant it is Vancouver with its ever-changing views of mountains and ocean. This restaurant at the top of the Landmark Hotel offers excellent West Coast and Asian food with unobstructed views of the city.

Le Crocodile ($$$)
909 Burrard Street, entrance on Smithe Street tel: 604/669–4298
Chic, French and challenging *Bishop's* for the title of the city's best restaurant.

Earl's On Top ($–$$)
1185 Robson Street, corner of Bute Street
tel: 604/669–0020
First choice in downtown for good, moderately priced food. Casual, with outside terrace.

Gallery Café ($)
Vancouver Art Gallery, 750 Hornby
tel: 604/688–2233
Relaxed, popular and stylish café that has outdoor seating available all year). Excellent for lunch—and you do not need a gallery ticket to eat here.

Le Gavroche ($$$)
1616 Alberni Street tel: 604/685–3924
Le Crocodile may be a touch better, but this other formal and romantic French restaurant is not far behind.

Hon's Wun Tun House ($)
108-268 Keefer Street at Gore Street
tel: 604/688–0871; 1339 Robson Street
tel: 604/685–0871
Good food and low prices.

Liliget Feast House ($$)
1724 Davie Street, near Denman
tel: 604/681–7044
Despite its unlikely location in a basement, this First Nations restaurant is a marvelous experience. Try their wood-grilled salmon, alder-smoked oysters, toasted seaweed and other Northwest coast cuisine.

Pink Pearl ($)
1132 East Hastings, at Clark Drive
tel: 604/253–4316
The city's biggest Cantonese restaurant (650 covers) and one of the most authentic. Arrive early for weekend *dim sum* to avoid the lines. Not in the best part of town.

Stepho's ($$)
1124 Davie Street tel: 604/683–2555
The best Greek restaurant close to downtown, but it has long line-ups.

The Teahouse Restaurant ($$)
Ferguson Point, Stanley Park
tel: 604/669–3281
This pretty restaurant is the best place for lunch during a walk or ride round Stanley Park.

Tojo's ($$$)
777 West Broadway at Willow
tel: 604/872–8050
The city's best Japanese food.

Villa del Lupo ($$–$$$)
869 Hamilton Street tel: 604/688–7436
Italian restaurant in a renovated old house between the library and Yaletown. A treat.

VANCOUVER ISLAND

Pacific Rim National Park

Canadian Princess Restaurant ($$)
Boat Basin, Ucluelet tel: 250/726–7771
Seafood is the specialty of this restaurant aboard a 72m (236ft) long ship moored in Ucluelet's Boat Basin.

The Loft ($$)
346 Campbell Street, Tofino
tel: 250/725–4241
Reliable for breakfast, lunch and dinner.

Wickaninnish Restaurant ($$)
Long Beach, 16km (10 miles) north of Ucluelet tel: 250/726–7706
Housed in part of the building used as the national park information center, this place on the beach-front has a lovely rustic interior.

Victoria

Bravo on Wharf ($$)
1218 Wharf Street tel: 250/386–2900
A very casual but elegant place with an interesting contemporary menu.

Camilles ($$$)
45 Bastion Square tel: 250/381–3433
Closed: last week Dec, first week Jan.
Intimate room showcasing creative West Coast cooking in generous portions. Dijon-mint lamb, served with blackberry port glaze and gorgonzola whipped potatoes, is a perennial favorite. Dinner only.

Demitasse Coffee Bar ($)
1320 Blanshard Street near Pandora
tel: 250/386–4442
A great place for coffee, snacks and inexpensive, filling lunches.

Herald Street Café ($$)
546 Herald Street tel: 250/381–1441
Well worth the walk north of the Inner Harbour, this long-established restaurant has a Pacific Northwest bias to its cooking.

Julia's Place ($–$$)
609 Courtenay Street tel: 250/388–7111
A cozy little place, with both Italian and Greek dishes. Open for breakfast, lunch and dinner.

Pagliacci's ($)
1011 Broad Street between Fort and Broughton tel: 250/386–1662
Lively and good-natured, this well-known Italian downtown restaurant has live music most nights. Arrive very early to avoid the lines.
The Tapa Bar ($–$$)
620 Trounce Alley tel: 250/383–0013
This restaurant on charming Trounce Alley is a tapas bar serving Latin fusion cuisine.

THE ROCKIES

Banff

Balkan Village ($$)
120 Banff Avenue tel: 403/762–3454
The place to come for Greek food in Banff.
Barbary Coast ($–$$)
119 Banff Avenue tel: 403/762–4616
Hidden upstairs in the mall, this laid-back restaurant, decorated with sporting memorabilia, offers salads, burgers, pizza and steaks. There is also a lively, separate, bar.
Le Beaujolais ($$$)
212 Buffalo Street at Banff Avenue tel: 403/762–2712
By far Banff's most elegant eating place; the food is French and the wine cellar is extensive.
Evelyn's ($)
201 Banff Avenue tel: 403/762–0352
Among the best of Banff Avenue's many cafés serving breakfast, coffee and snacks.
Melissa's ($$)
218 Lynx Street tel: 403/762–5511
Probably the first choice for a moderately priced lunch or dinner, Melissa's serves excellent steaks, salads and burgers, in its log cabin dining room.

Jasper

Beauvert Dining Room ($$$)
Jasper Park Lodge tel: 780/852–6052
You'll find some of the best food in the Canadian Rockies at this luxurious resort.
Becker's ($$$)
Just south of Jasper townsite on Highway 93 tel: 780/852–3535
Fine dining with superb views of the Athabasca River and Mount Kerkeslin. Closed Oct–end Apr.
Earl's ($$)
600 Patricia Street, Jasper tel: 780/852–2393
This casual dining place has a great view.
Jasper Pizza Place ($)
402 Connaught Drive, Jasper tel: 780/852–3225
Popular with locals and visitors, and serving gourmet pizza from a wood-fired stove.

Lake Louise

Bill Peyto's Café ($)
Lake Louise Village tel: 403/522–2200
Part of Lake Louise's smart youth hostel, this easygoing café is open to all, not just those staying in the hostel. It is the best choice in the area for a good, fairly priced meal.
Laggan's Mountain Bakery ($)
Samson Mall, Lake Louise Village tel: 403/522–2017
A popular, constantly busy café that is great for snacks, desserts and coffee.
Moraine Lake Lodge ($$)
Moraine Lake tel: 403/522–3733
A small café and airy restaurant in a tasteful lodge hotel. The restaurant makes a lovely spot to enjoy the lake and mountain views.
Post Hotel ($$–$$$)
200 Pipestone Street, Lake Louise Village tel: 403/522–3989
This rather formal hotel restaurant is one of the best in the Canadian Rockies.

YUKON

Dawson City

Jack London Grill ($$)
In the Downtown Hotel, 2nd Avenue tel: 867/993–5346
Dawson is not blessed with great restaurants, but this period-style dining room, with outdoor terrace in summer, is enjoyable.
Klondike Kate's ($)
3rd Avenue and King tel: 867/993-6527
Good food is served throughout the day, but the place is probably better for breakfast and lunch than for dinner.

Whitehorse

The Cellar ($$)
10 Main Street tel: 867/667–2572
One of the two good dining rooms in the Edgewater Hotel. The Gallery is the less formal alternative.
Klondike Rib and Salmon Barbecue ($$)
2116-2nd Avenue, tel: 867/667–7554
Let's face it, you are not in Yukon for gourmet dining. This unique place in the heart of downtown offering fish and meat smoked locally is an experience.

THE PRAIRIES

Calgary

Chianti Café ($$)
1438 17th Avenue SW tel: 403/229–1600
Dark, noisy and fun, this unpretentious Italian restaurant is a favorite. Make reservations.
River Cafe ($$)
Prince's Island Park tel: 403/261–7670
Specializing in Canadian market fare, this restaurant combines the serenity of nature with an urban backdrop. Good lunches, too.

Churchill

Trader's Table ($$)
Arctic Trading Post, 141 Kelsey Boulevard tel: 204/675–2141
This is the best (and most expensive) of a generally poor selection of eating places in Churchill. Try northern delicacies such as caribou and Arctic char.

Edmonton

Bistro Praha ($$$)
10168 100A Street at Jasper Avenue tel: 780/424–4218
Elegant, and with an Eastern European flavor.

Earl's Tin Palace ($–$$)
11830 Jasper Avenue tel: 780/488–6582
Part of a chain providing good food in pleasant surroundings. This is one of the most central of the Edmonton outlets.

Café Select ($$$)
10018 106th Street tel: 780/423–0419
This intimate, first-rate bistro is perfect for a relaxed meal close to the heart of downtown. Call ahead for reservations.

Packrat Louie ($$)
10335 83rd Avenue tel: 780/433–0123
In Old Strathcona, an interesting section of the city, this is an informal restaurant specializing in fresh market cuisine and fine wines.

Winnipeg

Le Beaujolais ($$$)
131 Provencher Road tel: 204/237–6276
Urbane and sophisticated French restaurant; the city's first choice for a formal dinner.

Hy's Steak Loft ($$)
216 Kennedy Street tel: 204/942–1000
For years, a downtown byword for steaks.

Muddy Waters Smokehouse ($$)
15 Forks Market Road, The Forks tel: 204/947–6653
In the popular Forks area (see page 155), this is a "deep south" restaurant. Try their barbecued ribs from the smoker.

Picasso's ($$)
615 Sargent Street tel: 204/775–2469
A vibrant Portuguese neighborhood café downstairs; a more sedate restaurant upstairs.

ONTARIO

Niagara Falls/Niagara-on-the-Lake

Old Angel Inn ($)
224 Regent Street, off Queen Street tel: 905/468–2651
Hotel, pub and fine restaurant that dates from the 1820s.

Skylon Tower ($$)
Niagara Falls tel: 905/356–2651
The Revolving Dining Room (one rotation an hour) is the place to be if you must eat dinner near Niagara Falls. The food is good, and the colorful floodlit views of the falls are superb.

Ottawa

Le Café ($–$$$)
National Arts Centre, Elgin Street at Confederation Square tel: 613/594–5127
Overlooking the Rideau Canal, and offering Canadian specialties, this restaurant has a less expensive outdoor café open in summer.

Courtyard ($$)
21 George Street tel: 613/241–1516
Built in 1827, Courtyard in the Byward Market area offers classic French cooking.

Les Muses ($$$)
100 rue Laurier, in the Canadian Museum of Civilization, Hull tel: 819/776–7009
This elegant restaurant overlooking the Ottawa River and the Parliament Buildings, with outdoor seating in the summer months, serves good French food. The cafeteria below it is less expensive, and has the same views.

Toronto

Agora ($$)
117 Dundas Street West, in Art Gallery of Ontario tel: 416/979–6612
After visiting one of the AGO's exhibitions, there is no better place for an elegant, original lunch than this—the gallery's restaurant—in an attractive atrium full of sculpture, with views of the surrounding park.

Arcadian Court ($)
8th Floor, The Bay, 176 Yonge Street at Queen tel: 416/861–6611
You come to this in-store café for the extraordinary dining room, lit by chandeliers and decorated in a pastiche of Classical Rome and Greece. Lunch only.

Auberge du Pommier ($$$)
4150 Yonge Street tel: 416/222–2220
Resembling a romantic French country house, this popular but pricey restaurant offers food to match its location.

Bistro 990 ($$)
990 Bay Street tel: 416/921–9990
Better-than-average French food; bistro setting.

Centro ($$$)
2472 Yonge Street tel: 416/483–2211
You need to dress up a little to eat here, and your wallet will take a knock, but this restaurant serves the best Italian food in the city. It's intimate inside, and the food and the service are both excellent.

The Coffee Mill ($)
99 Yorkville Avenue, near Cumberland Street tel: 416/920–2108
This café with attractive terrace has good sandwiches among other plates for lunch or a light meal.

Future Bakery & Café ($)
St. Lawrence Market, 95 Front Street East; 739 Queen Street; 483 Bloor Street West.
Ideal for everything from coffee and cheesecake to snacks and light meals, this chain of cafés has blossomed from the single bakery in St. Lawrence Market.

Jacques Bistro du Parc ($$)
126A Cumberland Street tel: 416/961–1893
Formerly Jacques' Omelettes, this Yorkville institution now offers other delicacies of a more Californian nature in addition to the famous fluffy omelettes. Splendid for lunch.

Scaramouche ($$$)
1 Benvenuto Place tel: 416/961–8011
Considered the city's top restaurant by many critics, Scaramouche offers fabulous seafood and wonderful desserts. It's very expensive, but great for that "special" night out. Don't arrive without a reservation.

Bangkok Paradise ($)
506 Queen Street West
tel: 416/504–3210
Popular Thai restaurant in the west of the city.
Shopsy's ($)
33 Yonge Street at Front
tel: 416/365–3333
This is one of the city's oldest delicatessens and restaurants. It serves generous portions at reasonable prices.

QUÉBEC

Montréal

Beaver Club ($$$)
Queen Elizabeth Hotel, 900 boulevard René Lévesque ouest tel: 514/861–3511
Montréal's most famous restaurant, embellished with fur-trapping memorabilia recalling the 1785 origins of what was once a private gentleman's club. Fine French food.
La Binerie Mont-Royal ($)
367 Mont-Royal Est tel: 514/285–9078
Tiny, but very busy and much-loved café, serving beans and more beans (and only a handful of non-bean alternatives).
Le Bonaparte ($$)
443 rue St-François Xavier
tel: 514/844–4368
Traditional French food.
Le Caveau ($$)
2063 Victoria tel: 514/844–1624
A charming restaurant in an old house almost completely submerged by the highrise of the financial district. Worth the effort to find it.
Chez La Mère Michel ($$$)
1209 rue Guy tel: 514/934–0473
A well-known restaurant in downtown that offers good French food, with game and other seasonal dishes.
Eggspectation ($)
201 rue St-Jacques tel: 514/282–0119
A big, bright, appealingly modern place with a long and interesting menu. Good for lunch. Other outlets, too.
Fairmount Bagel Bakery ($)
74 rue Fairmount Ouest
tel: 514/272–0667 Open: daily 24 hours.
The city's best bagels. Take-out.
La Fornarina ($$)
6825 boulevard Saint-Laurent
tel: 514/271–1741
A good choice in Monteréal's Little Italy district for pizzas, pastas, seafood and other fine Italian staples.
Moishe's ($$$)
3961 boulevard Saint-Laurent at rue Duluth
tel: 514/845–3509
A city institution that has been preparing its superb steaks in the same way since 1938.
Le Paris ($–$$)
1812 rue Sainte-Catherine West
tel: 514/937–4898
Simple first-rate French cuisine in the heart of downtown. A bargain.

Schwartz's ($–$$)
3895 Boulevard Saint-Laurent
tel: 514/842-4813
Famous for its smoked meat, Schwartz's is one of the city's few surviving smoked meat emporiums (Montréal's smoked meat is marinated smoked beef). Fabulous sandwiches—don't count the calories.
Toqué! ($$$)
3842 rue Saint-Denis tel: 514/499–2084
Simply the best restaurant in town, which is saying a lot in a city well known for its cuisine. The menu changes daily to take advantage of the best the market has to offer. Reserve in advance, especially if you want to eat here on a Friday or Saturday.

Québec

À la Maison de Serge Bruyère ($$$)
1200 rue St-Jean tel: 418/694–0618
An excellent restaurant, but watch the wines: they start at around $25 a bottle and go up to $800. Reservations are essential.
L'Astral ($$)
1225 Place Montcalm tel: 418/647–2222
The setting is bland, and modern, the food adequate, but the city view—from this revolving platform on the 29th floor of the Hôtel Loews Le Concorde—is superb.
Café de la Paix ($$)
44 rue des Jardins tel: 418/692–1430
A French restaurant of the old school (established in 1952), with low lights, close-packed tables, traditional food and polished service.
Le Cochon Dingue ($)
46 boulevard Champlain
tel: 418/692–2013
The "Crazy Pig" in the Lower Town is a lively place to eat, with outdoor and indoor tables, old stone walls and fairly priced café-bistro food. Also at 46 boulevard René Lévesque, near the Parliament Buildings.
Gambrinus ($$)
15 rue du Fort tel: 418/692–5144
Comfortable setting, sedate service; pleasant plant and wood-paneled décor, and a more-than-reliable menu of Continental standards.
Le Saint-Amour ($$$)
48 rue Ste-Ursule tel: 418/694–0667
Bright, spacious and relaxed; the food is delicious but never stuffy or overformal.

THE MARITIME PROVINCES

New Brunswick

Brewbaker's ($)
546 King Street, Fredericton tel: 506/459–0067
The first choice for pasta and pizzas.
Le Château à Pape ($$)
2 Steadman Street, Moncton tel: 506/855–7273
Good Acadian cuisine. For something cheaper try Jean's 369 St. George Street.

Gables ($$)
143 Water Street, St. Andrews
tel: 506/529–3440
This is one of the best-located restaurants in St. Andrews. It has a waterfront patio, and there is licensed diving.
Grannans ($$)
Market Square, Saint John
tel: 506/634–1555
Three buzzing bars, and a harborside setting with outside dining in summer, make this excellent seafood restaurant St. John's first choice for eating out.
Harbour Front Restaurant ($)
225 Water Street, St. Andrews
tel: 506/529–4887
This is the place for great steaks and seafood in a romantic setting overlooking the ocean.
Lunar Rogue ($)
625 King Street, Fredericton
tel: 506/450–2065
The best pub in town, offering good light meals and a patio open in good weather.
M & T Deli ($)
602 Queen Street, Fredericton
tel: 506/458–9068
Here you'll find a first-rate choice of cold cuts, breads, cheeses and desserts.
Prospect Street Diner and Lounge ($$)
Auberge Wandlyn Inn, 958 Prospect Street, Fredericton tel: 506/462–4447
A local favorite.
Reggie's ($)
26 Germain Street, Saint John
A wonderful, very popular, old-fashioned diner.

Nova Scotia

Acadian Restaurant ($)
744 Main Street, Chéticamp
tel: 902/224–2170
In the Acadian Museum (see page 231), this cafe offers simple but delicious Acadian foods—fish chowders, meat pies, home-made desserts and so on.
Bell Buoy ($$)
536 Chebucto Street, Baddeck
tel: 902/295–2581
One of the best of the restaurants on Cape Breton Island.
Five Fishermen ($$)
1740 Argyle Street, Halifax
tel: 902/422–4421
This is one of Halifax's oldest restaurants, and it's the best in town. The great seafood menu features local specialties such as Digby scallops and Malpeque oysters.
The Old Fish Factory Restaurant ($$)
68 Bluenose Drive, Lunenburg
tel: 902/3333
A good variety of seafood, and terrific views of the harbor, are to be found at the Fisheries Museum of the Atlantic (see page 227).
Ryan Duffy's ($$)
Dresden Row, 5640 Spring Garden Road, Halifax tel: 902/421–1116
This place is known for its excellent steaks.
Satisfaction Feast ($)
1581 Grafton Street, Halifax
tel: 902/422–3540
Well-regarded vegetarian restaurant.

Prince Edward Island

Claddagh Room Restaurant ($$–$$$)
131 Sydney Street, Charlottetown
tel: 902/892–9661
Irish-owned restaurant offering a warm welcome and live folk music in the bar; the seafood is some of the best in town.
Lobster Suppers ($$)
Informal fixed-price lobster suppers are a feature of the PEI summer.Try: Fishermen's Wharf Lobster Suppers in North Rustico, Route 6 (tel: 902/963–2669); New Glasgow Lobster Suppers, Highway 258 off Highway 13 (tel: 902/964–2870); and St. Ann's Church Lobster Suppers at Hope River, Highway 224 (tel: 902/621–0635). But there are others—check locally for latest details. Seasonal.
Lucy Maud Montgomery Dining Room ($$)
4 Sydney Street, Charlottetown
tel: 902/894–6868
This restaurant is operated by the Culinary Institute of Canada, and meals are prepared and served by students. It's good value.
Off Broadway ($$)
125 Sydney Street, Charlottetown
tel: 902/566–4620
Charlottetown's best restaurant offers classic local dishes and more innovative modern food. The emphasis is on fish and seafood, but desserts are also excellent.

NEWFOUNDLAND

Aqua ($)
310 Water Street, St. John's
tel: 709/576–2782
One of the several innovative cafés and restaurants that have appeared on Water Street.
Cellar Restaurant ($$)
152 Water Street and Harbour Drive, St. John's tel: 709/579–8900
Historic, waterfront building. More refined and expensive than most places in St. John's.
Ches's ($)
9 Freshwater Road at Lemarchant, St. John's tel: 709/722–4083 Also at 655 Topsail Road and 33 Commonwealth Avenue
The best fish and chips in the city.
Duck Street Bistro ($)
250 Duckworth Street, St. John's tel: 709/753–0400
Initimate and long-popular bistro with a wide range of creative dishes, including fish and meat.
Ocean View Motel Restaurant ($)
Main Street, Rocky Harbour tel: 709/458–2730
The seafood specials will fortify you during your exploration of Gros Morne National Park.

Index

Bold figures denote the main entry of a particular subject.

B

C

D

E

F

G

I

J

U

Picture credits

The Automobile Association would like to thank the following photographers, libraries and associations for their assistance in the preparation of this book.
THE BRIDGEMAN ART LIBRARY 27 *Indian Encampment on Lake Huron* by Paul Kane (1810–71) (Royal Ontario Museum, Toronto), 28b *The Cabot Brothers leaving Bristol*, 1497 by Board, Ernest (City of Bristol Museum & Art Gallery), 32/3 *A View of the City of Quebec taken from the Ferry House, October 3rd 1784* by J. Peachy (C18), (Natural History Museum, London), 34a *Signing the Declaration of Independence, July 4th 1776* by John Trumbull (1756–1843), (Yale University Art Gallery, New Haven, CT), 67 *Incidents on a Trading Journey: HMS Terror Thrown up by the Ice*, March 1837 by Lieutenant Smyth (Hudson Bay Company, Canada), 184b Huron moosehair embroidered screen, *c*1840–50 (detail) (Bonhams, London); BUTCHART GARDENS LTD 87, 265; CANADIAN TOURIST OFFICE 20b, 146, 151b, 164, 212b, 217; C COE 23, 36a, 83, 97, 134, 155, 163, 165, 170, 172/3, 174, 222a, 223, 228, 270; (MARY EVANS PICTURE LIBRARY 28a, 29, 31, 38a, 39, 66/7t, 185, 246a; GETTY IMAGES 32b, 40a, 40/1, 66; HUDSON'S BAY COMPANY ARCHIVES, PROVINCIAL ARCHIVES OF MANITOBA 168a (1987/363-T-200/21,N83-157), 169 (P.383,N13086); IMPERIAL WAR MUSEUM 44b; © 2005 FRANS LANTING 107; McMICHAEL CANADIAN ART COLLECTION 176b (Arthur Goss/Arts & Letters Club), 177 (Gift of Col. R S McLaughlin 1968.1.12); NATIONAL ARCHIVES OF CANADA 22a (The Montréal Gazette, PA117519), 34b (C168), 35 (C5456), 36b (C7727), 45 (R Brasseau, PA163903), 156a (Taconis, Kryn PA/65442), 156b (St. Nihal Singh, PA44418), 157 (C8891), 224b (C6643); DR. ECKART POTT/NHPA 145; DOC WHITE/NATUREPL.COM 212t; NOTMAN PHOTOGRAPHIC ARCHIVES, McCORD MUSEUM OF CANADIAN HISTORY 30a, 30b, 38b, 42/3, 43, 44a, 126a, 126b, 148/9; PHOTODISC 106b, 144; PICTURES COLOUR LIBRARY LTD 11, 69, 84/5, 112/3, 130, 133a, 137, 143, 154, 218/9, 220, 227, 232, 234/5; PICTURES LTD 106b, 212a; THE PROVINCE OF BRITISH COLUMBIA 75, 81; REX FEATURES LTD 19a (D Lewis), 22b, 24 (J Vinnick); SPECTRUM COLOUR LIBRARY 102, 138/9, 142a; TOURISM VANCOUVER 61; VISUAL IMAGES (Alberta Economic Development & Tourism) 147; YUKON TOURISM 120/1, 123, 125, 128:
The remaining pictures are held in the Association's own library (AA PHOTO LIBRARY): J. BEAZLEY 159; P. BENNETT 90cb, 106t, 153, 259; C COE 3, 4a, 4b, 6/7, 6, 9a, 10b, 12/3a, 13, 14a, 14b, 15, 16a, 18b, 21, 25b, 37b, 37c, 41, 47, 52, 53, 55, 56a, 56b, 57, 58/9, 60a, 60b, 62, 64, 65a, 65b, 71, 73, 77, 78a, 78b, 79, 80, 88, 89, 92, 93, 95, 98/9, 100, 101, 102/3, 104, 109, 116, 117, 119, 124, 127, 129, 131, 132a, 133b, 135, 138, 142b, 148, 149, 150, 168b, 168c, 252, 253, 255, 259c, 261, 264, 267, 271; M. DENT 51, 63, 72, 105, 111, 114; J. F. PIN 2a, 2b, 5a, 5c, 7, 8, 10a, 12, 16b, 17, 20a, 25a, 26a, 26b, 33, 37a, 161, 162, 167, 171, 175, 176a, 178, 179, 181, 182, 183, 186, 187, 190, 191, 192, 193, 194, 195, 196, 197, 200, 201, 202, 203, 205, 206, 207, 208, 209, 210, 211, 213, 214, 215, 222b, 224a, 225, 226, 230a, 230b, 231, 236, 237, 239, 240, 241, 242/3, 242, 243, 245, 246b, 247, 248, 248/9, 250, 260, 262, 263, 269; C. SAWYER 48, 74, 108, 115, 256; P. TIMMERMANS 5b, 9b, 19b, 70, 82, 251b

Contributors

Revision editors: Apostrophe S Limited
Revision verifier: Tim Jepson **Indexer**: Marie Lorimer